Dreamers of

Philippe Jullian

Dreamers of Decadence

Symbolist painters of the 1890s

Phaidon

Translated by Robert Baldick

Phaidon Press Limited
5 Cromwell Place, London SW7 2JL

First published in Great Britain 1971
under the Pall Mall Press imprint (hard cover)
2nd edition 1974
Originally published as *Esthètes et Magiciens*

ISBN 0 7148 1651 5

Printed in the USA

To Professor Mario Praz

Wer die Schönheit angeschaut mit Augen,
Ist dem Tode schon anheimgegeben;
Wird für keinen Dienst auf Erden taugen,
Und doch wird er vor dem Tode beben,
Wer die Schönheit angeschaut mit Augen.

August Graf von Platen (Tristan)

He who has seen Beauty with his eyes
Is condemned to Death;
He can serve no purpose on earth,
Yet he will tremble before Death,
He who has seen Beauty with his eyes.

Contents

Half-title page: Gustave Moreau: *La Chimère.*

Title page: Gustave Moreau: *Ganymède.*

Contents page: Henry Bataille: Drawing for the programme of *Ton Sang.*

Preface

I would like first of all to thank those collectors who preceded me in the study of a long-neglected period and who have not only allowed me to reproduce certain items in their collections, but have also given me the benefit of their knowledge and experience. H.R.H. the Princess of Hesse and the Rhine allowed me to study the piously preserved setting which was that of her father-in-law the Grand Duke Ernest Ludwig. Monsieur and Madame Wettamer received me in the Maison Solvay, one of the few dwellings of that period which have remained intact. Madame Schnerb placed at my disposal the library of Pierre Lièvre, her father. Monsieur P. E. Flament, who is preparing a thesis on the Rosicrucians, M. Seton, Mme. Legrand-Kappferer, M. Michel Lévy and M. Manoukian helped me by contributing a great many ideas and documents.

Miss Nathalie Barney's conversation and the advice of M. Patrick Walberg and M. Paul Hassaerts proved very valuable to me, and once again I must thank M. François Chapon for acting as my guide to the Symbolist poets whose works and papers are kept in the Bibliothèque Doucet. On the subject of the etchings and bibliophilia of the period, M. Henri Petiet's erudition was indispensable.

I owe a considerable debt to M. Paladilhe, Curator of the Musée Gustave Moreau, who placed at my disposal the painter's unpublished notes as well as his library. At the British Museum, Mr. John Gere showed me the Pre-Raphaelite drawings; in Brussels, Madame Legrand was my guide to the Belgian Symbolists to whom she had devoted a memorable exhibition; and in Berlin, Doctor Brauer assisted me in my research with tireless courtesy.

In the art galleries I also received considerable encouragement: in Paris, notably from Madame Myra Jacob, whose exhibitions at the Bateau Lavoir kept alive André Breton's tastes, from M. Lesieutre and from M. Gérard Lévy; in Milan, from Signor Bertonati; and in London, from the Piccadilly Gallery, whose exhibitions have for some years been rehabilitating the painters who are the subject of this book, from the Fine Arts Gallery, and from Hartnoll and Eyre.

In the United States I was greatly assisted in my research by Miss Mongan, Director of the Fogg Museum, by the Houghton Library of the University of Harvard, by the Library of the New York Art Institute, and by Mr. Robert Cashey. In Italy, the admirable exhibition organized by Signor Carluccio in Turin taught me a great deal, as did the exhibitions of the Galleria del Levante in Milan.

No bibliography is given in this book, as any I appended to it would be too vast. But I must express my gratitude here to Professor Mario Praz, Doctor Hoffstatter, M. Michaud and M. Vax. These authors will have no difficulty in recognizing how much I owe to their works. While I regret that I was unable to acknowledge my borrowings on every occasion, I would like to offer them my thanks for the valuable assistance they have given me.

To the names of these writers I would like to add that of Nelly Kaplan, whose admirable film on Gustave Moreau is well known.

I also wish to thank my friend Francis Spar, editor of *Connaissance des Arts*, for providing many of the colour illustrations.

Lastly I would like to thank my friend John Calmann whose helpful comments enabled me to adapt and enlarge this book in its English edition, M. Jean-Claude Peissel who designed it, and Dr. Robert Baldick who took so much trouble over the translation.

NOTE. To avoid overloading the text of this work with quotations, all the examples taken from literature have been given at the end of the book, and divided into two sections, the first constituting a repertory of the themes of the Decadence, and the second illustrating the theories of the artists I have studied. The figures in the text refer to these quotations.

Introduction

There are fashions in painting as in hats: what is considered sublime one season becomes commonplace within ten years and comic after thirty. In the sphere of art, this process is a little slower than in the field of millinery, but it is speeding up: thus the reign of abstract art lasted a mere ten years. Speculation and a feverish desire for novelty are rapidly gaining ground on aesthetics, and today's masterpieces are doomed to be tomorrow's daubs. Naturally the great masters, who have created a style and gone beyond it, suffer less from its decline than do their imitators; but in the long run, if their output has been considerable, they lose some of their prestige with fastidious collectors, in a period when masterpieces are sold all over the world. After all, it cannot be denied that Renoir was prolific and Monet uneven, or that there is something odd about a Cézanne watercolour fetching a higher price than a Greek statue.

Yet no proscription is forever, no oblivion is permanent: the academic painters of the Third Republic are beginning to emerge from the attics to which it was thought they had been relegated for all eternity. Meissonier is fetching high prices once again, and there was a Bouguereau Room in the museum Dali founded a few years ago. Revivals are traditionally most successful in the Anglo-Saxon countries, which tend to be more sentimental than other nations. The English have always found the Pre-Raphaelites touching, while the French rejected Gustave Moreau. Enchanted by the Impressionist sunlight or, more often, blinded by the dust which painters such as Gérome and Bouguereau threw into their eyes, our art-lovers generally failed to appreciate the bizarre geniuses who captivated a poetic Europe, such as the Wagnerian Böcklin, Hodler, Munch and Klimt. It was only fashion in the decorative arts that led discerning collectors to accept the Pre-Raphaelites. The present-day return to 'anecdotal painting' and 'painting in the grand manner' can partly be explained by period charm, and partly by psycho-analysis which enables us to glimpse unsuspected horrors underlying the most academic works. Thus it was the most

1. *Overleaf:* Gustave Moreau: *Les Chimères.* All the myths, religions and preoccupations of late Romanticism and the Decadence are to be found in this huge canvas on which Gustave Moreau worked for twenty years, but never finished. It presents a vision close to that of Goethe in the second part of *Faust*, and that of Flaubert in *La Tentation de Saint Antoine*.

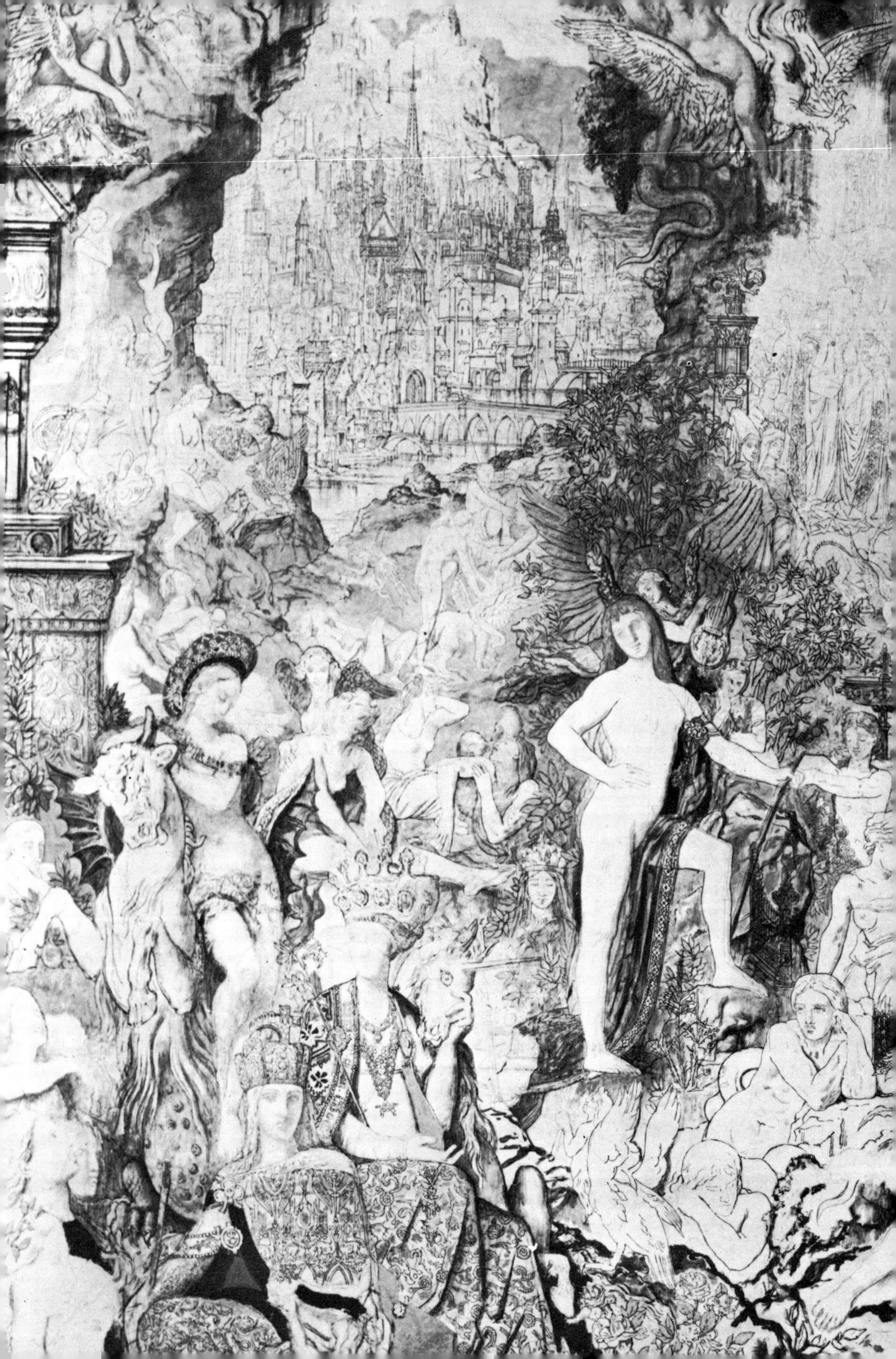

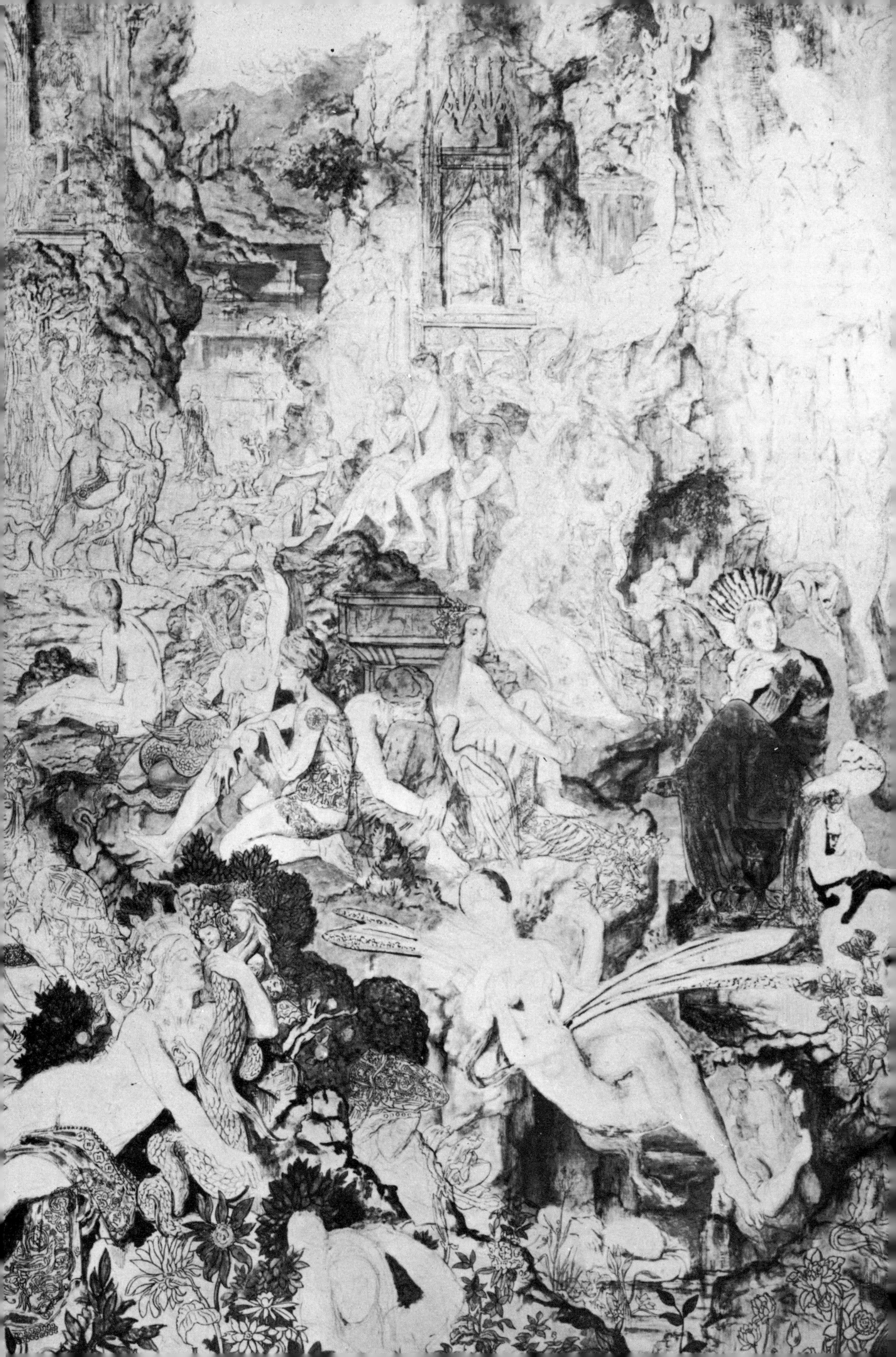

descriptive paintings which were the first to regain favour with the public: the works of Millais and Meissonier. They reappeared in all their glory at the exhibition entitled *The Imaginary Salon* held in Berlin in 1968, which in spite of its ironic intentions, contributed to a re-evaluation of such neglected masters as Mackart, Delaroche and Alma-Tadema . . . The younger generation, despite its addiction to the naïvety of Pop Art, admired the subtlety of their themes, the profundity of their thought. We began to witness a return towards museum painting, considered as a form of escapism – which was what Gustave Moreau had advocated: 'Everywhere, on the walls of museums, how many windows open on to artificial worlds which seem to be carved in marble and gold, and on to spatial regions which of necessity belong to the imagination . . .'

But it was Belgium which, the same year, in the exhibition entitled *Allégorie et Symbole*, asserted the importance of Symbolist painting which had become a force in that country as early as 1884. In 1965, the remarkable *Art Nouveau* exhibition in Ostend had already revealed many forgotten painters. In the spring of 1969, the important exhibition *Il Sacro e il Profano nell'Arte dei Simbolisti* brought together with their inspirers (Burne-Jones, Redon, Puvis de Chavannes, Moreau and Böcklin) those painters who had also derived undeniable inspiration from poetry, and whom modern art critics thought they had condemned to perpetual oblivion by labelling them 'literary'. The exhibition was so successful that it was later shown in Canada. This was followed by an exhibition in Paris of the French Symbolists whose influence was so great on certain painters, who, in turn, became more and more famous.

Thus it can be seen that next to the fashion that invents there is the fashion that rehabilitates, and here the whims of the art historians are as unpredictable as those of the customers of the great couturiers. The Mannerists, for example, highly praised twenty years ago, have now been relegated to the sphere of consecrated art. Up-to-the-minute experts are now full of admiration for the Neoclassicists and the Nazarenes. And finally, for the last ten years or so, *Art Nouveau* has been exhaustively studied, notably in Germany by Schmulzer and Hoffstatter, but also in Italy by Cremona and in France by Guerrand. The critics have puzzled over the evolution of a style whose roots went so deep but which flowered for so short a time. They have admired its audacity, which contrasted so sharply with the historicist tendencies of the nineteenth century, and its grace, which degenerated so rapidly into the vulgarity of *Modern Style*. This *Art Nouveau* has been compared to the Rococo and the Flamboyant, from which, incidentally, it derived its inspiration, and its empire has been mapped out, with Brussels and Glasgow, Vienna and Darmstadt as its capitals. In all their investigations, the experts have tended to consider *Art Nouveau* painting simply as one aspect of a movement which found its highest expression in decoration. That is unfair: there were some great *Art Nouveau* painters, just as there were some great Symbolist poets, but, unfortunately for them, they were not the only painters of their time, whereas in architecture Gallé and Horta stand head and shoulders above their colleagues.

When dealing with the paintings of the period from 1880 to 1910, the experts mention a score of artists, from Seurat to Matisse, without ever saying what they owed to masters who are ridiculed because they attached importance to ideas. And when the debt is obvious and undeniable, as in the case of Gauguin and Redon, their spiritual orientation is regarded as an intellectual accident, instead of being connected with the great idealistic movement which gave them both a faith and a style. Besides, Renoir and Monet dazzled the world so late in life that they are still thought of as modern painters. Let us follow Breton's example and repeat two quotations which allow us to leave the Impressionists in the rich international collections without any scruples or regrets:

Redon: 'The ceiling of the Impressionist boat is far too low.'
Gauguin: 'The Impressionists search around the eye and not at the mysterious centre of thought.'

Today stars which were thought to be dead, such as Klimt and Khnopff, are the darlings of the museums. They, with many others, form the ring round that planet which, like Saturn, lay for a long time under a curse: Gustave Moreau. It is therefore in relation to Moreau that we propose to study poetic painting in the last third of the nineteenth century – to study it in its own right, with its own qualities which sixty years of so-called modern art, sometimes brilliant, but over-abundant, have led us to forget.

In the first place, after admiring so many Matisses and so many abstracts, it takes a considerable effort to admit that the subject of a picture is important. Paul Valéry decreed fifty years ago that the subject was irrelevant. In subsequent years, countless painters supported him, and Cézanne's fruit-dish assumed the proportions of the Parthenon. Once the subject had been outlawed, shapes became all-important, only to fall into ridicule in their turn; and then painters such as Pollock and Dubuffet swept the debris of these disasters onto canvases which were undeniably effective, but boring in the long run. People began to wonder whether Heliogabalus or Salome might not be more interesting subjects than a fruit-dish, or the fragments of a fruit-dish hurled onto a canvas. In 1958 Breton replied to Valéry:

If there exists a cliché which is capable, by itself, of giving the full measure of those who use it, it must be the application of the epithet *literary* to any painting whose ambition goes further than offering us a picture of the exterior world or, failing that, seeking its final justification in the pleasure of the eyes . . . In absolute opposition to this realistic art, with its futile depiction of externals, there exists an art which represents a reaction against the world, by virtue of an inner need experienced by the artist. In this art, priority is no longer given to sensation, but to the deepest desires of heart and mind.

For twenty years Breton was the only visitor to the Musée Gustave Moreau, the building which Proust had described as an 'august and familiar' dwelling. That museum, to which the public has at last found its way, contains an immense unfinished canvas entitled *Les Chimères* (The Chimeras), in which all the painter's failings are clearly revealed: an inability to complete an over-ambitious task, artificial composition, a tendency to sacrifice the whole to the details, an abuse of oddities, and a superfluity of historical bric-à-brac. It was in reference to this apparently unsuccessful experiment that Moreau wrote to his mother:

I attach the greatest importance to this work: with its novel initiatory character, it is a work that attacks the whole of French art, which has never been able to rise to epic heights and which has never been able to understand anything beyond the wretched reporting of positive facts, even among its greatest exponents . . . but in that respect I am forging a link with Italian and Flemish art, while at the same time sounding a note which is profoundly personal and fundamentally French.

A statement which helps us to understand Moreau's connections with an alien art – the art of Böcklin and Burne-Jones, and the reason for his lack of success in France outside a small literary and poetic circle.

Anybody who makes an effort to enter into this picture, as one enters into an engraving with the aid of a magnifying-glass, will find himself carried off into a dreamworld by its beauties. Each of the ambiguous or monstrous creatures in the picture seems to be murmuring to the visitor the words which the Chimera shouts to Flaubert's St. Antony:

I am joyful and light of heart! I reveal to men dazzling prospects with paradises in the clouds and distant felicities. I fill their hearts with the eternal follies, plans for happiness, projects for the future, dreams of glory, declarations of love and virtuous resolutions. I urge them to embark on perilous travels and vast undertakings . . . I search for new perfumes, bigger flowers, unknown pleasures.

Some of the chimeras which can be seen flying out of the huge trees recall the strange creatures escaping from the foliage in Bresdin's pictures, while others look like witches on their way to the sabbath; Michelet devoted one of his finest books to them. The crags on the horizon suggest the Chinese-style spurs of rock that Leonardo painted around his Virgin. And those towers and spires, towards which legendary princesses are riding, soar into the air like those of a Mont Salvat or of some mystic castle such as Ludwig II of Bavaria was building in the same period. Confronted with those swarming hordes, one is reminded of Faust's vision on the Brocken, with his Helens of Troy and his dead gods, of the gorgeous Pasiphae whom Titian might have created, the Melusina who resembles the Lady with the Unicorn in the famous tapestry. In the foreground, is that Ophelia drowning in the midst of water-lilies drawn by Gallé? That woman dressed in the costume of a German Emperor comes out of Hugo's *Légende des Siècles*, and those beauties about to accept the Chimeras' advice are Baudelaire's creations. All those hybrid creatures, bejewelled and beflowered, all those buildings hidden in the trees, also remind us of some Indian temple choked with creepers, among which can be glimpsed calm or terrifying faces, languid bodies and unknown animals. If one wanted to describe those chimeras, it is the vocabulary of the poets who admired Moreau's work that would come to one's pen: porphyries and amethysts, guivres and gryphons, sylphs and succubi – the glorious words of the Parnassians, the precious words of the Symbolists.

Accordingly, in the course of this book, we shall constantly be returning to this picture or to other works of this great master, whose misfortune, which he shared with Delacroix, was to have been born in the nineteenth century. In the vast or tiny rooms of the Musée Gustave Moreau, a fabulous world has lain asleep for too long under dusty sheets of glass. Those drawings, worthy of Ingres, and those watercolours, sometimes close to Turner, reveal the characteristics of all the artistic styles which moved a generation of poets in Europe: a classical corruption which corresponds to the work of Feuerbach and Böcklin (the only artist with affinities with Moreau); an eroticism comparable to that of Rops, but without his vulgarity; visions foreshadowing those of Odilon Redon; and an idealized medievalism, more disturbing than that of Burne-Jones. In Moreau one can find all the artists we are going to meet, just as in his great unfinished canvas one can find all the feelings which inspired them.

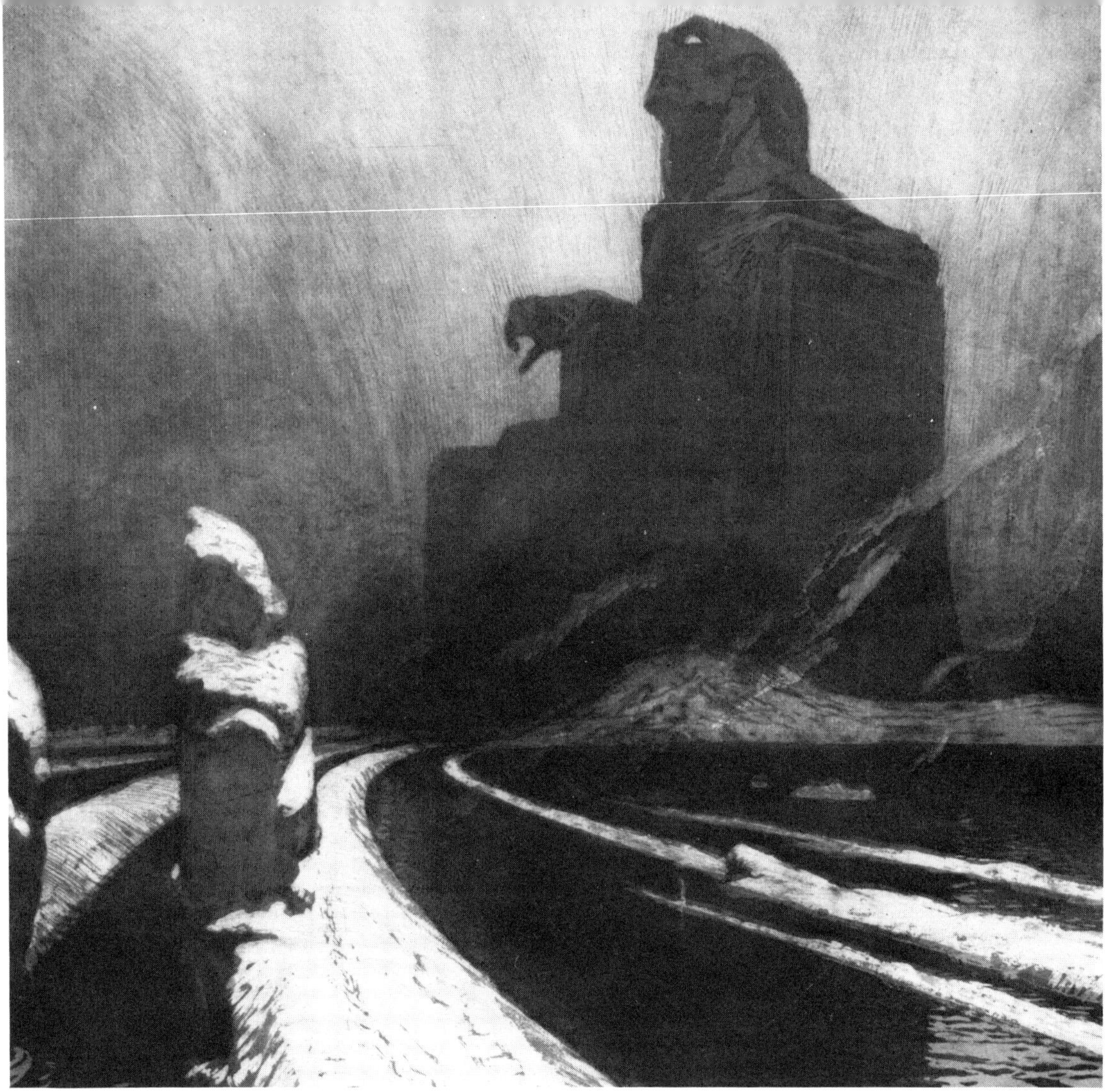

2. Frantisek Kupka: *Resistance – The Black Idol.* The Colossus of Memnon in the world of Kafka. This picture is typical of the metaphysical anxiety harboured by the Slav intelligentsia at the end of the last century.

These chimeras were listened to by poets and painters, and some thought that they could tame them, in that *fin de siècle* which seemed to them to be dominated by the machine. They carried the dreamers away, 'anywhere out of this world'. Many of them fell by the wayside, and others became figures of fun; but some of them went far. This is generally agreed to have been the case with Odilon Redon, and people are beginning to realize that it was also true of several others. We are therefore going to follow the chimeras along the various paths on which, either through imagination or with the help of a poetic fashion, they lured the painters and poets of the period which proudly called itself the Decadence. But first of all we shall see why the period in question gave rise to such an extraordinary flowering of talent: we shall ask ourselves from what mythical or aesthetic models the chimeras borrowed their masks, their plumage and their song.

To begin with we shall listen to the *legendary* chimera, the one whom Moreau depicts in a crown or a hennin. This is Clio in the guise of a fairy, and we shall follow her into her kingdoms, Byzantium or Thule. Then the *exotic* chimera will take us to India, whose thought Europe had just discovered, and also introduce us to a corrupt antiquity – that of Bactria and Cappadocia, familiar to the readers of Flaubert, Gautier and Swinburne.

The *mystical* chimera, Isis holding a lily, the female pope of secret religions, surrounded by ambiguous angels, flies towards Wagnerian basilicas; witch that she is, she conjures up spirits – occultism dominated the *fin de siècle* – and does not hesitate to dip her wings in the mire of Black Masses. Her sister, the *erotic* chimera, is a daughter of Baudelaire, present everywhere in Moreau's picture, sad and even cruel in character; once eroticism had become a priestly function, as against the frivolity of the *Belle Époque*, it gave as much pain as pleasure.

We shall also see another chimera, or rather a figure of nostalgia: she did not tempt Moreau, but she inspired Verlaine, Maeterlinck and a few other poets with tired wings, for she is the muse of dead cities and melancholy music, the one who inspired *Pelléas*, the masterpiece of that period.

Before following the chimeras, we shall try to discover why they spread their wings about a hundred years ago, and who were the artists who prepared their coming. Following the custom of the times, we shall use the word *artists* to describe poets as well as painters. Hoffmann and Poe, Delacroix, Gustave Doré and the Pre-Raphaelites opened the cages in which, ever since the end of the irrational ages, sphinxes, ghouls and sirens had been kept.

We shall salute certain personages who, braving misfortune and even vulgarity, embodied those fantasies: Ludwig II, Sarah Bernhardt, Oscar Wilde. We shall visit the cities of their empire, from Benares to Bruges, going by way of Florence. We shall linger especially in Byzantium, for there an anxious Europe saw a prefiguration of its destiny, even in the explosion of its vices. In a final chapter, we shall learn how they disappeared or how they adapted themselves to a new world, and we shall also discover the use made of them by the Surrealists, the cinema and psychedelic art. Finally, in an appendix of pictures and poems, we shall take an inventory of the chimeras and their treasures, gathering together some of the recipes by means of which philosophers and poets hoped to fight them or control them.

Thus this book will be not so much a history of fantastic art in the last third of the nineteenth century as a study of the myths which made possible such a blossoming of curiosities and which, on occasion, gave birth to marvels. The best painters and the best poets are often not the most representative; consequently the literary and pictorial illustrations will be more often chosen from among the worst than among the best. If pride of place has been given to Jean Lorrain and Toorop, that is not to say that they are regarded as greater than Verlaine or Redon; they are simply more typical. Good taste has all too often prevented the chimeras from taking wing. There is even reason to fear that people of taste may regard this book as a catalogue of horrors; but they can console themselves by devising an aesthetic manichaeism which will condemn the chimeras to hell.

The art we are studying was the prerogative of a very small number of people, a few thousand at the most; the others, even the most intelligent, allowed themselves to be swept away by the excitements of the *Belle Époque*, tore each other to pieces in political quarrels, or else fell asleep in their religious convictions. Disquiet was therefore an artistic ferment for only a handful of initiates – far fewer than the Romantics had been – but from that anguish was born the first truly European style, which can be discovered in some marvellous poems and in a few pictures whose beauty is beginning to be recognized. The poets and painters of the imagination played an important role, for they enriched what Gombrich calls 'that common stock of images which makes a style' – a style which, for the first time, was elaborated by the unconscious and made age-old images its own. The painters of this group – much less of painters than the Impressionists who freed painting from all styles – have to be classified, in the history of art, with the Mannerists. Like the Mannerists, they were the product of an uneasy period; like them, they did not scorn certain affectations; and they opened the way to the Surrealists – though the latter went much further than their predecessors, the *Idéistes*.

There was never a clearly defined Symbolist school, but only a number of Symbolist centres of which the most important were the Rosicrucian Group, the *Salon des XX* in Brussels, and later the Viennese *Sezession;* but the influence of the Symbolists can be seen upon certain artists who lost little time in shaking it off. The first Signacs and the early Maillols could well figure in this book beside Maurice Denis. About 1895, Cross, K. X. Roussel, Desvallières and Vallotton went through a Symbolist phase, and it is fair to say that Rouault remained marked by Symbolism throughout his life. The Pointillist atmosphere delighted the painters of the imagination, who often imitated it. Art-dealers and the organizers of exhibitions are often tempted to hang next to the Symbolists painters of an earlier period who were also attracted by mystery, painters who were often academic but also filled with a sense of poetry: Watts, Carrière, Henner, Fantin-Latour, and above all Carzin (1841–1901), whose melancholy canvases had as much influence as those of Puvis de Chavannes.

A writer has to limit himself in time as well as space. It is undeniable that, while the principal influence on the Symbolist artists was that of the Pre-Raphaelites, painters such as the German Nazarenes at the beginning of the nineteenth century and the school of the Lyons mystics a little later, had prepared a section of the public for the appearance of a mystically oriented art. And it is possible to speak of a Symbolist school in Belgium before any other country, for Wirty's homeland, the mystical land where Balzac set his novel *La Recherche de l'Absolu*, was ready before all the rest to seek out that world of symbols which had been the world of Bosch and Memling.

This book may therefore be read, on the one hand as a guide to *Art Nouveau*, though it makes no claim to tell the story of that movement yet again, and on the other hand as the history of an idealistic society which produced those two archetypal characters: the aesthete – in other words, the hero of Proust's fictional world – and the magician, whose mission the Surrealists were to continue. Some readers may regard these images, especially those which come from Germany (Klinger, Von Stuck, Klimt), as illustrations of Freudian symbolism. Others will be reminded by these poems and visions, of forgotten aesthetes and lonely magicians, the last witnesses of a period which tried to be sublime.

Today Miss Nathalie Barney, whose beauty embodied the *fin de siècle* ideal, can still communicate to us some of the ardour which fired so many of her friends mentioned in this book: Rémy de Gourmont, Milosz, Montesquiou, d'Annunzio, Renée Vivien . . . learned and mysterious personages who emerge from oblivion with their arms filled with lilies. All of them, with varying degrees of success, have lived for the sake of a spiritual adventure and had set off, in spite of certain eccentricities which the common herd call vices, in search of an aesthetic Grail.

The realm of the imagination is ethereal only for the artist: for anybody else trailing the chimeras to their lair it can appear to be rather more like an underground passage. So this book will not be a flying lesson, but a visit to a marvellous, dilapidated palace, closed to the light and noise of the world, a palace which houses the mythical menagerie Wilde was impatient to open up:

> When that day dawns, or sunset reddens, how joyous we shall all be! Facts will be regarded as discreditable, Truth will be found mourning over her fetters, and Romance, with her temper of wonder, will return to the land. The very aspect of the world will change to our startled eyes . . . Dragons will wander about the waste places, and the phoenix will soar from her nest of fire into the air. We shall lay our hands upon the basilisk, and

see the jewel in the toad's head. Champing his gilded oats, the Hippogriff will stand in our stalls, and over our heads will float the Blue Bird singing of beautiful and impossible things, of things that are lovely and that never happen, of things that are not and that should be.

For a long time the chimeras have slept, stifled by the images they have inspired, and for a long time the sphinxes have asked no questions. Dust covered the books of poetry on the shelves, and hid the pictures beneath a grey mist. Feather-duster in hand, we are going to walk through mythical galleries, some of which lead to Freud. We shall light up the portraits of those who were the faithful servants of the monsters, lingering more with mad or unsuccessful artists than with recognized masters such as Redon or recently discovered figures such as Klimt. We shall open only a little way the doors leading to the world of those privileged individuals, such as Gauguin and the Nabis, who have seen the sirens. Finally, we shall not open the palace windows onto the garden of Impressionism. The sun is the worst enemy of the chimeras: their favourite star is an opera chandelier, the flame of a punch-bowl, the gaslamp from which Gérard de Nerval hanged himself. Their palace is also a library. The artists find their inspiration in books, and seek to make each picture a 'work of art' – an art so representative that it succeeds in recreating the other world, that of the scholarly artists who reconstruct Babylon and Florence. That is why a large number of the pictures represented in this work are book illustrations. (At the same time, in fact, as a revival of the decorative arts, the *fin de siècle* witnessed a revival of the art book and the creation of *de luxe* reviews such as *Pan* or the *Yellow Book*.)

This palace naturally resembles the castles of Ludwig II of Bavaria, but with the bad taste of historical pastiche corrected by Symbolist preciosity and Decadent exaggeration. For a long time it was thought that it had crumbled beneath the mockery of those who regarded it as Sodom rather than as Mont Salvat. In fact, for twenty years most artists had forgotten the way to the keep, the living heart of Europe, which had raised its drawbridge on the appearance of modern fashions. A hideous vegetation had then spread over all the roads. In the rooms of the palace, smelling of opium or the grave, there are treasures which will fascinate those who ask psychedelic art, yogis or drugs to take them out of this world. But the guide on this tour will be an aesthete, an admirer of Walter Pater who endowed the chimeras with the Mona Lisa's smile, an admirer of Wilde who tamed the sphinx in the fashionable boudoirs, an admirer of Jean Lorrain who so often regarded himself as a faery spirit. The aesthete is well aware that fantastic art is created from man's ancient fears, long after he has ceased to take them seriously. He knows that Jung is right when he declares that the artist's intuition manages to translate the realities of the collective unconscious, giving them a new life in pictures or poems.

This sorcerer's apprentice of a guide will therefore deliberately employ expressions such as 'the Beyond', in a book dealing with the irrational, knowing that Hugo and Strindberg and many others frequently derived inspiration from spiritualist experiences. He will look about him with admiration rather than mockery as he stands in the flower-filled, ruined precincts of the castle of the arts, at the foot of the ivory tower which is also the manor of Nosferatu and the house of Usher. *Art Nouveau* was born here, Romanticism suffered a strange death-agony here, and Surrealism stripped the place of its treasures. We in our turn can forget in its galleries the '1984' or 'Brave New World' which awaits us.

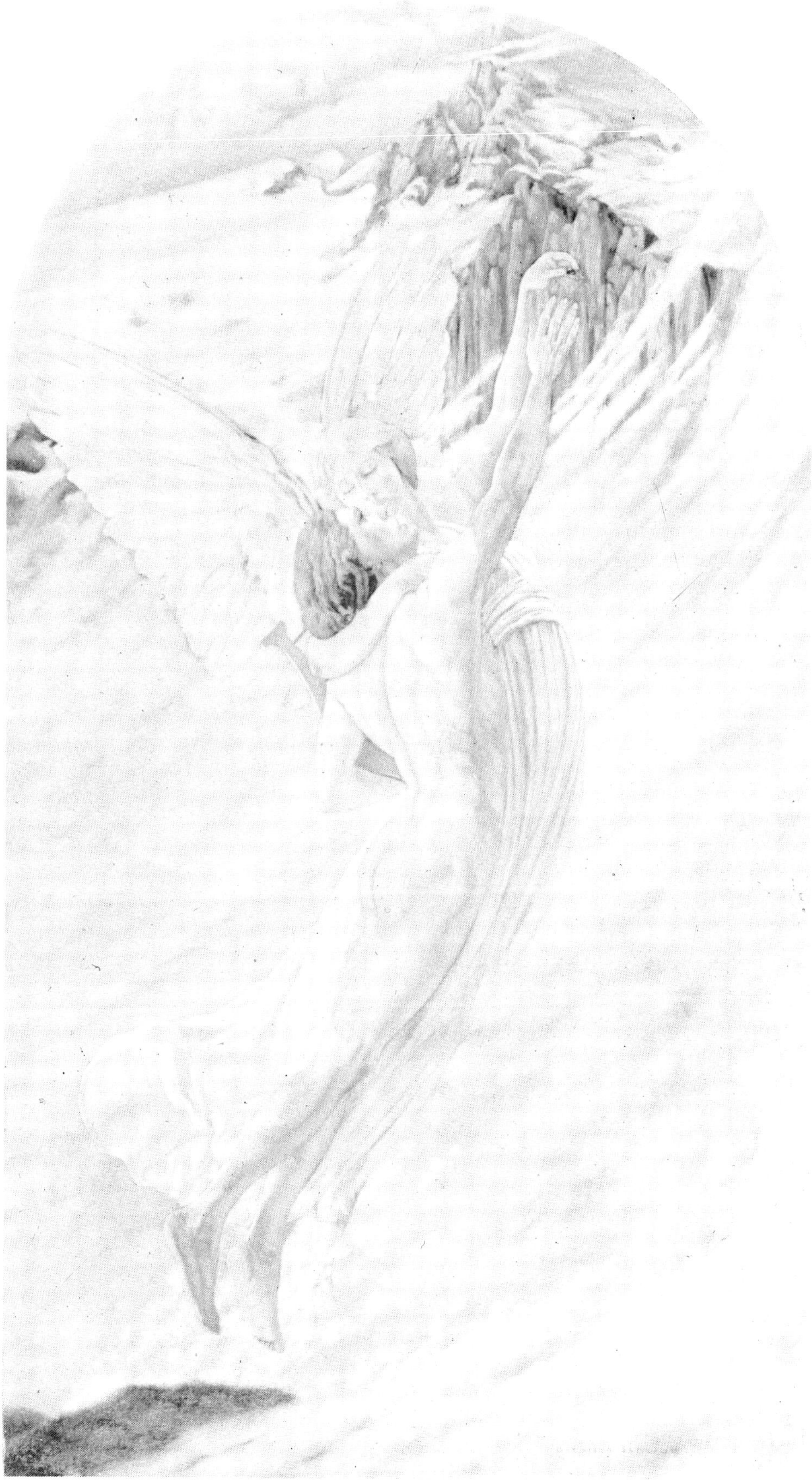

1 Fin de siècle

PESSIMISM. 'Our century is not moving towards either good or evil: it is moving towards mediocrity.' These words, uttered by Renan when the last quarter of the nineteenth century was just beginning, were scarcely calculated to encourage young people endowed with any imagination. But who at that time said anything that might be described as encouraging? Leaders of expanding industries and generals in need of soldiers to defend a province or conquer a colony: that was nearly all. The Church was losing many of its faithful, and the intransigent attitude adopted by the Vatican Council was unlikely to bring them back to the fold; the bourgeoisie, terrified by the Commune, was finding it impossible to recapture the sense of security it had known in the middle of the century; while high society felt ashamed of having enjoyed itself too much under the Second Empire. Consequently, as the century drew towards its close, a feeling of uneasiness became apparent in every class of society. There was no fear that the end of the world was in sight: at that time the possibility seemed incompatible with science. However there *was* a fear of the end of civilization, a sort of *millennium* whose destructive forces would no longer be the angels of the Apocalypse, but either Socialism or the Machine or the Yellow Peril. In the case of particularly sensitive natures, this fear became sheer anguish; it took the form either of insolent rebellion against an unstable society, or of escape into the world of dreams. But the Intellectuals were divided: some of them, led by Zola, accepted the materialism of their age, however much this might horrify more delicate souls. The *fin de siècle* malady was much less anti-social than the Romantic *mal du siècle* had been, but it was also much less widespread than in 1830, for the mass of society wanted nothing but material satisfaction. This anguish was therefore the privilege of a young élite. The form it took varied according to the country and period in which it appeared, but it found expression everywhere in the cult of death and melancholy.

England went through this crisis when, at the time of the Industrial Revolution, the spirit of competition and excessive conformism

3. Carlos Schwabe: *L'Idéal*. Schwabe was a Belgian painter, one of the first Rosicrucians; in this picture he shows the artist lifted up to the peaks of thought as a reward for a lifetime of suffering.

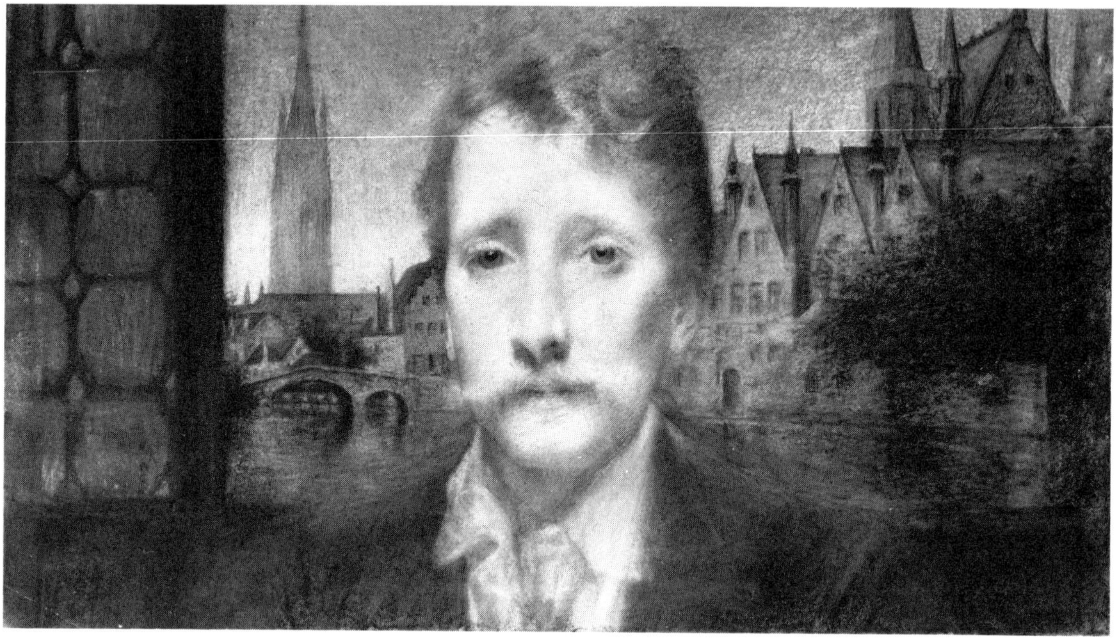

4. Lucien Lévy-Dhurmer: *Georges Rodenbach.* The Belgian writer who typified the Decadent dandy, portrayed in front of a canal in Bruges. His works, notably *Bruges-la-Morte*, inspired many painters.

weighed too heavily on social life. The resulting revolt was more moral and artistic than literary. The idea was a return to the purity which some pious individuals and a few artists believed to have existed in the Middle Ages. The most ardent advocates of this purity founded the Pre-Raphaelite Brotherhood in 1848, having found in Ruskin a champion for their ideas. For these painters and their prophet, the idea of Beauty was inseparable from a reformed society. They accordingly depicted the Middle Ages as a mystical, Socialist period to which they attributed all the virtues they had searched for in vain in the Victorian era. They hoped to regenerate society by ridding its surroundings of vulgar industrial manifestations, and they set off with admirable courage on a crusade. Many never came back – for if William Morris became the respected patriarch of *Art Nouveau* and Millais the richest of the academic painters, Rossetti succumbed to drugs, and his admirers Swinburne and Wilde, each in his fashion, both suffered the vengeance of society. The dramas of the Pre-Raphaelite Bohemia foreshadowed the dramas of the *fin de siècle* Bohemia, just as Chelsea's fashions would be copied a dozen years later on the other side of the Channel.

Those fashions were adopted by men who were looking, above all else, for a soul, while the English Decadence was chiefly a revolt in matters of taste, and ridicule was the chief danger that it braved. Wilde, thanks to his sense of the theatre, managed to become an ill-starred poet, a *poète maudit*, at the end of a delightful life; but that was a French fashion. There were hardly any *poètes maudits* in England, only a few poor wretches who died of hunger in complete obscurity, while their French contemporaries, ill-starred or not, were famous. Thus James Thomson, the author of *The City of Dreadful Night*, and Francis Thompson remained unknown. In France, only Germain Nouveau could be compared to these successors of Thomas de Quincey.

One of the greatest influences, that of Edgar Allan Poe, came from the United States, where Decadence would not set in until over a century after the poet's death. Poe had an immense influence on Redon, for example, who made lithographs entitled *Le Pèlerin d'un monde sublunaire* (and here we can see the continuity of fantasy down to Lovecraft), *La Cosmologie du poème 'Eureka'*, and *Le Souffle qui conduit les êtres est aussi dans les sphères*; many other *fin de siècle* figures saw the world lit by the cabbalistic star of Gérard de Nerval, Poe and the Victor Hugo of *Ce que dit la bouche d'ombre:* the Black Sun.

THE AESTHETES. The most important consequence of this English movement was probably the appearance of a character who was new to Europe (he had existed for a long time in China): the aesthete, the ardent servant of beauty, often incapable of creating anything himself, but skilled in devising a décor or setting a tone. Unlike the art-lover, however, he was eager to play a part in artistic creation, and he served as a link between the various forms of artistic expression. The aesthetes had no fatherland, no ideal other than Beauty, no enemies other than ugliness and stupidity. These *fin de siècle* Knights Templar were violently attacked by those who envied their gifts, and also by those who were annoyed by their insolence. The aesthetes, following in the wake of the Pre-Raphaelites, succeeded in giving Europe a new style and fashioning a new type of beauty, leaving anguish to the artists. But the aesthete, with a perversity he calls humour, sometimes makes fun of what he most admires; thus we see the rarest flower of aestheticism, Aubrey Beardsley, casually toying with all the religions and all the vices which tempted him. For forty years, thanks to the Pre-Raphaelites, and then to Beardsley, English art was to be a source of images from which all dreamers would draw inspiration. On the other hand, the ideas of the English aesthetes were less representative of the movement, in spite of Ruskin, Pater and above all Wilde, who was the Holy Ghost, or rather the Blue Bird, of the aesthetic trinity.

France, on the contrary, was to be a great source of poetic themes, thanks to Baudelaire, who was recognized by the time he died as the first modern European poet, and then, later on and to a lesser degree, thanks to Mallarmé and Verlaine. Baudelaire dominated all Swinburne's work, and the Germans admired him more than their own poets. All the themes of *Les Fleurs du Mal* were taken over by the artists we are going to consider: satanism, dandyism, exoticism and above all eroticism – in fact, everything the bourgeois regarded as decadent. However, we shall only rarely quote Baudelaire, preferring to pass over well-known texts in favour of less familiar passages of prose and poetry steeped in his thought, which are glosses on it and sometimes seem to be parodies of it. Thus, while England was Aesthetic, France was Decadent. There were few Decadents in England, apart from certain disciples of Wilde, and few Aesthetes in France, although she can lay claim to the most exquisite of them all, Robert de Montesquiou, who was the model for the Duc Floressas des Esseintes in Huysmans's novel *A Rebours* before becoming Proust's Baron de Charlus. *A Rebours* was published in 1884, an important date also for painting, with the first *Salon des Indépendants* in Paris and the first *Salon des XX* in Brussels.

5. Aubrey Beardsley: Vignette for *La Morte d'Arthur*. Beardsley provided the Decadents with the ambiguous images called for by their poets; this boy is very similar to certain figures in Moreau's work.

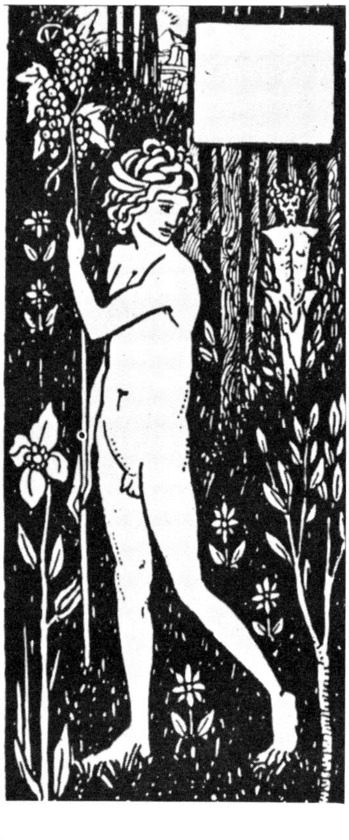

The Decadence found more remarkable expression in France than anywhere else because in that country the *fin de siècle* anguish was rooted in two separate preoccupations. First of all, after the disasters of the Franco-Prussian War and the Commune, people had the feeling that they were living in a period of political degeneration, a suspicion confirmed by the many scandals of the Third Republic. With a democratic government, France was afraid of becoming a second Spain. One of the strangest figures of the period, Joséphin Péladan, whom we shall come across frequently in the course of this book, was to give vivid expression to this horror of democracy about 1890, when he declared: 'I believe in the inevitable and imminent putrefaction of a Latin world without gods and without Symbols.' Twenty years earlier, on hearing the news of the defeat of Sedan, Flaubert had written: 'We are witnessing the end of the Latin world'; and it is said that Renan once retorted to the chauvinistic Déroulède: 'Young man, France is dying: don't disturb her death-agony.' Refusing to recognize Germany's intellectual superiority, the French drew a parallel between the Byzantine Empire and the Second Empire on the one hand, and the barbarian world and Bismarck's Germany on the other.

The other reason for pessimism was one which France shared with Germany and England, for like those powers, although to a lesser degree, she was feeling the effects of prosperity, or in other words materialism. Everybody who had retained a certain sense of honour, whether religious, aesthetic or literary, felt threatened by the machine as well as by the masses who served the machine. They were conscious of the hostility of the advocates of progress typified by Flaubert's Homais and certain characters in Dickens's

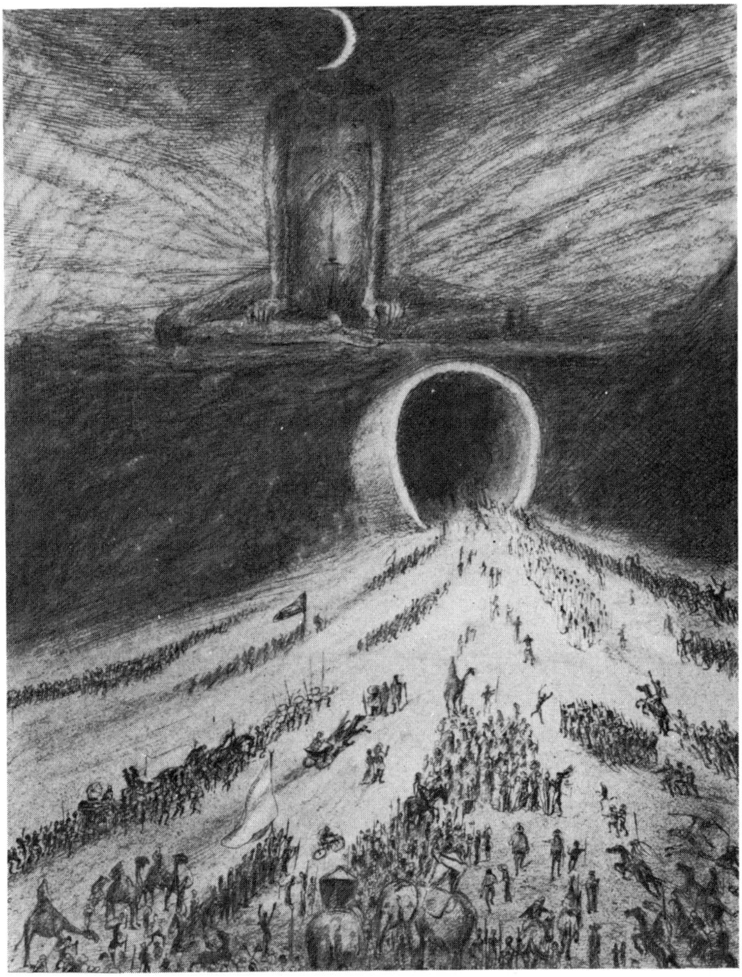

6. Alfred Kubin: *The Way to Hell.* This Czech artist comes very close here to Ensor, but there is an oriental influence which is not to be found in the Belgian painter's work.

novels. Since the Revolution of 1848 nobody in France could seriously believe in democracy. Baudelaire and Renan both condemned it, the former on behalf of the dandies – who, it should be noted, were the progenitors of the aesthetes: 'Day after day, the rising tide of democracy, which is spreading everywhere, is drowning the last representatives of human pride.' Renan for his part wrote: 'Democracy is the most powerful solvent of virtue of any kind that the world has ever known.'

Young people who were not attracted by the nationalist movement for *la revanche* or revenge on Germany, a movement which in any case began only in the late 1880s with the Boulanger episode, could find hardly anybody to inspire them at the beginning of the *fin de siècle*. Hugo regarded himself as God, the Parnassians were first and foremost academicians, and Renan's pronouncements, as we have seen, were anything but encouraging. If they turned towards the fine arts, they met with a similar disappointment. On the one hand there was academic art, and on the other Impressionism, whose language was still difficult to understand

and which offered nothing to the imagination. Gustave Moreau was to be both a Baudelaire and a Delacroix to this frustrated generation. One has only to read Huysmans's *Salon* of 1889 to realize that the youth of a whole era found their dreams and their despair reflected in Moreau:

> Spiritual onanism . . . a soul exhausted by secret thoughts . . . Insidious appeals to sacrilege and debauchery . . . Goddesses riding hippogryphs and streaking with their lapis-lazuli wings the death-agony of the clouds . . . The crushed globes of bleeding suns and haemorrhages of stars flowing in crimson cataracts . . . Contrary to Taine's theory, environment stimulates revolt: exceptional individuals retrace their steps down the century, and, out of disgust for the promiscuities they have to suffer, hurl themselves into the abysses of bygone ages, into the tumultuous spaces of dreams and nightmares.

All the themes of the *fin de siècle* are gathered together in these few lines which place Moreau among the poets rather than among the painters; and indeed, his influence was to be greater upon the former than upon the latter.

If England provided the images of the *fin de siècle* and France the poetic themes, Germany supplied the doctrine – that of her philosophers, and above all the most pessimistic of them – and also gave the world Wagner, who was the god of the time. The young German Empire had too much self-confidence to give birth to Aesthetes and Decadents. Even the most unusual of its painters had something robust about them. It was the crumbling Austro-Hungarian Empire which would provide the German representatives of the *fin de siècle*: Rilke and Klimt.

In Russia, another crumbling Empire, mysticism occupied a far more important place than aestheticism. The Russian Decadents are represented by Dostoevsky's *The Possessed* and the Nihilists, while Tolstoy became the guru of a Europe which was already drawn towards Asia. Leontiev, a writer despised far too long as a reactionary, was a 'Knight of Beauty' like Stefan Trofimovich in *The Possessed*, but also a narcissistic anti-Christian without any social preoccupations who declared that Poetry was the sole reality: his influence was confined to only a few artists.

From the artistic point of view, the Scandinavians made a much greater contribution: first through a revival of traditional decorative themes, and secondly through the close connections with the Beyond which Scandinavians from Swedenborg to Strindberg had maintained since the late eighteenth century. The same phenomenon, incidentally, was to be observed in Ireland, where the Celtic Revival was inseparable from spiritualism

THE THINKERS. Swedenborg is scarcely known today except to readers of Balzac, who expounded his theories in the novel *Seraphita*, thus becoming a hero for the Symbolists – at once sage and aesthete, spiritualist and dandy. The Norwegian visionary found a new public when artists discouraged by a world dedicated to progress began to seek refuge in fantasy. Baudelaire had rediscovered the first of Swedenborg's principles when he had written in his *Paradis Artificiels*: 'Natural things exist to only a limited degree; reality lies only in dreams,' and again in his tribute to Théophile Gautier: 'It is this admirable, unchanging instinct for beauty which leads us to regard the world and its sights as manifestations of heaven. The insatiable hunger for all that belongs to the after-life which is revealed to us by life on earth is the clearest proof of our immortality.' The whole outlook of Symbolism is to be found in these lines inspired by Swedenborg, and later the theorist of the Symbolist movement, Albert Aurier, was to cite the visionary as his principal authority (87).

A few quotations from Guy Michaud's fine work, *Le Message Poétique du Symbolisme*, will show us what the enemies of Realism

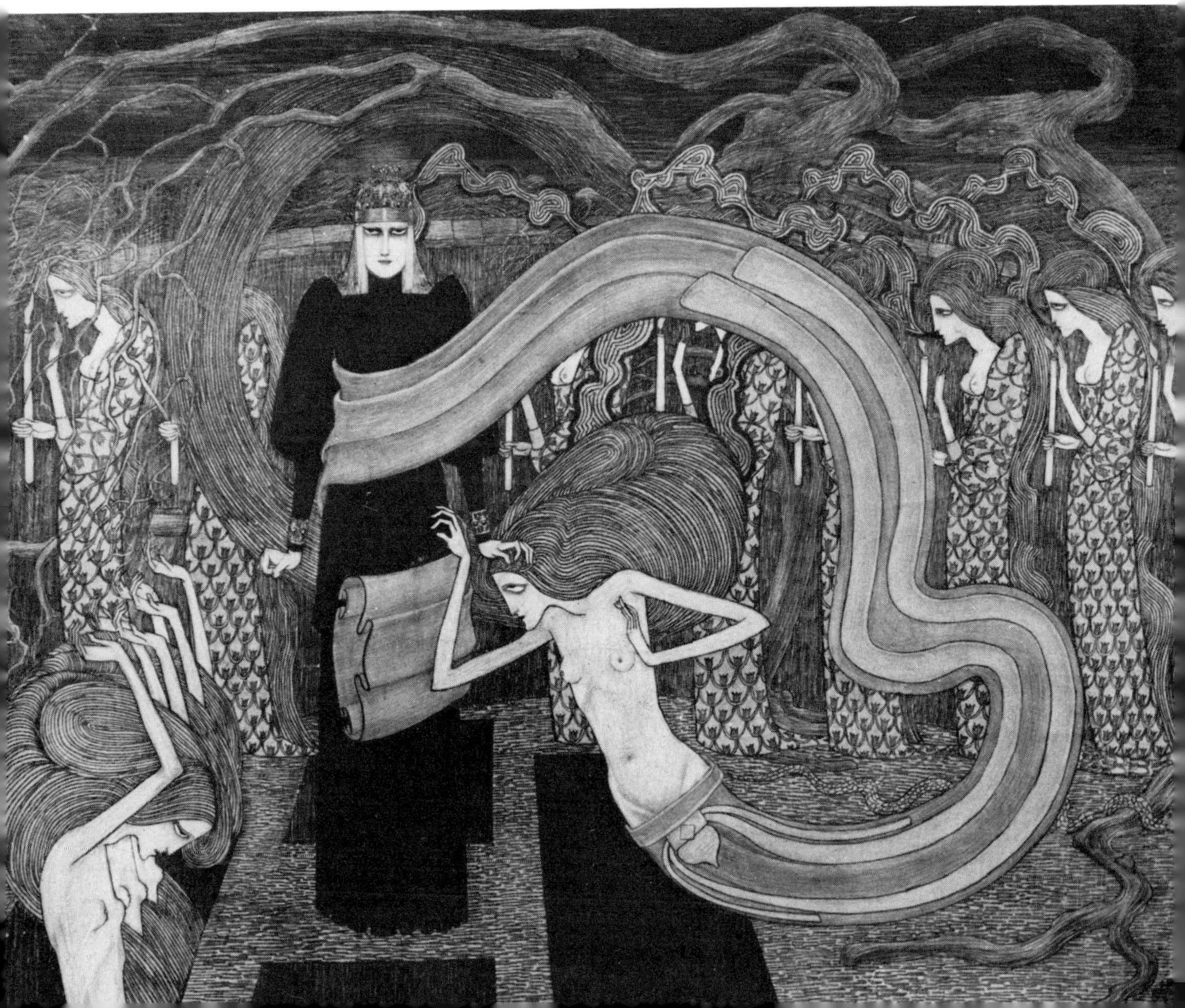

7. Jan Toorop: *Fatalism*. Nearly all the themes of the Decadence are combined in this drawing, made about 1890, by the half-Dutch, half-Javanese artist: a Strindberg heroine, Maeterlinck maidens, and a Pre-Raphaelite 'soul' which foreshadows Klimt.

expected from the philosophers. Thus Taine introduced Carlyle to them in the following terms: 'Ideas transformed into hallucinations lose their solidity. Human beings take on the appearance of dreams. Mysticism seeps like a vapour through the overheated walls of the crumbling mind . . . The distinguishing feature of Carlyle as of any mystic is his ability to see a double meaning in anything and everything.' Here again we note the Baudelairean idea of correspondences, as does this dictum which sheds light on a great many figures in the paintings of Moreau and Burne-Jones: 'The hero is a messenger sent from the impenetrable infinite, bearing news for us' (Carlyle).

Any theory which undermined the rationalism inseparable from materialism was welcome. Thus Jules Laforgue, excited by Hartmann's *Philosophie des Unbewussten*, looked forward to 'a system of aesthetics in harmony with Hartmann's philosophy of the unconscious, Darwin's theory of evolution, and Helmholtz's studies on the physics of colour.' As for pessimism, Schopenhauer's works encouraged it in its darkest forms. He was just as popular in society drawing-rooms as he was at the Sorbonne, and the caricaturist Caran d'Ache frequently poked fun at his female readers; in 1879 Elme-Marie Caro, the so-called 'ladies' philosopher', gave a series of lectures on Schopenhauer which were attended by a painter we shall often meet again, Khnopff. Schopenhauer's influence was countered by Nietzsche's success, but in 1893 Rémy de Gourmont could still write, in connection with a Filiger drawing entitled *Idealism*:

> Idealism is an immoral, antisocial, inhuman doctrine of despair, and therefore an admirable doctrine in a period when what matters is not preservation but destruction . . . Everything I think is real . . The only reality is thought. Schopenhauer's pessi-

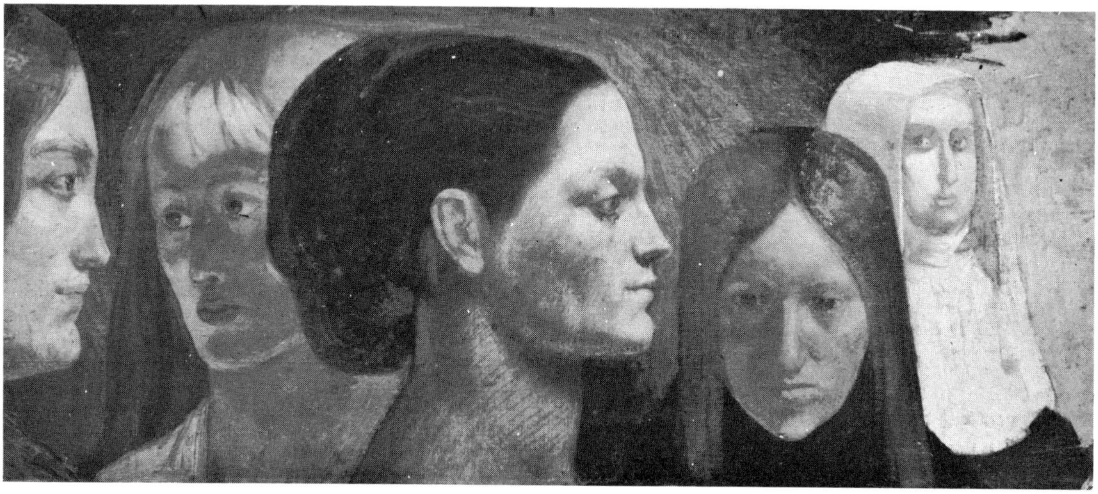

8. Fabry: *La Prison*. Inspired by Rops, these women prisoners have the expression of fallen angels which the era required.

mistic ideal culminates in despotism; Hegel's optimistic idealism results in anarchy. One has only to apply the differential method to see that Schopenhauer is in the right.

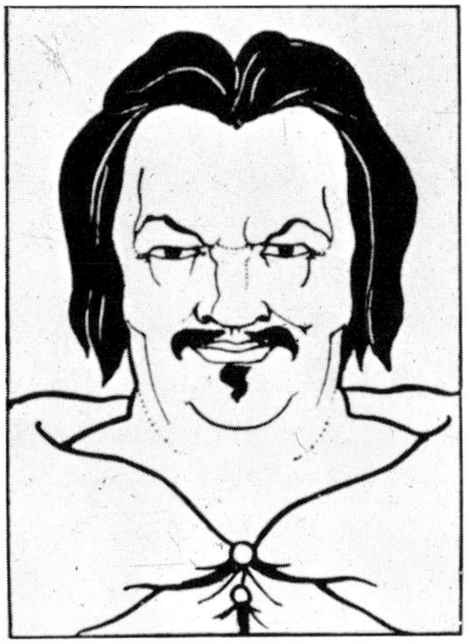

9. Beardsley: Cover design for Balzac's *Comédie Humaine*. Balzac was the writer most revered by the *fin-de-siècle* generation, both for his belief in the supernatural and for having treated ambiguous subjects such as that of *La Fille aux Yeux d'Or*.

Two French thinkers, whose reputation in their own day astonishes us now, were greatly influenced by the philosophers we have just quoted. They were the teachers of all the *fin de siècle* dreamers. In 1889 Edouard Schuré published his *Grands initiés*, which for several generations was the bedside book of high-minded Frenchmen, much as the works of Teilhard de Chardin are now. In it he wrote: 'Deprived of the sight of the eternal horizons, literature and art have lost the sense of the divine. Positivism and scepticism have produced nothing but a desiccated generation without ideals, without inspiration and without faith, doubting in itself and in human liberty.' Schuré wanted to rediscover 'the profound learning, the secret doctrine and the occult influence of the great initiates, prophets or reformers'. Ernest Hello, a Breton mystic who, in Léon Bloy's happy phrase, was 'a man of genius with flashes of the commonplace', also tended to be pessimistic. 'Between the eighteenth century,' he wrote, 'and the century I shall call the twentieth, even if it begins tomorrow, the clock of the earth marks a slow and awful hour, an hour of transition: the terrible nineteenth century. Waking slowly from its nightmare, it possesses nothing, but it yearns, my God, as the world has never yearned before.' Hello had a certain influence on the art of his times, for, before Huysmans, he violently attacked the Sulpician style and all commercial art based on the work of Hippolyte Flandrin and Ary Scheffer.

It is essential to mention these thinkers, because the painters we are going to consider read their works with fervent admiration. In their writings they found a justification for their own dreams, and arguments which enabled them to despise the age in which they lived, the age of their *bête noire* Zola. Nerval, Poe, and sometimes E. T. A. Hoffmann, as well as the inevitable Baudelaire, provided them with the ferment their imagination needed. Their world, unlike that of the Impressionists, was a library with its windows closed to nature.

THE DECADENTS. 'I love the word "Decadence", all gleaming with crimson . . . It is made up of a mixture of carnal spirit and melancholy flesh and all the violent splendours of the Byzantine Empire . . . The collapse into the flames of races exhausted by sensation at the invading sound of the enemy trumpets' (Verlaine). 'Slowly and surely a belief is growing in the bankruptcy of Nature which promises to become the sinister faith of the twentieth century, if science or an invasion of barbarians does not save an over-reflective humanity from the fatigue of its own thought' (Paul Bourget, *Essais de psychologie contemporaine*, 1884). These quotations are taken from K. W. Swart's interesting thesis, *The Sense of Decadence*. We are often surprised to find that Bourget was taken seriously, but we should not forget that Nietzsche admired him and that Wilde, in *Intentions*, imitated his *Dialogues esthétiques* of 1883. If Bourget, famous thinker and triumphant snob, was a pessimist, what else could be expected of a poor, unknown poet such as Jules Laforgue? Here is a note found among his papers about a novel he planned to write: 'It is an autobiography of my person and my thought transferred to a painter, to a painter's life and ambitions, but to a philosopher-painter, a macabre and pessimistic Chenavard. A failed, virgin genius, who dreams of four great frescoes: the epic of mankind, the *danse macabre* of the last period of the planet, the three stages of illusion.' The same anguish in the face of the absurdity of the world, this time taking the form of frenzy, is expressed in a letter from the young Belgian poet Verhaeren to Odilon Redon: 'I fly into a fury with myself because every other form of heroism is forbidden to me. I love things that are absurd, useless, impossible, frantic, excessive and intense, because they provoke me, because I feel them like thorns in my flesh . . .'

The society of Zola's Rougon-Macquarts certainly offered the pessimists countless reasons for despair, with the result that the atmosphere of the *fin de siècle* Bohemia was more bitter and dramatic than that of the Romantic Bohemia of the 1830s. The difference is illustrated quite well by the choice of drinks: the Decadents drank absinthe, the so-called 'green fairy'; the 1830 generation, on the other hand, preferred punch. A little later, opium had had its adepts, often in the form of laudanum, as with Nerval and Rossetti. Other drugs appeared on the scene about 1880; for a time morphine was in fashion, and then ether which could produce madness fairly quickly; but more often than not, absinthe was regarded as sufficient. Consequently much of the literary life of the Decadence was spent at the café, and every group had its own, for very few *salons* were open to young artists before 1892 or 1893. The appearance of these artists was often very peculiar; we can get some idea of how they looked from today's hippies, who likewise take drugs and are attracted by the East. In the absence of any Decadent *salons*, artists' studios also played a great part. Wilde enthused over the studios, with their more or less luxurious bric-à-brac, the company of the models, chats on the divans and discussions in front of the easels. The studio was as important as the café for another reason – painters, poets, thinkers and even musicians

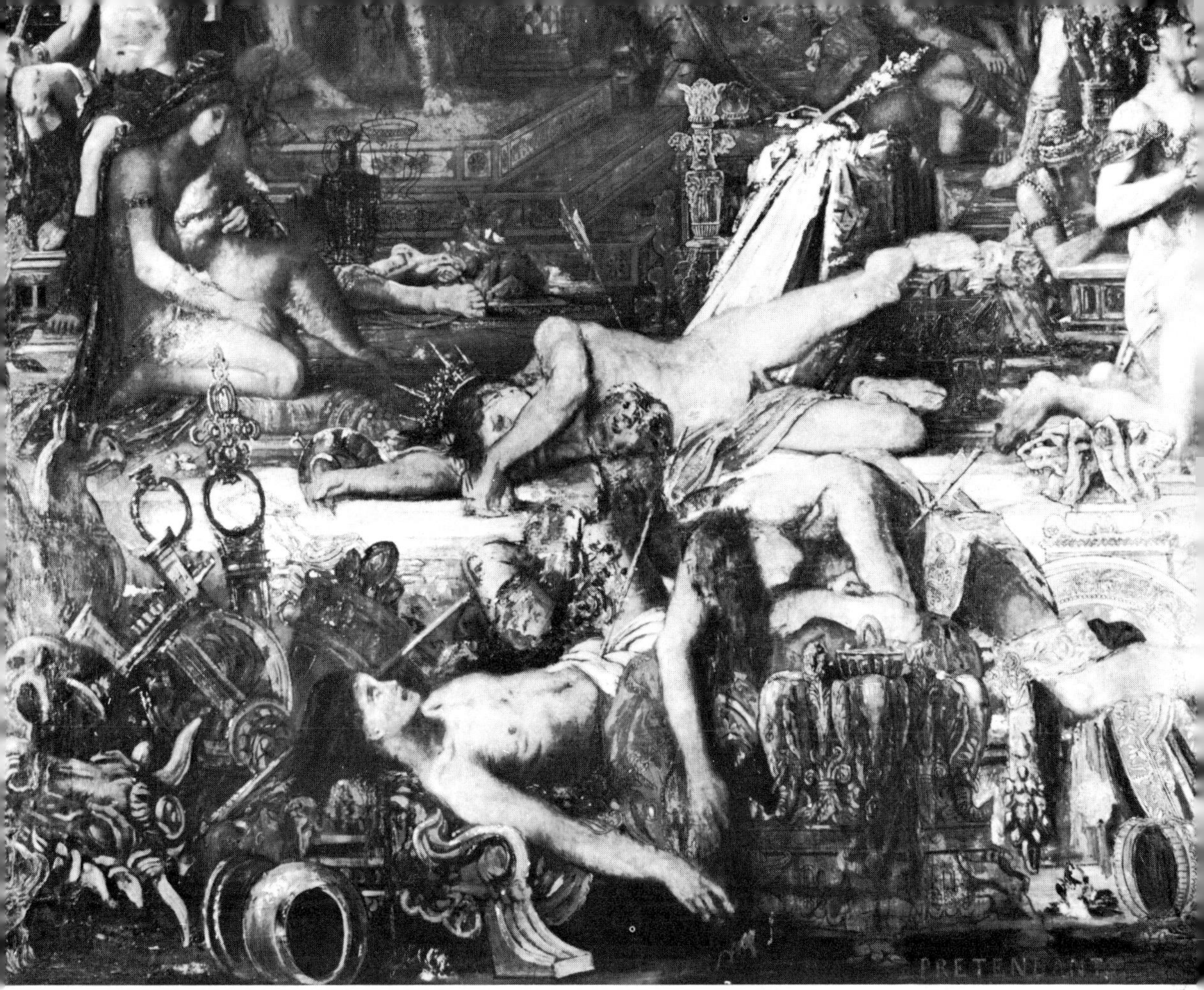

10. Moreau: *Les Prétendants* (detail). The Decadents had a premonition of disaster, and many poets identified themselves with the princes killed by Athena while courting Ulysses's wife Penelope.

dreamed of a mingling of all the arts, and dabbled in everything. Studios were equally suitable for costume parties and spiritualist seances, two ways of travelling 'anywhere out of this world'. Here we are close to the hippies, to whom drugs offer an all too easy means of escape, and we shall see again and again that from their physical appearance to their metaphysical aspirations, the generation which was twenty years old in 1970 has much in common with the Decadents – although far fewer in number – who were twenty in 1890.

The extravagances of the Decadents can best be seen in their language. While the Aesthetes prided themselves on speaking a precise language, studded with expressions of ecstasy, the Decadents enriched the opulent vocabulary of the Parnassians and the Goncourt brothers' *écriture artiste* with fresh neologisms. It is not always easy to see where originality ended and pastiche began, and reviews such as *La Plume* and *Le Décadent* unhesitatingly accepted hair-raising contributions from fake Rimbauds. The best known satire on the language of the Decadents is *Les Déliquescences d'Adoré Floupette*; it is worth quoting instead a few definitions from the *Little Glossary for the Understanding of Decadent and Symbolist Poets* published by Jacques Plowert (Paul Adam & Félix Fénéon) in 1887:

AMPHICURVED: Curved on both sides. 'Age-old nightmares in love with amphicurved orbs' (Moréas).

(TRANSLATION): Succubi with their feet on the ground and fond of bottoms.

VESANIC: Mad. 'Tormented by vesanic neuroses' (Fénéon).

BALSAMYRRHED: Steeped in balm. 'And the solitary plic-placs of balsamyrrhed, opaline fountains' (Laforgue).

The black humour which the Surrealists would try to achieve is to be found on every page of this glossary. People laughed in 1890 too, but a little hysterically. There were countless corpses in the works of poets and painters, who were fond of describing themselves as doomed. This macabre preciosity, cultivated in the studios of Montmartre, found an echo in Beardsley, Klimt and many foreign writers, the most famous of whom was d'Annunzio, for such extravagances, which reconciled the fashionable pessimism of the period with the exuberance of youth, were successful throughout Europe. It was thanks to the Decadents – and at that time Mallarmé and Verlaine, Moreau and Redon were classified as Decadents – that France, despised and denigrated after her defeat, recovered her prestige among the European *avant-garde*. This movement prolonged the Pre-Raphaelite movement in an increasingly bizarre direction: Wilde, for instance, came to Paris to take lessons in 'deliquescence' from Rollinat and Lorrain. Thus the so-called 'mauve Nineties' derived their sinister glow from the Celtic twilight as well as from the gaslamps of Paris. 'They delight in the rare and push worship of the unique to the point of decadence.' It was in 1884, in *Taches d'Encre*, that Barrès used this last word for the first time to describe the new spirit. And satirists were quick to seize upon the Decadents' affectations. Octave Mirbeau, the great friend of the Impressionists, who was always hostile to the Aesthetes and the Decadents, was one of the first to show his teeth. He invented a painter called Loys Jambois, modelled on Whistler and Montesquiou. The bric-à-brac surrounding this character (30) recalls des Esseintes's drawing-room, Sarah Bernhardt's studio, Dorian Gray's boudoir, and the Duke of Brunswick's palace. Exoticism and historicism combined in it to form the culture in which *Art Nouveau* would be born and the chimeras raised.

This religion had few martyrs, but it found a great many worshippers among those new phenomena in French society: the snobs. The word *snob* became current in France about the same time. The snobs were those Aesthetes who were in the latest fashion; the beauty they admired was novelty, and that is why

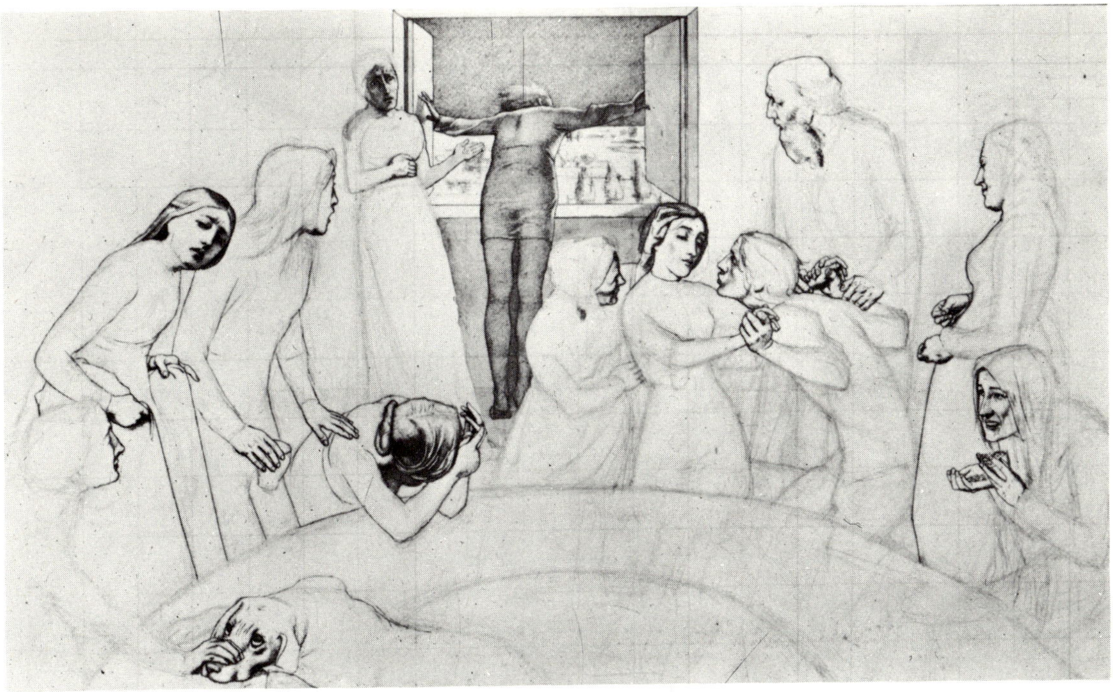

11. John Everett Millais: *The Eve of the Flood.* One of the first works expressing the spiritual anguish of the nineteenth century. The postures foreshadow the stage directions of the Symbolist theatre.

their enthusiasms lasted so short a time. As we shall see, their influence was immense and eventually disastrous, since it thrust a number of masters into unjustified oblivion after a brief hour of fame. The alliance of the snobs and the artists created, by the end of the nineteenth century, an aristocracy of taste served by Toorop, Khnopff, Klimt, all the exponents of *Art Nouveau,* an élite which itself had been nurtured on the works of the Pre-Raphaelites and especially of Moreau.

Jean Lorrain wrote in *Sensations et Souvenirs:*

> Oh, that man [Moreau] can boast of having broken open the door of Mystery; that man can claim the honour of having disturbed his entire century. He infected a whole generation, sick today with a mystical nostalgia for the Beyond, with a dangerous passion for dead beauties, beauties of bygone ages which he resuscitated in the Mirror of Time . . . And that painful obsession with the symbols and perversions of the old theogonies, that curiosity about the divine debaucheries worshipped in the dead religions, has become the exquisite sickness of the refined souls of this *fin de siècle.*

These lines state once again the themes of the first art to be deliberately decadent: the taste for death and occultism, the combination of mysticism and eroticism. But it would be a mistake to see in these tendencies a pose or a vice: they revealed above all else a compulsive need to escape from a materialistic society.

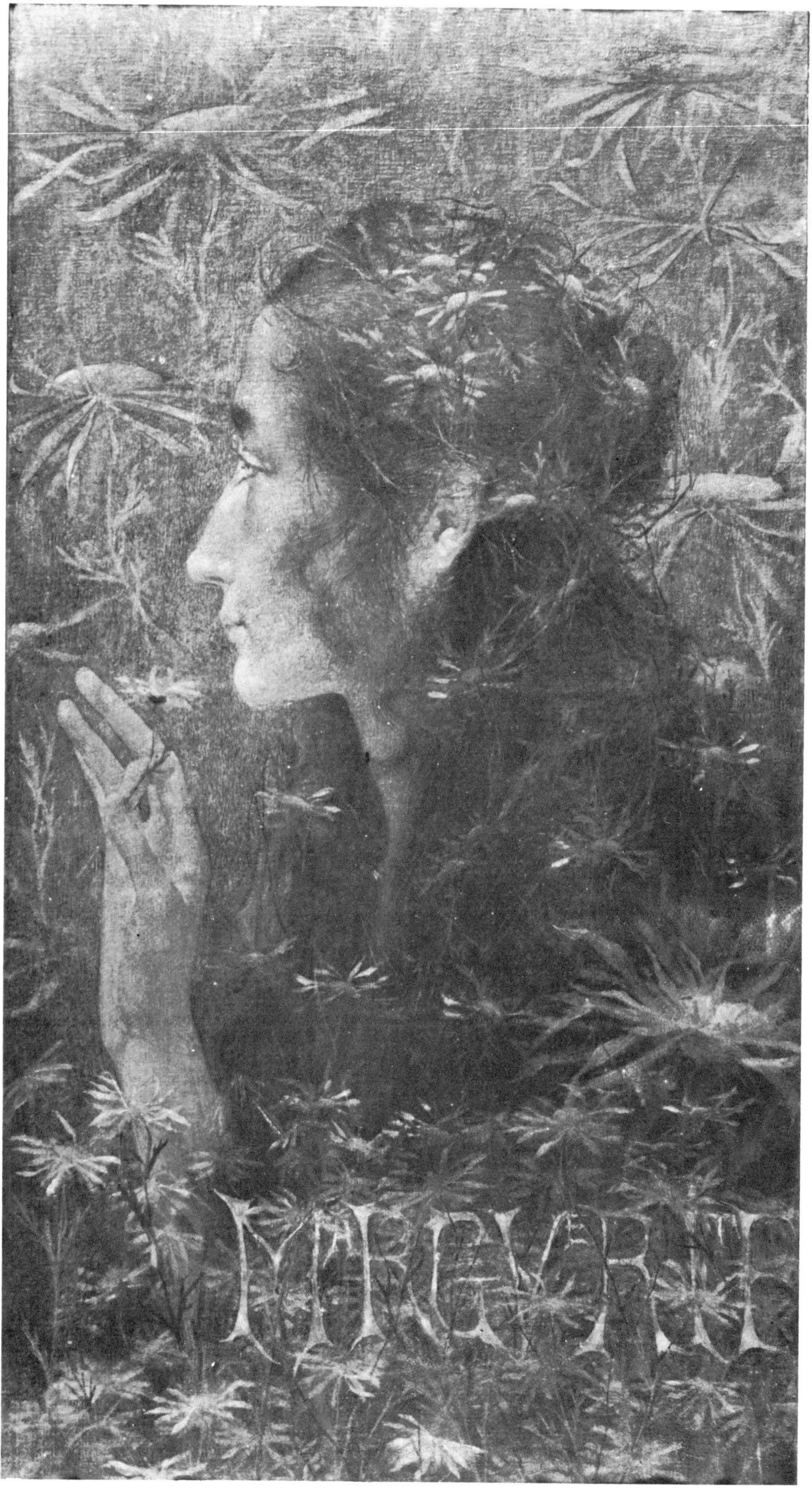

2 A New Beauty

THE MONA LISAS. Every new style proposes an original type of beauty which derives less from fashion than from the secret aspirations of a generation. The first Romantic movement had promoted a masculine ideal of Byronic gloom rather than a feminine ideal, because the public was tired of the images of martyred women offered by the Gothic novel, and even more hostile to the dead women painted by Delacroix. Only Princess Belgiojoso had had the courage to personify that funereal type of beauty, which we are going to consider now. With the triumph of the opulent beauties of the Second Empire, it was thought that the extravagances of minor poets and the illustrations of German ballads or exotic novels had brought permanent ridicule upon the lovely spectres of the Romantics. A prosperous and often vulgar period refused to be touched any longer by these skeletal beauties, let alone imitate them. The Second Empire woman was the woman Courbet painted, who already foreshadowed Renoir's models. But when, together with pessimism, there came a distaste for realism, and, in certain English circles, a revulsion against the opposite sex, Romantic feminine beauty at last came into its own – the fatal or doomed beauty of Baudelaire's poems, which could be distinguished as early as 1860 in the pictures of Dante Gabriel Rossetti and Gustave Moreau. For about thirty years we propose to follow the development of this ideal from the sad sensuality of Rossetti's models to the cadaverous type in vogue at the end of the century. The worm was in the fruit; the melancholy of the Pre-Raphaelites already pointed the way to the madness of the Decadents, and in *The Critic as Artist* Wilde passes quite naturally from Rossetti's Beatrice to the Baudelairean ideal '*Sois belle et sois triste*: Be beautiful and sad.'

At the beginning of his admirable book, *The Romantic Agony*, Professor Mario Praz recognizes this fatal beauty in the lithograph by Delacroix showing Goethe's Margaret, white-faced, with a red line around her neck, being carried off by devils. Goethe compares this vision with the Medusa's head. The ancient Greek sorceress is

12. Lévy-Dhurmer: *Marguerite*. In the early part of his career Lévy-Dhurmer was the artistic counterpart of Jean Lorrain. He was the most gifted of all the French Symbolist painters. The predominant colours are blue-grey and dark green, and the lettering is an imitation of Primitive paintings.

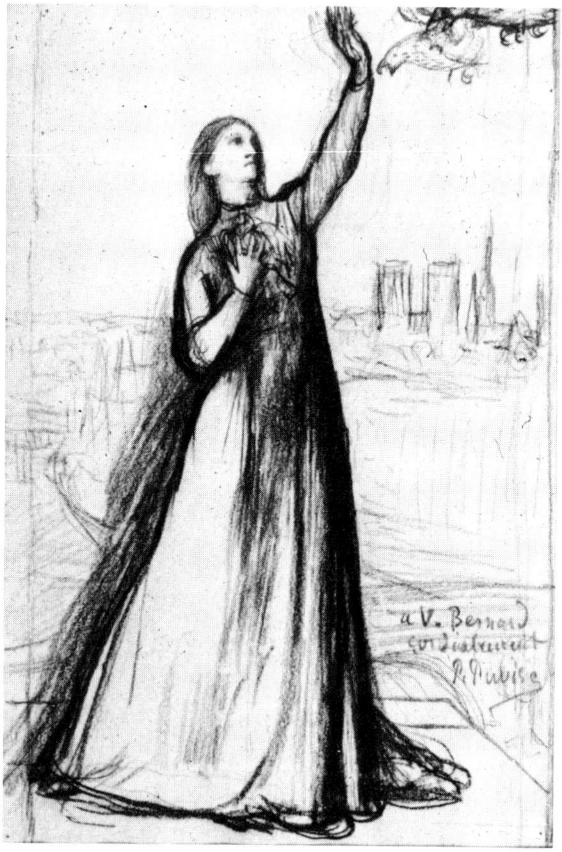

13. Pierre Puvis de Chavannes: Study for *Le Siège de Paris*. In this allegory, in which France is protecting Paris from the German Eagle, it can be seen how close Puvis was at times to Rossetti.

in fact the ancestress of all the chimeras, whether conceived by Moreau or by Klimt. After seeing a picture of her in the Uffizi Gallery, Shelley had paid homage to her in these words:

> Its horror and its beauty are divine.
> Upon its lips and eyelids seems to lie
> Loveliness like a shadow, from which shine,
> Fiery and Lurid, struggling underneath,
> The agonies of anguish and of death.

This picture, attributed at the time to Leonardo da Vinci, but in fact the work of an unknown follower of Caravaggio, shows a severed head, deathly pale and surrounded by writhing serpents. Shelley saw Leonardo's art in a sinister light, and Walter Pater's famous work, *Studies in the History of the Renaissance* (1873), endows this fatal beauty with the ambiguities of the painter of Bacchus and St. John. His passage on the Mona Lisa, in which so many painters and poets were to find their inspiration, deserves to be quoted here:

> It is a beauty wrought out from within upon the flesh, the deposit, little cell by cell, of strange thoughts and fantastic reveries and exquisite passions. Set it for a moment beside one of those

white Greek goddesses or beautiful women of antiquity, and how would they be troubled by this beauty, into which the soul with all its maladies has passed! All the thoughts and experience of the world have etched and moulded there, in that which they have of power to refine and make expressive the outward form, the animalism of Greece, the lust of Rome, the mysticism of the Middle Ages with its spiritual ambition and imaginative loves, the return of the Pagan world, the sins of the Borgias. She is older than the rocks among which she sits; like the vampire, she has been dead many times, and learned the secrets of the grave . . . Certainly Lady Lisa might stand as the embodiment of the old fancy, the symbol of the modern idea . . .

Subsequently, there were to be countless Mona Lisas in the works of the *fin de siècle* – ludicrous in Sâr Péladan, terrifying in d'Annunzio, Parisian in Jean de Tinan.

There was no lack of heroines whom poets and painters could endow with this same terrible beauty. First there was Helen, as depicted in the Second Part of *Faust*, and as painted by Moreau, and then Sappho, whose perversity added to her mystery. Not to mention the empresses dear to Swinburne, and even Böcklin's robust sea-nymphs.

We can find the same smile on Moreau's faces, and lighting up the masks Khnopff gives his sphinxes. Odilon Redon's monsters have it too, even though his archangels have known 'strange thoughts, mad reveries and rare passions'. And, of course, the Pre-Raphaelites had treated the same theme as early as 1850, when painting Beatrice or Morgan, so that one may wonder whether all that Pater discovered was found in the da Vinci portrait or in those which Rossetti painted of Elizabeth Siddal, his model, his mistress, and finally his wife. A pale yet sensual beauty, simple clothes and languid poses – everything about Elizabeth Siddal was a protest against Victorian tastes. The effort of embodying the new ideal was too great for this delightful woman, who was never known to laugh; she died of tuberculosis at the age of twenty-seven.

This ideal of a mysterious or melancholy beauty conquered the studios, and then other artists, thanks to two casts: the Wax Head in Lille Museum, attributed to Raphael, and the cast of the Unknown Woman of the Seine. Like the Mona Lisa, these masks showed Symbolist faces, but with closed eyes. Many portraits of the time were to show eyes closed to conceal an inner world, thus giving an impression of silence.

14. Louis Lessieux: *Ondine*. This mediocre picture is a good example of the way in which *Art Nouveau* themes were debased after the 1900 exhibition.

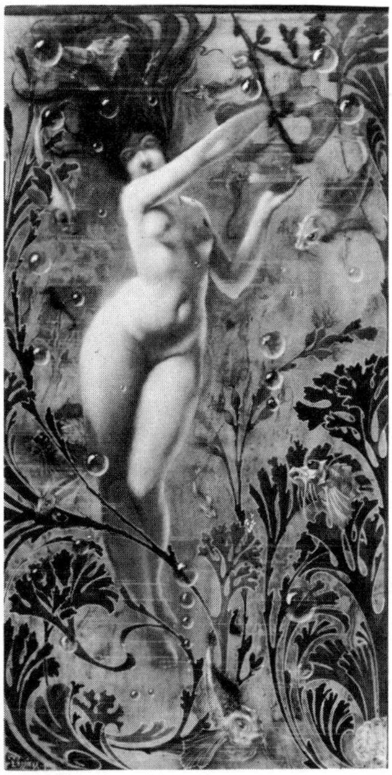

THE BEATRICES. Chelsea about 1870, Montmartre about 1890, and Munich and Vienna about 1900, swarmed with replicas of

Elizabeth and the Mona Lisa, and then of Botticellis, for as fashion took hold of the myth, it made it more insipid. Jean Lorrain (whom we shall be quoting often in this work, for he was the best observer of a milieu of which he was also the worst ornament) shows us what Pater's ideal became in a *fin de siècle* Parisienne:

> The disturbing pallor of the host, a thin oval face with an expression of spiritual suffering, and wide eyes of an ultramarine colour bordering on black, with bluish rings around them tinged with mother-of-pearl; this strange and fragile creature embodied the psychic beauty of the twentieth century ... Where had I already seen that delicate nose with the vibrant nostrils, or the panting of that flat chest?

Perhaps this was Wilde's friend the Baronne Deslandes, the French incarnation of the New Woman invented by the English Aesthetes, the woman who copied her floral dresses from Botticelli's *Primavera.* The spirit of spring is a virginal Mona Lisa, as ambiguous as da Vinci's creation, but not burdened with terrible secrets. Liberty's of London copied Quattrocento materials for these creatures, who abandoned their contemporaries' bustles and held lilies in their hands. All these images were derived from Rossetti's pictures of Beatrice, the inaccessible Egeria. Her masculine equivalent was to be invented by Burne-Jones.

Princess or artist's model, sphinx or succubus, Sappho or Ganymede, the *fin de siècle* insisted that the face should be moulded by the soul, and this was the mask which obtained the greatest success. In order to be desirable in a milieu which had turned its back on materialism, woman had to become a lily, if she did not want to be condemned as vulgar by the Aesthetes. If woman could not be childlike and innocent, she was expected to inspire evil desires, with the result that the poets were fond of confusing women with boys. The Florentine décor lent itself to this sort of confusion, for it will be remembered that Botticelli used long-haired boys as his models, just as Shakespeare's heroines, on the stage at least, were always transvestites. Thus an ambivalence was created in many minds which is very clearly expressed in a poem by Jean Lorrain (32) comparing Ophelia with Renaissance page-boys.

We are entering here into a period even more anaemic than the first Romantic movement: at that time pallor had been the effect of overwhelming passions, whereas for the Decadents it showed that a person was a soul before all else, and that he could enter Death's domain at any moment, gracefully and with no regrets. Octave Mirbeau, who always preferred the common-sense point of view, expressed indignation over these external signs of spirituality, which he noticed particularly in Burne-Jones's paintings:

'The rings under the eyes . . . are unique in the whole history of art; it is impossible to tell whether they are the result of masturbation, lesbianism, normal love-making or tuberculosis.'

THE OPHELIAS. The melancholy, ambiguous beauty of Moreau's picture is that of a creature who has listened to the chimeras. For an explanation of this expression we have to turn, not to Pater this time, but to Poe, who writes: 'The death of a beautiful woman is without doubt the most poetic subject in the world.' One thinks of all Poe's dead fiancées, Delacroix's *Ophélie*, or, better still, Millais's *Ophelia*, for which Elizabeth Siddal posed fully clothed in a bath, with her hair spread out, during interminable seances. These drowned women are the sisters of the beautiful female corpses Delacroix was so fond of painting lying on the steps of Constantinople, bleeding in the sunshine of Chios, or with their throats slit on the funeral pyre of Sardanapalus. We know how much Baudelaire loved them too, and it is interesting to read these lines by Delacroix endorsing the opinion of the poet of the dead: 'Baudelaire says in his preface that I recall in the field of painting that feeling for an ideal which is so strange and so pleasant in its terrifying effects. He is right' (*Journal*, 1856). These Ophelias are the figments of sadistic imaginations, just as the Mona Lisas are the creatures of masochistic dreams.

All the dead women of the *fin de siècle* are certainly closer to Poe than to Shakespeare: drowned Botticelli beauties, their hair and dresses floating in the current, or those macabre Rossetti arabesques

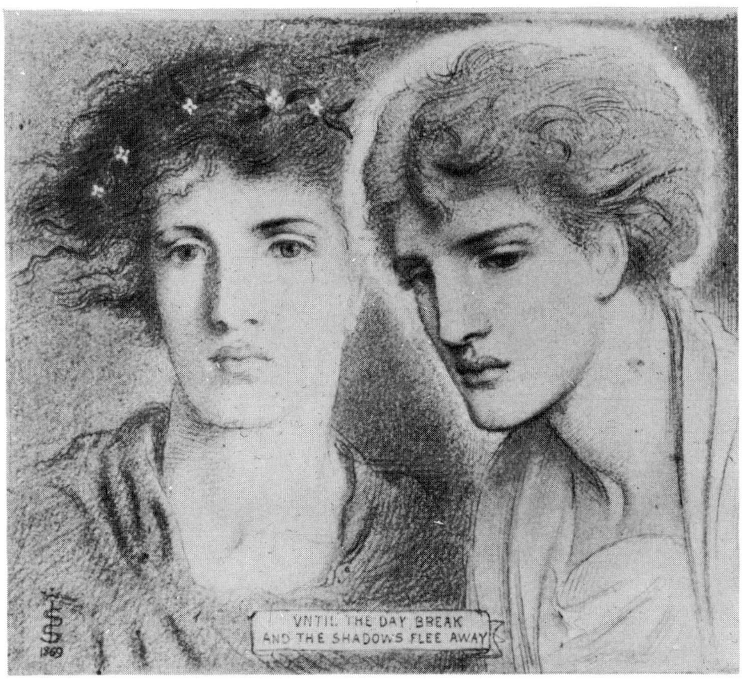

15. Simeon Solomon: *Until the Day Break*. A charcoal drawing which exemplifies Walter Pater's ideal of beauty. This gifted draughtsman ended his days as a pavement artist in the 1890s.

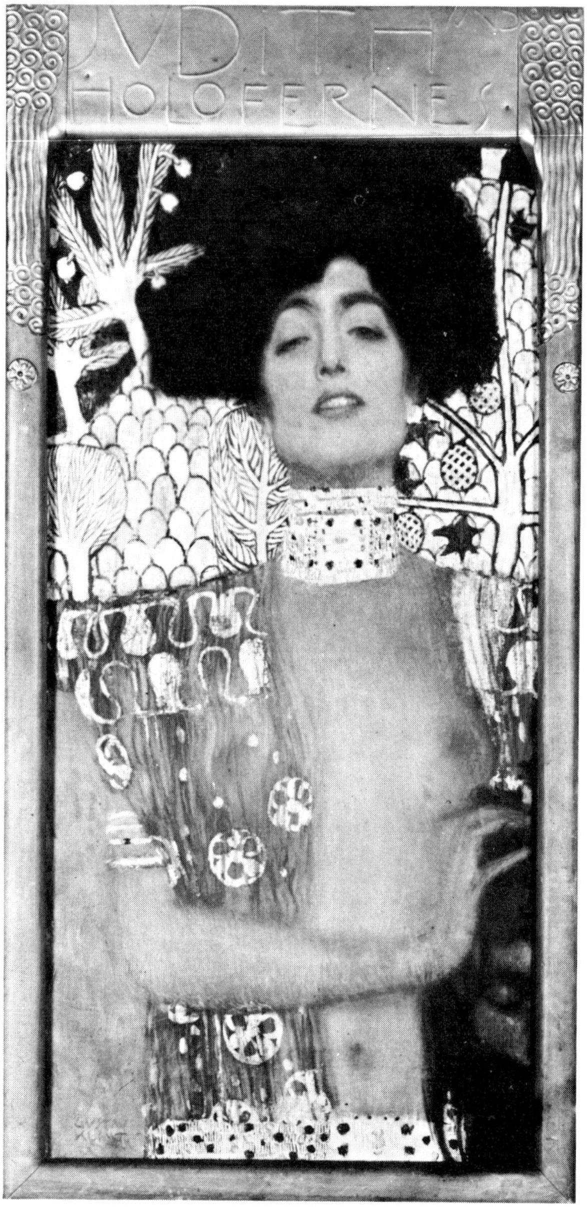

16. Gustav Klimt: *Judith*. A Viennese Mona Lisa pictured against a gilded Byzantine background, wearing the jewels of Theodora. The frame is already in the *Arts Décoratifs* style of 1925.

illustrating Tennyson's *Lady of Shalott*, which could still be discerned, forty years later, by anyone peering into the canals of Bruges-la-Morte. The woman seen through the water, a siren rather than a chimera, was often treated by writers as well as painters: Wilde's story *The Fisherman and his Soul* is the best known example. These Ophelias, so much more Florentine than Scandinavian in character, inspired a great many poets, and one of the first examples, a very *Art Nouveau* creature, is Rimbaud's:

Sur l'onde calme et noire où dorment les étoiles
La blanche Ophélie flotte comme un grand lys,
Flotte très lentement couchée en ses longs voiles . . .

On the calm, dark waters in which sleep the stars
Pale Ophelia floats like a great lily,
Floats very slowly lying in her long veils . . .

17. Edward Burne-Jones: *St. George*. This tall canvas, painted in tones of red and sepia, which are unusual for Burne-Jones, dominates the *Jugendstil* room in the favourite château of the Grand Duke of Hesse, the chief patron of *Art Nouveau* in Germany. The work had considerable influence.

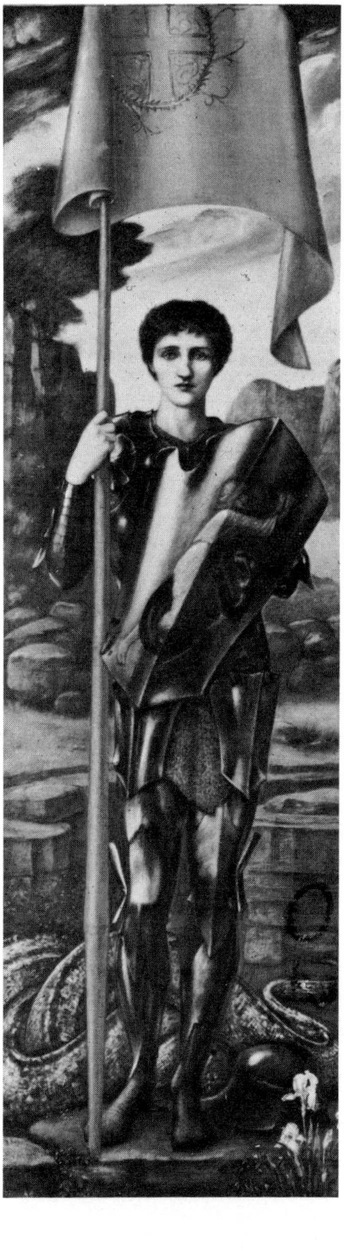

The Pre-Raphaelites and Moreau created a new type of beauty when they imposed on their contemporaries a choice between a threatening or sacrificed version of the Renaissance ideal, and the Baudelairean woman. Hitherto it had been the painters who had followed the beauty of their time, but with the aesthetic revolution the reverse occurred, enabling Wilde to remark that 'Nature imitates Art'. That, of course, was true in only a limited circle, but a circle which represented the most sensitive elements in every country. Renoir's models, who have never been troubled by even the shadow of a thought, lack that aura of dead flowers which was so dear to Edgar Allan Poe – 'the incense of these slumbering roses'.

Let us return to Poe and go from the siren to the vampire. If Lady Madeline is a sister of Ophelia's – 'the flower beneath the foot' – her brother Usher is the prototype of the decadent aesthete. He foreshadows certain characters in the works of Jean Lorrain and above all the Duc Jean Floressas des Esseintes of Huysmans's *A Rebours*.

THE HERMAPHRODITES. *A Rebours* gives the impression of being a Realistic gloss on Edgar Allan Poe's Romantic story. Usher and des Esseintes read the same books: Swedenborg, the *Directorium inquisitorum*, the Gnostics and the obscurer theologians. They resemble each other physically:

> A cadaverousness of complexion; an eye large, liquid, and luminous beyond comparison; lips somewhat thin and very pallid, but of a surpassingly beautiful curve; a nose of a delicate Hebrew model, but with a breadth of nostril unusual in similar formations; a finely moulded chin, speaking, in its want of prominence, of a want of moral energy; hair of a more than web-like softness and tenuity; these features, with an inordinate expansion above the regions of the temple, made up altogether a countenance not easily to be forgotten.

This face will be found again in Toorop's paintings. Small wonder that the literary descendants of such characters were described as unhealthy, even before less unusual pleasures than necrophilia earned them the condemnation of the critics and the sympathy of the Aesthetes.

Let us return to the room in the Musée Gustave Moreau where *Les Chimères* hangs, and let us consider its unfinished pendant, *Les*

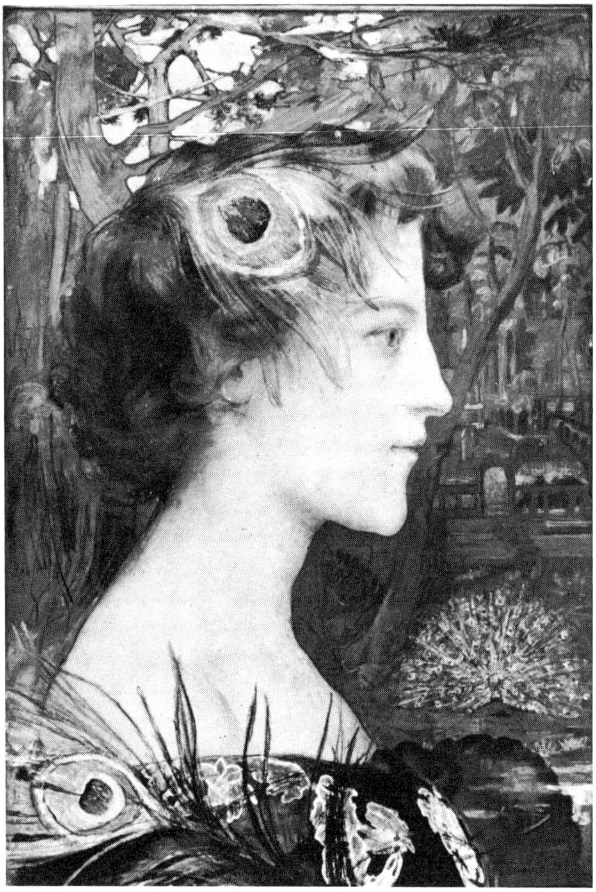

18. Edgar Maxence: *Femme dans un Parc.* Later to become famous at the Salon for his pictures of medieval ladies at prayer, this painter gave way in his youth to the fashion for peacocks and mysterious parks.

Prétendants (The Suitors), in which the only figures are a goddess and some men. Among the beautiful victims covered with jewels the Aesthetes recognized themselves, or at least their ideal. The virile beauty of the first Romantic movement was that of Byron's Satan; however, the beauty of Decadent Romanticism would be hermaphrodite in character. In 1886 the review *Le Décadent* decreed: 'The delicate faces of the new generations shall be smooth and immaculate. Already the Decadents, precursors of the society of the future, are close to the ideal type of perfection. The few fine, silky hairs on their faces are only remotely reminiscent of the animal. Man is growing more refined, more feminine, more divine.' Péladan and Rachilde would describe this ideal *ad nauseam* (16, 21).

The Don Juan Satan lost a great deal of his prestige about 1880. Perhaps it was thought that he looked too much like the paunchy tenors singing Mephistopheles in Gounod's *Faust*. Baudelaire would certainly have felt no desire to repeat his dictum that 'the most perfect type of manly beauty is Satan, as described by Milton'. With the passing of the years, this dandyish Satan had become a vampire; he was usually to be found in some Carpathian castle as dilapidated as the House of Usher, lying in wait for innocent victims. The *fin de siècle* Satan had lost his Romantic beauty, and his features lacked distinction, except in a Redon lithograph which endowed him with a Leonardo smile; he had become a Priapus of the sacristy, conjured up at Black Masses by Huysmans's heroines.

Let us return to the victims in Moreau's pictures, which inspired first Proust, then the Baron de Charlus. With what tender devotion Moreau adorned the poets in his pictures with all the treasures of Asia, from the *Oedipe*, which made his name, to the *Jason* which death prevented him from finishing! And how tenderly he spoke of his heroes in his notes! On the other hand, he had nothing but loathing for the women for whose sake these young men had died: 'This bored, capricious woman, with her animal nature, deriving very little pleasure from seeing her enemy defeated, for she is easily disgusted by any satisfaction of her desires . . .' All Moreau's work cries out with a secret which the official painter did his best to conceal, but which the poets all guessed.

19. Dante Gabriel Rossetti: *Elizabeth Siddal*. A pen-and-ink drawing of the prototype of the woman artist, the original 'soul'. Thirty years later, the women associated with the Symbolists would try to look like her.

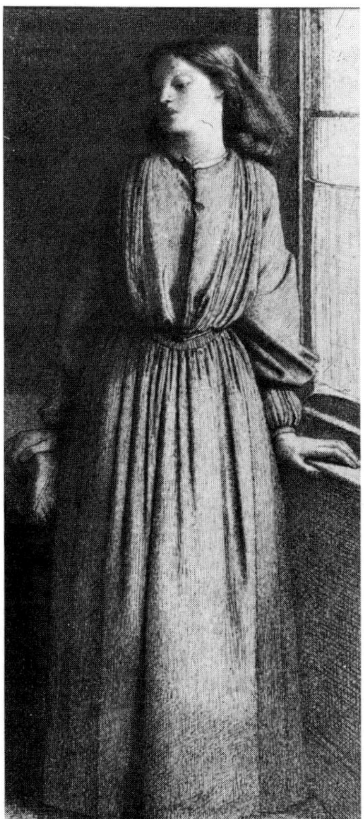

Nevertheless the same physical type occurred in the pictures of Burne-Jones, whose private life was above reproach; the English painter drew the inspiration for his ephebes from Mantegna rather than Botticelli. Huysmans, who was not attracted by young boys but who swam with the Decadent tide, spoke of this type of beauty with curious enthusiasm in connection with an Italian primitive. His description (24) would apply just as well to one of Burne-Jones's knights of the Round Table. With a more robust physique and a less anguished expression, the ephebe might have been an Oxford undergraduate.

These young boys were to be found in both the Paris Salon and the London Royal Academy: witness Lévy's *Le Tepidarium*, Lecomte du Nouÿ's *Le Porteur de Mauvaises Nouvelles* (which made such an impression on the young Julien Green), the flower-bedecked slaves in Alma-Tadema's pictures of antiquity, and the works of other painters who delighted in confusing Oxford with Ancient Greece. The Germans found more robust specimens of manhood in the works of Böcklin and Klinger; and as early as 1860, in the strongly classical pictures of one of Thomas Couture's pupils, Feuerbach, they could discover a Baudelairean anxiety in the faces of a Medea or an Aspasia. They could even be aroused by the ephebes in a vast painting by the same artist entitled *Plato's School*. Moreau was therefore not the only painter to depict youths adorned with jewels, and this is why his works did not create the scandal one might have expected.

On the other hand a very handsome, very talented young English Jew, a friend of the Pre-Raphaelites called Simeon Solomon, drew some boys for Walter Pater who were frankly lascivious, in spite of their angelic attributes. Another of his admirers, Swinburne, describes them for us in the following terms: 'Grecian form and beauty divide the allegiance of his spirit with Hebraic shadow and majesty: depths of cloud unsearchable and summits unsurmountable of fire darken and lighten before the vision of a soul enamoured of soft light and clear water, of leaves and flowers and limbs more lovely than these.' Solomon was in the habit of illustrating and describing his dreams in the Blake manner, and this is how Love appeared to him in a vision: 'Ever and again his feet, wherefrom sprang glowing wings, touched the earth and caused it to bring forth flowers; his head was bound with a fillet of violet, and violet blossoms breathed upon by Love; he carried a mystic veil of saffron colour, which depended from his head upon his shoulders even to the ground, and his shining body was halfgirt with fawnskin' (*Vision of Love Revealed in Sleep*, 1871). Unfortunately young Solomon donned the same costume for a few notorious Chelsea parties, and his life in society ended in a terrible scandal. Wilde owned several drawings by Solomon.

Later on, in 1891, a friend of Wilde's called Ricketts illustrated his stories in the same style, with languid athletes rather like those of Burne-Jones and supple fishermen in love with sirens. Around Wilde there was formed an ideal of male beauty which was close to the ideal created in Rossetti's studio twenty years before. Lord Alfred Douglas is the counterpart of Elizabeth Siddal. But the 'love-boy' inspired no works of art to match the admirable drawings Rossetti has left us of his beloved. Perhaps Wilde fell in love with Lord Alfred because he resembled, in rather more robust form, Burne-Jones's models and above all Watts's knights. This ideal rapidly degenerated. It can be found in antique guise in the photographs of that Baron de Gloeben who drew so many visitors to Taormina, and in that dismal 'sanctuary of art' at Locarno whose walls were covered with more or less antique visions by a Russian painter called Elisarion, or in the vast paintings by d'Annunzio's friend Aristide Sartorio, full of handsome warriors who are always naked and generally dead. In our own day certain American periodicals, supposedly devoted to the cause of physical culture, offer their readers pencil drawings of ephebes who are the great-nephews of Moreau's and Burne-Jones's heroes. It is interesting to compare these insipid productions with the 'Beardsley Boy' as described by the artist himself: 'Sporion was a tall, slim, depraved young man with a slight stoop, a troubled walk, an oval impassible face with its olive skin drawn tightly over the bone, strong, scarlet lips, long Japanese eyes, and a great gilt toupet.' Beardsley's Ganymedes and Sporions do indeed possess an elegance which is entirely lacking in the works of the painters cited above. And though

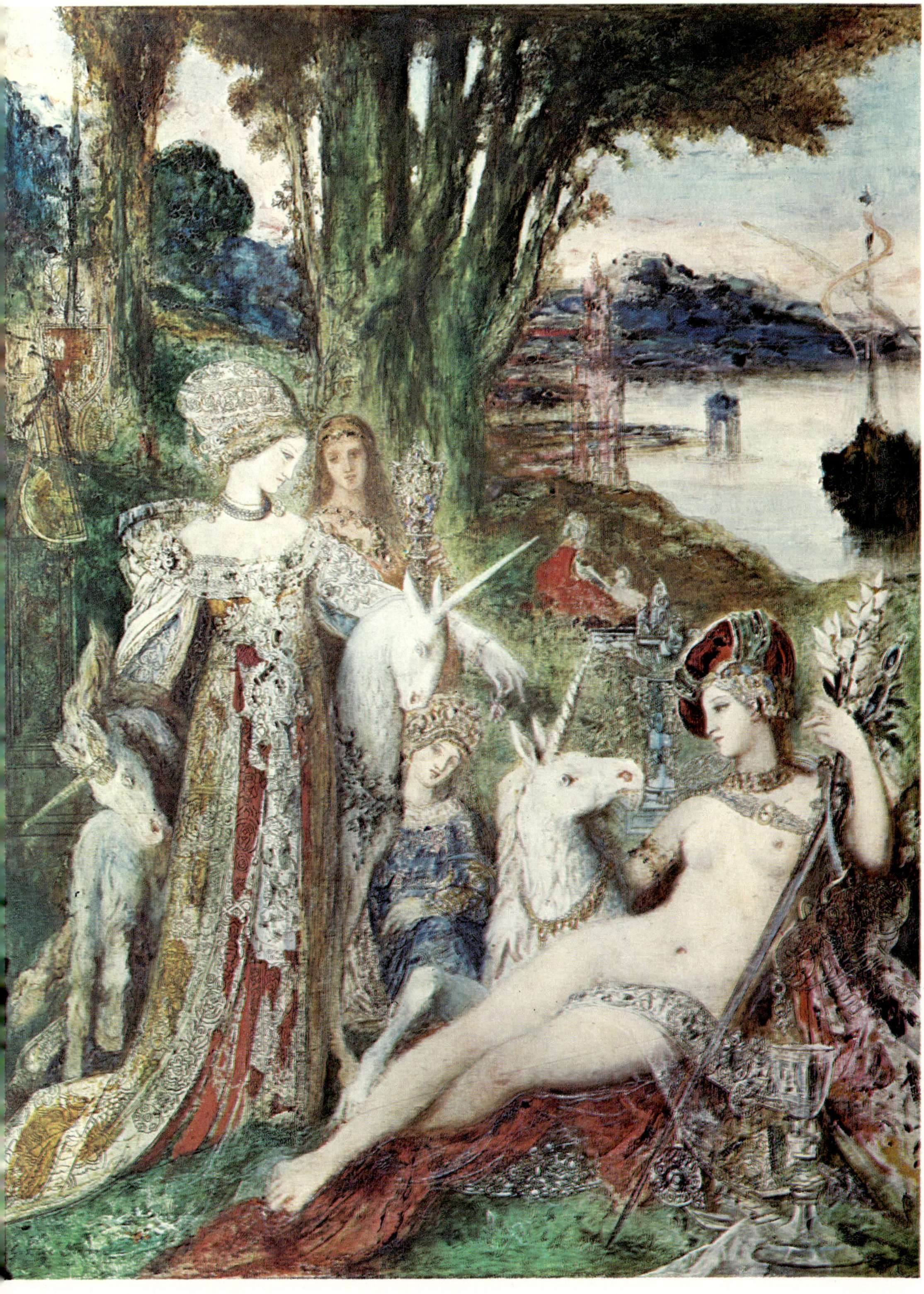

20. Moreau: *Les Licornes.* Painted in about 1885, this work was inspired by the flowery Middle Ages of legend, the famous tapestries of the Musée de Cluny with their misty beauty, and the landscapes of Leonardo, with the costumes deriving from Pisanello. The unicorn, of course, could only be tamed by virgins.

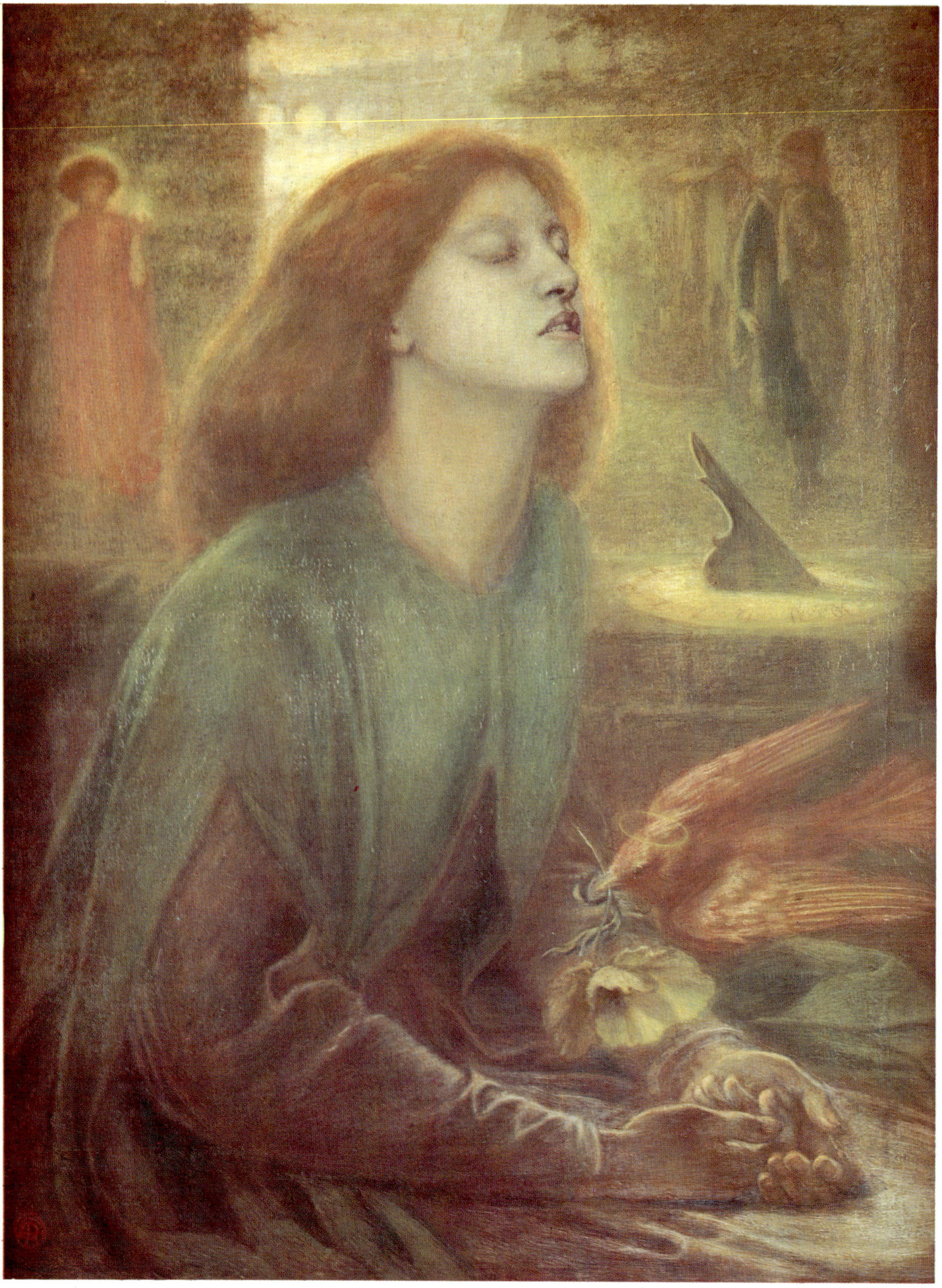

one may remain untroubled by the cynical expressions on Beardsley's faces and the implacable strength of his line, the same is not true when one sees these same creatures loaded with enormous chignons and wearing Japanese crinolines or Byzantine night-dresses slit where the sexes differ only slightly. There can be no doubt that the 'Beardsley Woman' who followed the Pre-Raphaelite 'New Woman' was a transvestite.

In Beardsley too we find a more dynamic type of male beauty in the shape of the faun. The faun in the English artist's drawings bears a certain resemblance to the faun in Verlaine's poems, but he is only distantly related to the hairy, red-faced creature we see pursuing the nymphs in Böcklin's paintings. This Teutonic Pan gave his name to the splendid German review of the *Jugendstil*; the *fin de siècle* version continues the theme of the wild man treated so often by Cranach and other late medieval artists, and it is in his old domain, the Germanic forest, that he enjoys the greatest vogue. He also emerges from the Russian forest in the strange paintings of Vroubel, who seems to have inspired Stravinsky's music even more than Mallarmé's poem. Mallarmé's Faun, leaping from rock to rock, is indeed not as disturbing as the devilish Pan, to whom Arthur Machen devoted a book which was translated by Toulet and adorned with a Beardsley cover. Lévy-Dhurmer and Henry de Groux too were inspired by the primitive myth. Pan is undoubtedly the most eloquent of those dead gods whom Renan had wrapped in 'a crimson shroud': he alone, in this strange period of the *fin de siècle*, represents the natural instincts.

21. Rossetti: *Beata Beatrix*. Elizabeth Siddal depicted between the ghosts of Dante and Beatrice. An almost mediumistic picture painted in purples and greens shortly after Elizabeth's death. Every element in this work is a symbol of the past or a symbol of the life to come. This was also Rossetti's last masterpiece.

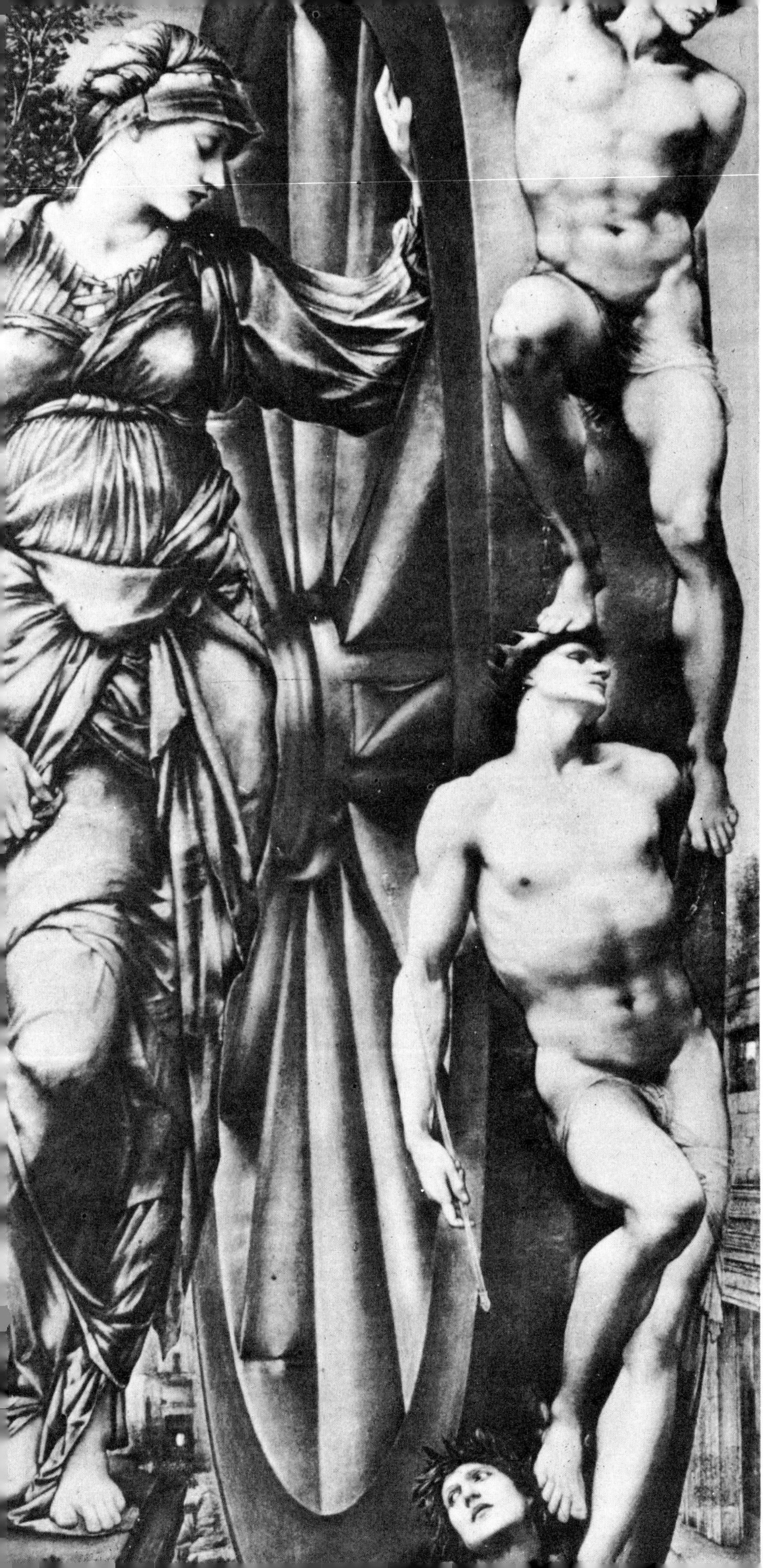

3 The Legendary Chimera

22. Burne-Jones: *The Wheel of Fortune* (detail). This strange *grisaille* is perhaps the painter's masterpiece. It embodies the physical ideal of Wilde's stories: the bodies are taken from Michelangelo, the expressions from Leonardo da Vinci.

HISTORY. In the left-hand corner of Gustave Moreau's great painting, in the shadow of the Byzantine monument surmounted by a sphinx, there are three women who, from the ornaments they are wearing, seem to form a link between Myth and History. The tallest of the three, a sort of Europa, being carried off by a bull, has the face of Raphael's Joan of Aragon; at her feet, stroking a unicorn, there is a Melusina, naked apart from a hennin, and loaded with chains, who seems to come straight out of a tapestry; and lastly there is a pensive girl wearing Charlemagne's crown on her blond tresses and bowed beneath a dalmatic embroidered with eagles, who could be the embodiment of Germania. Perhaps she is an allegory of History, which occupied such a large place in the thought of the last century, that History made woman, cruel or sublime, portrayed with a certain disquiet by Michelet, or the visionary, messianic History of Hugo's *Légende des Siècles*. As for the architectural elements scattered about the picture, they are excellent examples of historicism, the name used by art historians to denote the various pastiches which took the place of style during the Victorian era. The Viollet-le-Duc décor deliberately situates the picture in an atmosphere of Christian fantasy. The Gothic arches and pinnacles had been depicted forty years earlier by the illustrators of Hugo's *Notre-Dame de Paris*, and bear a close resemblance to Merovak's imaginary cathedrals. They were known, about 1880, under the name of 'the *Chat noir* style' – a reference to the Montmartre tavern fitted with stained-glass windows and imitation tapestries where the young poets of the period recited their verse. This is one of the rare examples of the Gothic style to be found in Moreau's work, as he usually prefers to depict antiquity with a flamboyance more like Garnier's Opéra than the Parthenon.

Like his contemporary Leconte de Lisle, Moreau attaches considerable importance to accurate detail. In this and other respects, he is more of a Parnassian than a Symbolist. The images themselves bear the mark of their century, and this accumulation of archaeologically accurate details betrays the time in which the picture was painted: the Second Empire. A remark by Degas bears this out: 'Moreau reminds us that the gods wore watch-chains.' It is in this attention to historical detail that Moreau is representative of his time; thus these three allegorical figures of his can be linked with three nudes loaded with Renaissance accessories who can be seen strutting in the middle of Hans Mackart's huge picture, very famous in its day, *Charles the Fifth's entry into Antwerp*. The same resemblance can be seen in the famous watercolour entitled *Légende*, which shows women wearing hennins surrounding a unicorn. However, the disturbing gravity of Moreau's women eliminates any suspicion of vulgarity. They also resemble Gustave Doré's fairies, but fortunately their lips wear an enigmatic smile which distinguishes them from those period creations. Nor do they recall Delacroix, whom Moreau admired so much, for Delacroix's women are real women and not symbols.

Deserting Versailles, History had become a middle-class muse, imitators of Delacroix had entered the Institut, and the poets had turned away from their gloomy *tableaux vivants*. Chilly Jean-Paul Laurens and pompous Gérôme can perhaps still make us dream a little, thanks to some odd feature of décor or subject, when we meet their work in a provincial museum or reproduced in Larousse or the *Encyclopaedia Britannica*. There can be no doubt that *L'Excommunication de Robert le Pieux* and *Les Énervés de Jumièges* would have appealed to the Decadents, if only they had not been painted in an academic style. It is only now that our eyes, opened by psycho-analysis, are able to discover in the most grandiloquent of these canvases a good deal of ingenuous and unconscious perversity.

The same phenomenon has helped, in the last fifteen years, to bring the Royal Academy's Victorian painters back into fashion. The Pre-Raphaelites' technique and sentimentality had imposed themselves on the world of art as early as 1875, and would last until 1914. Painters such as Byam Shaw and Waterhouse went on painting Round Table pictures well into this century. Ricketts too exerted a considerable influence and had two excellent imitators in E. R. Frompton and the Scot Eric Robertson. In France the same can be said of Luc Olivier Merson, Edgar Maxence and that charming Irishman Roderic O'Connor (1860–1940), who lived in France in almost complete obscurity, carrying on the tradition of Ford Madox Brown; while among the Germans one can cite Friedrich Stahl (1863–1940), a native of Munich who lived in Florence, and who depicted Pisanello characters in gardens which were a little too green to be genuinely Italian.

The one history painter who found favour in the eyes of the French poets now strikes us as merely comical, his intentions are so obvious. This was Rochegrosse, a distant cousin of Flaubert's who, on the strength of this relationship, seemed to spend his entire life illustrating episodes from *Salammbô* on enormous canvases. True, he did produce a few massacres of emperors, a couple or so *Last Days of Babylon*, and a few *Légendes des Siècles* with a social message. But the odd settings and the abundance of ornaments keep bringing us back to a papier-mâché *Salammbô*. Now and then Rochegrosse reminds us of Moreau, when he paints embroidered garments trailing in pools of blood, but more often he recalls Rops, who must have liked all those fat ladies massacred in the midst of flowers. More than Moreau or even Rops, Rochegrosse brings to mind a visionary called Henry de Groux, who painted better pictures and had a better mind.

THE FAIRIES. But it was the Chimera of Legend which most inspired Moreau and his literary disciples. It was she to whom Wagner listened, just as it was she whom Flaubert followed in *La Tentation de Saint Antoine*. The love of legend is more than a con-

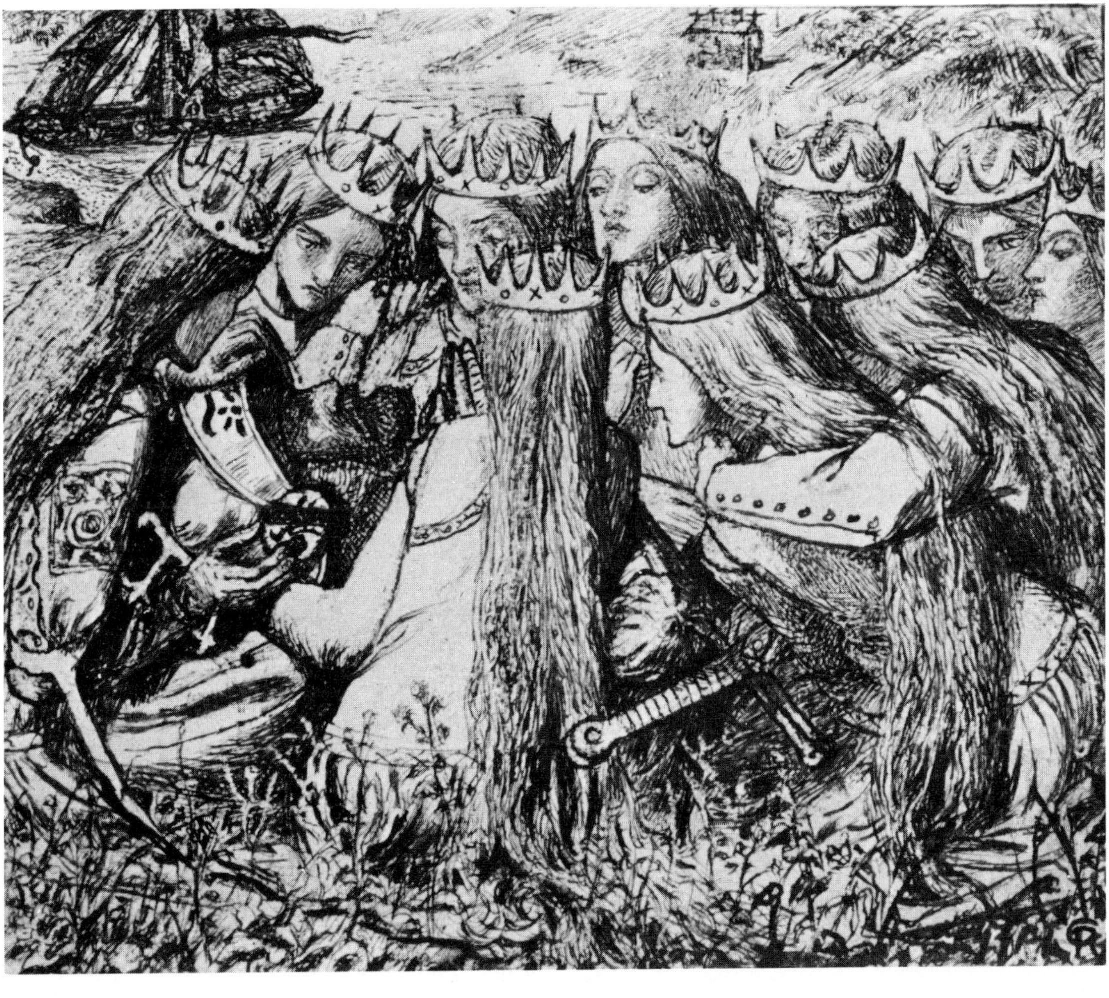

23. Rossetti: *King Arthur and Weeping Queens*. The whole of Maeterlinck's world is already to be seen in this illustration to Tennyson. Thanks to the Moxon edition, the works of the Pre-Raphaelites became known all over the Continent.

cession to fantasy justified by History. As M. Guy Michaud observes in his admirable book on Symbolism:

> The return to the fabulous settings, primitive legends and ancient traditions of folklore marks a deliberate effort towards deeper truths, a surer awareness of hidden realities. It is no longer a recourse to the individual subconscious, but to the collective unconscious, to the race memory and the legends in which it finds expression . . . In the depths of these forests, in which our reason seems to lose its way, there lies the Sleeping Beauty, in other words our soul . . .

In the course of the nineteenth century, scholars had collected and reproduced in modern parlance the Nordic sagas, the Germanic myths and the Arthurian legends. The Germans and the English were to draw on these sources much more deeply than the French, in spite of Edgar Quinet's poetic and scholarly study *Merlin l'Enchanteur*. About 1880 a regular invasion of fairies took place. Jean Lorrain, always in the forefront of fashion, went looking for them in *La Forêt Bleue* (13), and with them all sorts of charms and spells, including the mandrake whose evil properties are depicted in several engravings: 'In the lukewarm blood and the green oil, the root slept inert beside a grim hour-glass.' A periodical illustrated with more or less naïve pictures, entitled *L'Album des Légendes*, provided a wide variety of fairies in every number. They are either depicted in the English fashion, dressed in delicate lace by innocent imitators of Beardsley, or else in a style recalling those Gothic maidens painted by Armand Point, Edgar Maxence, and Waterhouse. In the same album we can read the scenario of a play by Jacques des Gachons, with scenery by Andhré des Gachons: *Le Prince Naïf*, a *lumino-conte* in sixteen tableaux, first performed at the Théâtre Minuscule on 2 December 1893. The tableaux carry titles such as *The Bloody Castle*, *The Hopeless Appeals*, *The Flight to the Beyond*, and *The Fair-Haired Maiden*. Some of these pictures foreshadow Méliè's fantastic films. The best illustrations are those by Séon; the others are pastiches of Walter Crane (1845–1915), that disciple of William Morris's whose albums helped to spread the new style across the Continent.

Crane's influence would have been less considerable if people had seen his paintings instead of his book illustrations, for he was a chaste Rochegrosse who entrusted his fairies with the task of preparing the way for Socialism. His style of line-drawing and his symbolic ornaments had a great influence on *Art Nouveau*, but there was nothing decadent about the man himself. The closest of all English artists to the Germans, Crane drew his inspiration from Grimm and Wagner, and handled philosophical symbols clumsily.

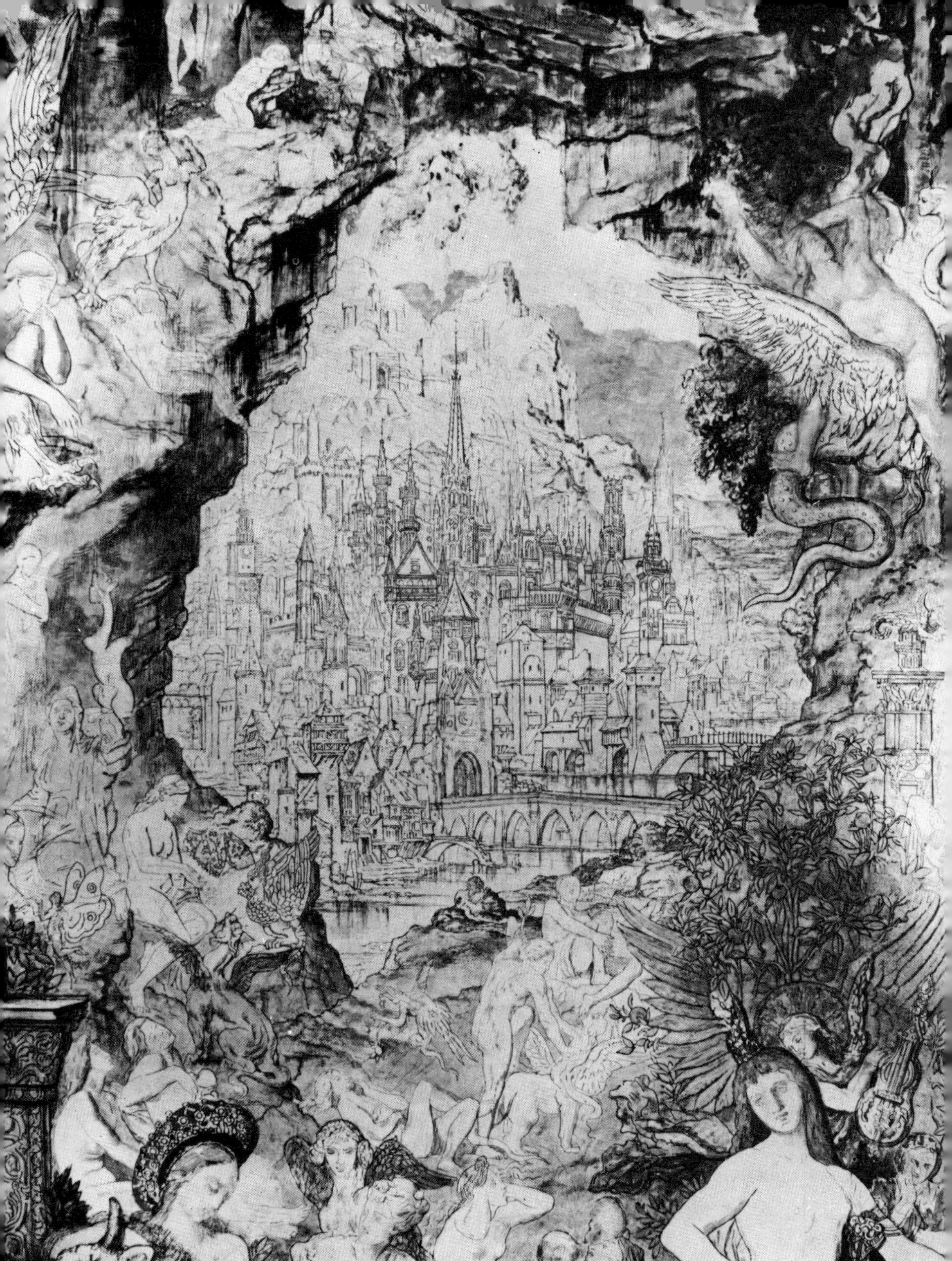

24. Moreau: *La Ville maudite* (detail of *Les Chimères*). Nuremberg and Florence rub shoulders in this vision reminiscent of Viollet-le-Duc's restorations. The monsters on the rocks signify that this is a city of evil and not an ideal city like those of the Pre-Raphaelites.

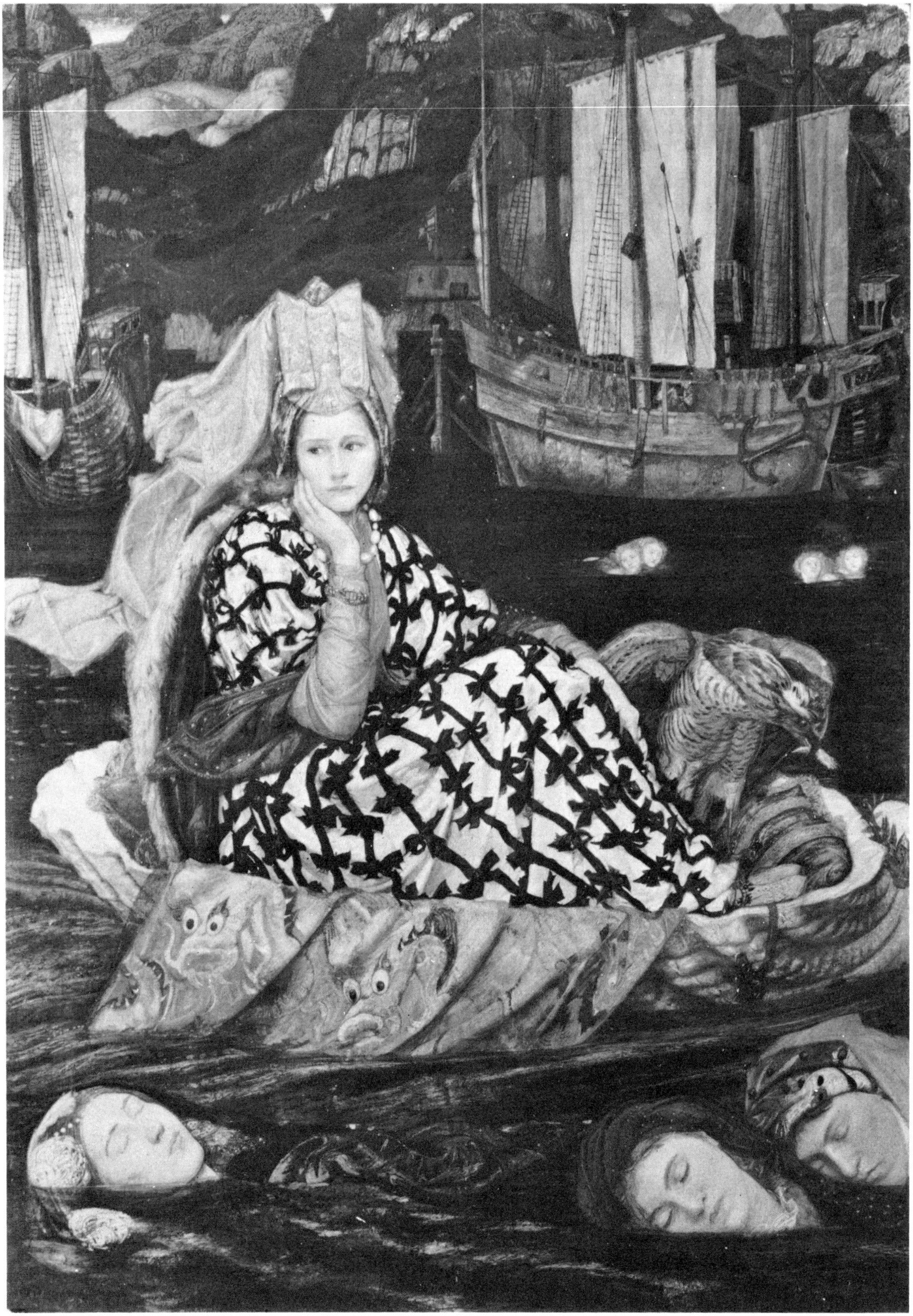

25. Henry A. Payne: *The Enchanted Sea*. This work by a late Pre-Raphaelite takes up a favourite theme of the Symbolists, that of drowned and drowning women.

He undoubtedly influenced Klinger who, while going much further in the direction of the fantastic, also produced coloured bas-reliefs; his best paintings are those which are reminiscent of bas-reliefs, such as *Les Chevaux de Neptune*, which is a veritable frieze. A little later, the Swede Carl Larsson carried on where Crane had left off, with a series of albums which did as much as the sagas to spread the Swedish decorative style. A forgotten Pre-Raphaelite, A. F. Sandys (1837–1904), showed a tousle-haired *Morgan le fay* at the Royal Academy, as well as a *Medea* who also seems to be uttering 'the fairy's cry'. Similarly the Swiss Albert Welti (1862–1912), who lived at Munich under the lingering influence of Maurice von Schwind, painted legendary but faintly morbid pictures, but with much less grace than his Romantic precursor.

The Pont-Aven School, in its Celtic setting, was particularly partial to fairies; thus in one of his best paintings Sérusier shows them as aesthetic young ladies walking in procession through a wood, in front of Breton peasants respectfully doffing their hats. Brittany, with its legends, provides the French setting for the Celtic Revival, and a letter from Sérusier to Maurice Denis sets the tone of this return to the past: 'Alas, Armor calls me, beautiful Armor, the land of pious men, and he who is about to leave will never again this year set eyes on your beloved face, before the red leaves fall' (1889). Émile Schuffenecker shows fairies wandering among ruins, while Paul Ranson, more of an image-maker than a painter, depicts dragons and serpents against a Breton background. And one of Émile Bernard's first paintings, *La Madeleine au bois d'amour*, remains one of the masterpieces of this trend.

All these fairies, both winged and medieval, had already been described by E. T. A. Hoffmann in his story *Klein Zach*. Compared to Hoffmann's creations, which may be fragile but are deeply disturbing because of their connection with age-old fears, Perrault's fairies are nothing but *deae ex machina*. The best portraitist of these fairy princesses, born of a mist, a rainbow or a dead leaf, is Arthur Rackham; admittedly he owes a great deal to Moritz von Schwind, who illustrated Grimm's fairy tales and whom Walt Disney was to imitate, but Rackham is a Schwind with Majorelle roots and Gallé Titanias, and with knights and Ophelias in the Burne-Jones or rather the Ricketts manner. Rackham's illustrations for La Motte-Fouquet's *Ondine* or for Barrie's *Peter Pan* would carry the poetry of Symbolist fairies far into the twentieth century. His rival, Edmund Dulac, was more influenced by Persian miniatures. There were countless fairies too in the stories published in the Christmas numbers of the more expensive magazines: some of them, drawn by Carlos Schwabe or even Rochegrosse, ethereal creatures, and the rest, as painted by Weber, more comic than

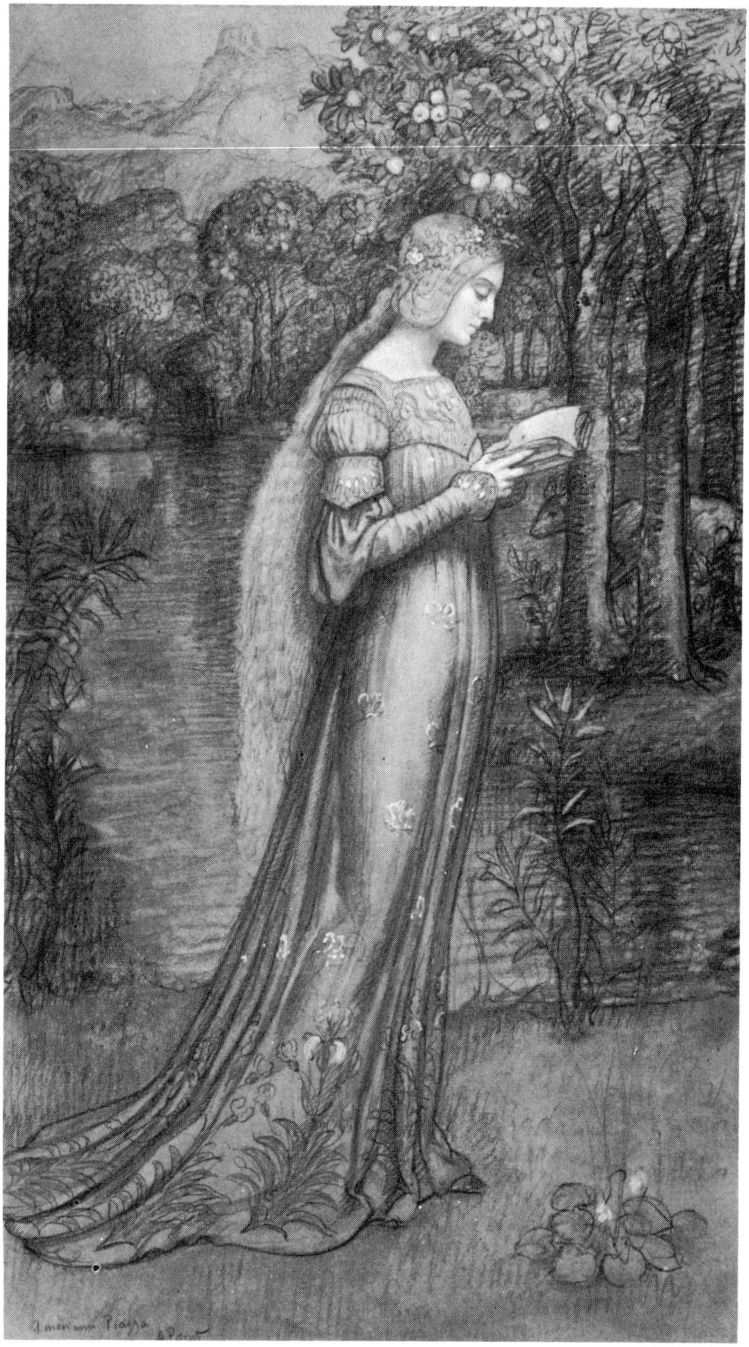

26. Armand Point: *Légende*. An excellent draughtsman, Point here shows the style of drawing 'souls' then current.

poetic, fashion-plate princesses surrounded by dwarfs who look like left-wing deputies. Rostand liked Weber's anti-democratic message, and commissioned him to decorate one of the drawing-rooms at Arnaga, his Basque palace near Biarritz.

These fairies answered an urgent longing for escape; their magic wand was a protest against Edison's inventions. It was also, in a rather insipid form, a return of the old gods. So they came crowding into the Celtic countries, elegant apparitions in the margins of story-books, clad in gowns by those charming lace-makers called Jessie M. King and Annie French; or else almost vegetable in appearance, in the green and silver *cloisonnés* with which Margaret MacDonald covered the walls of the tearooms her husband Mackintosh built in Glasgow. With their enchanting faces, their melancholy hues, and their willowy figures, they were much less fashionable than the fairies dreamt up by de Feure, who look as if they were modelling Redfern dresses.

The fairies also wove their spell over the first works of two extremely gifted American artists who unfortunately went over to commercial art: Maxfield Parish (1870–1965) and Arthur Davies (1862–1928). The former, with a minute attention to detail, invested his New England landscapes with a haunted atmosphere; his fairies belong to the realm of Rip Van Winkle. Davies loved unicorns, naked ladies in silent gardens, a legendary antiquity owing something to both Böcklin and Whistler.

The fairies have always appealed to young painters; some can be found in the first works of Kandinsky. They are a link with childhood, and the most beautiful of all illustrated fairy-tales – *Peter Pan* and *Ondine* with Arthur Rackham's drawings – date back to the 1900 period.

Jeanne Jacquemin's fairies, pale-faced ladies in hennins wandering in the forest of Broceliande, have the melancholy appearance of magicians who have lost their way or are fleeing from the modern world. They are obviously more complex creatures than their Scottish sisters, and they look as if they had read that book by the Sâr Péladan entitled: *How to Become a Fairy. Instructions for the Two Methods of Becoming Beatrice and Hypatia. Ascesis of Transcendent Sexuality. Restitution of the Forgotten Feminine Initiation . . .*

All of them – disillusioned magicians, delicious giantesses, ambiguous charmers – come from the Pre-Raphaelites. Rossetti's Fata Morgana is really one of those fair-haired sorceresses, hungry for the souls of handsome young men, such as we find in Wilde's fairy tales, captivating incarnations of the Uffizi Medusa. Burne-Jones remains the best painter of legendary subjects; his characters seem to emerge from the misty depths of memory, and look as if they are bent under the weight of remorse which would link the heroes of antiquity with Christian fantasy. And Wilde's fairy tales, which skilfully transpose Hans Andersen to a Byzantine or medieval setting, while allowing a little mist to hang around the characters, are also steeped in Burne-Jones. Ricketts, who illustrated these prose poems, was a delightful artist and a pioneer of the *Modern Style*, but his work lacks the morbidity of Burne-Jones's paintings, and his characters have none of those shadows under their eyes which Mirbeau attributed to masturbation.

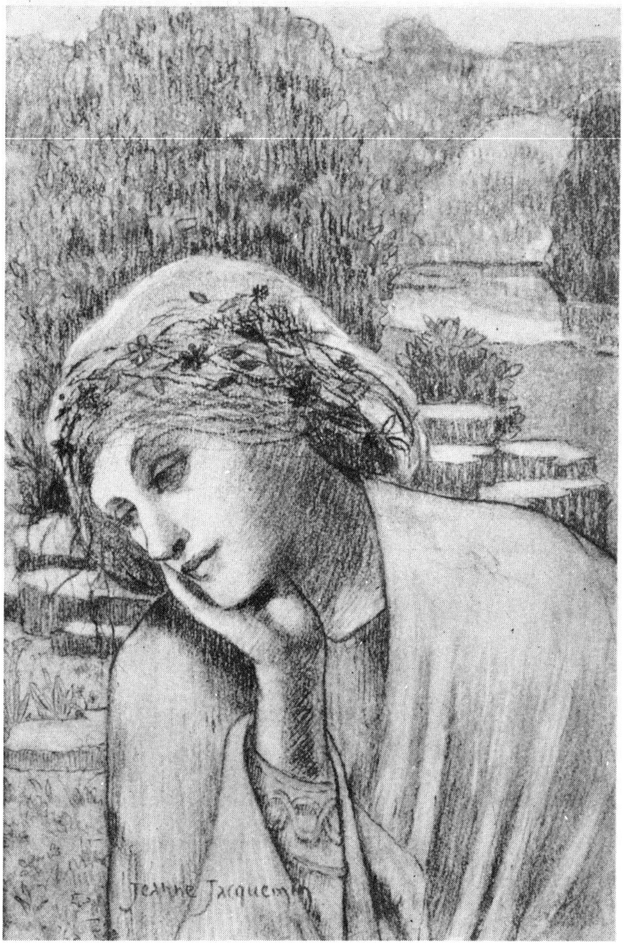

27. Jeanne Jacquemin: *Mélancholie*. Nothing is known of this very gifted artist, who worked in the style of Puvis de Chavannes, except that she aroused great enthusiasm in Jean Lorrain and other art critics when she exhibited in 1893.

In a very interesting book devoted to Moreau and Burne-Jones, and written shortly after their death in the same year, Léonce Benedict compared the two artists, classing them with Böcklin and Watts – all of them 'rare thinkers who, throughout the vicissitudes of the century, held high the Apollonian torch of idealism and the dream'. Burne-Jones represents an ideal which the Decadents distorted and deformed: the ideal of aesthetic chivalry. (Grand Duke Ernest Ludwig of Hesse, who himself embodied that ideal, had a large picture of St. George by Burne-Jones in his study, and the whole room was decorated to complement the painting.) Compared with Moreau, the man of the Renaissance, Burne-Jones seemed closeted and confined within his Victorian Middle Ages. Moreau's legends spring from the fiery heat of the Mediterranean, Burne-Jones's from the rainy Celtic world; even his Perseus contemplating Medusa's head in a fountain looks as if he had been posed in an Oxford garden: his works are steeped in the damp atmosphere of an English park, in a grey June twilight. Brambles cling to the dresses of his young maidens and water seems to have stuck their flimsy draperies to their bodies. There is another respect in which Burne-Jones is much more a man of his time than Moreau: he believes in a moralizing art, and like William Morris, wants to create beauty for the people. For him women are always modest, desirable, vulnerable, never cruel. Perhaps he was not a very intelligent man. His dream is simple: 'A beautiful romantic country of things which have never been and will never be – a country which cannot be defined, which nobody can remember, and which has simply been desired.' Wilde, who preferred Moreau to Burne-Jones, expressed the same aspiration much better with the aid of hippogryphs and phoenixes.

These enchanted princes and half-awakened princesses embodied the world of Maeterlinck before he described it with his pen. *Pelléas et Mélisande* ought to have been produced with settings by Burne-Jones; and indeed Maeterlinck must surely have been thinking of the English painter when he sent Lugné-Poe these suggestions for his characters' costumes: 'Don't you think that, instead of green for Mélisande, something mauve from Liberty's might be better? Pelléas for his part should be in green – a very simple, very long dress, hanging loosely round the body, with a jewelled belt, and purple ribbons plaited into the hair, or just a little unusual foliage.' It would have been interesting to see, if not to listen to, *La Belle au Bois Dormant*, by Henri Bataille and Robert d'Humières, when it was produced in Paris at the Théâtre de l'Œuvre, in 1892, with settings by Burne-Jones and Rochegrosse. We can obtain

28. Georges Rochegrosse: *Le Chevalier aux Fleurs*. This Parsifal surrounded by rather too Parisian girl-flowers obtained a great success at the 1900 Salon. An excellent example of the vulgarization of Symbolist themes.

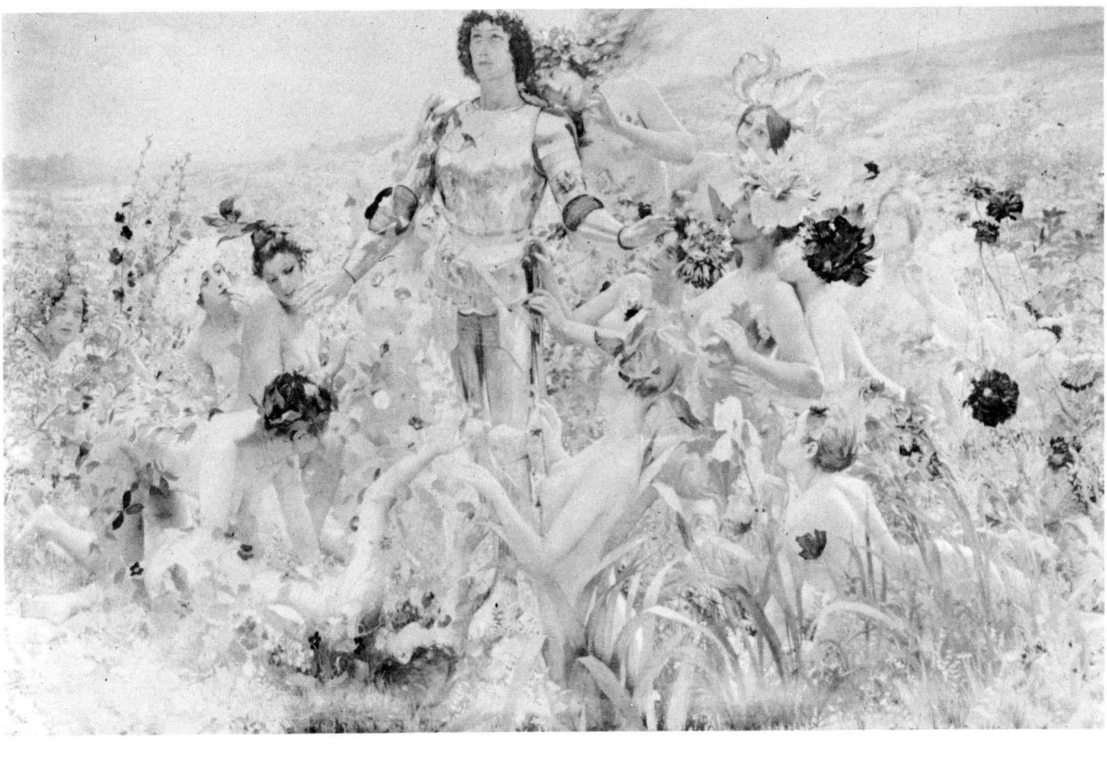

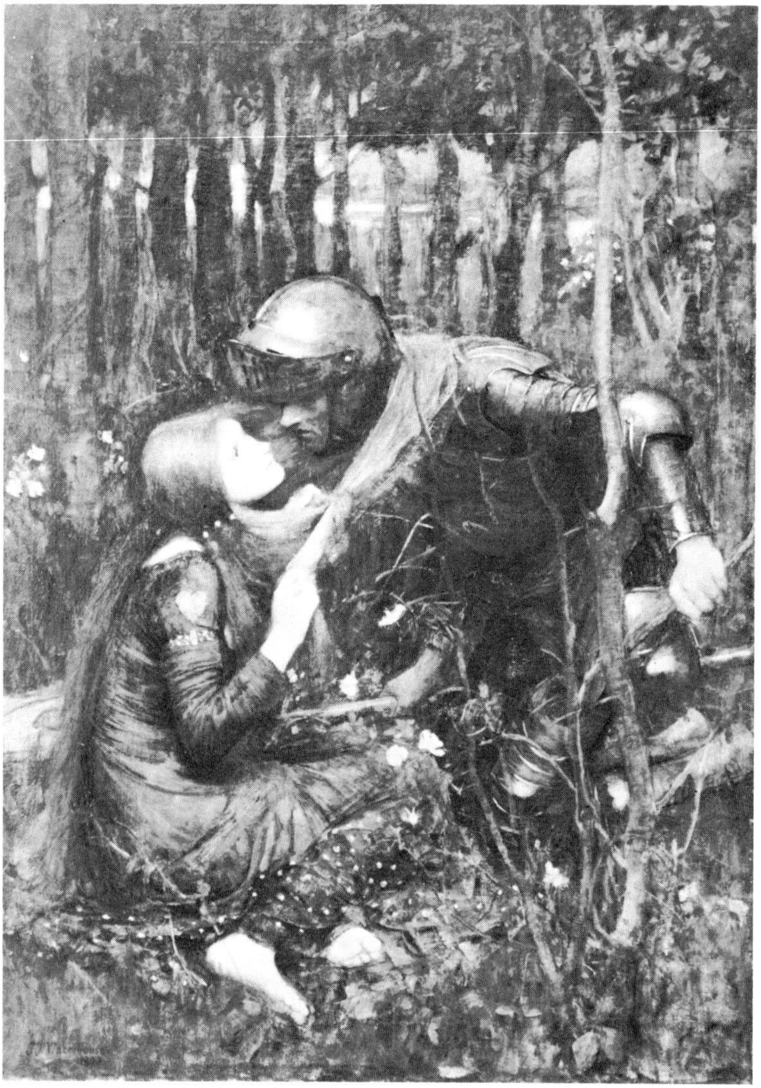

29. J. W. Waterhouse: *La belle Dame sans Merci.* A belated Pre-Raphaelite joins the Symbolists in this very common theme of the knight trapped by the lady's hair. Waterhouse went on exhibiting at the Royal Academy up to the 1920s.

some idea of Rochegrosse's contribution to this partnership by looking at his *Chevalier aux Fleurs*, shown at the Salon of 1894, which combines the influences of both the Pre-Raphaelites and Wagner.

WAGNER. Thanks to Wagner, Isolde was to become the ideal of all adulterous and artistic women of the *fin de siècle*, yet very few artists ventured to depict her, apart from William Morris, in the margin of his famous edition of tales of the Round Table, and Beardsley, a little later, in some excessively witty drawings. The best pictorial representation of Tristan is Watts's *Sir Galahad.* Jean Cocteau, remaining faithful to the myths of his childhood, rediscovered the Pre-Raphaelite atmosphere in his play *Les Chevaliers de la Table Ronde*, and the drawings he did then are pastiches of William Morris (just as in *La Machine infernale* he had previously rediscovered the Sphinx, and his drawings at that time had parodied Ingres, who was more fashionable than Moreau in the Cubist era).

If Beardsley is far too sophisticated to give us touching pictures of Isolde, or for that matter of Parsifal – the frail English artist lacked Wagner's robust good health – he offers us a splendid caricature of the typical Wagnerian audience: the women the cartoonist Forain called the Jewesses of art, sharing the ecstasy of the aesthetes in the course of performances which were a cross between opera and the Mass. One is reminded of the last chapter of Élémir Bourges's novel *Le Crépuscule des Dieux*, when, at the official opening of the Bayreuth opera-house, the German Emperor greets the bankers; the tormented, ecstatic faces in Beardsley's drawings recall the Duke of Brunswick's incestuous children in the Bourges novel, who are given the parts of Siegfried and Sieglinde to sing. (Years later Thomas Mann took up this theme again in his story *The Blood of the Walsungen.*) A striking letter from Gauguin to Redon bears witness to the authenticity of this fervour: 'A saying of Wagner's explains what I think: I believe that the disciples of great art will be glorified, and that, wrapped in a heavenly cloak of rays, scents and melodious chords, they will return for all eternity into the bosom of the divine source of all harmony. So, my dear Redon, you see that we shall meet again.'

Another text bearing witness to the Wagnerian fervour of the times is this quotation from Péladan's 1890 *Salon*: 'Monsieur de Egusquiza alone has understood how Wagner and his *leitmotiven* could carry on Delacroix's passionate art . . . One day he will unveil the astonishing fruit of his mysterious labours. His vocation as

30. Franz von Stuck: *The Sphinx*. A portrait of a Munich Jewess: an example of academic art in the service of the Decadence.

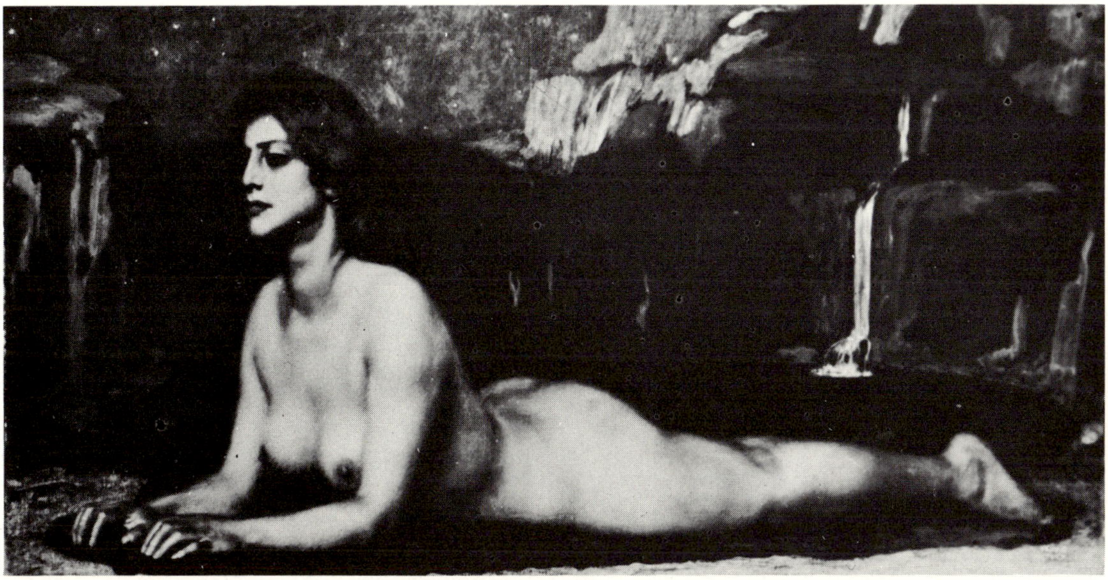

a great painter was determined at Bayreuth as was my genius as a tragedian.' Monsieur de Egusquiza, alas, never unveiled the astonishing fruit in question. On the other hand, Albert Ryder (1847–1917), a lonely American, was inspired by Wagner no less than by Poe. Siegfried and the Flying Dutchman can be dimly distinguished through the darkness created as much by this painter's morose character as by the poor quality of the paints he used.

In one of his notes Moreau comments harshly on the Wagner cult, in connection with the book in which Catulle Mendès claimed that all Wagner's poems are steeped in legend: 'This is a trap, a trick to deceive people of inferior intelligence; seeing themselves plunged in a dim, mysterious atmosphere of legend, they will believe that what they are experiencing is transcendental, poetic, anti-bourgeois *Art Nouveau* . . . Inspiration is never to be found in the subject of a work of art, but in the artist's soul, and the choice of subject is a matter of indifference.' This judgement may have been inspired by the irritating memory of a lady he had heard exclaim: 'Wagner is Manet in music!' Noting down the remark of this bluestocking enthusiast for modern art, Moreau comments: 'A large-scale incursion into the arts by the opposite sex would be an irremediable disaster.'

It should not be forgotten that Wagner was the great master of intellectual eroticism. To take only one of many examples, Henry de Groux, after imposing the name Sieglinde on his young mistress, offered her the score of *Tristan* with these words: 'So that she may know everything about love.' If *Lohengrin* and *Tristan* were a revelation for the Opera public, *Parsifal* gave much more to artists (35). Witness Odilon Redon's admirable lithographs, Verlaine's famous poem on the subject, and countless other poems in the *Revue Wagnérienne*, together with now famous texts by Villiers de l'Isle-Adam and Mallarmé.

In *Parsifal* there is one very decadent character, namely Klingsor, the eunuch-magician, the keeper of the girl-flowers, and the doomed aesthete in whom Wilde or Robert de Montesquiou might have recognized themselves – it was Montesquiou who had sent Gallé to Bayreuth to look for inspiration in the magic garden. And it is surely the vegetable architecture of Klingsor's palace which Villiers describes in *L'Ève future*:

> An underground Eden. Huge pillars, spaced out at intervals, supported the front of the basalt dome. Their decoration, in which the Syrian style was rejuvenated, represented large sheaves and bluish convolvulus reaching all the way up. From the middle of the ceiling a powerful lamp hung at the end of a long golden stem, a star whose electric rays were dulled by an azure globe.

31. *Opposite:* Thorn Prikker: *The Bride of Christ.* This large painting in mauve and grey is one of the masterpieces of Christian Symbolism. As early as 1890 this artist, with Toorop, gave Holland an important place in the Symbolist movement. Towards the end of his life he produced some curious stained-glass windows under the influence of Cubism.

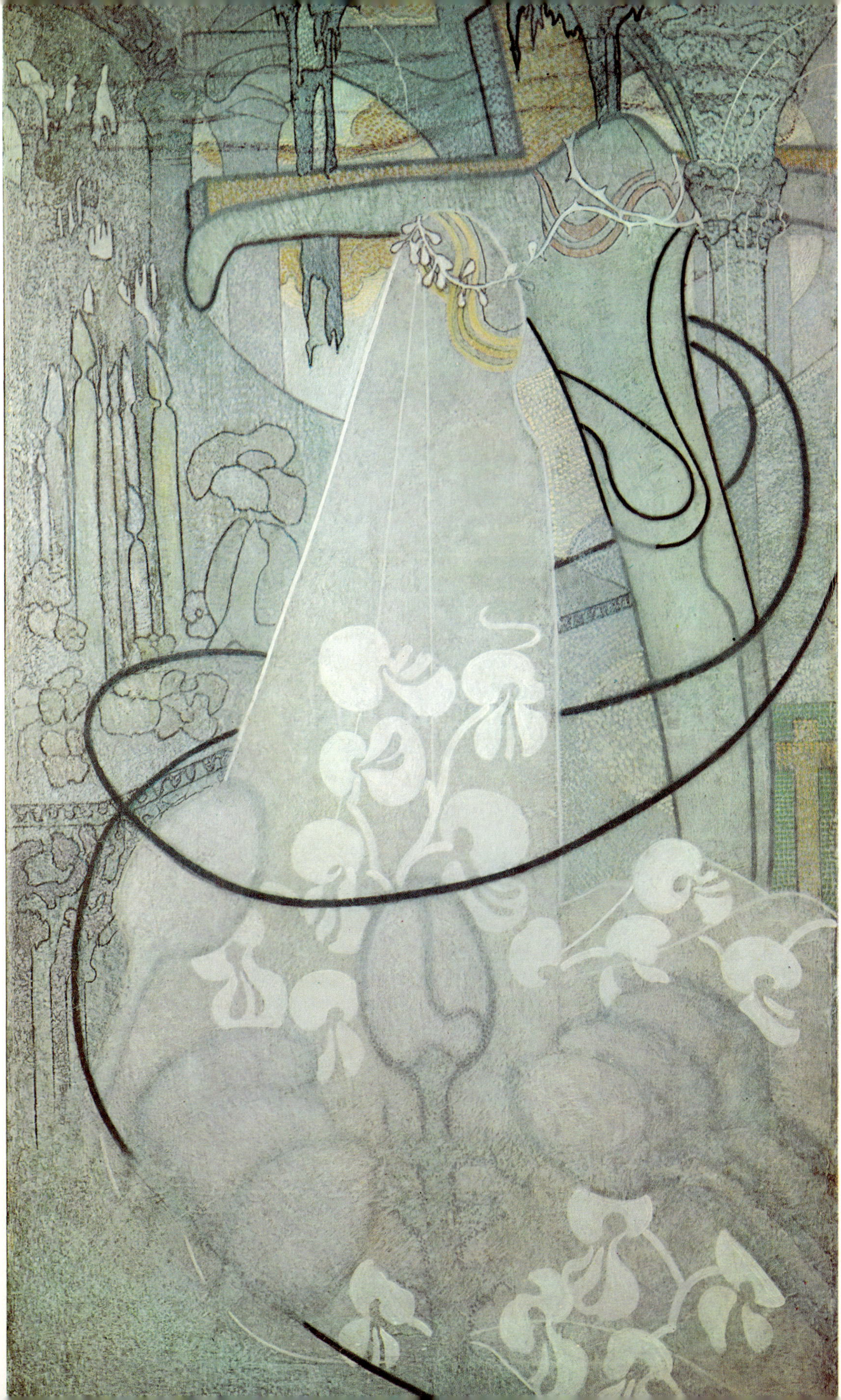

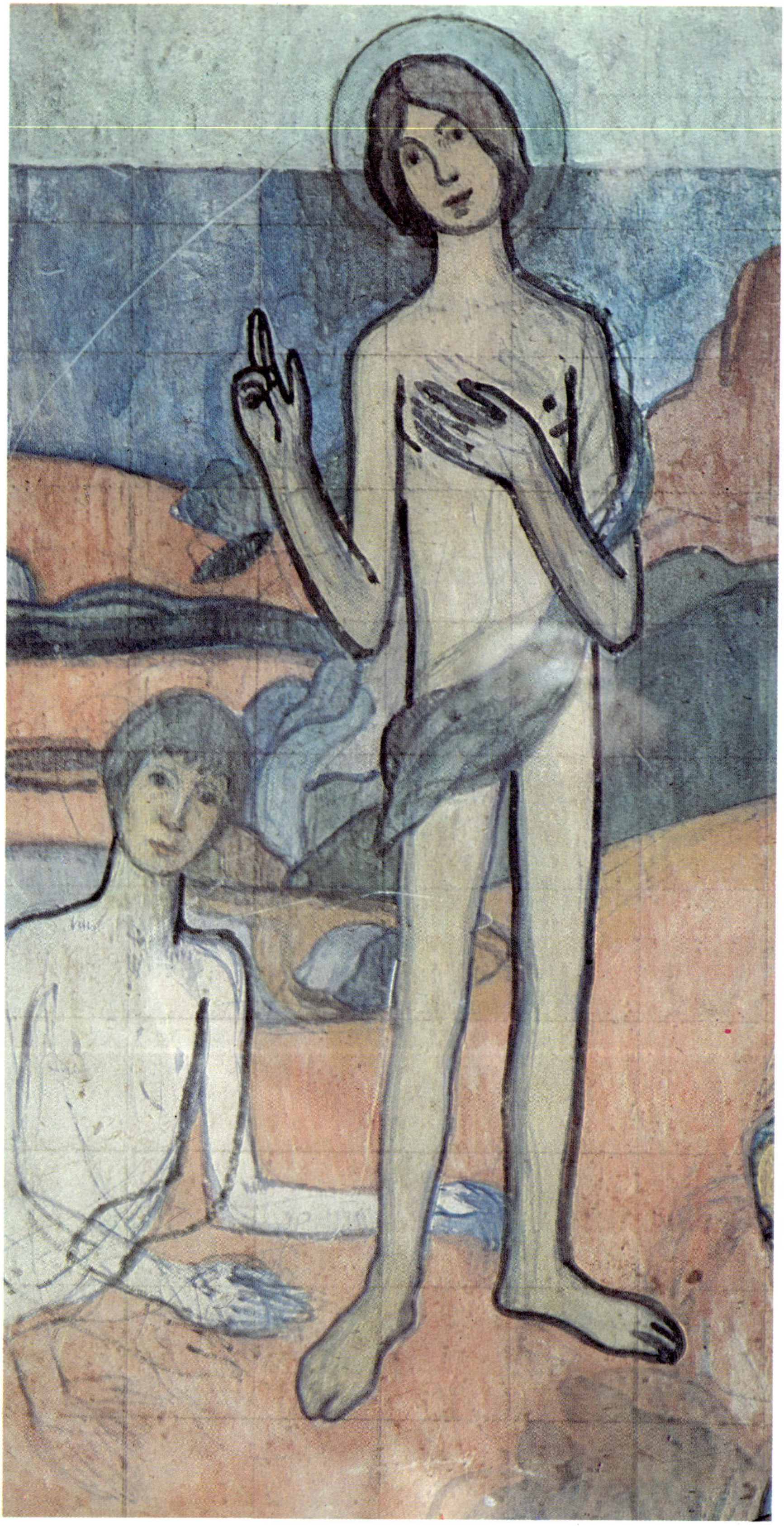

The tree which formed the end wall of the room, facing the threshold, was surrounded with rich slopes like gardens; on them waved thousands of creepers and Eastern roses, island flowers with luminous pistils and leaves oozing with thick fluids.

Gaudí set out to build in just such an architectural style, and he is said to have designed the façade of the Sagrada Familia with certain Wagnerian themes in mind, notably the *Siegfried Idyll.* Decorators working for Ludwig II of Bavaria had entwined a whole world of plants around medieval motifs, with capitals spreading out in branches and pedestals in roots. This plastic animism corresponded to Wagner's ambition to express the innermost voice of Nature, to glorify instinct.

However, the setting of Wagner's mystical drama was to be much more Byzantine than Gothic in character, like the great hall in the castle of Hohenschwangau, which recalls the Oriental splendours of the Holy Roman Empire. As for the *Tetralogy*, it was one of the factors which led to a revival of the barbarian motifs of traceries and dragons which had been used a thousand years before, from Norway to Ireland. Wagner would have liked to have nobody but Böcklin to stage his works, for Böcklin's world of fauns and knights comes out of a gloomy forest, the same forest from which the Wagnerian heroes had emerged. As Jules Laforgue writes: 'The Mother Nature of the true German is a pantheistic Nature, the sacred forest of Wagner's national theories, in which the great melodious voice of the forest is made up of the thousand-voiced symphonies of trees and things, and dominates them, and inhabited by that fantastic, ephemeral mythology of a Midautumn or Midwinter Night's Dream: ghosts from the Brocken or Wilis of Novalis's poems.'

32. Charles Filiger: *Saint Jean-Baptiste.* Here the most gifted of the Rosicrucian painters comes very close to his friend Gauguin. The landscape and the colours are characteristic of Pont-Aven. The composition and the postures recall Puvis de Chavannes, but with a homosexual note.

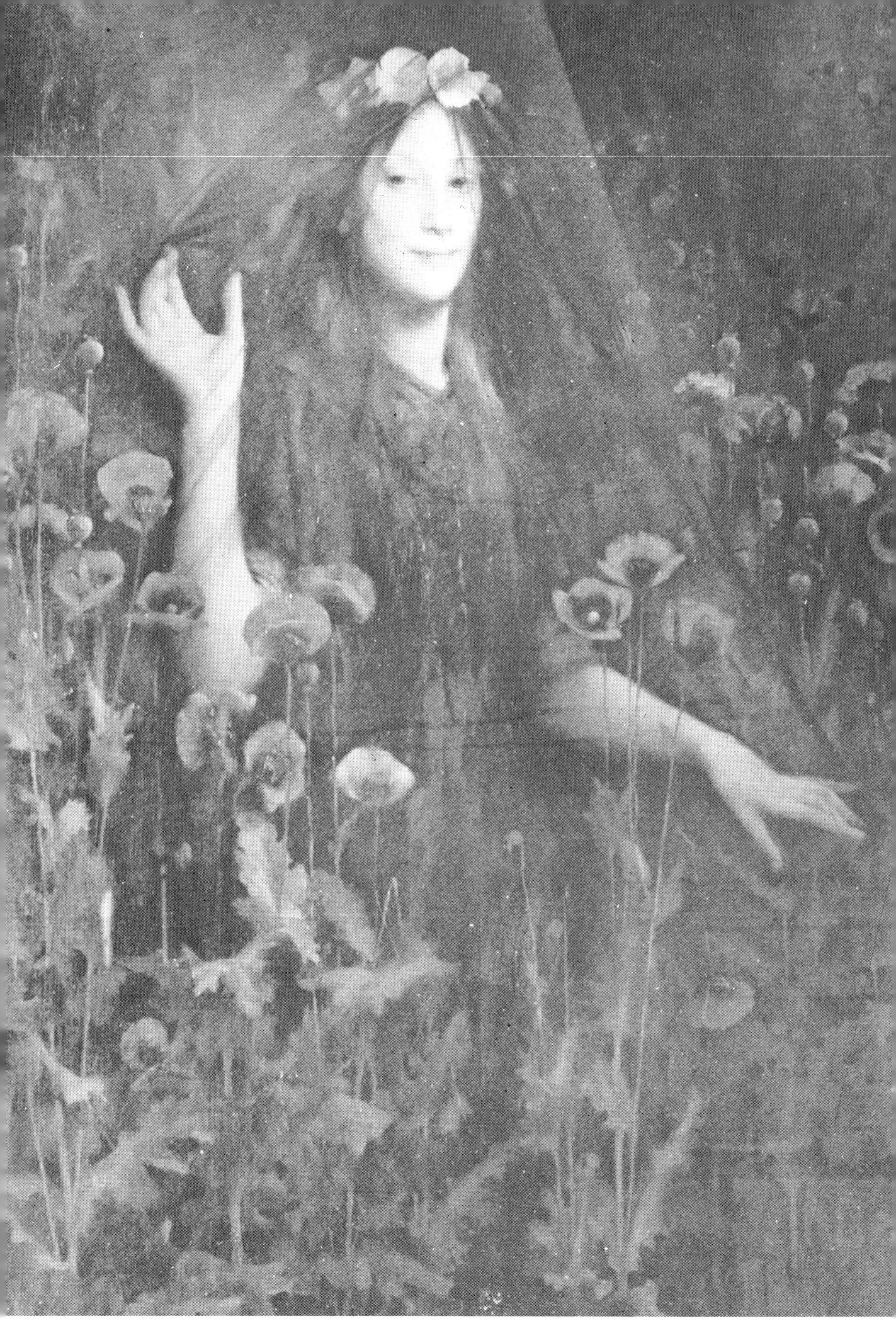

4 The Mystical Chimera

SOULS. Souls are to Symbolism what angels were to Romanticism, but they play only a distant part in the life of the emotions; they float 'incorruptible' above the most appalling horrors. A little melancholy at having to pass through this world, their faces reveal that 'wistfulness of exiles' which Pater discerned in Botticelli's creations. The Symbolists' souls dream of knowing the bliss or the disgrace of the angels, and often hesitate between God and Satan. It is by way of art that they approach the divine; they follow the mystical chimera, but it is rarely that they attain their heavenly goal.

This profusion of souls is not so much the result of a return to Christian belief as of a horror of materialism. Catholicism, after the Vatican Council which had consecrated its most retrograde ideas as dogmas, was utterly repellent to every rationalist, but by the very irrationality of its propositions proved attractive to a generation which preferred Verlaine and Villiers de l'Isle-Adam to Zola or Taine, and which was excited by certain pages of Léon Bloy. Souls began to make an appearance in Montmartre as early as 1880. The mystery plays performed as shadow performances at the *Chat noir*, and the brasseries with waitresses wearing angel wings, showed that spirituality was in fashion. The *chansonnier* Rodolphe Salis declared that 'mysticism and hoaxes go well together,' and for the poets who frequented his tavern, mysticism and eroticism went together just as well. On a much higher level, the neo-Gothic *Chat noir* décor occupies as we have seen an important place in Moreau's *Chimères*. It consists of a town rather like Nuremberg, bristling with pinnacles whose Freudian significance is obvious. With infinite care and futile precision Moreau has depicted every machicolation and every bartizan of this sinister town, revealing in his attempts at historical accuracy his commitment to the enthusiasms of his time. If Flaubert's Bouvard and Pécuchet had taken up mysticism, they would have tried to reconstruct just such a town, and even Mallarmé is not entirely free from the picturesque religiosity of the *Chat noir* or Flaubert's hagiography (41).

33. Thomas Cooper Gotch: *Death the Bride*. Painted by a late Pre-Raphaelite, this figure of Death with her Mona Lisa smile walks through a field of poppies, the symbol of oblivion.

The saints are simply a higher category in the order of souls. Some artists depict them as pale creatures clad in nightdresses, in the Puvis de Chavannes style and the Flandrin tradition, while the rest see them as Byzantine or Florentine. The angels, on the other hand, are more disturbing: witness the one Rémy de Gourmont shows us in one of his first books, *Le Château singulier* (1894). The strange woman at Christ's feet, whose veil the Dutchman Thorn Prikker has decorated with a phallic pattern in his picture *The Bride of Christ*, could well serve as an illustration to Gourmont's text. The Symbolists raised great hosts of angels to fight the rowing men of Impressionism and the stevedores of Naturalism. In Moreau's pictures, alas, such as his *Sainte Cécile* and *Sainte Élisabeth de Hongrie*, they are somewhat unconvincing angels, with stiff wings and expressions which reveal the boredom of chastity rather than mystical ecstasy.

The French looked for models for these souls in England. As far back as the beginning of the nineteenth century, thin, sinuous, thoroughly *Modern Style* visions had appeared in William Blake's drawings. Then, about forty years after the great visionary's death, the Pre-Raphaelites had rediscovered his work. For Rossetti and Burne-Jones, spirituality was an attitude of mind, an aesthetic concept, rather than a faith. As a reaction against the vulgarity of Victorian prosperity, they rejected artifice of every kind and insisted on simple styles, handmade furniture. Their Fair Rosamunds and Beatrices carried the English public far away from their weekday machines and their gloomy Sundays; they imposed their fashions on a group of elegant and cultured young women who came to be known as 'the souls'; their pictures are perhaps erotic reveries rather than mystical visions. And it was high seriousness more than religious fervour which led Rossetti to explain with a sonnet carved into the frame of a picture which made his reputation, *The Childhood of the Virgin Mary* (1849), the symbolism of the furniture (15).

The mysticism of the Round Table provided Burne-Jones with the opportunity to paint a great many souls, but none of them was to have the magical vulgarity of Holman Hunt's picture *The Light of the World*. This painting, with Millais's *Bubbles*, the most popular picture of its time, but later regarded as the nadir of art, has a nightmarish quality in the minuteness of its detail. Following this mystical, phosphorescent, but purple-blue Christ, the same artist's *Scapegoat* bogged down in the salty mud of the Dead Sea became a symbol in which countless lost souls recognized themselves. (It is interesting to note, incidentally, that Catholicism, which exerted a considerable influence on the best English poets of this period, contributed nothing to the fine arts.)

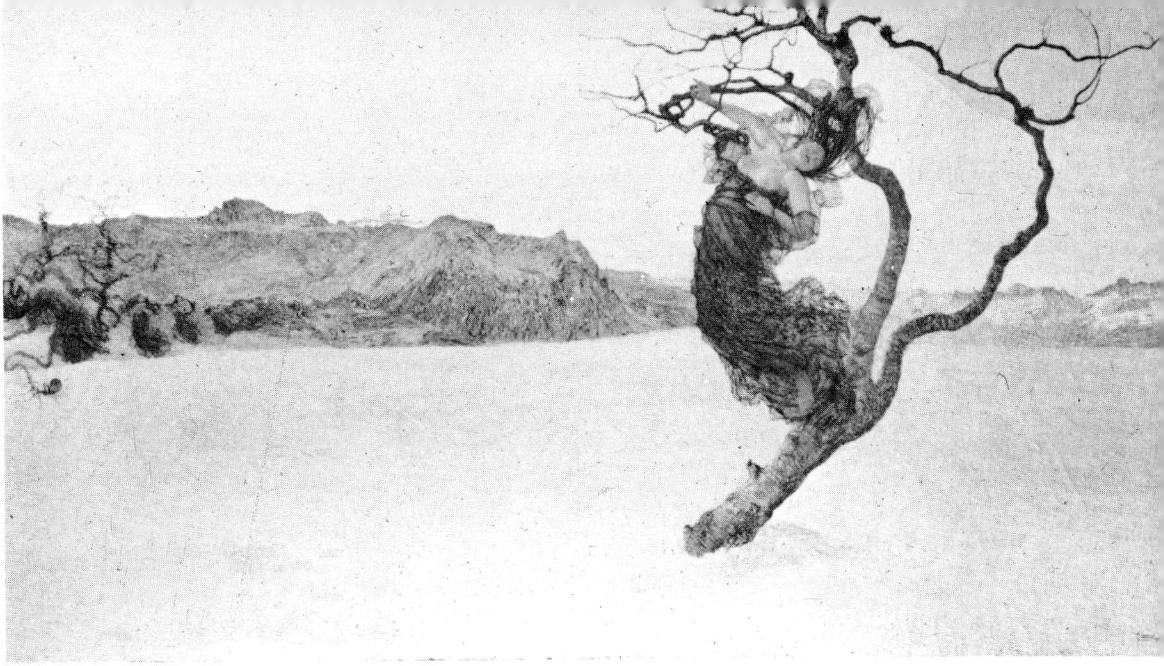

34. Giovanni Segantini: *Böse Mütter*. The most famous of the Italian Symbolists found his inspiration in the Alps, where the 'souls' occasionally went to breathe the air of the peaks.

As well as the symbolism of objects in the work of these painters steeped in mysticism, the symbolism of colours is also very important. There is a profusion of purples and violets, which are difficult colours to handle. Even Odilon Redon is not always successful with these hues, frequently associated with mystical experiences. The acid greens, strident yellows, and insipid pinks of the Symbolists alienated not only the traditionalist public of the Salons, but also the public attracted by the Impressionists. Stained-glass windows had a considerable influence on the Rosicrucian group, who insisted on seeing the world through cathedral window-panes – hence their flat but brilliant colours and their dark lines, like the strips of lead round the pieces of glass. Filiger, whose *Notations chromatiques* are miniature rose-windows, and Rouault offer the best examples of this influence, which can occasionally be seen also in Gauguin or Toorop. Decorators such as Tiffany and Grasset also deliberately imitated stained-glass windows when they did not actually make them.

After Hunt, mention should also be made of Watts, whose mysticism was rather philosophical in character, a less interesting painter and a lion of the Royal Academy, but an artist who had a great influence on the Continent. Reminiscences of Watts and Holman Hunt can be found in an American painter, Elihu Vedder (1836–1923), who treated subjects such as *The Questioner of the Sphinx*, *The Lost Mind* and *The Lair of the Sea-Serpent*. His draughtsmanship and his subjects would entitle this solitary artist to be cited with the leading precursors of *Art Nouveau* if his style were not so academic and his palette so dull. Like so many literary artists, he drew much better than he painted.

THE BEYOND. In England as in France, fresh proof of the existence and immortality of souls was found in spiritualism. Works such as Alain Kardee's *L'Imitation de Jésus-Christ selon le Spiritisme* (1864) and Madame Blavatsky's *Secret Doctrine* (1893) made countless converts, while Flammarion's works lent a scientific appearance to this interest in the after-life. It is well known that in Victor Hugo's house on Guernsey the tables turned merrily, although their confidences and the poem in the *Légende des siècles* which they dictated are only pale reflections of the master's mind. Much more convincing are the poet's medium-like drawings and his poem, *Ce que dit la bouche d'ombre*. There is something very curious, too, about the drawings done in a state of trance by that down-to-earth person, Victorien Sardou, and several poems by Robert de Montesquiou. The correspondence between Montesquiou, who had just served as a model for Huysmans's des Esseintes, and Gallé, is a compendium of spiritualist vocabulary (90); so it is scarcely surprising that the works of the master of Nancy, seen through layers of more or less opaque glass, should look like visions of another world. Gallé would sometimes reply with cards painted with very thin watercolours: wandering shadows in the Celtic twilight, ectoplasms in the shape of plants, shadowy faces and outstretched hands, glimpsed in the course of spiritualist seances.

It is impossible to overestimate the immense influence of spiritualism on the *fin de siècle*. Rossetti had carried out a great many experiments in 1866 with his friend William Howitt, author of a *History of the Supernatural*, and it is possible that Gustave Moreau too tried to make contact with the spirit world. Several books in his library bear witness to his interest in occultism, notably Eliphas Lévi's work *Fables et Symboles*, with its explanations of the secrets of universal magnetism and the basic principles of the Philosopher's Stone. In Lévi's book we find these words: 'Occult philosophy is basically mystical and symbolical.' And it is with cabbalistic symbols that Moreau illustrated La Fontaine's *Fables*, in the admirable series of watercolours commissioned by Doctor Hayem in 1882. Next to Eliphas Lévi's book we find the famous collection of Catherine Emmerich's visions, *La Douloureuse Passion de Notre-Seigneur Jésus-Christ*. What affinities there are between the painter's work and the pictures which illustrate the writings of the Rhenish mystic. Another book, more poetic than mystical in character, bears the inscription: 'To the painter of profound mystery' – *L'Illusion* by Henri Cazalis (better known as Jean Lahor).

Moreau had not had a religious upbringing, but he had worked out a religion for himself which, if we are to believe one of his notes, was connected with Schuré's theories (70). In any case he considered himself to be one of the Great Initiates, and in his great canvas he painted some mystical chimeras rising heavenwards, borne by angels' wings. Let us follow them now with a man they were long held to have involved in irrevocable ridicule.

THE SÂR PÉLADAN. Joseph Péladan was born in Lyons, in 1858, into a milieu obsessed with occultism. He had spent some time in Florence before visiting Bayreuth, where he had astonished the Master with his opinions on his work. In 1884 Péladan imposed himself on the Parisian public by publishing *Le Vice Suprême*, a fantastic mystico-erotic novel in which poetry alternates with a no less studied prose: 'Faithful to your monstrous vice, O daughter of da Vinci, corrupting Muse of the aesthetics of evil, your smile may fade from the canvas, but it is engraved for ever in my heart.'

Péladan, who changed his name from Joseph to Joséphin, described himself as 'the sandwich-man of the Beyond', exhumed a mystical society founded in Germany in the late Middle Ages, declared himself its leader, and crowned himself Sâr Merodac, a title which enabled him to dress himself up in a costume reminiscent of Lohengrin and Nebuchadnezzar. He was a dark, handsome man, with bushy hair and a bushy beard, ready to swallow – and utter – all sorts of nonsense. In the despairing Paris of his day, which he convinced of its decadence, Barbey d'Aurévilly sang his praises, and young men such as Jean Lorrain and d'Annunzio

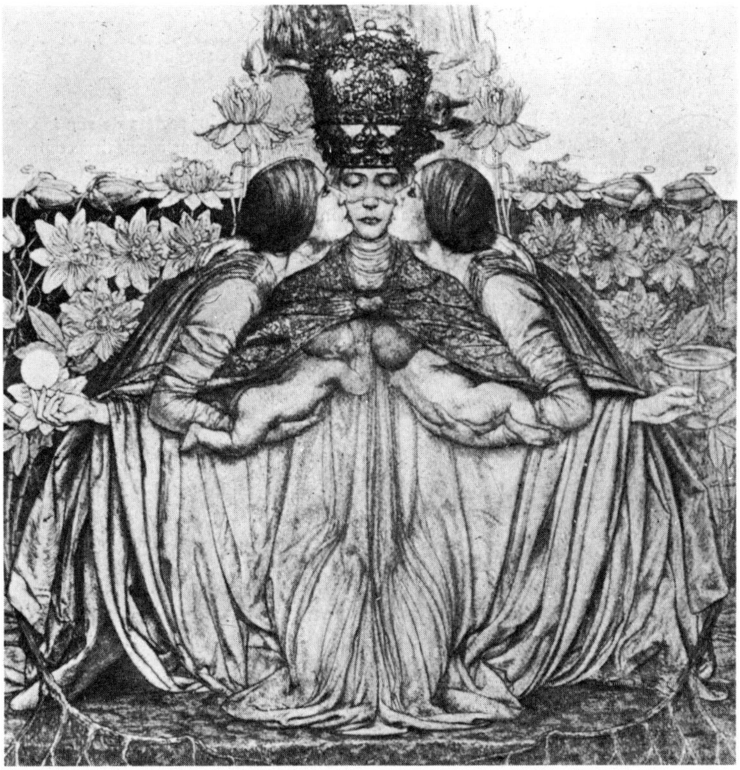

35. Schwabe: *La Passion* (detail). One of the most curious book illustrations by this excellent illustrator who was greatly influenced by the Primitives. If the draperies are reminiscent of Memling, the floral setting is typically *Art Nouveau*.

copied him. How, indeed, could they have failed to admire a man who declared: 'Artist, you are a priest . . . artist, you are a king . . . artist, you are a mage'? Péladan obtained immediate fame, drawing on two sources from which all those who were disgusted with materialism would drink: occultism and aestheticism. His books came out in rapid succession, under the general title of *La Décadence Latine*. The brief extracts from them which we have been able to quote give some idea of their eccentricity, but not of their importance. They depicted an ideal type bearing a certain resemblance to the vague inventions of Gustave Moreau or Burne-Jones. Sensible people laughed at Péladan: they were making a mistake. Strong enough to brave any sort of ridicule, he was also an extremely cultured man, determined to fight against the vulgarity of what we call *la Belle Époque*. He declared that the arts were inseparable, and that he was going to unite poetry, music, and painting as Wagner had already tried to do. Péladan did in fact succeed in linking a certain type of painting with poems by Maeterlinck or Samain.

In order to put his theories into practice, he decided to set up, in opposition to the official Salon, the *Salon des Rose+Croix*. The first was opened in 1892, at the Durand-Ruel gallery, to the sound of Erik Satie's trumpets. The Comte Antoine de La Rochefoucauld put up the funds for this first Salon, the rules for which were strictly laid down. There were six Rosicrucian Salons from 1892 to 1897. The first was a triumph, yet the three artists whom Péladan most admired – Gustave Moreau, Odilon Redon, and Puvis de Chavannes – did not send in paintings. These solitaries must have been put off by all the publicity surrounding Péladan, but they were represented by a great many imitators. We shall not dwell on those artists who exhibited in the *Salon des Rose+Croix* and then hurried off in other directions: Maurice Denis and Rouault remained faithful to the mystical tendency, but it is well known how Émile Bernard, Bourdelle, and Vallotton developed. The chief attraction of the exhibition was a Swiss work, *Les Ames Déçues*, by Hodler, a sort of Puvis de Chavannes but with more vigour in concept and execution, one of the first characteristic works of *Art Nouveau;* Hodler's influence was considerable, and can be seen in painters as different as Toorop and Maurice Denis, Munch, and Klimt. Unfortunately a somewhat too academic style in his finished works removes much of the strangeness which characterizes his sketches. Macabre or cosmic allegories, Swiss naïvety scattering flowers around chaste nudes, and the use of colour symbolism – all this struck Hodler's contemporaries as exemplary but touches us much less today, for he keeps his feet firmly on the ground. The most admired of all the foreign exhibitors were

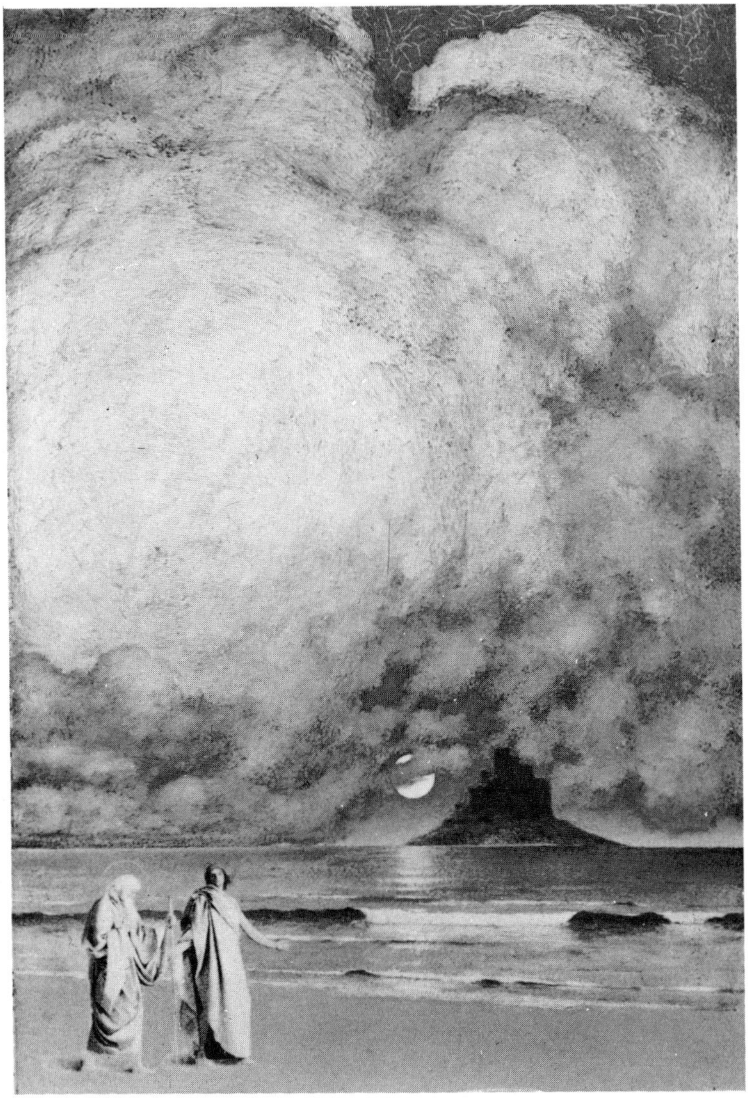

36. Maxfield Parish: *The Apostles.* At the beginning of his career this American painter was an excellent image-maker with a poetic imagination, deriving from the Pre-Raphaelites.

Khnopff and Toorop, whom we shall meet again in later chapters.

A lesser known artist whom this Salon revealed to the public was Jean Delville (1867–1951). His *Orphée* recalls Gustave Moreau's figures, is faithful to Péladan's hermaphrodite ideal, and possesses the weird symbolic richness of a page by Villiers de l'Isle-Adam. Similarly, the portrait of Madame Stuart Merrill entitled *Mysteriosa* could have been a portrait of Villiers's Future Eve. Delville spread Péladan's ideas throughout Belgium and exerted a considerable influence. But his most extraordinary canvas, entitled *Le Trésor de Satan*, shows a red-haired archangel with fiery wings stepping over entwined bodies; the wings are fitted with octopus-like suckers, for the scene, despite the murky colouring, is set on a coral reef under the sea. Thanks to Delville's admirable draughtsmanship, this work is a success, and indeed may be described as one of the finest paintings of the mystical Decadence. With Christ, as was often the case, Delville was less successful. His huge *Jugement Dernier* (Michelangelo bodies among Horta clouds) is one of the most pathetic pictures ever painted in an attempt to express the universal. Delville's teacher and friend, Xavier Mellery, is far inferior to him. His allegories have nothing mystical about them, notably his *Justice Embrassant l'Humanité*, which was intended for the Brussels Palace of Justice. On the other hand, another Belgian, Émile Fabry (1865–1966), who exhibited with the Rosicrucians twice, was an admirable draughtsman who occasionally recalls William Blake.

Henry de Groux began by being considered a new Michelangelo, in spite of the pretentiousness of his ideas and the inadequacies of his palette. A squalid, lascivious mystic and a dazzling conversationalist, he dominated a shrinking circle of admirers, of whom Léon Bloy was the most vehement; under the inspiration of the Catholic polemist, he painted a *danse macabre* of anarchy called *Le Grand Chambardement*. His life was an epitome of all the failures of his generation; the most spectacular episode, his liaison with his niece Sieglinde (a girl who bore an astonishing resemblance to Dürer's *Melancholy*), ended, after a stay in Florence, with the genius being incarcerated in a lunatic asylum. His huge canvases, the most famous of which are *Le Christ aux outrages* (1890) and *La Veille de Waterloo*, are kept in the store-rooms of various Belgian museums. His thoughts, noted down in a private diary, are an interesting document on the taste for suffering which characterized the Decadence (92), being variations on Flaubert's dictum that 'all suffering is an aspiration'. He has a few points in common with Ensor, but he is grandiloquent where the painter of *L'Entrée du Christ à Bruxelles* is caustic.

37. A. Osbert: *Vision*. This large painting has the soft colouring of a pastel drawing. The influence of Puvis de Chavannes can be seen in the mauve Joan of Arc, and that of Seurat in the painter's technique.

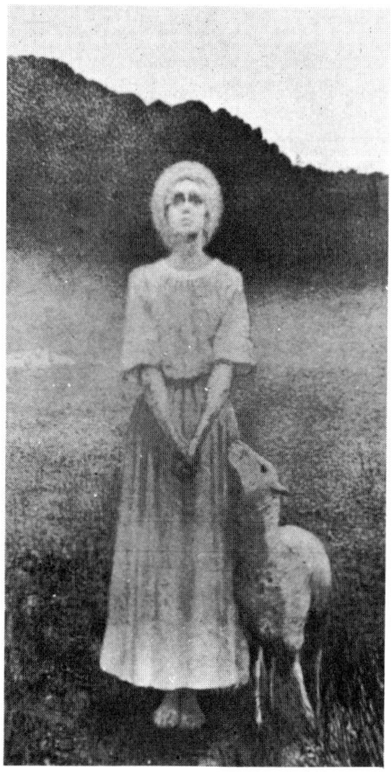

Carlos Schwabe (1866–1926) had a certain influence on Mucha through his posters and illustrations; his gracefully angular models – Ophelias or Beatrices – appear in beautiful watercolours and drawings which recall Burne-Jones, but a Burne-Jones influenced not by Mantegna, but by Memling. His elegant drawings and his adventures in floral decoration make him the most exquisite illustrator of his period – as, for example, in Haraucourt's *Évangile de l'Enfance*.

The most interesting of the French painters is Filiger (1863–1928), a friend of Gauguin's who moved from Pont-Aven to join the colony of German Naïfs at Beuron. Filiger painted little pictures of female saints in the Byzantine style, for he was scrupulous in applying divisionist principles. He was a friend of Jarry and Gourmont, and he died in 1928, in Brittany, penniless and completely forgotten. His work is modest in quantity but brilliant; he has assimilated Duccio and Cimabue without pastiching them, and

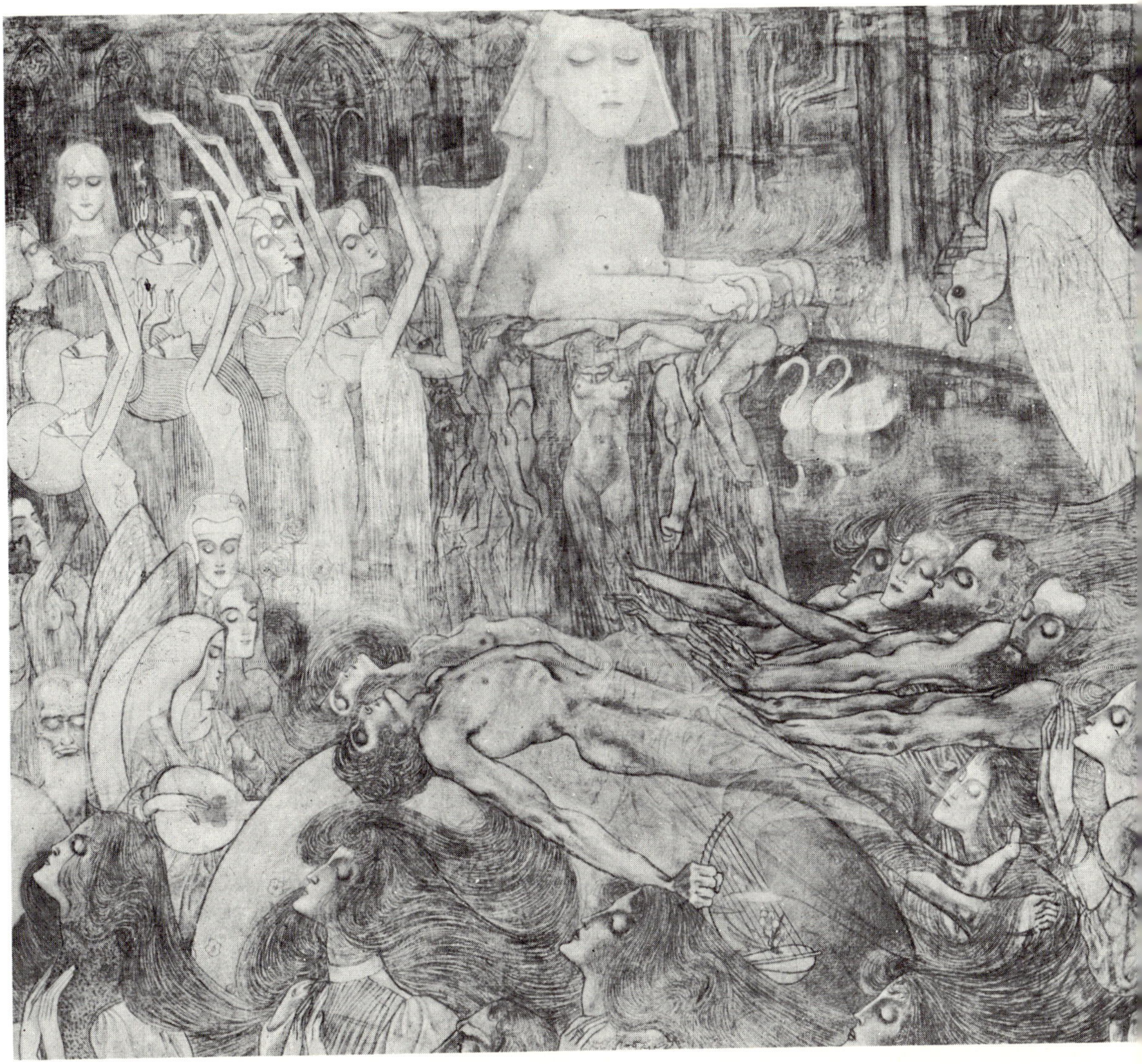

38. Jan Toorop: *The Sphinx*. This drawing brings together all the themes of the Decadence in a river of human hair: madonnas, dead girls, swans, roses, water-lilies, Egyptian and Gothic art, angel musicians, and the Buddha.

there is no ambiguity behind the inclusion of the young Bretons he loves in his Biblical scenes. Of all the Rosicrucians, Filiger is the one who approaches most closely to a state of sanctity. André Breton, who had discovered him after reading Jarry's enthusiastic article, hung a series of Filiger's watercolours over his bed, explaining that 'their beneficial influence combats the evil spells exhaled by the idols brought back from Mexico'. Jarry's article, the only example of his art criticism, appeared in the *Mercure de France* in 1894. Taken as a whole it explains the whole mystical revival; here there is space only for a short passage:

> These resigned Bretons, oval-shaped and almost lozenge-shaped, are made for the torments from which they will not budge . . . I would find them even more beautiful crucified, but then, they all bear the crucifixion at the heart of their eternally motionless faces . . . Of the two eternal principles which cannot exist with-

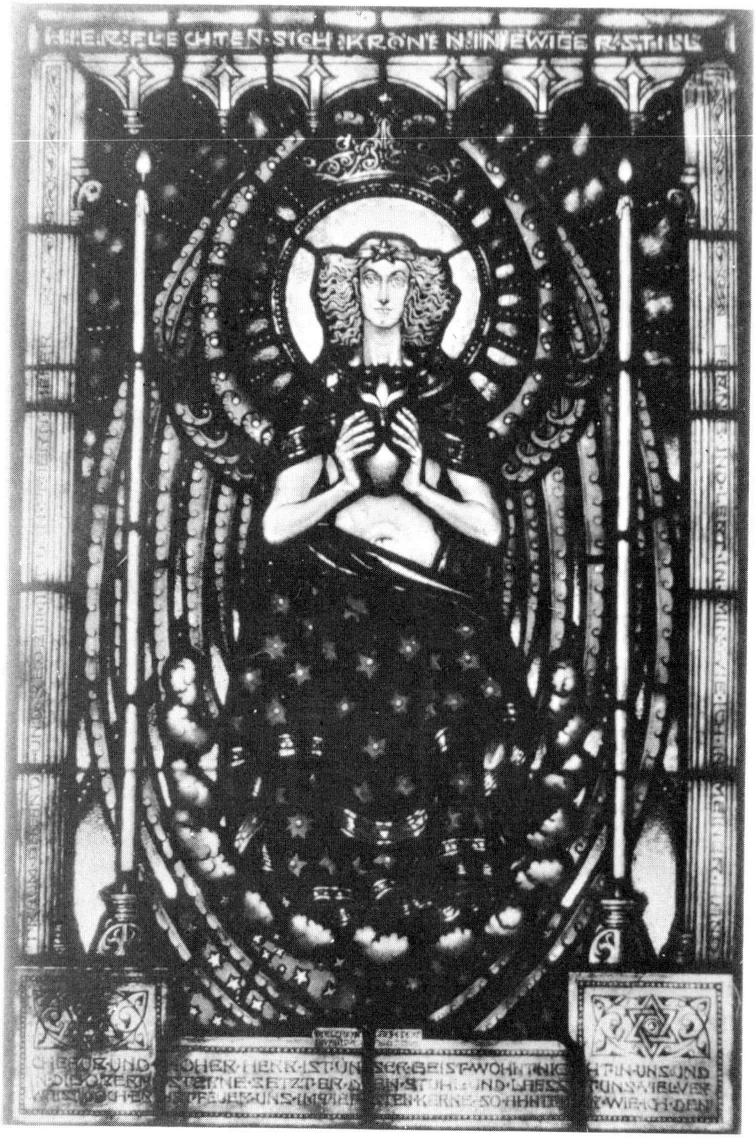

39. Melchior Richter: *Christ.* A stained-glass window of 1916. Christ in the guise of a Stefan George hero in a Rosicrucian setting. Unfortunately the Symbolist painters rarely had the opportunity to do stained-glass windows, but they imitated their mystic colours and strong lines.

out each other, Filiger has not chosen the worse. But beware lest the love of purity and piety send that other purity, evil, back to material life. Under the hollow cardboard hide of the rhinoceros, Maldoror embodies a God who is beautiful too and perhaps holier . . . That is why Filiger's art surpasses him with the innocence of his chaste heads and their expiatory Giottist expressions.

Filiger could have been a far greater painter than Denis if he had not been handicapped by scruples, the difficulty of finishing a work and a feeling of indifference towards the world. Maurice Denis, whose tremendous importance has been revealed in recent exhibitions, was to derive enormous benefits from mysticism. He took the roses of religious painting, leaving the thorns to Desvallières, the favourite painter of *avant-garde* priests until the day the Dominicans discovered Matisse. Denis wrote to Odilon Redon in 1893: 'We are all preoccupied with God. Today Christ is alive. Not for a long time has there been a period more passionately interested in religious Beauty.' Péladan's influence on the Nabis was considerable, but diminished in face of the more critical attitude of the *Revue Blanche*.

Two of the stars of the *Salon des Rose+Croix* have fallen into an oblivion which does not deserve to be permanent: Alphonse Osbert (1857–1939) and Alexandre Séon (1857–1917). Both of them greatly influenced by Puvis de Chavannes, they created pale, stiff figures not far removed from those of Picasso's Blue Period, and sent the 'souls' of their day into ecstasies. These two painters were also connected with the Lyons Mystics, a school fairly similar to the German Nazarenes. Like them, they were excited by ideas which they transposed into stiff pictures painted in inoffensive colours. Forty years earlier, Jeannot had attracted Baudelaire's attention: his *Poème de l'âme* (1847), which could easily have been painted by Osbert or Chenavard, pointed the way to Henry de Groux. It should not be forgotten that Péladan was a native of Lyons.

Séon painted some frescoes at the *Mairie* of Courbevoie, among which the critic of *L'Art et l'Idée* particularly admired *Vesprée Hiemnale* (*Winter Evening*). He too had depicted the chimera: 'A learned logician, he was determined to possibilize his winged gymnocephalous feline.' A close friend of Péladan's, Séon drew frontispieces for his *Ethopée* which tempered the Sâr's wild imagination and earned the artist this tribute: 'You have pictured the nabi of impavid ideality in his purple robes, confronting his infamous epoch as it insults him.' However, Séon's chaste pictures are very different from the painting the Sâr attributes to his hero, the ambiguous Nébo: 'It was a medley of limbs, torsoes of young girls of the night, the thin, wiry legs of Mantegna, astonishingly delicate hands, gaunt but powerful arms, and small bellies – all painted with such hermaphroditic preoccupation that the princess blushed.' Perhaps it is the description of a Toorop which has caused the princess's embarrassment: anything is better than good health, which is a more serious obstacle to mysticism than any of the vices.

Séon was a great friend of Seurat, whom he brought under the influence of the Rosicrucians just before he died. Séon painted some small landscapes on the island of Bréhat, simple but minutely detailed works in dawn or sunset colours, very superior to his figure-paintings, even to his *Désespoir de la Chimère* which attracted attention at the time because Moreau's influence was recognized in it as well as that of Puvis de Chavannes.

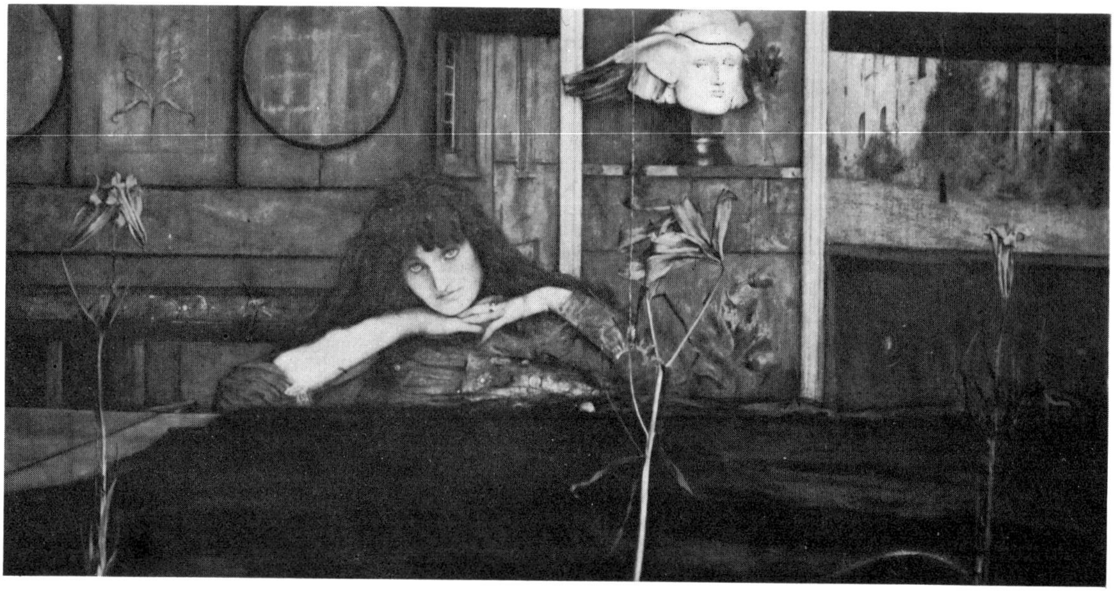

40. Fernand Khnopff: *I lock my Door upon Myself.* One of the most famous of all Symbolist pictures, inspired by a line of Christina Rossetti's poetry. The cast represents silence, and the window is open on a dead city.

Osbert, also a friend of Seurat's from his early days, was greatly influenced by Pointillism. He had first exhibited at the *Salon des Indépendants*, with *Les Edens*. The frames were decorated with verse explaining the artist's intentions, a habit borrowed from Rossetti which gave his work a medieval quality. His *Harmonie Virginale* and his *Mélancolie du Lac* have curious combinations of purple and pistachio-green. His huge picture *Vision* was the main attraction of the second Independents' Salon. Osbert is the painter of quiet blue twilights, and for this sincere artist 'art is a prayer, a resting-place on life's journey, and is necessarily literary since it translates emotions'.

Another star of the *Salon des Rose+Croix* was Armand Point (1861–1932), whose chimeras, too closely imitated from those of his master Moreau, give us some idea of what academic fantasy can be like. Point had ambitions to become the French William Morris, but his studio at Hauteclair was only briefly successful. Until 1925 he went on painting figures in colours and with expressions borrowed from da Vinci; his Dutch disciple Sareluys had been much admired by Wilde – but for his physical beauty. Another of Moreau's pupils, Piot, who was influenced by Delacroix, was torn between his instincts as a colourist and his Symbolist tendencies. In his case, as in Émile Bernard's, ideas unfortunately condemned a genuine talent to tasks which did not suit it. Yet another pupil of Moreau, whom nobody who has looked through the old numbers of *L'Illustration* devoted to the Salon can possibly forget, was Edgar Maxence (1871–1954), who every year until the outbreak of the First World War sent to the Grand Palais paintings of Gothic ladies kneeling with their hands joined in prayer before rich missals. Then there was a young American, Pinky Marcius-Simmons, who exhibited at the *Salon des Rose+Croix* small, exquisitely detailed canvases of mystical inspiration or skyscapes of fantastic clouds.

Finally, mention must be made of the Comte Antoine de La Rochefoucauld, not on account of his paintings, which were clumsy rather than naïve, but because of his generosity. It was thanks to him that Péladan was able to organize the *Salons des Rose+Croix*, and that many members of the brotherhood were saved from poverty. His review *Le Cœur* disseminated the theories of Rosicrucianism until the time when the Count, weary of Péladan's eccentricities, turned his interest to the Nabis, who had likewise been alienated by the Sâr, although they had often drawn inspiration from his ideas.

Some little reviews went into ecstasies over these exhibitions, as we have seen, but a good many remained cool. The opinion expressed in 1892 by Félix Fénéon, one of the most intelligent critics, sets the tone:

> The Regulations and the Monitory listed the subjects which would be welcome 'even if the execution should prove imperfect'. Incidentally, M. Joséphin Péladan referred to himself by the pseudonym of 'Maccabaeus of Beauty'. However, it must be admitted that the *Salon de la Rose+Croix* only partly keeps the promises of merriment implicit in these documents. And one would gladly sing its praises if the 150 pictures on show were not so often reminiscent of other works.
>
> Towards *La Mer*, in a flosculous decoration in the Gustave Moreau manner, Jan Toorop's *Hétaïre* moves beneath the Monticellian machicolation of a light-coloured dress, her face pencilled on a plaque of papier mâché and contrasted with the Malayan masks of the fishermen and handmaidens.
>
> Among the sculptural exhibits: some Bourdelles, a huge work entitled *Le Torrent* by Niederhausen-Rodos, a candelabrum by Alexandre Charpentier, and an exquisite *Virgo Admirabilis* by Pézieux, embossed in gold and painted with purples, pinks and metallic blues.

Mirbeau's mockery had a greater effect. In an article entitled 'Lilies! Lilies!' published in the *Journal* in 1895, the champion of the Impressionists laid into the Symbolist painters. It is difficult to tell whether he was referring to Bernard, Ranson or Sérusier when he wrote: 'I beheld yellow scrolls on blue surfaces; knock-kneed Christs whose outstretched arms ended up in bleeding lilies; wingless birds in scarlet skies pecking at weird stars which looked like prostitutes' eyes; and mystical forests in which the tree-trunks had vaguely human shapes . . .' A year later Mirbeau returned to the attack with another onslaught on 'mystical, mystico-larvist, mystico-vermicelli art'.

It was not long before Fénéon's and Mirbeau's opinions carried the day. The public made the necessary effort to accept the Impressionists, who at least did not require it to think, while the collectors finally turned their backs on the painters of ideas. Péladan's message was discredited by ridicule – the inevitable consequence of any change in fashion – souls, the Middle Ages and Byzantium were relegated to crystal-gazers' ante-rooms, and the Rosicrucians' works fell into oblivion. It is amusing to note the tone of commiseration in which Rouault's biographers, as if faced with a youthful folly, admit that he sent thirteen religious studies to the last of the *Salons des Rose+Croix* in 1897.

Yet Péladan's personality weathered the storm, thanks to the success obtained by certain painters into whom he had injected the courage to depict their inner lives in spite of public opinion. But his reign was a brief one: as early as 1900 his disciples began looking for another guide. Thus Schuffenecker became a theosophist, producing pastel Buddhas which are sometimes reminiscent of Redon; Delville ended as a disciple of Krishnamurti; and Sérusier, after his retreat at Beuron, also devoted himself to depicting Hindu myths. The Catholic-Aesthetic movement therefore turned towards Asia, and particularly towards those sects inspired by Ger-

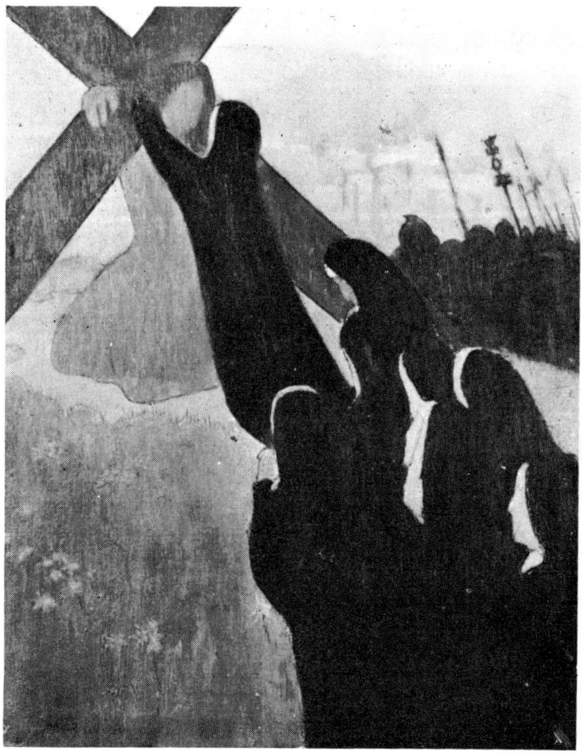

41. Maurice Denis: *Montée au Calvaire*. This canvas is one of the most characteristic of the Pont-Aven School.

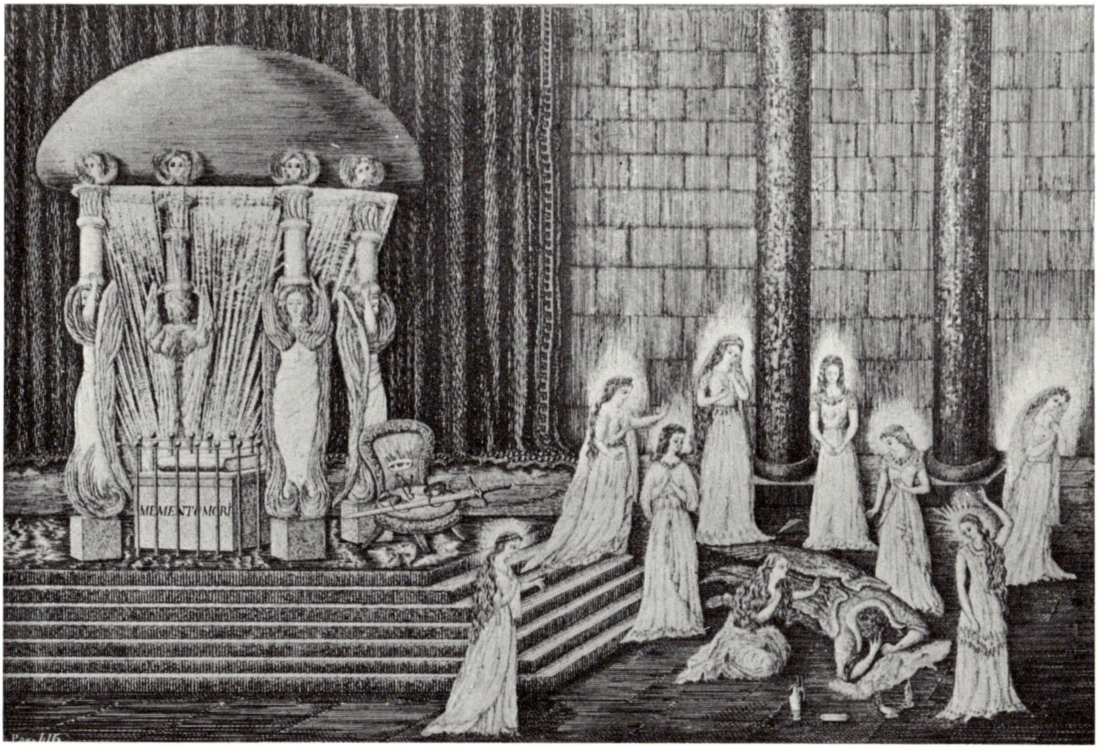

42. Frederika Bodmer: *Automatic Drawing*. This drawing, executed in a state of trance by a Victorian medium, recalls William Blake and at the same time foreshadows *Art Nouveau*. In it can be found themes from biblical symbolism, grouped around an altar to the dead.

man philosophers to which the skull-shaped *Goetheanum*, built for Steiner near Zürich, remains as a curious monument.

Beside Péladan, a place must be made for a less flamboyant but more perspicacious figure, the critic Albert Aurier. His articles, gathered together under the title *Les Isolés*, link names which at first sight seem far apart: Moreau, Gauguin, Sérusier, Maurice Denis, and Van Gogh. In Aurier's opinion, Van Gogh 'is a Symbolist, for he expresses something beyond everyday reality'. Aurier explains very clearly, in terms of the mysticism of the period, Gauguin's strange picture *Vision après le Sermon*, by imagining the Breton church and the priest's sermon which had inspired this vision. The following lines by Gauguin confirm the critic's intuition and might serve as the Credo of all Symbolist painting, reaching far beyond Pont-Aven: 'Truth is to be found in a purely cerebral art, in primitive art . . . Our only salvation lies in a return to principle. This can be accomplished by Symbolism in Poetry and in Art.' One of the most famous of all Gauguin's pictures, the one in Boston Museum painted in 1899 at the time when he was obsessed by death, *Que sommes-nous? D'où venons-nous? Où allons-nous?*, by virtue of its title as well as its composition undoubtedly deserves to be regarded as the masterpiece of Symbolist painting. It is impossible not to see in the same light Picasso's picture of 1901, *L'Enterrement de Casagenas*. And Symbolist mysticism can still be discerned in *La Vie*, which he painted in 1903.

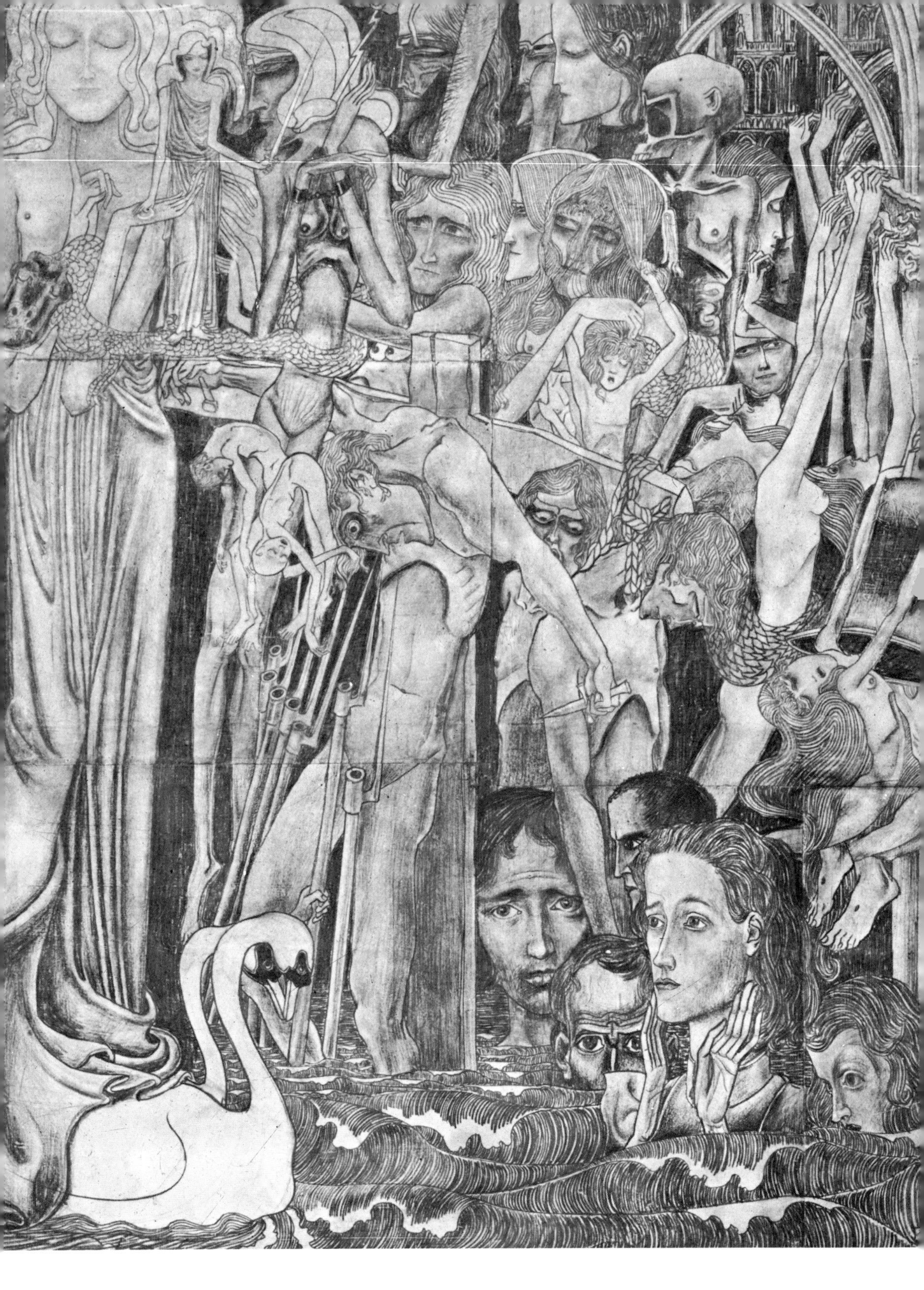

43. Toorop: *Disintegration of Faith*. In this charcoal sketch the artist comes close to Hieronymus Bosch, with the disproportion between the figures, the birds of ill omen, and the mixture of mysticism and torture. This is the Symbolist hell in a half-submerged cathedral.

5 The Macabre Chimera

VISIONARIES. The artist who would have been the most admirable of all the exhibitors at the *Salon des Rose+Croix*, Odilon Redon, kept out of the way, for the chimera he was following was as timid as the Unicorn, and shunned the sort of publicity favoured by the Sâr. A lonelier figure than Moreau, who was very conscious of his magical power and even of his genius, as he sometimes hinted with a certain complacency, Redon admittedly profited from an exhibition of Moreau's work in Bordeaux in 1868, as also from the lessons Bresdin gave him; but with astonishingly simple resources he went much further than his masters. No vampire branches or Asiatic treasures clutter up his visions of another world, visions which were received and not searched for. It seems that Redon was never a spiritualist; his life, judging by his notes *A Soi-même*, was simple and straightforward. And it is indeed astonishing that such a man should have had such amazing visions – visions occasionally mingled, it must be admitted, with insipid pieties, first-communion pictures with vaguely Buddhist overtones. Where Redon comes closest to the Oriental vision is not in the borrowing of external forms but in his conviction that the world is a series of variations on a single theme and reflections of a single being, and in his desire to 'place the logic of the visible at the service of the invisible'. Unlike the vague dreamers who were legion in his time, Redon was a precise dreamer who used minute observation as a springboard to reach the sublime. His familiarity with the supernatural is so complete that he goes further than Flaubert in his series of lithographs inspired by *La Tentation de Saint Antoine*: for him the text is a means of producing visions, much as Tarot cards and coffee-grounds stimulate fortune-tellers (76). Like Moreau, and contrary to what usually happens, Redon influenced painters less than writers. Some of his finest lithographs served as frontispieces to the first works of Verlaine and Ivan Gilkin. This is how Gilkin pays tribute to the artist:

Rouge, rouge saigne le soir
Sur un merveilleux paysage,

J'ai vu un terrible visage
D'un majestueux ange noir.
Red, red bleeds the evening
In a wonderful landscape,
I have seen a terrifying face
Of a majestic black angel.

It need scarcely be added that Redon was infinitely superior to the literature he inspired.

Huysmans was one of the first to bring Redon to the attention of the general public, in a passage in *A Rebours* too well known to be quoted here. Already, in his 1881 *Salon*, he had written: 'Here is a nightmare turned into art. Imagine, in a macabre setting, terrifying, sleep-walking figures with a vague resemblance to those of Gustave Moreau, and you may be able to form some idea of this bizarre talent.' After, so to speak, launching the painter, the novelist had become a friend of his. When Redon sent him a lithograph depicting the hero of *A Rebours*, des Esseintes, Huysmans thanked him in a letter which is particularly interesting in that it stresses the current vogue for occultism: 'He strikes me as a des Esseintes who is more satanic and Hoffmannesque, more obsessed with the occult sciences than mine, who perhaps was not so to a sufficient degree, given the current now sweeping so many people towards these shores . . .'

Even Redon's most devoted admirers have not paid sufficient attention to two themes which recur constantly in his work – and often in the work of the other Symbolists, but without the same significance: the Eye and the Flower. The Eye, which appears in the lithographs inspired by Poe, is important as the means of entering into another world. As for the Flower, in *Les Origines*, the lithographs in which he looks for connections between the animate and the inanimate, animal and vegetable, in an evolutionary spirit, Redon has a plate on which he makes the following comment: 'When life awoke in the depths of darkest matter, perhaps there was a first vision attempted in the Flower' – flowers which are either Baudelairean, or Buddhist lotus-blossoms, or bouquets in stained-glass-window colours gathered in dreams.

In 1894, writing about a Redon exhibition at the Durand-Ruel gallery, Jean Lorrain called his article 'A Strange Juggler' (57). He mentions Wagner in connection with the painter who published some of his finest lithographs in the *Revue Wagnérienne*, and whose hero was Parsifal. At a time when matter was becoming the sole interest of most painters, Redon's art drew this naïve comment from Bonnard: 'What strikes me most about his work is the combination of two completely opposed qualities: very pure plastic expression and very mysterious expression.' That judgement shows what harm rich, complex pictures such as Moreau's had done to inspirational painting. In fact, the visionary Redon was anything but indulgent in his comments on the magician of the Rue La Rochefoucauld: 'What wonderful embroidery on faded, old-fashioned silks for the cushions of a few old ladies, dreamers of luxurious dreams, whose past was unblemished except for the fact that they kept their eyes closed to poverty.'

Unlike Moreau, a solitary who was rarely alone and a greatly respected master, Redon had no disciples; however, he exerted a considerable influence on certain Scandinavians, Strindberg for example, who wrote of his own pictures: 'Every painting has two sides – an exoteric side, visible, though only just, to everyone, and an esoteric side which is visible only to the painter himself and the "elect"; it should be added that my canvases are painted in a dark room and cannot stand the light of day.'

The exhibition entitled *Les Sources du XXe Siècle* (Paris, 1961) revealed two Swedish painters: Hill and Josefson. Both men went mad when they were about forty, and both, like Strindberg's characters, were obsessed with the Beyond. Again, both men had worked in France. Hill had been there in 1877, so it is doubtful that he ever knew Redon's work. But the resemblances are amazing, even in the titles of Hill's pictures, such as *Prophet in a landscape of immemorial time* and *Men-Cathedrals*. Josefson, after fighting for years against the academic art of his country, settled in Brittany. His *Soul of the Flower* and *Sun-God* are likewise titles and pictures in the Redon manner.

Later on, Redon's influence can be distinguished in the watercolours of the German Emil Nolde, although the Biblical inspiration of that visionary places him closer to Moreau. The combination of the influences of Strindberg, Redon, and Gauguin explains the conversion of the 'Naturalist' Munch to Idea Painting. Munch was the first to express the anguish of the individual in the face of society and death; he was also one of the inventors of the ectoplasm line. Munch's figures emerge from the lithographic darkness like apparitions at a seance, yet their problems are those of ordinary people: jealousy, loneliness, and syphilis (then very common, very badly treated, and a source of several masterpieces). He once declared: 'I do not paint what I see, but what I have seen; the camera will never be able to rival painting as long as it is impossible to use it in Heaven and Hell.' Munch's ghosts are not those of pontiffs and princesses: they are characters such as Strindberg created: 'When the sun goes down, and night falls, and dusk turns mortals into ghosts and corpses, at the time when they go home to don the shroud of their bed and abandon themselves to sleep, that simulacrum of death reconstructs life; this faculty for suffering comes to us from Heaven or from Hell.' Munch is the illustrator of a black Symbolism, unrelieved by the smallest lily. Verhaeren's poems are as dark as Redon's and Munch's works: witness these lines from *Soirs* (1898), which was published with a lithograph by Redon:

Du soir! Et dans les cieux pleins de nuages ivres,
Du noir toujours! Et dans les cœurs pleins de caveaux!
Et c'est du noir encor qui nous tombe des livres
Que nous avons élus pour dorer nos cerveaux.
Evening! And in the skies full of drunken clouds
More darkness! And in our hearts full of vaults!
And it is darkness too that falls from the books
We have chosen to gild our brains.

Again, the spermatozoa writhing around Munch's Madonna recall these lines by Verhaeren:

Les rigides phallus, tordus d'efforts,
Cassés, et par les mares de la plaine
Les vieux caillots de la semence humaine.
The rigid phalluses, twisted with effort,
Lie broken, and in the pools on the plain
Float the old clots of human seed.

The Decadents were fond of dwelling on such horrors, partly out of a desire to shock, but largely out of a sort of fury at being

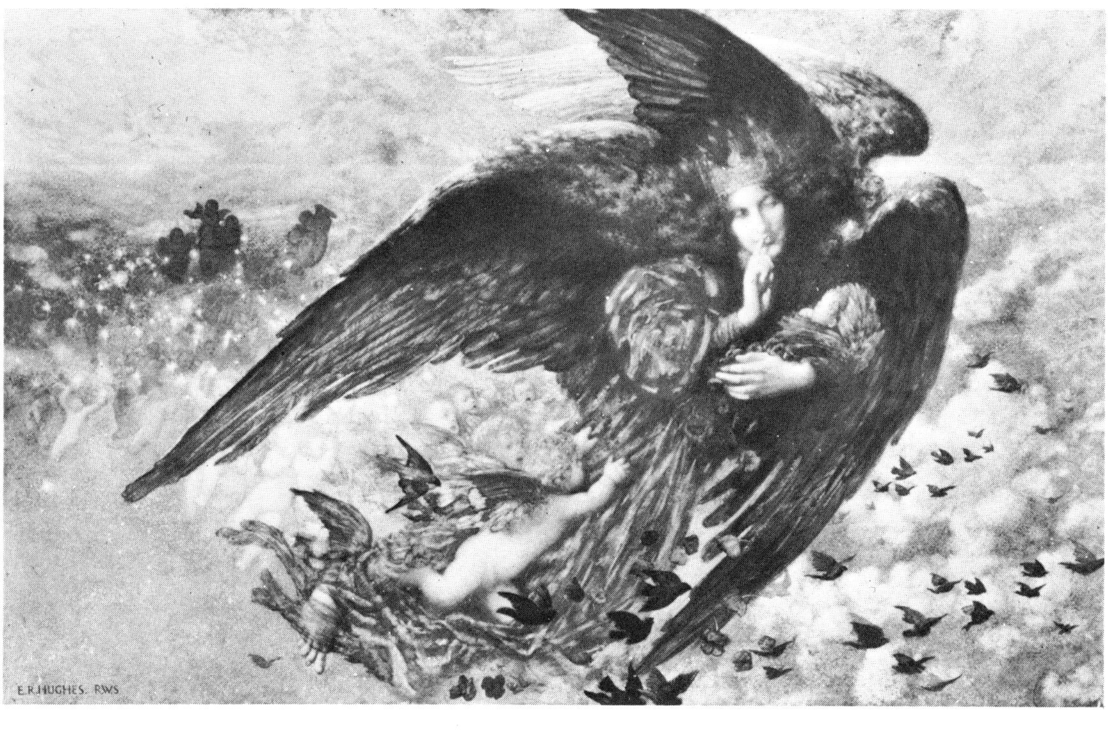

44. E. R. Hughes: *Night with her Train of Stars and Gift of Sleep.* This angel painted in black and midnight blue has the expression of the Mona Lisa; he (or she) is carrying in his arms small dead babies who are perhaps to become stars or birds. It is one of the most typical portrayals of Victorian sentiment with regard to death.

unable to find a faith or love to match their illusions. These weird visions were the deliberately sacrilegious themes of the Satanists. Redon's apparitions on the other hand came from a personal Beyond. The Rosicrucians' pictures were the products of a carefully cultivated dream; Munch's ghosts showed the suffering of 'souls' in the face of everyday life. But when occultists tried to give pictorial expression to evil aspirations, most of their works were vitiated by an unspeakable vulgarity, for in the arts it is vulgarity, not ugliness, that is the expression of evil.

BLACK MAGIC. An indication of this tendency is to be seen in the devil who forms the frontispiece to the works of Eliphas Lévi. He is to be found again in the countless occultist reviews which mushroomed at that period, the best known of which is the *Voile d'Isis* edited by Papus and Guaita. Satanism, often linked with spiritualism, was taken very seriously, and Charles Morice wrote in *La Littérature de Tout à l'Heure*: 'The occult sciences form one of the principal cornerstones of Art. Every true poet is instinctively an initiate; the reading of books of spells awakens in him secrets of which he had always possessed an inborn knowledge.' A complete error from the aesthetic point of view, as we shall see.

In the last third of the nineteenth century people played with evil as children play with fire. Some were burnt to death, such as Stanislas de Guaita, the most brilliant of Barrès's friends in his youth, who died in mysterious circumstances after publishing revelations about occultist circles in *Le Temple de Satan* and *Au Seuil du Mystère*. A native of Germany, who spent part of every year in a lonely castle in the Ardennes, this occultist aesthete had a great influence on Barrès's first novels. Quarrels between the inoffensive Péladan and the practitioners of a certain variety of black magic divided the devotees of the Beyond, and made several victims among those who allowed themselves to be led into sinister adventures. Of these adventures the most innocent were such purple passages as this from Jean Lorrain's *Monsieur de Phocas*:

> To the chanting of a liturgical prose, and standing stiffly against the tapestry of vague figures and floating lights, the tragic actress seemed to be embodying a rite, a rite from some forgotten religion which she had resuscitated, in a gesture and in the rigid curve of her loins.

This is the posture of certain figures depicted by Klimt against a background of skeletons swathed in scarves, and the grotesque phantasms in Kubin's drawings seem to have come from similar witches' sabbaths. The chimeras of Occultism, which Moreau undoubtedly intended to depict, led the poets into evil company in that Paris where – to talk like the author of *Monsieur de Phocas* – 'snobbery exacerbates vice'. Moreau did not hide this aim in his long explanation of his chimeras, from which I need quote only a few phrases to reveal the influence of Satanism: 'Woman, in her essential nature, the irrational creature, obsessed with mystery and the unknown, and in love with evil in the form of perverse and diabolical seduction . . . that satanic enclave, in that circle of vices and guilty passions . . . creatures whose souls have been abolished, waiting by the roadside to see the lascivious goat go by, ridden by lust.'

One of the monsters in Moreau's picture, a goat with three serpent heads, is carrying a fat, naked woman, riding backwards on its scaly back, towards a Gothic tabernacle. One is reminded of Madame Chantelouve, Huysmans's heroine, going to the Black Mass described in *Là-bas*. And indeed there were countless horrors thought up at the time by bad priests and neurotic women, in their hatred for a Christ who had not brought them peace. It was for them that Rémy de Gourmont wrote this dreadful litany, quoted in *Monsieur de Phocas*, with its strange *fin de siècle* flavour bordering on the infamous (8):

> *Et ce rubis impie de volupté, tout sanglant et tout froid:*
> *C'est la dernière blessure de Jésus sur la Croix . . .*
> *Et la boucle améthyste qui tend la jarretière de soie,*
> *C'est le dernier frisson de Jésus sur la Croix . . .*
> *O douloureux saphir d'amertume et d'effroi!*
> *Saphir, dernier regard de Jésus sur la Croix.*
> And this unholy ruby of pleasure, bleeding and cold,
> Is the last wound of Jesus on the Cross . . .
> And the amethyst clasp holding the silk garter
> Is the last shudder of Jesus on the Cross . . .
> O painful sapphire of bitterness and fear!
> Sapphire, last look of Jesus on the Cross.

Huysmans's famous description of Grünewald's Christ prepares the reader of *Là-bas* for the sacrilegious Christ of the Black Mass. That was a Christ Huysmans had already seen and studied in *Le Calvaire*, an engraving by Rops, the artist who copied the satanic and erotic aspects of Baudelaire with a laborious persistency which earned him a considerable reputation during the *Belle Époque*. Huysmans's delirious description of the Rops print in *Certains* deserves to be quoted here: 'The unspeakable Beast hangs there with his money-box mouth and his walrus teeth. Smiling, his chin in the air, he reaches out with his unnailed feet, grips the mane of a naked woman standing before him, and slowly strangles her with the locks of her hair, while she, terrified, her arms outstretched,

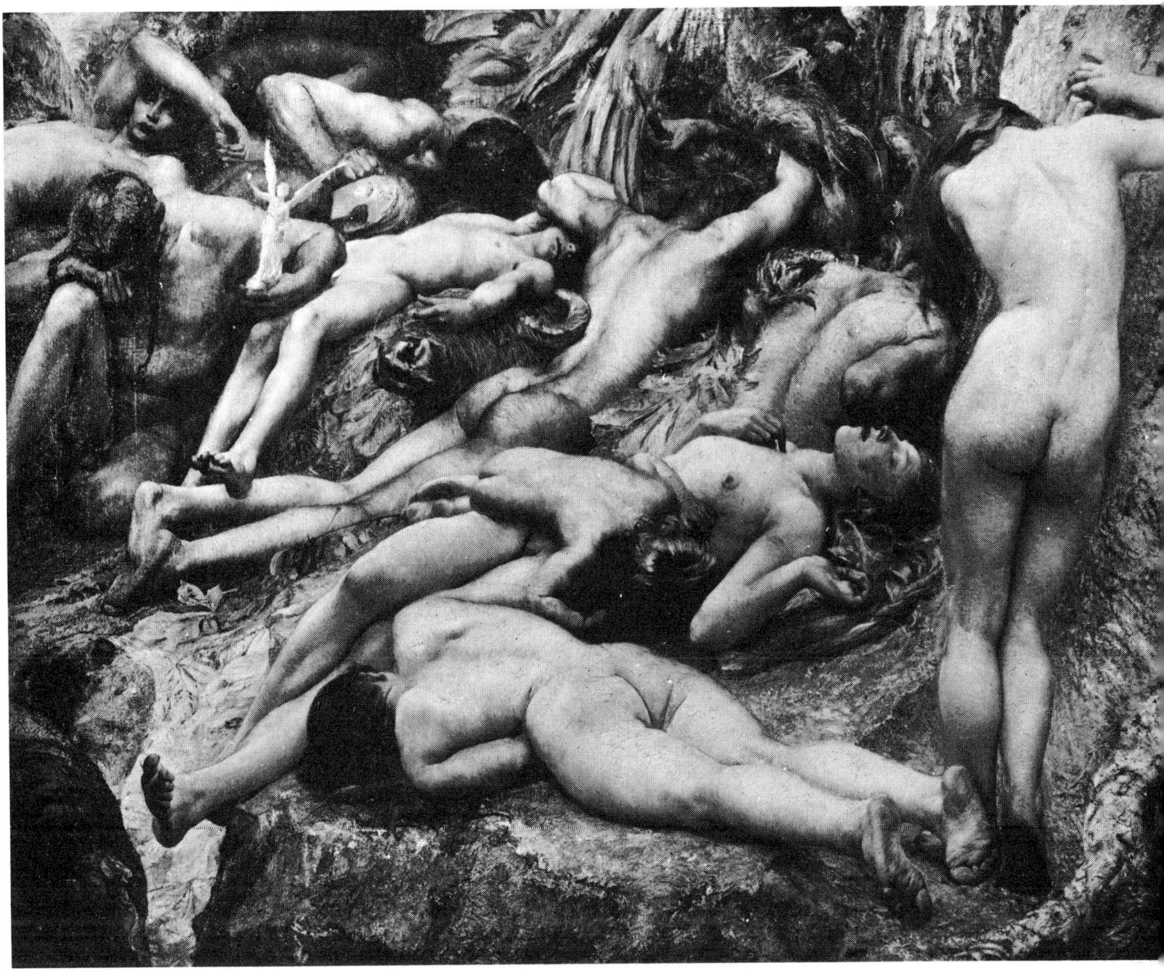

45. Sartorio: *Diana of Ephesus* (detail). This work, by a favourite illustrator of d'Annunzio, could depict one of his goriest dramas. Eroticism and death have been blended with great skill.

dies in a spasm of atrocious pleasure . . .' And in another work Huysmans writes: 'He has celebrated the spirituality of lust which is Satanism, depicted in imperfectible pages the supernatural of perversity, the immortality of evil.'

Another German Christ inspired a great many painters: the *Dead Christ* in the Basle Museum which Holbein is said to have painted from a Jew found drowned in the Rhine. It was copied by Böcklin in a *Descent from the Cross* in which Mary Magdalen, looking rather like a widow of 1870, has clothed her nudity in filmy crape. It was also imitated by Käthe Kollwitz and by that strange Finnish artist Alexis Gallen Kallela. There one is also reminded of Vallotton (but why, one wonders, is there a swan in the background of the picture?).

The Decadents treated the Virgin Mary no more respectfully than they treated Christ (28), but as she could not be profaned in the shape of the Eucharist, she escaped the full fury of the Satanists. Many of the poems about her are variations on *L'Ex-Voto* in the Spanish style, the finest being Swinburne's *Dolores*, who could be

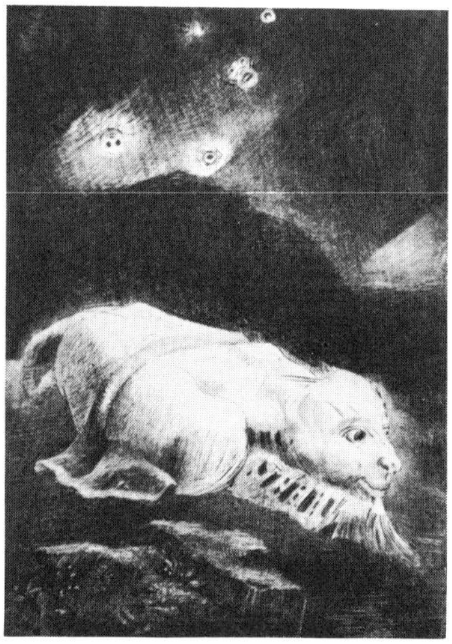

46. Odilon Redon: *Quand s'éveillait la Vie*. In this, the first of his lithographs to be influenced by a Darwinian friend, Redon depicted his vision of the first living beings in a way reminiscent of Bosch as well as of the monsters conjured up by Flaubert in the *Tentation de Saint Antoine*.

called Our Lady of the Masochists. The Belgians, brought up in a more pious atmosphere than the French, depicted some very curious Virgins. The English, on the other hand, did not go so far in the way of Satanism, possibly because the Catholic Church had an exotic charm for them, and going over to Rome was as momentous a step as becoming a Satanist for a Catholic. Simeon Solomon, following in Wilde's footsteps, fell under the spell of incense, confessions, Rome; and Beardsley died a convert to Catholicism. The latter had practised spiritualism with Father Gurney, who had a great influence on him in his youth. Some of Beardsley's works, full of branches, bare roots, and black flowers, can be linked with a poem which was greatly admired at that time: *The Valley of Vain Desires*, by John Addington Symonds (11).

One of Beardsley's less successful drawings shows a neophyte being initiated into black magic. Bad taste is in fact inseparable from this sort of activity, the tradition of which was continued into the nineteen-thirties by the so-called magician Aleister Crowley, one of the last of the Decadents and the hero of Somerset Maugham's novel *The Magician*. Among these late-comers, mention must also be made of the German Alastair, who looked like Nosferatu and adapted Beardsley to the taste of Berlin in 1920. Alastair was involved in the esoteric movements then agitating Germany, and represented the most corrupt aspect of the Decadence. He indulged in excesses far worse than Beardsley's, for his world was one of Black Masses in transvestite clubs; and in his illustrations of Wilde's *Sphinx* he cruelly caricatures the ideas which had passed through the mind of the author of *Dorian Gray*. For Alastair as for Rops, bad taste led to hell more surely than the elegant caprices of the English. He lived to nearly a hundred, but only his early works show any inspiration.

GHOSTS AND SKELETONS. Death is ever-present in the works of those who have tried to penetrate its secrets. Some of Rops's engravings are actually suggestive of necrophilia, but it is easier to deal with the horrors of decomposition in literature than in art. In spite of countless scenes of vampirism in literary works and the heaps of female corpses in Delacroix's and Géricault's pictures, the human corpse in an advanced state of decomposition did not inspire the Romantic painters. There is certainly no decaying flesh in the work of another bizarre individual, a Belgian like Rops, Baron Léon Frédéric (1856–1940). Apart from several social allegories, he painted a triptych entitled *Le Ruisseau*, *Le Torrent*, and *L'Eau dormante*: the stream in question is an Alpine Styx sweeping along hundreds of dead children who, from a distance, might be taken for pink and yellow pebbles; swans are gliding about among these bundles of humanity. None of the Surrealists ever attained the insipid horror of this huge canvas with its cold colours but impeccable draughtsmanship. Another Belgian obsessed with death was Ensor, who is chiefly remembered for his masked skeletons. But his bright colours take away much of the force of his pictures, which are far less macabre than the poems of, say, Verhaeren and Gilkin (10,30). As for the Italian Sartorio, he littered his huge canvases with vast numbers of naked heroes struck down by d'Annunzio goddesses.

Dead women were painted by the hundred by tardy academic imitators of Delacroix. The oddest of them all, without the slightest doubt, is *Jeanne la Folle* by the Spanish painter Francesco Pradilla. But the finest study of necrophilia is offered to us by the *Petit Journal*, with an engraving showing the famous Sergeant Bertrand removing a girl's body by moonlight from the family

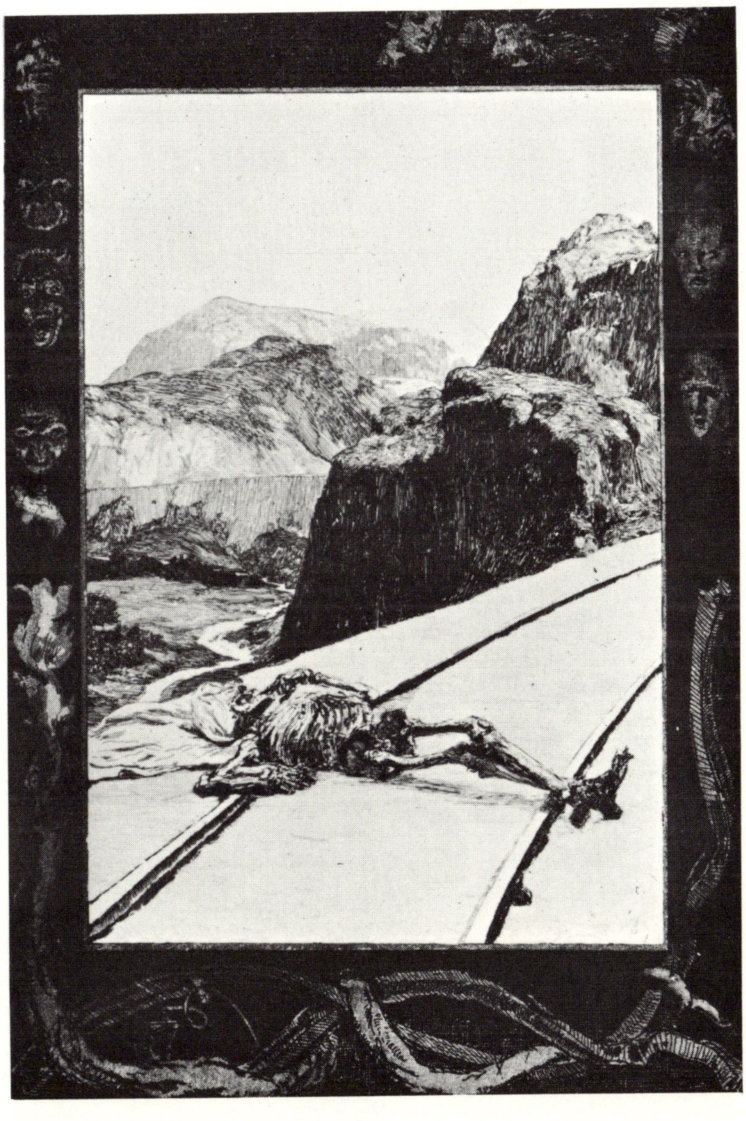

47. Max Klinger: *Death is there*. In the tradition of the German *danses macabres* of Holbein and Rethel, this etching done about 1885 is noteworthy for its frame, which influenced Munch among others.

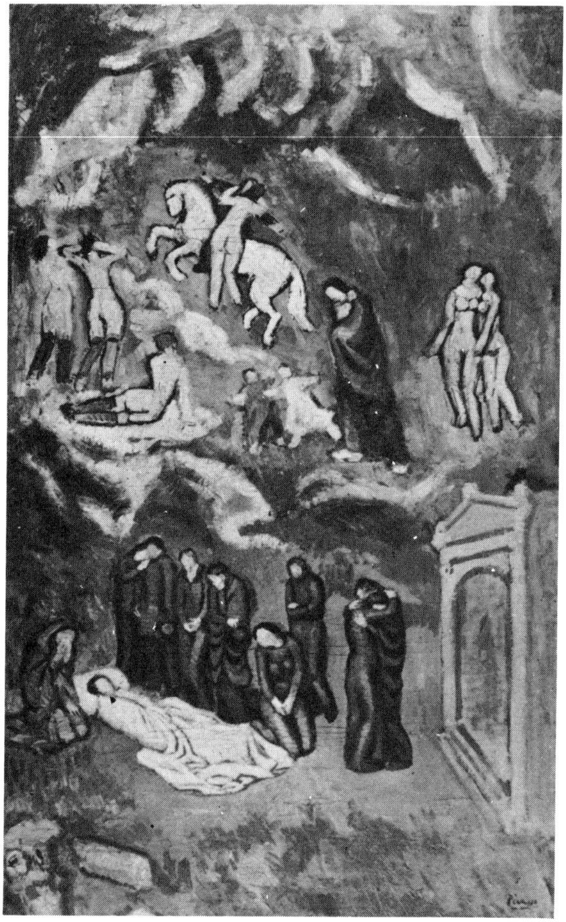

48. Pablo Picasso: *Evocation*. Using the grey-blue tones beloved of Puvis de Chavannes, the young Picasso has evoked scenes from Symbolist dramas, grouped about the tableau of the death of a friend.

vault in Montparnasse Cemetery. None of Max Ernst's collages, made up of engravings of similar inspiration, attains the poetic quality of this picture.

The most poetic of all the macabre episodes of this period – and also the most typical, for it might have been born in Poe's imagination – was the exhumation of Rossetti's poems buried in Elizabeth Siddal's coffin. In 1862, on the death of the girl who had embodied the concept of the New Woman, the poet placed the collection of poems Elizabeth had inspired next to her face and under her long hair before the coffin was closed. During the following months, obsessed by his memories of her, he depicted her once more as Beatrice, but this time as a ghostly apparition from another world: the result was his masterpiece, *Beata Beatrix*, painted with her eyes closed against the background of a misty Florence. It is a picture rich in symbols: thus the bird is red, the colour of death, while the dress is green, suggesting springtime, but against the purple background of grief. At that time Rossetti moved a great deal in spiritualist circles; then he fell under the influence of less ethereal creatures, including Mrs. William Morris, whose Jewish beauty inspired his pictures of Oriental goddesses. But he found that he was no longer capable of writing. It was then that some friends suggested that he should retrieve the poems he had buried. After several years of hesitation, Rossetti, now completely neurotic, gave way to the exhortations of a certain Howell, a picture-dealer and blackmailer, and instructed him to make arrangements for the exhumation. Some mysterious signs – a bell ringing of its own accord and a sparrow perching on his hand – told the poet that Elizabeth gave her consent. On 4 October 1869, in Highgate Cemetery, the coffin was taken out of the grave. A bonfire had been lit to dispel any unwholesome vapours which might be released – a fire of dead leaves as in Millais's admirable picture *Autumn Leaves*. In the light of the dancing flames the coffin was opened, revealing the dead woman, still radiantly beautiful. The manuscript was removed. A long lock of golden hair remained stuck to the paper. No Decadent has ever painted a stranger scene. After being duly disinfected, the poems were sent to Rossetti's publisher and, when they appeared the following year, gained a huge success. But then their sensuality, and perhaps the ill-guarded secret of their exhumation, led certain critics to pass harsh judgements on their author. Elizabeth Siddal was the first dead heroine of Symbolism.

Death was always present to Maeterlinck, from his first poems to the metaphysical speculations which occupied his robust old age. Doudelet's wood-cuts illustrate admirably a ballad published in *Pan* in 1895:

Et j'ai vu la mort
(J'entendis son âme)
Et j'ai vu la mort
Qui l'attend encore . . .
And I saw death
(I heard his soul)
And I saw death
Waiting for him still . . .

If the Death lying in wait in the corner of Laforgue's poems reminds us of a Rops engraving, the Death which inspired Redon had been imagined by Flaubert: 'It had a death's head with a crown of roses, above a woman's torso of mother-of-pearl whiteness. Below, a shroud speckled with gold dots forms a sort of tail; and the whole body undulates like a gigantic worm standing up' (*La Tentation de Saint Antoine*).

Death, the great obsession of the pessimistic *fin de siècle*, was rarely depicted by the artists of the period in the familiar and doubtless over-precise form of the skeleton, although that is the usual

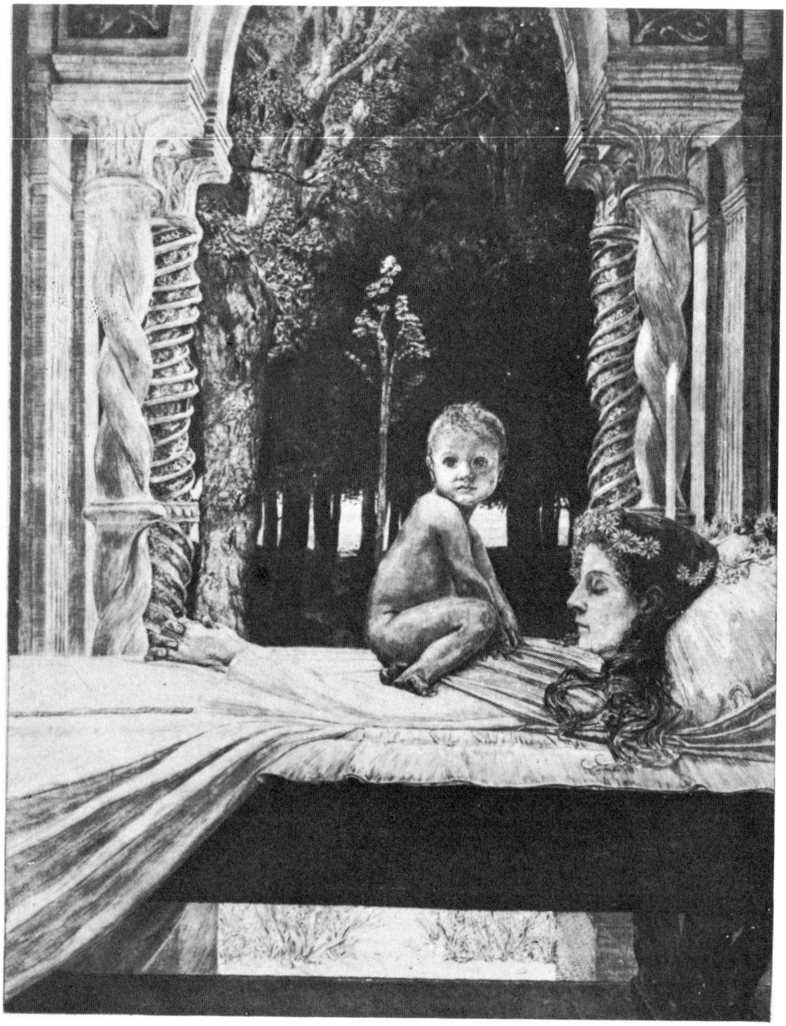

49. Klinger: *Dead Mother*. This etching, by the strangest of all German artists, seems to illustrate a Freudian case-history, and is close to Surrealism in its symbolism. The saplings in the dark forest and the flowers underneath the tombstone represent the renewal of life.

theological symbol. Unlike the Death of the Baroque artists, the Death of the Decadents is bejewelled, by Ensor and Rops, in a manner Baudelaire would have approved. For one thing, a skeleton could not have inspired desire in Poe or his imitators. For another, ghosts – and this was a period devoted to the occult – never appear in the form of skeletons. The most striking evocation of this hallucinatory death is to be found in Toorop's drawing *The Disintegration of Faith*, in which bodies can be seen turning into skeletons, and phosphorescent faces emerging from shrouds. In its preciosity, in the deliberate disproportion of faces and planes, and in the incongruous presence of swans, this Symbolist hell is close to Bosch. Toorop alone has succeeded in depicting the stage of decomposition on the journey to hell without disgusting us or making us laugh. His damned souls are sinking into a quagmire of sulphur, like Bosch's, with birds flying among them, but, as in Poe, passing-bells or alarm-bells make his figures vibrate like Javanese silhouettes pictured by Rossetti. As we shall see in connection with Bruges,

Toorop was also the painter of hallucinations born of stagnant waters.

Rodolphe Bresdin likewise reminds us of Bosch, by establishing a detailed ambiguity between the human and the vegetable, and by creating a poisonous flora which seems to hold captive sad and exotic figures; skeletons and roots merge together, and skulls are the fruits of this infernal vegetation. Huysmans's des Esseintes described a Bresdin engraving (11) in terms which revived the public's interest in an artist whom Baudelaire admired. But, astonishingly enough, a few lines by Théodore de Banville go further than Huysmans in analysing Bresdin's dreamlike equivalences: 'The stagnant water and rotten matter engender winged souls; there is a terrifying link between the gaze of the lakes and that of human beings. The tree-roots are monsters crawling under the ground; the bestial postures adopted by the branches can only be the result of memory and cannot have been learnt in their immobile lives.' Bresdin's world is dominated by Death, like the world of Lautréamont, another Decadent before his time. The typically Second Empire chalets depicted in two of Bresdin's engravings have something hallucinatory about them and Lautréamont's Maldoror might well have made them his home. Marcel Brion once summed up Bresdin's art in a happy phrase when he wrote: 'He imagines what he sees.' There are skeletons too in Klinger's engravings, in which we can recognize the themes of Rethel's famous *Totentanz* (1849), but, like Bresdin, Klinger is more disturbing in those works where he does not depict a too explicit Death.

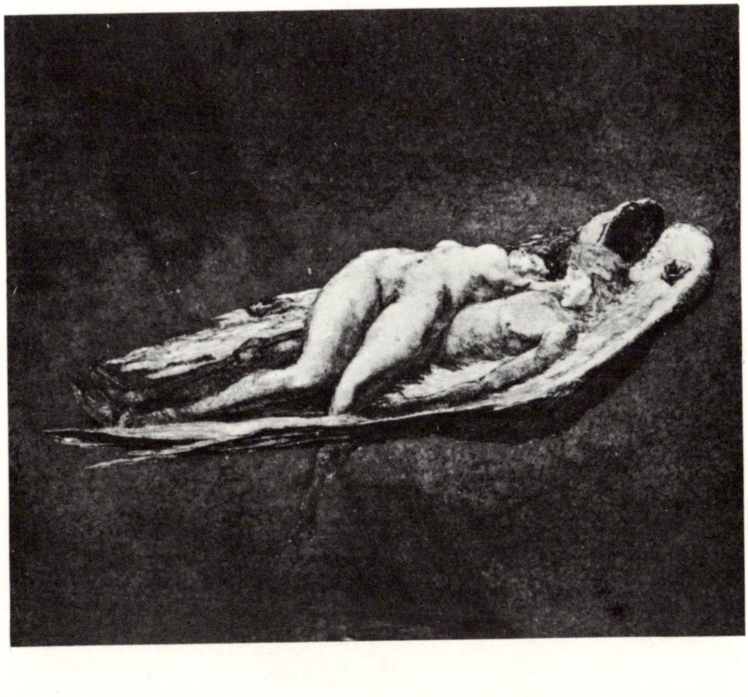

50. Klinger: *Death of the Lovers* (detail). Freudian symbolism is foreshadowed in this etching which, in spite of its minute detail and its eroticism, is reminiscent of Redon.

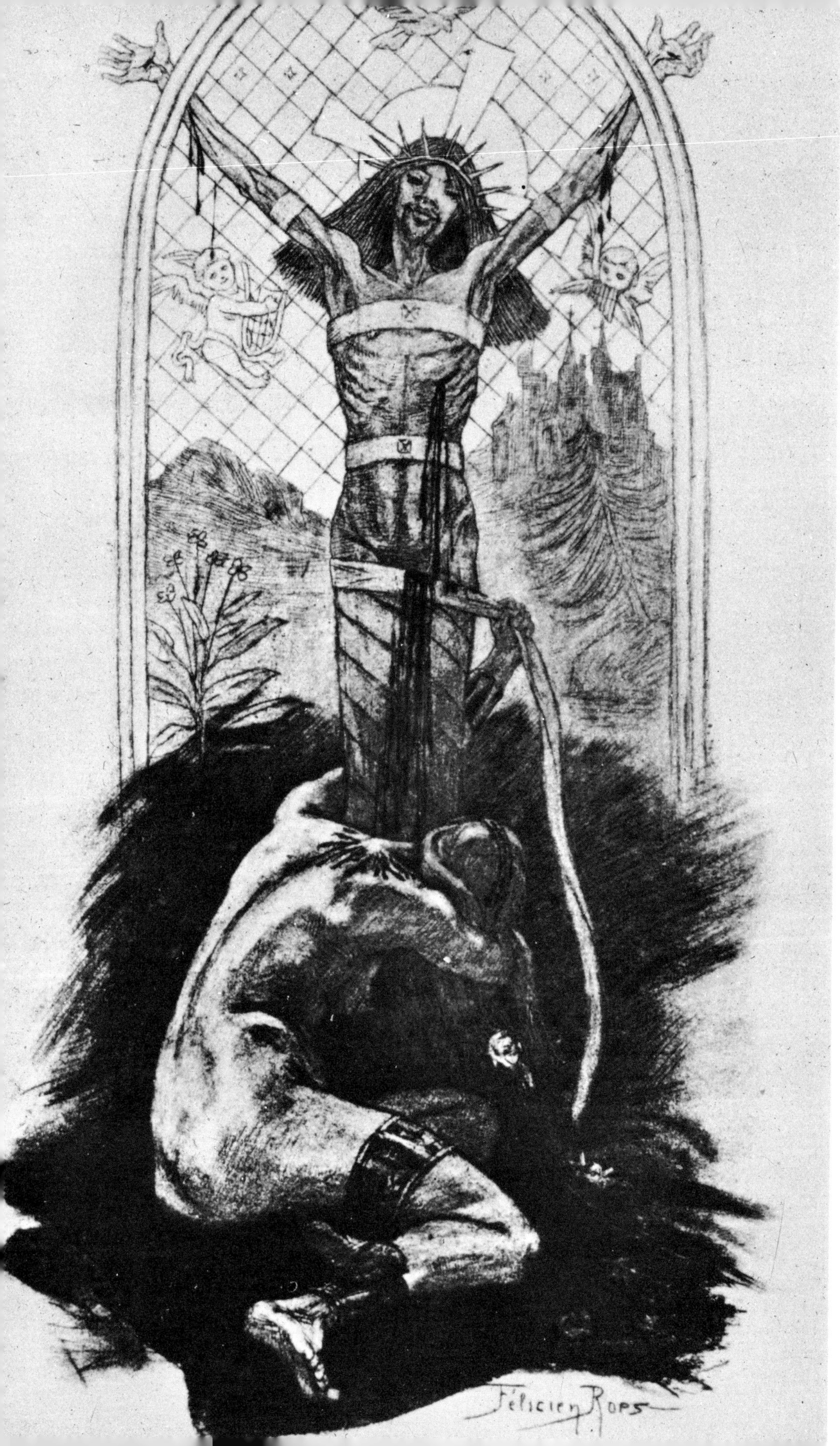
Félicien Rops

6 The Erotic Chimera

THE DECADENT EROS

Très vieux malgré mes vingt ans,
Usé, blasé,
Car je suis né
Sur un lit de roses fanées,
Je suis un Eros vanné.
Very old though only twenty,
I am worn out and bored,
For I was born
On a bed of faded roses,
I am an exhausted Eros.

This Maurice Donnay song, made famous by Yvette Guilbert, was illustrated by a Lautrec lithograph showing two fashionable ghouls making fun of a limping Cupid. What is the explanation of the song and illustration?

The twenty-odd years known as the *fin de siècle* which tried, in a Sardanapalian apotheosis, to destroy all moral principles, were dominated by the twin forces of mysticism and eroticism. As we have just seen, the Mystical Chimera is often very close to the Erotic Chimera; the former carries the artist out of the world, while the latter allows him to brave it – for there is eroticism every time a prohibition is flouted. This eroticism was displayed with a freedom which astonishes us today, and which helps us to understand Freud, whose ideas were conceived in an environment which now strikes us as sexually obsessed. As Patrick Walberg has observed in his *Eros Modern Style*, brutal animal realism was to be found side by side with hazy and sometimes demented intellectualism. We propose to confine ourselves to the latter. All the roads, or nearly all, along which the Chimeras have taken us so far passed by way of eroticism. Odilon Redon and Puvis de Chavannes are almost the only artists we have considered who did not enter that domain, and who avoided the vulgarity which is inseparable from pictorial eroticism. Witness most of the illustrators of Baude-

51. Félicien Rops: *L'Amante du Christ*. There is more than a touch of Montmartre about this picture, which was very famous in its time: the sails of the Moulin Rouge protrude beyond Christ's halo, the stained-glass window is based on those in the *Chat noir*, and the Mary Magdalen with the leather bracelet looks as if she had a masochistic clientele. As for Rops's Christ, he shows us the closeness of the resemblance between the Decadent poets and the Hippies of today.

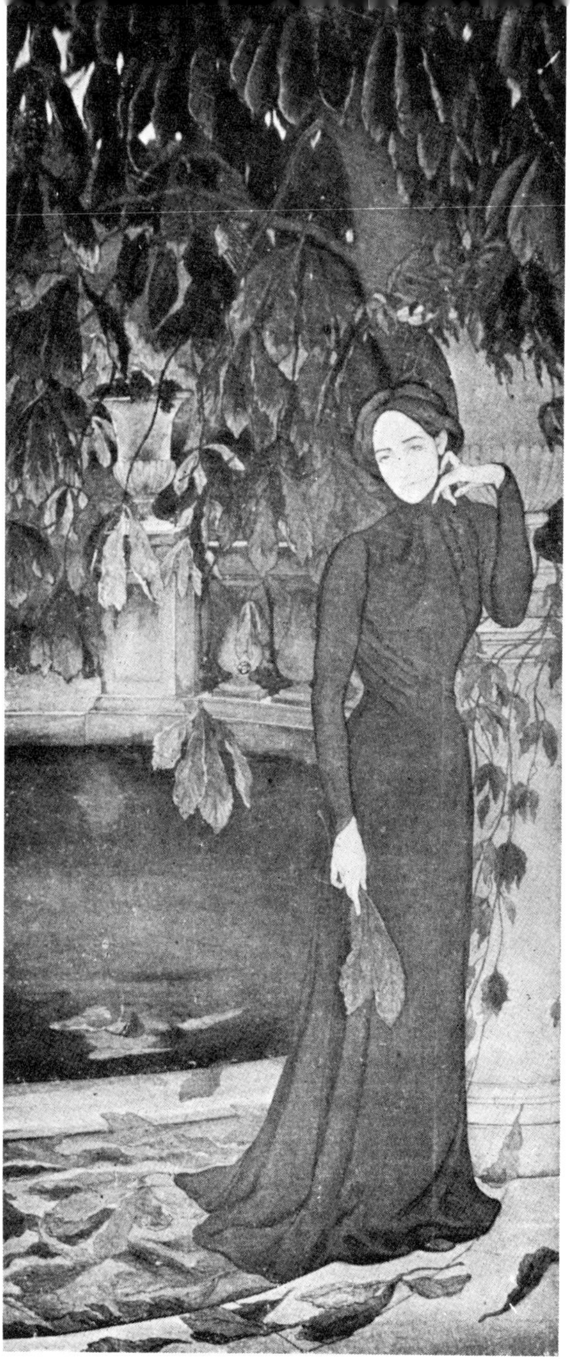

52. Hubert de La Rochefoucauld: *Promeneuse*. This respected painter, a patron of the Rosicrucians, here gives us a picture of a particularly distinguished 'soul'.

laire – although of course *Les Fleurs du Mal* was the favourite work of true artists as well as of those who turned to it for voluptuous and ambiguous images. Baudelaire's *femmes damnées* can be found again in works as different as those of Rodin and the naïve Séguin (1869–1903) of Pont-Aven. For a long time Rops seemed to be the artist closest to the poet – perhaps because the latter had admired his first drawings – but Moreau's haughty, bejewelled heroines, under their 'vast porticoes', are to us much closer to the Baudelairean ideal.

For most of the painters and writers whose reveries we are studying, however, the transgressive element is more important than the satisfaction of creating phantasms. Beardsley's insolence, for example, purifies even his most obscene drawings; they become extravagant and comical, and as everyone knows, laughter is the worst enemy of Eros. Sade, by contrast, is boring and disgusting as long as his inventions fail to touch our personal eroticism; he is never funny. The same can be said of Rops, who also took himself very seriously. This could be said too of many of Huysmans's and Lorrain's writings, if their stylish experiments did not so often raise a smile. But there was a public at the time which was ready to swallow anything – a public described as follows by Laurent Tailhade (*Le Chat noir*, 1884) on the publication of Lorrain's poems *Modernités*.

> Fellatrices, catamites, pimps, ponces, madams, club-owners – all those who traffic in lust are pictured here in all their hideous ugliness. Pale from the kisses of Lesbos, girls of sixteen beg for superhuman embraces, and, to make them fertile, crave the clutches of a monster. Crazed with perverted lust, the damned souls of love hold out their bloated faces to young males stronger than oaks.

Erotic imagery even invaded the realm of the sublime; thus Péladan could write in *A Cœur perdu*: 'My lust for the ideal, turning to the past, violated the tombs in which the miracles slept, and assaulted young ideas which will not blossom until another century has passed.' It was eroticism which made *Art Nouveau* and experiments in poetry known to the public, thanks to magazines with titillating covers. In France there was *Le Rire*, to which Toulouse-Lautrec and Vallotton contributed; in England *Pick-me-up*, illustrated by Beerbohm and some of Beardsley's imitators; and in Germany, *Jugend*, a periodical with considerable artistic pretensions, which gave its name to the German form of *Art Nouveau*. Everyday objects became pretexts for nude studies and drawings of ecstatic faces framed in flowing locks.

This artistic freedom forced the poets of the time to go further than ever in order to astonish their readers. Take, for example, this extract from Rollinat's *Névroses* (1883):

> *Je me livre en pâture aux ventouses des filles,*
> *Mais raffinant alors sa tortuosité,*
> *La fièvre tourne en moi ses plus creusantes vrilles.*
> I abandon myself to the whores' suckers,
> But then, in a tortuous refinement,
> Fever twists its deepest gimlets inside me.

Samain, the best known of these poets, exclaimed:

Je te salue, ô très occulte, ô très profonde
Luxure, étoile triste au ciel pourpre du monde.
Hail to thee, O occult, O profound
Lust, sad star in the world's purple sky.

And Maeterlinck himself gave way, at least on paper, to some strange temptations:

O les glauques tentations
Au milieu des ombres mentales
Avec leurs flammes végétales
Et leurs éjaculations.
O, the sea-green temptations
In the shadows of the mind
With their vegetable flames
And their ejaculations.

Khnopff's 'sphinx-women' looked down impassively on these horrors, though sometimes the master evoked the sinister charms of the goddess who had given way to 'Animality' (2). But it is Rops whom we always find behind these poems and pictures. His clever engravings are the antithesis of Symbolism, for, like Zola, he dwells lovingly on sordid detail and vulgarizes the Baudelairean dreams; and it is hard for us today to understand the vogue he enjoyed among people, who simultaneously made fun of artists such as Bouguereau. He had many imitators, of whom the best were the Munich artist, Otto Greiner, a disciple of Klinger, who specialized in erotico-satanist engravings, and a Viennese, the Marquis von Byros, who was also influenced by Beardsley, and whose work brings together the Venus in Furs and the Merry Widow.

The two attitudes to woman adopted by these artists – idealization, born of the failure to attain her, and prostitution in weird dreams, born of shame at surrendering to her – are both fundamentally misogynistic. The Symbolists experienced the disgust Baudelaire expressed so often for woman as a natural creature, contrasted with the dandy. If we substitute the word *aesthete* for *dandy*, we shall see that, here again, Symbolist eroticism is simply a gloss on a Baudelairean theme: loathing for Nature – in other words Realism – and contempt for those who represent it.

Moreau agreed entirely with this point of view, writing scornfully of 'the nature of woman who looks for unhealthy emotions in life and stupidly fails to understand the horror of situations . . .' One of the reasons for Rops's success is given in this remark by Huysmans, who admired him a little too much: 'He embodies the possession of woman or more precisely her degradation', and again: 'Woman is the great vessel of iniquity and crime; the

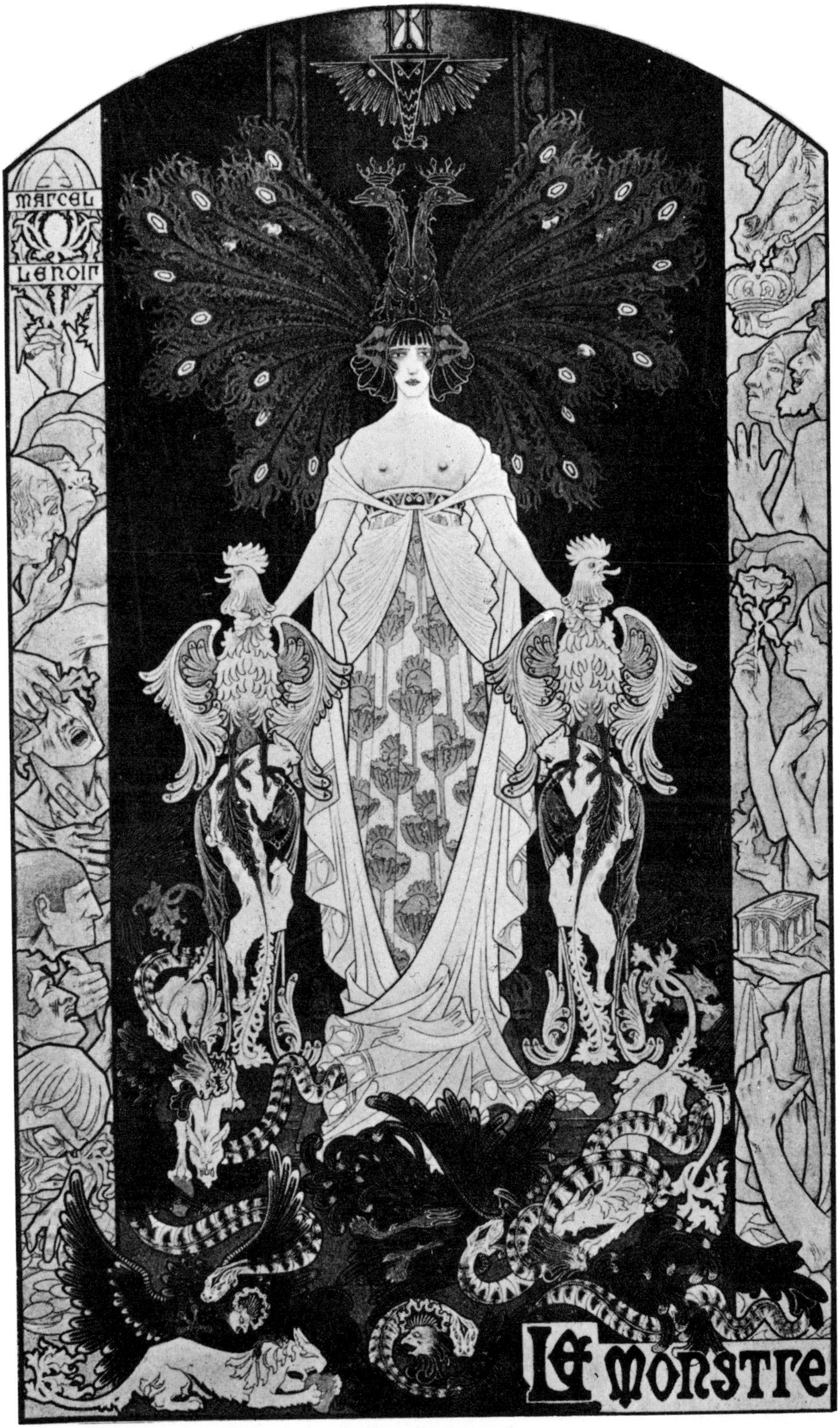

53. Marcel Lenoir: *Le Monstre*. This tinted drawing of a witch could serve as a decoration for a chapel used for Black Masses. Note the Masonic symbols. The figures on the sides recall those in stained-glass windows, and the animals resemble gargoyles.

charnel-house of misery and shame, the mistress of ceremonies who introduces into our souls the ambassadors of all the vices . . .' Rops's influence was immense, and Moreau was correct in thinking that he could discern it in Rodin's work: 'Macabre medievalism, still with elements of Rops sadism and the decaying detritus of modernism, an idiotic mixture of bar-room mysticism and boulevard pornography. The victim of critics he has made to measure, who have led him to believe that he is a profound thinker and a mysterious soul, when he was simply a sensitive, ardent craftsman . . .' Later on, he writes more succinctly: 'A Michelangelo dream flitting across the brain of a Gustave Doré.' But Rodin succeeded where Rops had failed; his work is a sublimation of physical love, and could be compared, according to a woman journalist of that time, to 'those violins in *Tristan* which produce a spasm of complete ecstasy'. The sculptor's *femmes damnées*, like d'Annunzio's heroines, are cases of *mithologia estetico-afrodisiaca* and *lussuria ossidionale*.

Rodin towered above *Art Nouveau*, just as Michelangelo dominated Mannerism. His *Portes de l'Enfer* were an undertaking comparable to Moreau's *Chimères*. He was the first to make *objets d'art* out of bodies twisted in the strange convulsions of pleasure: Carabin, who did the same thing, was more often than not ridiculous.

PSYCHOPATHIA SEXUALIS. We have already seen the types of beauty which Rossetti and Moreau had imposed on a Decadent Europe: the Mona Lisa, the ambiguous Botticellis, and a few 'visions of antiquity'. If we now consider these beauties in the context of the fantasies for which they were dreamt, we shall find ourselves faced with several examples from Krafft-Ebing's famous manual, which was published about the same time. Without going into pathological details, we shall have to distinguish between the dominating beauties and the dominated, between the beauties from Lesbos and those from Sodom.

Swinburne provides us with the most eloquent images of pitiless womanhood. His women are, of course, empresses whose slave the masochist poet would like to be: he lends them the features of the imposing horsewoman Adah Menken, at whose feet he did homage in the late 1860s. Here we must refer the reader to the chapter in Professor Mario Praz's book *The Romantic Agony*, entitled *La Belle Dame sans Merci*, after the poem by Keats:

> I saw pale kings, and princes too,
> Pale warriors, death-pale were they all;
> Who cry'd '*La belle Dame sans Merci*
> Hath thee in thrall'.

54. *Opposite:* Stuck: *Eve*. The famous Munich painter, who inhabits the same world as Stefan George and is a follower of Böcklin, sometimes reminds us of Khnopff, but his women are more voluptuous than those of the Belgian artist. They are very often shown with exotic animals.

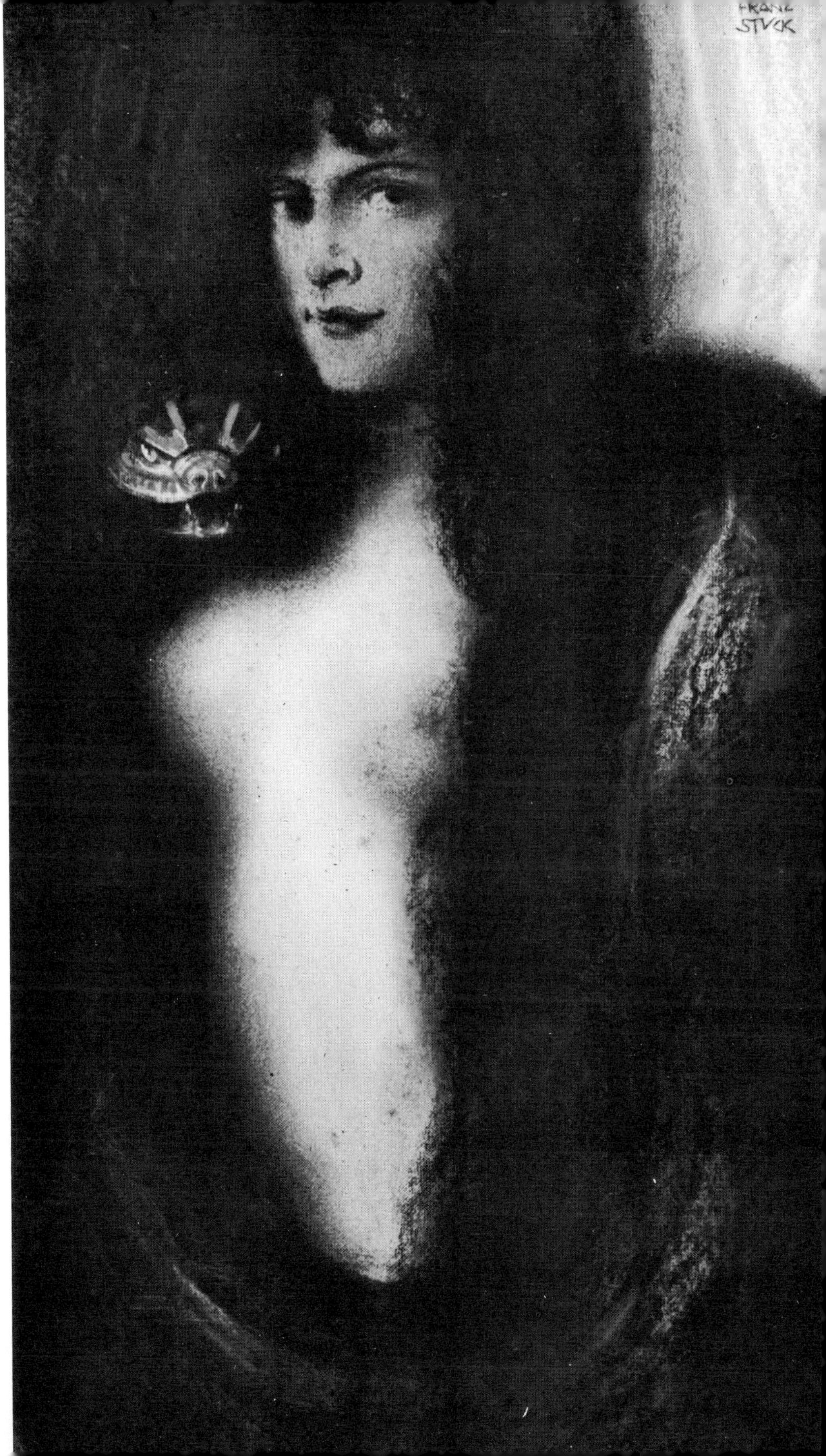
STVCK

The Keats heroine who holds a knight captive in her long tresses (see the Waterhouse picture) illustrates the principal object of *fin de siècle* fetishism: hair (18). From Baudelaire's poem *La Chevelure* to Rodenbach's novel about the widower who strangles his wife's double with a lock of the dead woman's hair, and from the golden head of Holman Hunt's Lady of Shalott to the liquid locks of Millais's Ophelia, loosened tresses repeatedly appear in literature and art. Perhaps, in a period of hats and chignons, all this cascading beauty signified a promise of unreserved intimacy. Loosened hair is also a symbol of woman reverting to a state of Nature, an animal's mane.

Swinburne found in Sade a justification of his tendencies, and pictures of his heroines in the works of his painter friends. Rossetti and Burne-Jones both painted imaginary portraits of Fair Rosamund, to whom Swinburne devoted one of his first poems, at the same time conjuring up a whole gallery of *femmes fatales*: Helen, Cressida, Guinevere. But painters can never go as far as writers, and Elizabeth Siddal's most sorrowful expressions only vaguely evoke the torments described in *Dolores*:

> O Daughter of Death and Priapus,
> Our Lady of Pain.

Swinburne outdoes Baudelaire in his treatment of the poet's subjects, and the Symbolists too play delicate variations on the theme of sensual suffering. '*L'Offrande Obscure*' in Maeterlinck's *Serres chaudes* is one of many examples of these variations. And in *Le Fouet*, with its references to the lengthy torments and slow refinements of the whip, Samain is nothing if not explicit.

It should be remembered that Sacher-Masoch had just written his *Venus in Furs*, in which we find once again the whip Beardsley depicts so lovingly, its cruel, supple thong seeming to pursue the lock of hair which will soon fall upon the ecstatic victim. Beardsley's black arabesque is the *Art Nouveau* line; it will reappear a little later in the work of Klimt, a devoted admirer of both the Englishman and Moreau. These three artists, incidentally, have a common heroine: terrified worshippers of Salome, they depict her so often that the little Jewish princess, who is also the heroine of Laforgue, Wilde, and Milosz, may be regarded as the goddess of the Decadence (42). To quote only a few lines from the well-known passage in *A Rebours*, she is 'the symbolic incarnation of undying Lust, the goddess of immortal Hysteria, the accursed Beauty exalted above all other beauties by the catalepsy that hardens her flesh and steels her muscles . . .'

All these themes and fetishes are epitomized and pastiched in Wilde's Salome, a figure as dazzling as the bronze veils trailed by

Moreau's princess or the scarves waved by Klimt's dancer to the sound of Strauss's music. Salome dances again in one of Picasso's first engravings, and the Lolita of our times keeps alive this *fin de siècle* myth of the capricious *petite fille fatale*. Similarly the Marlene Dietrich of *The Blue Angel* (1930) is the last *belle dame sans merci*. In the same period, Erich von Stroheim's sadly mutilated film *Queen Kelly* continues the dreams of Swinburne and Sacher-Masoch in a terrifying atmosphere.

The sophisticated, bejewelled Salome, the daughter of fire, is contrasted, in the mythology of the Decadence, by the innocent Ophelia, surrounded by flowers, the daughter of water. The former is the executioner, the latter the victim, and the victim has almost as many admirers as the executioner (32). She had had more of them during the first Romantic period: Delacroix, for example, who dreamed of treating women 'like the flower beneath the foot'. Then the popular serials of the nineteenth century made a great deal of the spectacle of downtrodden innocence: witness that working-class Ophelia, Eugène Sue's Fleur de Marie. And the 'flower beneath the foot' seems to have been depicted by more

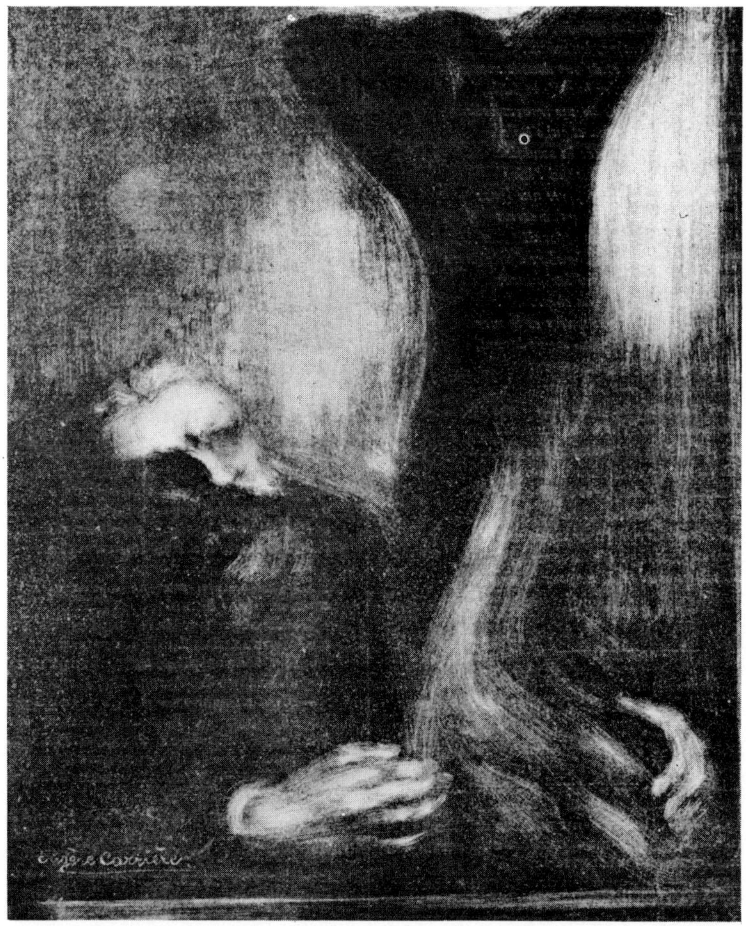

55. Eugène Carrière: Lithograph for the Rodin Exhibition. Rodin was one of the creators of the ecto-plasmic woman, the venerable prophet of the new eroticism. Painting motherly creatures through a mist, Carrière succeeded in making them poetic.

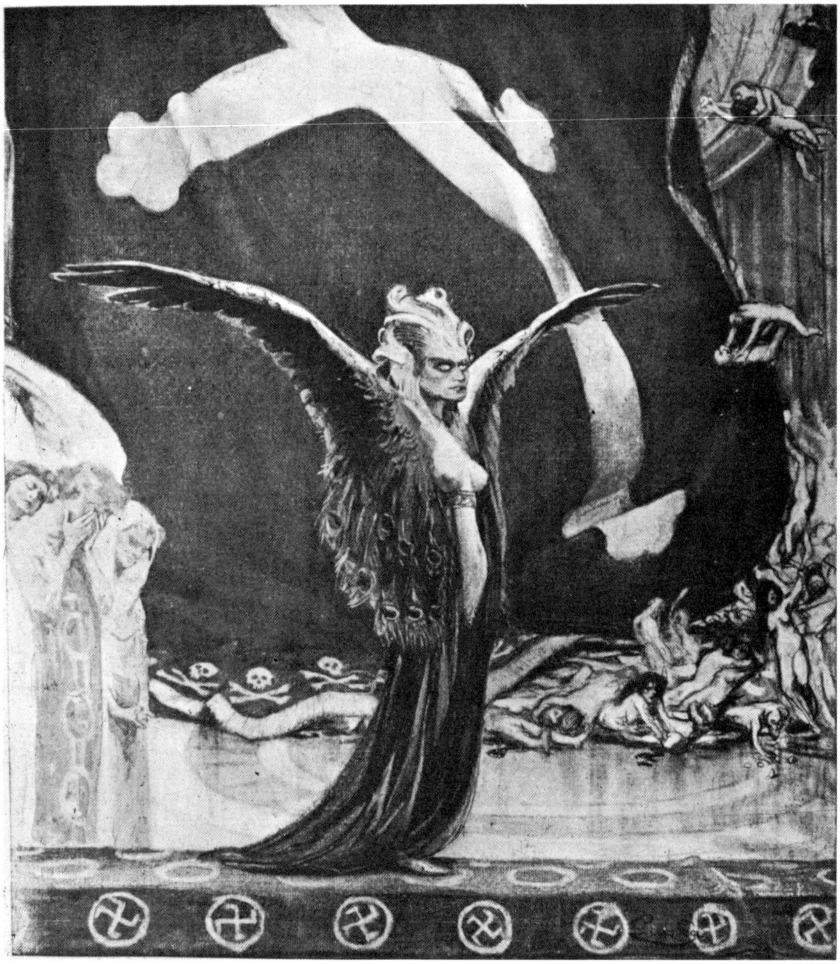

56. Kupka: *The Conqueror Worm*. A d'Annunzio-like vision on an Edgar Allan Poe theme.

painters than the *belle dame sans merci*. This is because she is a 'soul'. Margaret MacDonald's greenish nymphs and Maeterlinck's little heroines were Ophelias who could be found again, well and truly dead, in Toorop's famous picture *Les Trois Fiancées*. As for the seven princesses in one of Klimt's first pictures, one can sense them slipping towards the water surrounding their keep. And there was Mélisande too, that ravishing creature doomed to tears and ponds.

In Moreau's pictures it is not flowers but boys that Helen tramples underfoot beneath the walls of Troy and that Minerva strikes down with her anger. As Wilde observed, 'each of us kills the thing he loves'.

On a higher plane than these fatal or martyred women, but much less interesting, there is Venus. True, she appears in *La Tentation de Saint Antoine* and in *Tannhäuser* but simply as a cliché, like Böcklin's bluish Venus. Pierre Louÿs's *Aphrodite* aroused a feeling of genuine horror in Rémy de Gourmont, who wrote in 1896: 'All these women, all this flesh, all these screams, all this futile, cruel animal lust! The females nibble cerebella and eat brains; the mind escapes in ejaculation; the women's souls ooze out as if through an open sore; and all these couplings engender nothing but disgust, annihilation and death.'

The Venus of the *fin de siècle* is Villiers de l'Isle-Adam's synthetic *Ève Future*. This book, which reads like a Jules Vernes novel with an infusion of poetry, is in fact an erotic Nautilus (56). There are few Venuses in the works of the Pre-Raphaelites, and though mention must be made of the madly sophisticated Venus in Beardsley's *Under the Hill*, there are no Venuses at all in the paintings of Moreau, Toorop, and Klimt. Her good health must have struck the Decadents as vulgar, and the homage she was paid as very common; she was taken over by the Second Empire and brought into disrepute by Bouguereau, and when Renoir needed a Venus, he got his cook to pose for him.

On the other hand, as we have already seen in the preceding chapter on Occultism, there was a powerful current of necrophilia running through the *fin de siècle* in the best Romantic tradition. There are countless dead women in the Symbolists' works (10), and in his tragic story of Princess Phénissa (1893) Rémy de Gourmont goes as far as vampirism: 'Abandon the barely deflowered female lamb to the ingenuous embrace of a young wolf, and let him die devouring her. But do not expect her, enriched by your life, to lie down on your tomb and open up the rich gates of her sex to the funereal joker . . .'

SODOM AND GOMORRHA. Mirbeau could not bear what he called the 'soul-painters', and he regarded them as incapable of normal love-making. Here is a Decadent speaking in one of his articles:

> We, the sexless ones, in other words the superior beings, the intellectuals, beget by way of the brain. That is the ritual nowadays. It is from our brains that the seed of life spurts to fecundate the stars, those miraculous ovaries of the infinite . . . As for women, on the shores of poisonous lakes, on noxious beaches, among deadly flowers, they will couple among themselves, in acts of imperfect, painful, and demoniacal possession.

This parody is of interest in that it stresses the alienation of the sexes in those circles where contempt for the flesh was preached. True, the Decadents often refused to pay homage to Cythera only to render it to Lesbos. Gustave Moreau painted an admirable Sappho, while Rodin and Klimt drew some beautiful lesbians. Baudelaire and Verlaine both wrote of the tendency made famous by Gautier's Mademoiselle de Maupin (43), and Lorrain exalted lesbian love in countless poems. But Europe had to wait until the beginning of the twentieth century to see the high priestess of

Sappho, Renée Vivien. This beautiful Englishwoman, whose real name was Pauline Tarn and who wrote French poetry admired by Maurras, lived like one of Jean Lorrain's heroines, or rather like Balzac's *fille aux yeux d'or*: shut up by a rich baroness in a setting of Oriental luxury, in the midst of Buddhas, lacquered tables, soft cushions, and Chinese servants who, it is said, poisoned the young woman when her lover grew tired of her, Renée Vivien made no secret of her tastes: 'She sang of the ephemeral forms of love, of pallor and ecstasy and the loosening of hair . . . of the immortal pride which scorns pain and smiles in death, and of the charm of feminine kisses' (*La Genèse profane*, 1902).

Let us imagine the amours of these ladies in the setting described by Rachilde:

> The countess's room was lit by a magnesium lamp which spread jewelled varnish over everything it touched. The walls were hung with apple-green plush, framed in whorls of iridescent mother-of-pearl; from the ceiling, painted in enamel to imitate a cathedral rose-window, the bright light fell like a meteorite. The bed was very low, lacquered in iridescent mother-of-pearl, and curtained only by a canopy of gauze studded with Bohemian garnets; the counterpane consisted of three hundred blue points . . .

Let us also imagine, contorted on this bed, Rodin's models, rump in air, in embraces which, like the chimeras, were never satisfied. This connection cannot have occurred to Moreau, who, as we have seen, judged Rodin harshly. Redon, for that matter, was not indulgent towards Rodin either. Jacques-Émile Blanche used to relate how Rodin completely lost his head when he saw Nijinsky, and that the old Pan suggested some curious afternoon pastimes to the young faun in his studio. But that, of course, was simply a demonstration of his universal love of Beauty. If Rodin was excited by lesbians, men had inspired him to create works which were more academic than *Art Nouveau* in character.

It was to the academic painters that admirers of what was then called the third sex had to turn for studies of the ephebes whom the poets of the day depicted much more openly than the painters. Whole anthologies were devoted to the subject of Greek love, for the poets preferred to speak of 'ancient idylls' rather than of Sodom. But in fact it was Sodom, often called Byzantium, that the Decadents looked for in the shadiest quarters of London and Paris, as their review *Le Décadent* clearly indicated in the prologue to a poem by 'Mitrophane Crapoussin':

> In the green light of the Esoteric Temple, here, conjured up by some magician, are the young princes of frenzied Desire –

> Batthyllos, Antinous, and you, the Infant Bagoas, and you, cruel Alexis, created by the Mantuan. You Pallides, modern Ephestions whose flesh, bitten by our lips in the sacrilegious glow of the lamps, exhales beneficent decay. You timid Narcissi of the gaping Sodoms, athletes leaping like rhythms into the blue sky, and you frail hermaphrodites, the solamel of the crossroads.

Moréas wrote of 'the ambiguous mouths of smooth-faced good-for-nothings', and Verlaine justified his tastes by recalling how Shakespeare, abandoning Ophelia, Cordelia, and Desdemona, had praised in splendid verse 'the masculine form' (*Hombres*).

While Gautier and Baudelaire had often sung the praises of Lesbos, it was not considered good form, under the Second Empire, to stray too far in the direction of Sodom. In 1863 young Catulle Mendès had written these lines and earned himself an evil reputation which lasted all his life:

> *Toi seul, posthume enfant des époques sereines,*
> *Tu portes fièrement la honte d'être beau.*
> You alone, posthumous child of serene times
> Bear with pride the stigma of your beauty.

In *Hombres* Verlaine was much more explicit, but these poems were circulated only in private. Lorrain's short stories, the obscene novel *Télény* which is partly by Wilde, and *The Picture of Dorian Gray* are all tales of Sodom, just as Housman's poems are the countryside and Stefan George's works the basilica of that imaginary capital.

Those writers who did not dare speak openly of their unconventional amours attributed them to mad queens (39): Jarry's Messalina, Wilde's Jezebel (unfortunately mislaid in a cab), and above all Theodora, whose circus liaisons fascinated the generations which had seen performances of Sardou's play. All the jewels which Moreau's admirers were inhibited from wearing – Lorrain alone had the courage to wear bracelets on his arms and rings on every finger – were bestowed upon their heroines. The so-called 'mauve Nineties' were resolutely homosexual in character, and it was only the Wilde case which put a stop to their excesses. Even Bismarck's Germany, undermined by a wave of scandals at the Kaiser's court, took unashamed pleasure in Fidus's sentimental pictures.

The penchant for young boys became one of the accepted forms of non-conformity, and those who did not share the taste for them stopped half-way and praised or painted the hermaphrodites so dear to Péladan's heart (21). And there is an interesting comparison to be drawn between Beardsley's drawings and some of Rachilde's descriptions in *La Marquise de Sade*.

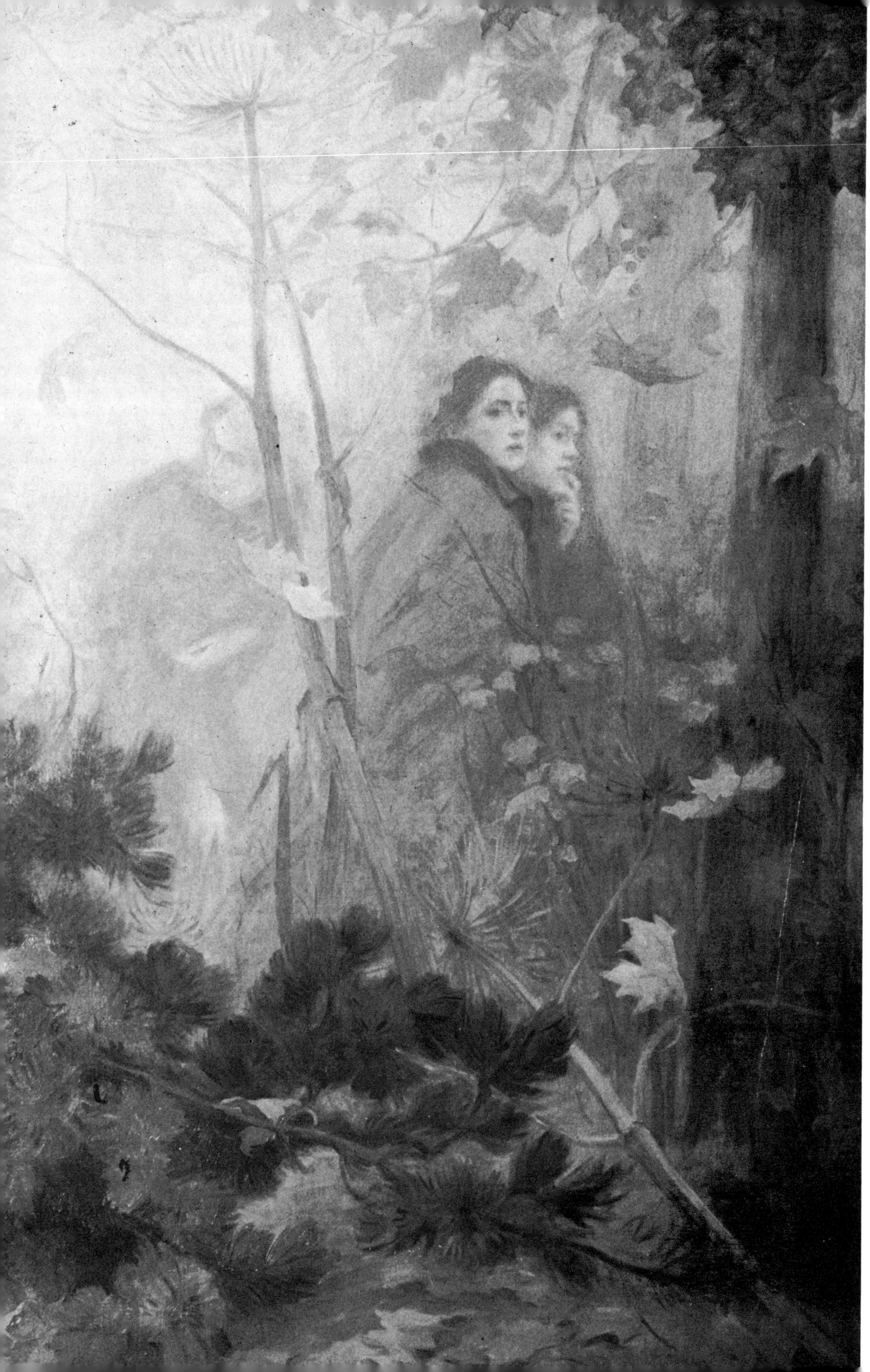

7 Nostalgia

FÊTES GALANTES. The disgust for the nineteenth century which drove Moreau towards antiquity, Redon towards the Beyond, and the Pre-Raphaelites towards a more or less erotic medievalism, led other imaginations, less well equipped for the high adventures of the mind, towards less remote refuges of silence and oblivion. Shuttered summerhouses, neglected parks, marble steps overrun with weeds, inspired dreamers almost as much as Benares and Byzantium. In the earlier part of the century Théophile Gautier, in the manor-house where Mademoiselle de Maupin donned her disguise, and Victor Hugo, in the folly where Cosette was brought up, had offered their readers welcome relief from scabrous stories and social dramas. Then Théodore de Banville and Verlaine peopled these gardens with figures who were perhaps a little quaint, but who were ready to satisfy all the whims of a sensibility revolted by Zola's novels. Among the Decadents, the most charming of the nostalgic poets was undoubtedly Stuart Merrill:

A l'ombre du bleu perron,
Dans les lis et les lauroses,
Les amours dodus dansent en rond
Comme en un crépuscule de roses.
(*Fastes*, 1891)

In the shadow of the blue steps,
Among the lilies and the oleanders,
Plump Cupids dance in a ring
As in a twilight of roses.

Verlaine's nostalgia spread like a mist to conceal a hideous world, allowing glimpses only of thickets, statues and above all paths strewn with dead leaves. His dead leaves, whose shape and colour were transferred by a sort of osmosis to so many pictures of the period, symbolized a beauty which was all the more touching in that it belonged to the past. 'Sadness remains when happiness has gone.' Camille Martin etched this dictum, between some red leaves, in the leather of a blotting-pad which can be seen in the

57. Victor Prouvé: *L'Automne*. Looking at the foreground of dead Queen Anne's Lace it is obvious that Prouvé was a friend of the jeweller and designer Gallé.

museum of the École de Nancy, next to Prouvé's paintings and Gallé's vases. In that autumnal atmosphere, summer was bound to seem vulgar and spring ingenuous. The Decadents' favourite season was the season of faded glory, with the result that towards the end of the century Versailles became to some degree the Venice or Bruges of France. Robert de Montesquiou wrote *Les Perles Rouges* there, and Henri de Régnier *La Cité des Eaux*. Versailles's perspectives appealed to dreamers of an aristocratic bent and a melancholy temperament, who were fond of quoting Samain: '*Mon âme est une infante en robe de parade*: My soul is an infanta in court regalia.' Some people, tired of the fearful and the sublime, and forgetting Poe and Wagner, caressed the marble statues with Mallarméan fans. The Second Empire and the Victorians had already looked back nostalgically towards the eighteenth century, but an eighteenth century of beauty spots and masked courtiers. Romako in Austria and Menzel in Germany had produced elegant pictures of a rococo society, but Monticelli had painted courtly entertainments in autumnal colours which were already melancholy, and the Symbolists for their part found anything but moonlight scenes unbearable. Their parks – like the deserted gardens often found in d'Annunzio's early poems – can seem just as sinister as those described by Poe, and one has the impression that the dazzling roses, fed on decay, are liable to decompose at any moment.

Painters of gay park scenes such as Albert Besnard are out of place here: Besnard's *L'Île Heureuse* is an *Embarquement pour Cythère* in the *Modern Style* manner. The painter's skill, his technique borrowed from the Impressionists, and above all his subjects, all far too serious for his palette, have created the impression that he was a master – and it is true that his influence on Klimt was considerable – but he was no poet. Aman-Jean, on the other hand, by introducing Pre-Raphaelite girls into provincial gardens, comes very close to the spirit of Verlaine's poetry. His world is the world of Duparc's melodies; his Symbolism is only faintly tinged with pessimism, and only his colours – blue hydrangeas and dead roses – show that 'his soul is a little grey'. Aman-Jean, whose portrait was painted by his friend Seurat, was a charming man. Next to his paintings one could hang the landscapes of Le Sidaner, who wraps the Trianon in the mists of Bruges. His world of purple shadows, and of summer-houses reflected in the water among dead leaves, is half-way between Symbolism and Impressionism, and appealed to Proust so much that he endowed Elstir with some of Le Sidaner's characteristics. As Camille Mauclair said of him, 'he applied the technical subtlety of the Impressionists to the expression of psychic, immaterial feelings that were almost musical

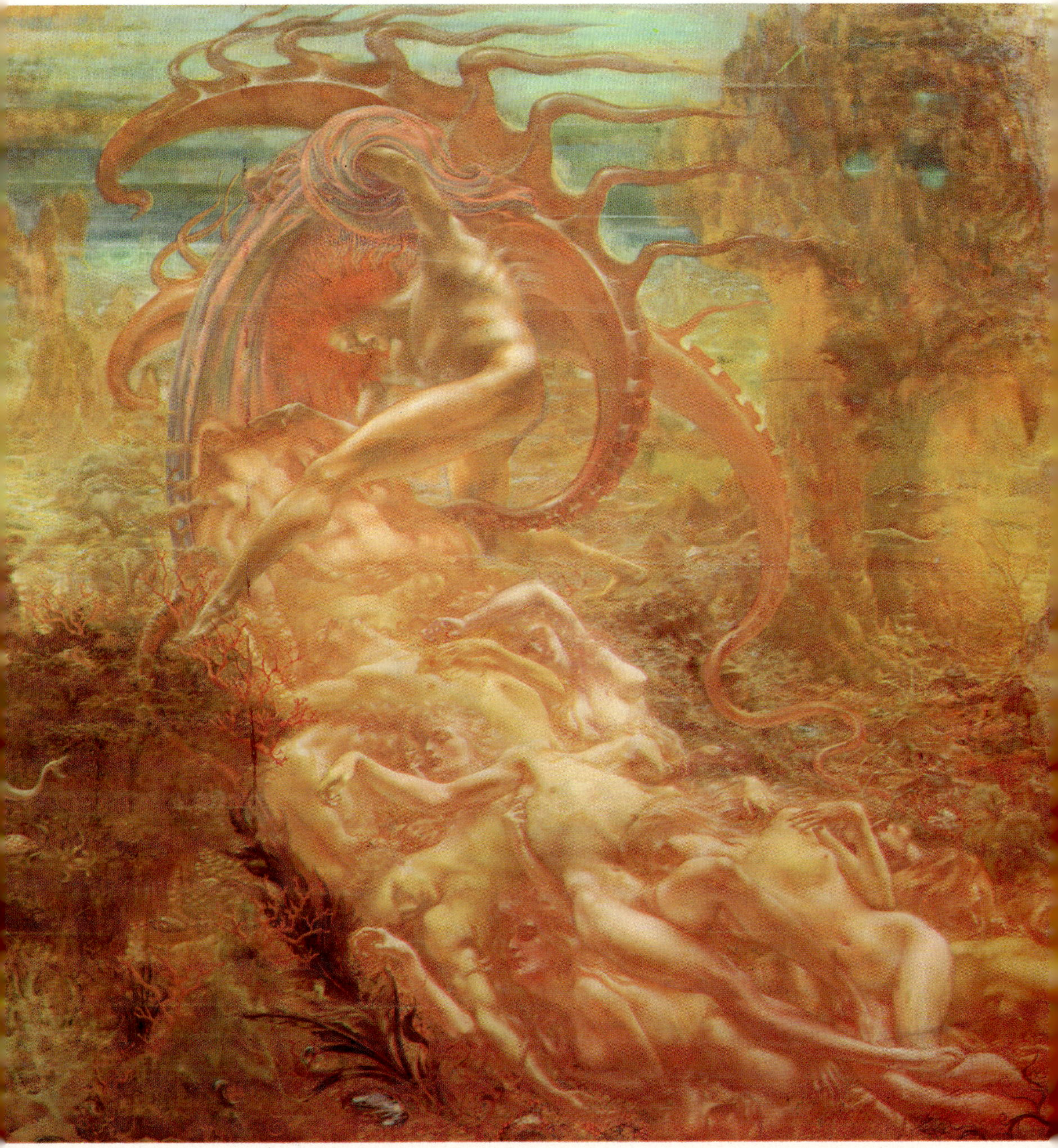

58. Jean Delville: *Trésor de Satan*. This immense canvas, which gives the impression of a conflagration in the depths of the ocean, with the figure of Satan in the centre, is the most important work of this mystic painter, who eventually became a theosophist.

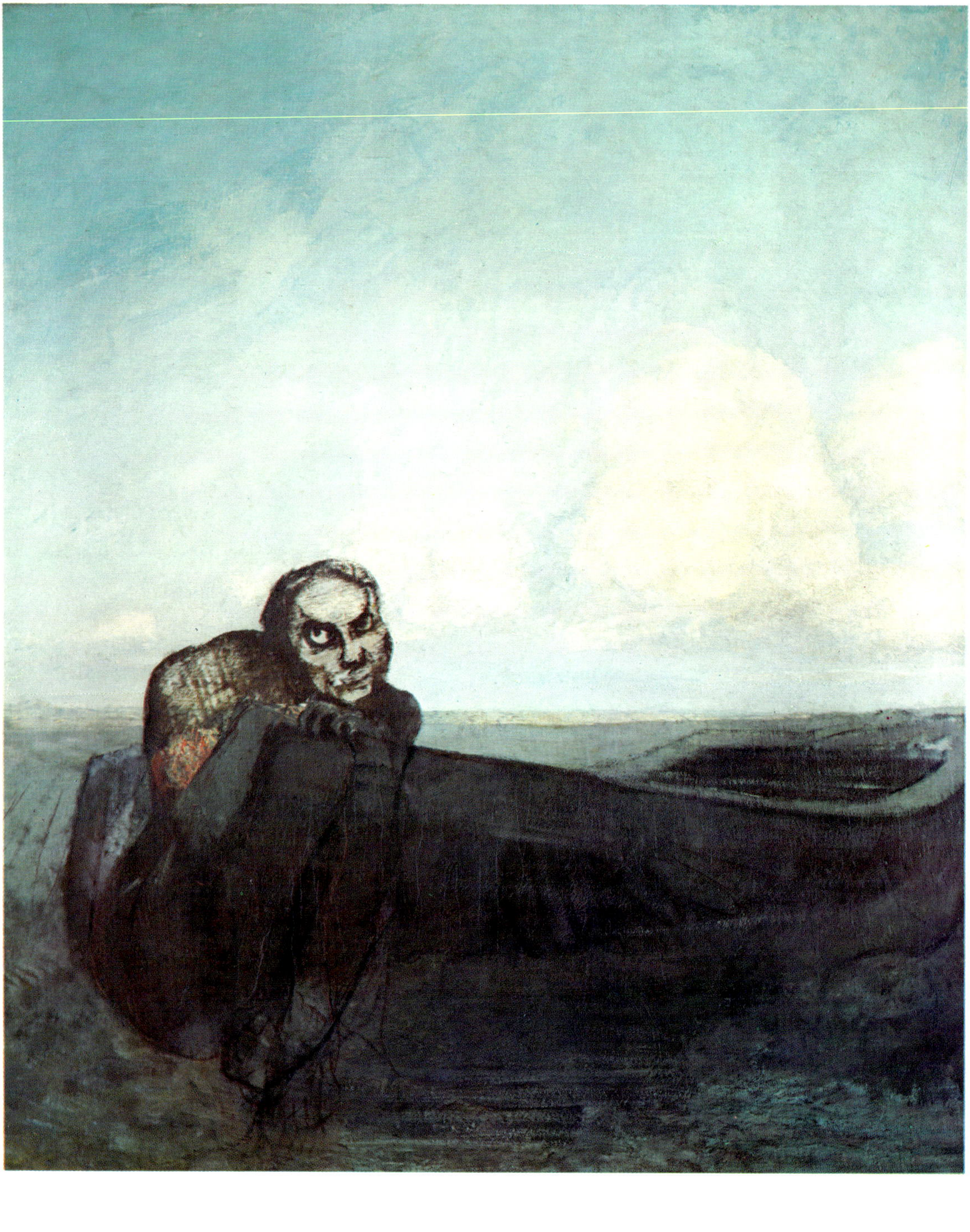

59. Odilon Redon: *L'Ange du Destin*. This malefic vision under a perfect sky is an exact expression of the contrasts to be found in the Symbolist imagination. The motif of the boat is probably borrowed from the funeral myths of ancient Egypt.

in their spirituality . . .' A tribute which could be paid even more to Maurice Denis, who brought the Florentine twilight to the gardens of surburban Paris.

There is something more sinister about the park in Khnopff's picture, *Memories*, showing some girls who have just been playing tennis. They are not ghosts, but the atmosphere is as oppressive as that evoked by Henry James in *The Turn of the Screw*. Here we are not far from the misty landscapes of *Le Grand Meaulnes*.

The art of the Symbolist landscape-painters is fundamentally an evocative, suggestive art, whether they use a Pointillist technique, like Le Sidaner and Van Rysselberghe, or, as is more often the case, employ flat tints. There are no picturesque details, indeed no details at all, in Henri Breton's long pictures of Breton ports in the twilight or autumn ploughing. His work has something about it reminiscent of Chinese painting, and recalls wallpaper friezes or porcelain from Copenhagen. The same could be said of the blue forest in which Osbert depicts his muses, and of Schuffenecker's green cliffs. Theirs is a Nature peopled with shadows, from which the sun is absent, as far removed as possible from Impressionism. One of Toorop's pupils, the Belgian Degouve de Nuncques (1867–1935) can sometimes be regarded as a link between Van Gogh and these painters of dream landscapes, but that is the effect of inadequate technique more than anything else; we are rather surprised nowadays by the admiration he aroused at the *Libre Esthétique* and *Vie et Lumière* exhibitions held in the nineties – an admiration exemplified by this quotation from A. de Ridder: 'His art consists of giving life to the scenes he discovers in Nature, whether they be humble or magical in appearance, by means of the supernatural quality contributed by his intelligence, his sensibility, his cultured refinement.'

The rather medieval nostalgia of the English was a nostalgia for the cloisters of Oxford. Thus Wilde advised Lord Alfred Douglas to go and cool his hands in 'the grey twilight of Gothic things'. However, Kate Greenaway chose instead to depict Regency cottages, with little girls in long dresses playing around them. She had a very great influence on aesthetic fashions from 1880 onwards, and then on illustrators such as Grasset. Her little innocents, playing battledore and shuttlecock among the holly-hocks, excited the ageing Ruskin, and he praised Kate's albums to the skies. Then there was Charles Conder, a great friend of Wilde and Lautrec, a giant of a man who painted fans and decorative panels in the colours of faded petals; his ladies in crinolines trying to catch the Blue Bird, and his masked revellers playing hide-and-seek among the colonnades, may be chocolate-box subjects, but are seen as in a dream. Conder lived a Bohemian life in Montmartre, and illustrated *La Fille aux Yeux d'Or* and André Lebey's *Automnales* in the *Centaure* of 1896. But the greatest Symbolist landscape-painter, an artist steeped in Swedenborgian mysticism, was already dead; he was Caspar David Friedrich, who lived in Hamburg at the beginning of the nineteenth century. His ruins, overgrown with huge dead trees, would provide the perfect setting for a production of *Axël*, Villiers de l'Isle-Adam's Wagnerian drama.

The Germans, too, found their way back to the parks; as for the forests, they had remained faithful to them, ever since Altdorfer. They greatly admired Hans Thoma (1859–1924), one of those Teutonic painters whose charms tend to be hidden by their vulgarity; but the charms are clearly visible in certain landscapes of the Taunus, bathed in a mysterious light, with the castle of Mont Salvat in the background. Wagner admired his *Wandervogel* so much that he hung it in the drawing-room of the Wahnfried. A more unusual artist was Carl Strahtmann (1866–1939), with his pictures of forest interiors like dark mosaics. Looking through copies of the review *Pan*, one can find countless views of stately homes depicted in the manner of Le Sidaner, with statues, belfries and swans. Klimt himself succumbed more than once to the nostalgia which inspired Hugo von Hofmannsthal's *Der Wind wäht durch kahle Alleen* (the wind blows through empty avenues) and Rilke's poems about gardens.

In Italy Pelizza da Valpedo (1868–1907) painted Roman villas in the twilight before studying the sun in his Divisionist pictures.

In the United States ladies of good family wrote poems about English gardens, the best example being Amy Lowell's *Waiting*,

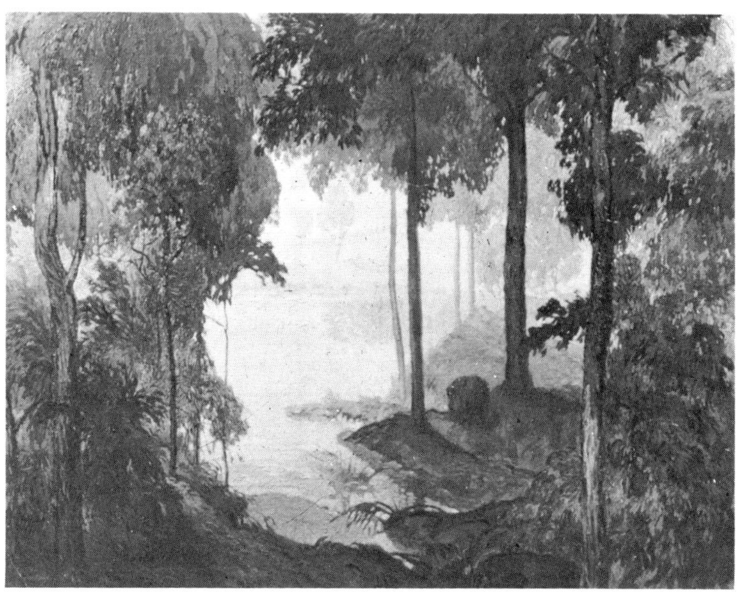

60. Georges de Feure: *Sous-Bois*. With its tones of blue-green, this oil painting could almost be used as the backdrop to a piece by Debussy.

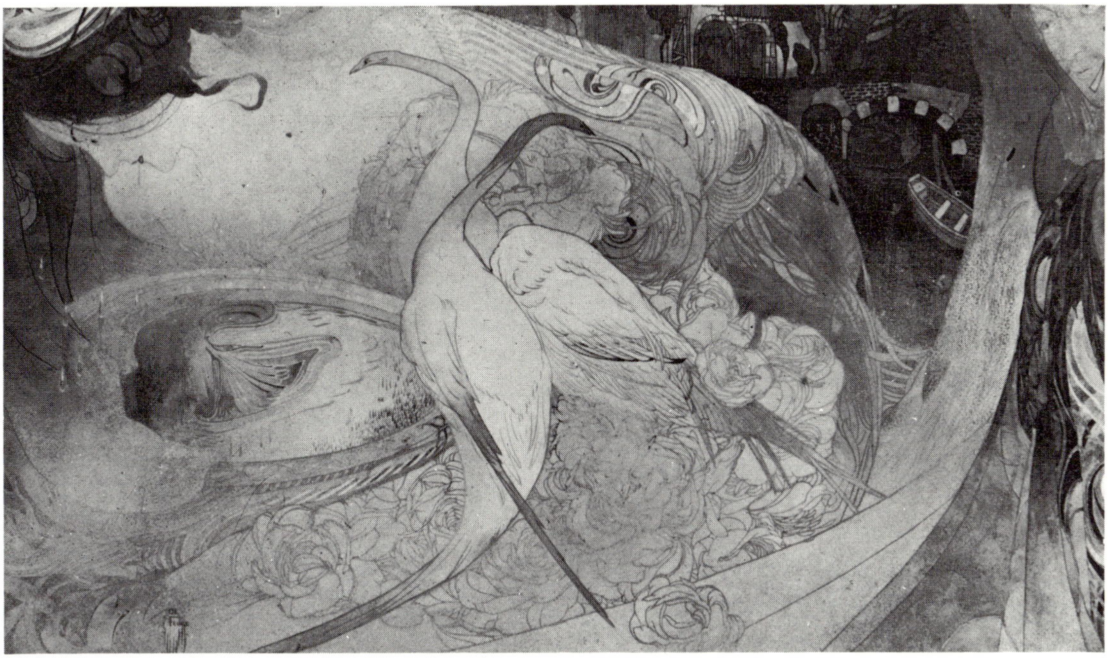

61. De Feure: *Lac des Cygnes*. In this watercolour de Feure excels in the depiction of materials. He was almost the only Symbolist to be influenced by the Japanese. The disproportion between the faces and the birds and the confusion between the flowers on the dresses and those in the park create a dream-like impression.

in which the lady of the manor learns in the midst of her flowers of her husband's death in action. When Maxfield Parish was quite young he illustrated Marion Warner Wildman's *Hill Prayer*, which contains these charming lines:

> I love thee with a Beauty-broken heart
> And worship thee, be whatever thou art.

Abbott Thayer depicted girls in white tunics in walled gardens. Tiffany painted strange, detailed watercolours of the flowers in his garden, in preparation for his stained-glass windows, while John LaFarge did a watercolour painting of a sort of garden fairy, *The Spirit of the Water-Lily*, for Isabella Stewart Gardner.

The Russians too, thanks to Sergei Diaghilev, rediscovered the palaces built by some of their whimsical empresses. The review *Mir Iskusstva*, inspired by Beardsley's drawings and Symbolist poetry, stimulated artists such as Sommov, who would have been the ideal illustrator of Verlaine's *Fêtes galantes*, and Alexander Benois, who recreated so many baroque extravaganzas for Diaghilev's ballets. If Diaghilev launched a neo-Romantic movement in St. Petersburg, Moscow returned to its barbaric splendours under Vroubel's influence. His *Swan Princess* was a tremendous success, and he had a considerable influence on the young Kandinsky, who painted at least one moonlight study in purple and green which could not be more Verlainesque.

MUSIC. If the Russians underwent to some extent the influence of Symbolism, they in their turn influenced the Symbolists greatly

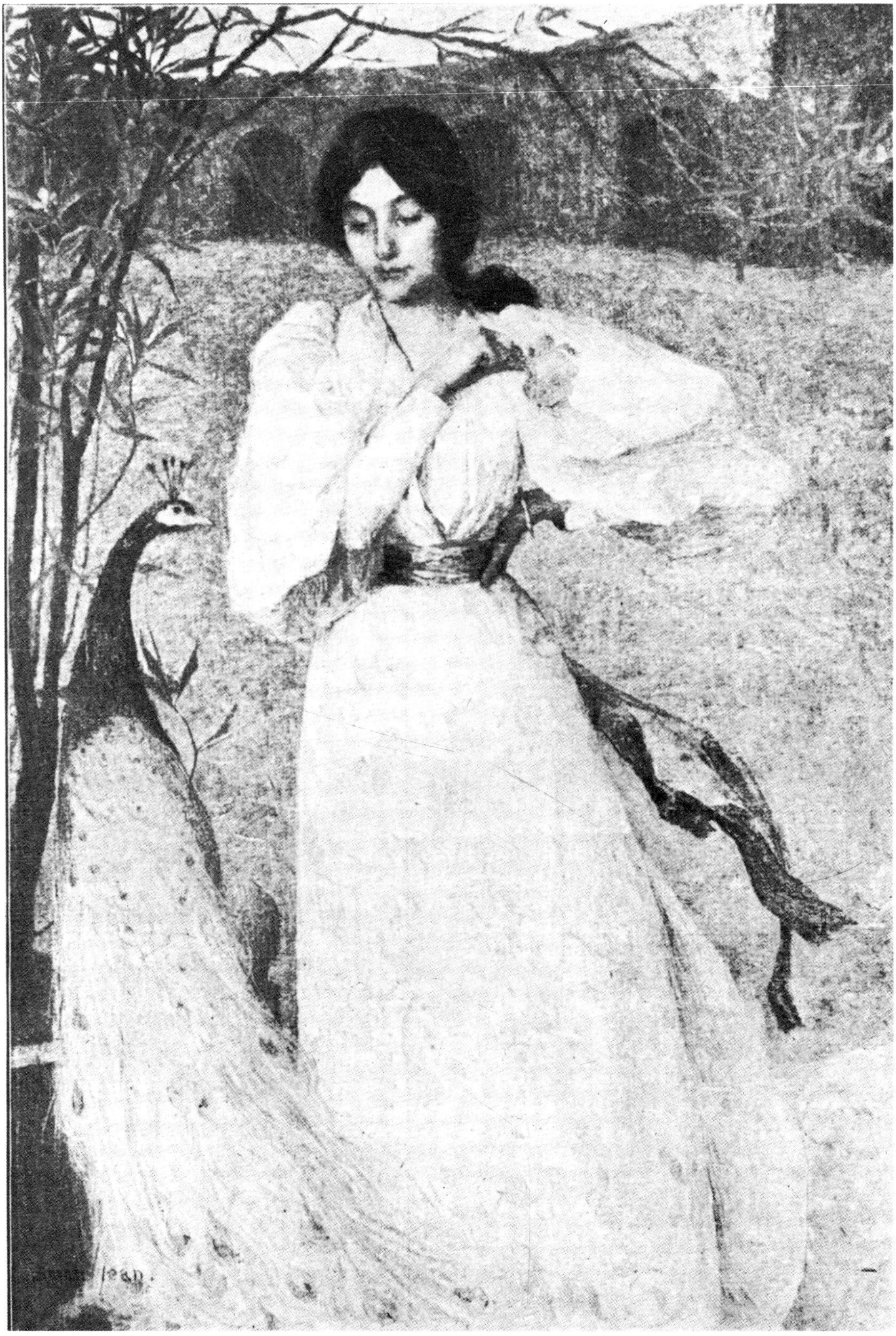

62. E. Aman-Jean: *La jeune Fille au Paon*. This could be the portrait of a heroine of Francis Jammes, or one of the Vergini delle Rocce of d'Annunzio.

through their music. Debussy in particular, who developed all the themes of the *fin de siècle* to a degree which painting could never equal, owed them an enormous debt. Thanks to his *Pelléas* certain images dear to a despised period have succeeded in retaining their poetic force in spite of changes in fashion: the rain-drenched gardens with a view through the trees to the sea, a dark sea gleaming with the lights of fishing-boats, hands full of roses, hair blowing in the wind, an old magician, an innocent child.

It is scarcely surprising that the masterpiece of a period devoted to dreams should have been a musical play, and music occupied indeed a large place in the intellectual life of the Decadence. There were countless pictures which were based on a musical inspiration. A picture by an Italian painter called Balestrieri which was often reproduced at the time shows long-haired poets and their mistresses in a smoke-filled studio in Montparnasse, listening to a pianist with their heads in their hands. The picture is called *Beethoven*, but should be entitled *Russian Music*, as is one of Ensor's canvases. There are many other figures in our Decadent gallery with their heads in their hands: witness Khnopff's *Listening to Schumann*, and an early picture with the same title by Klimt, who at the *Sezession* exhibition in Vienna in 1902 was to display his famous decorations around Klinger's polychrome statue of *Beethoven*. This period of great failures saw Beethoven as one of its gods: thus Henry de Groux devoted a great many grandiloquent pictures to the composer of the Ninth Symphony. It was the time of *The Kreutzer Sonata*, when Romain Rolland was preparing his biography of the musician. Lévy-Dhurmer gave his finest pastels the names of Beethoven's works, while, earlier on, Klinger's strangest engravings had been inspired by the *Brahms Phantasie*, op. XII. One of Maurice Denis's most charming portraits shows a girl at the piano playing the minuet from *La Princesse Maleine*.

An insipid disciple of Puvis de Chavannes, Henri Martin, painted ladies in nightdresses floating between poplars with lutes in their hands. The strains of lutes, lyres, and theorbos can also constantly be heard in Moreau's world, but Moreau's work evokes opera more than chamber music, notably Wagner, Fervaal's *Vincent d'Indy* and Verdi's *Otello*. Painters such as Makart or Rochegrosse, for their part, recall Mascagni or Puccini, for they were in tune with the pompous, heavy rhythm of conventional society, whose temple was the Opera. The Symbolists, who knew Wagner almost only through concerts, regarded that temple as The Temple of the Golden Calf; but for thirty years the Colonne and Pasdeloup concerts, in which classical and modern music were played, were among the liveliest poetic centres in Paris. Indeed, when Ernest Laurent, a friend of Seurat and the Symbolists, was preparing his vast painting *Au Concert Colonne*, he made an admirable series of pencil studies in which we can recognize the faces of the young artists and writers whose works we are studying now.

Redon emphasized this influence of music on young painters who understood it better than his contemporaries, when he wrote: 'The young people of today, moved more deeply than before by the supreme waves of music, necessarily open themselves up too to the spiritual fictions and dreams of plastic art.'

One could go on for ever comparing painters and musicians of the *fin de siècle*. Thus Böcklin is very close to Strauss in his Zarathustrian landscapes, but the Pandean pipes which he put in the hands of his Virgilian shepherds attracted hosts of Germans to Capri. Even Kandinsky passed through a Symbolist period: his *Blauer Ritter* is the last incarnation of Tristan, and in his book on the spiritual in art, he refers repeatedly to music, citing not only Wagner, but also Moussorgsky and Debussy. Similarly, Schoenberg's *Pierrot Lunaire* remains a Decadent oddity, out of place in modern music.

PIERROT. There are serenades, peacocks, swans, and roses in the park crossed by the cavalcades in *Mademoiselle de Maupin*. The English praised Gautier's book to the skies, Wilde calling it 'the holy writ of beauty' and Swinburne 'the most perfect and exquisite book of all time'. It was Beardsley's favourite book too, and he dreamed of illustrating it – very naturally, for such descriptions as this are highly reminiscent of one of the Englishman's drawings:

> The arms were bare to the elbow, and they emerged from a cloud of lace, round, white, and dimpled, as splendid as polished silver and with unimaginably delicate lineaments; the hands loaded with rings were languidly waving a huge fan of variegated feathers . . . However, these masculine garments were fitted in such a way as to suggest that they had a feminine lining: something wider about the hips and fuller in the chest, a flowing quality which draperies never have on a man's body.

Mademoiselle de Maupin was a dream of pleasures both facile and indecent, qualities which were unfortunately incompatible in Victorian England – a dream of which Beardsley was to produce a wildly exaggerated version in his story *Under the Hill*. But the frail young man was unable to do more than dream. His delicate constitution prevented him from indulging in even the simplest pleasures. Arthur Symons, who knew him very well, wrote that the characters in Beardsley's drawings 'desire more pleasure than there is in the world, fiercer and more exquisite pains, a more intolerable suspense . . . Here, then, we have a sort of abstract

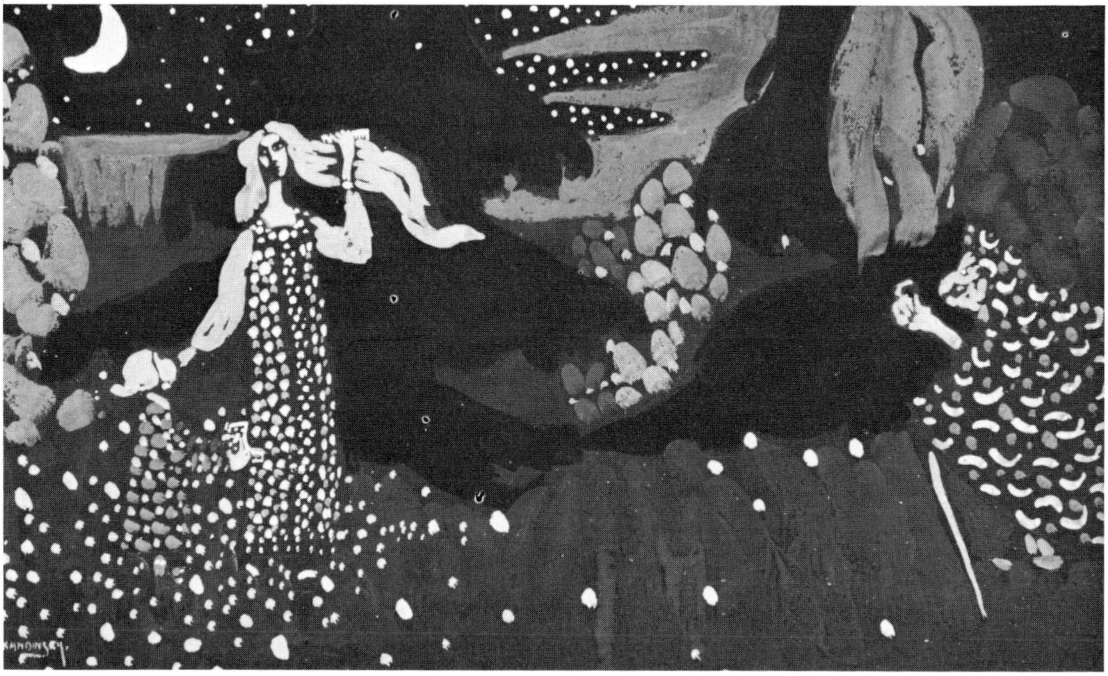

63. Wassily Kandinsky: *Night*. In this vision of Mélisande painted in Munich in 1907 one can see the beginnings of abstract art – the Symbolist universe disappears in a mass of coloured dots.

spiritual corruption, revealed in beautiful form; sin transfigured by beauty . . . And the peculiar efficacy of this satire is that it is so much the satire of desire returning upon itself, the mockery of desire enjoyed, the mockery of desire denied. It is because he loves beauty that beauty's degradation obsesses him . . .'

Symons continued his study by observing that Aubrey Beardsley identified himself with a figure he frequently depicted: Pierrot. This Pierrot is no longer the one of *fêtes galantes*, but rather the Pierrot Verlaine wrote of later, in 1883, a Pierrot who looks like a ghost (37). His poem shows that a wave of pessimism had swept away the gaiety of the Second Empire. All these *fin de siècle* Pierrots were to influence the melancholy acrobats of Picasso's Blue Period, and they can be compared with the Pulcinella who appears so often in Tiepolo's macabre caprices.

For the Decadents, Pierrot and Hamlet (19) were almost indistinguishable. Pierrot was the Montmartre Hamlet of Willette's drawings, which were published in the *Chat noir* review, and Pierrot-Hamlet was taken as his patron saint by a young man who, with Beardsley, was the most attractive of the Decadents: Jules Laforgue. His ironic pessimism, his cult of the moon, the post he occupied as reader to the aged empress Augusta, his engagement to a young Pre-Raphaelite painter, and his swift death, made him as fanciful a figure as the heroes of his *Moralités Légendaires*. In some of his poems, notably *Climat, Faune et Flore de la Lune*, his world comes close to Beardsley's (25). At other times he recalls Gustave Moreau at his most dazzling:

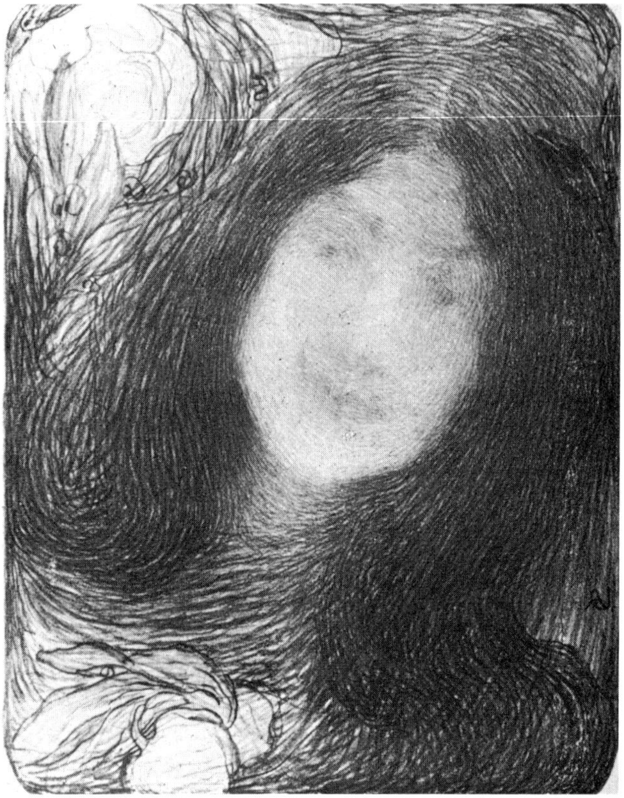

64. Aman-Jean: *Tête de Femme*. This lithograph by one of Seurat's friends shows us a Mona Lisa of the parks. Like many Symbolist painters Aman-Jean produced many good pictures while he was part of the general musical and poetic movement of the times. After 1905 he merely did work for the *Salon*. His best model was his wife.

O convois solennels des soleils magnifiques,
Nouez et dénouez vos vastes masses d'or.
O solemn processions of the splendid suns,
Tie and untie your vast masses of gold.

An admirer of the Impressionists, he imitates certain Monets: 'The sun on the horizon was pale gold; streaks of blood in patches of dead lilac and dull purple. Further up, the anaemic yellow sky melted into a milky-white mist, and here and there trails of violet, purplish-red, aubergine clouds . . .'

MASKS. For their melancholy parties and macabre serenades, the Decadents called for masks, and there are masks in plenty in their poems. Viélé-Griffin wrote of 'the sphinx-like smile of sweet masks' – which might almost be a description of a Khnopff. Henri de Régnier conjured up the masks of antiquity; Marcel Schwob wrote *La Porte des Rêves* (29), Jean Lorrain *Histoires de Masques*, and Wilde *The Truth of Masks.*

Beardsley is fond of unmasking his characters, and describes in detail the masks worn by the guests when Tannhäuser visits Venus:

> There were masks of green velvet that make the face look trebly powdered; masks of the heads of birds, of apes, of ser-

pents, of dolphins, of men and women, of little embryos and of cats . . . There were wigs of black and scarlet wools, of peacocks' feathers, of gold and silver threads, of swansdown, of the tendrils of the vine, and of human hair; huge collars of stiff muslin rising high above the head; tunics of panthers' skins that looked beautiful over pink tights; capotes of crimson satin trimmed with the wings of owls; stockings clocked with *fêtes galantes* and curious designs . . . Some of the women had put on delightful little moustaches dyed in purples and bright greens.

'A mask is always more expressive than a face,' wrote Wilde in a characteristic paradox, the only form of criticism which can be applied to those who have followed the Chimeras (77). And there are in fact countless masks in the works of our artists. There are Carrière's masks in polychrome ceramic, which look like mossy fauns, Klinger's masks in painted marble, a few masks in Redon's works, such as the mask sounding the alarm in the Edgar Allan Poe series, but above all expressionless faces which Khnopff transforms into masks to enable the mind to dissociate itself more easily

65. Ernest Laurent: Study for *Au Concert Colonne*. This charcoal sketch was one of a series for a picture which was much less interesting than the preparatory drawings. This friend of Seurat's succeeds brilliantly in conveying the almost religious atmosphere which surrounded these concerts.

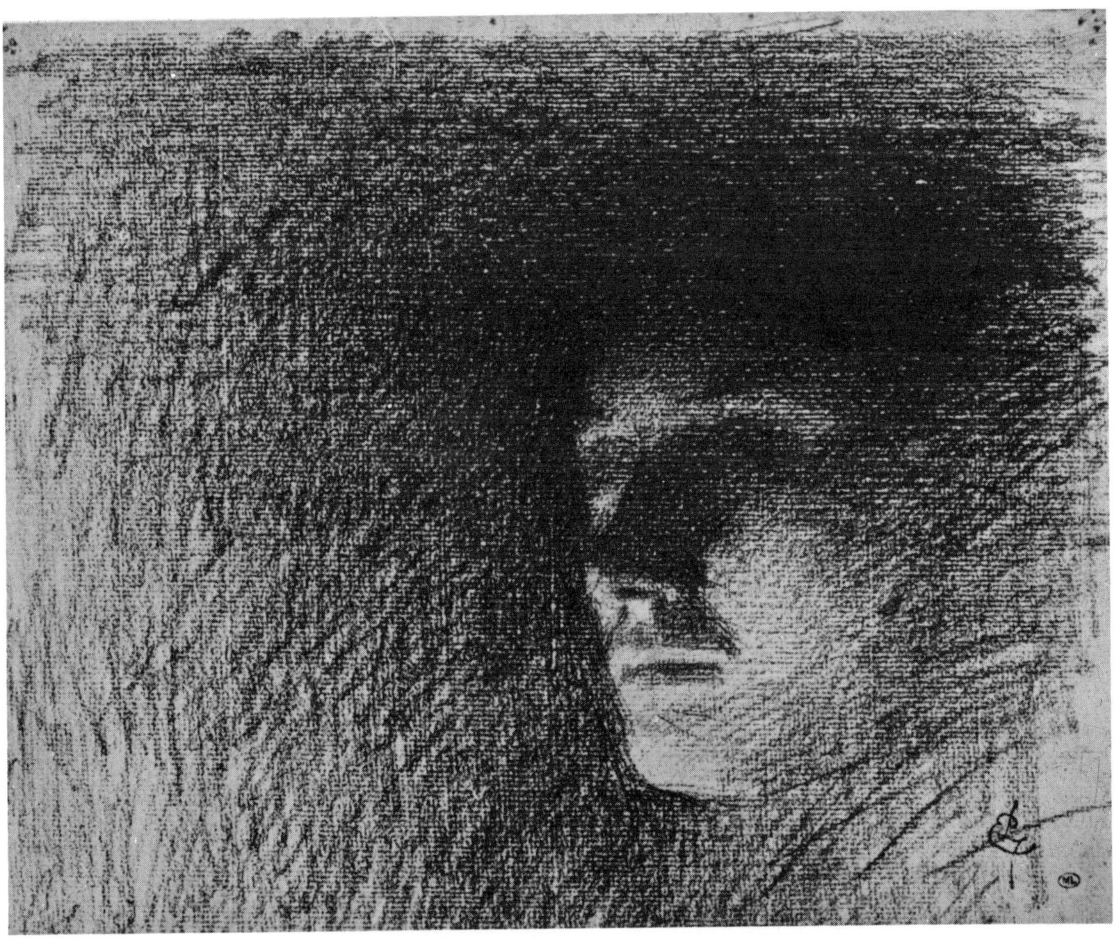

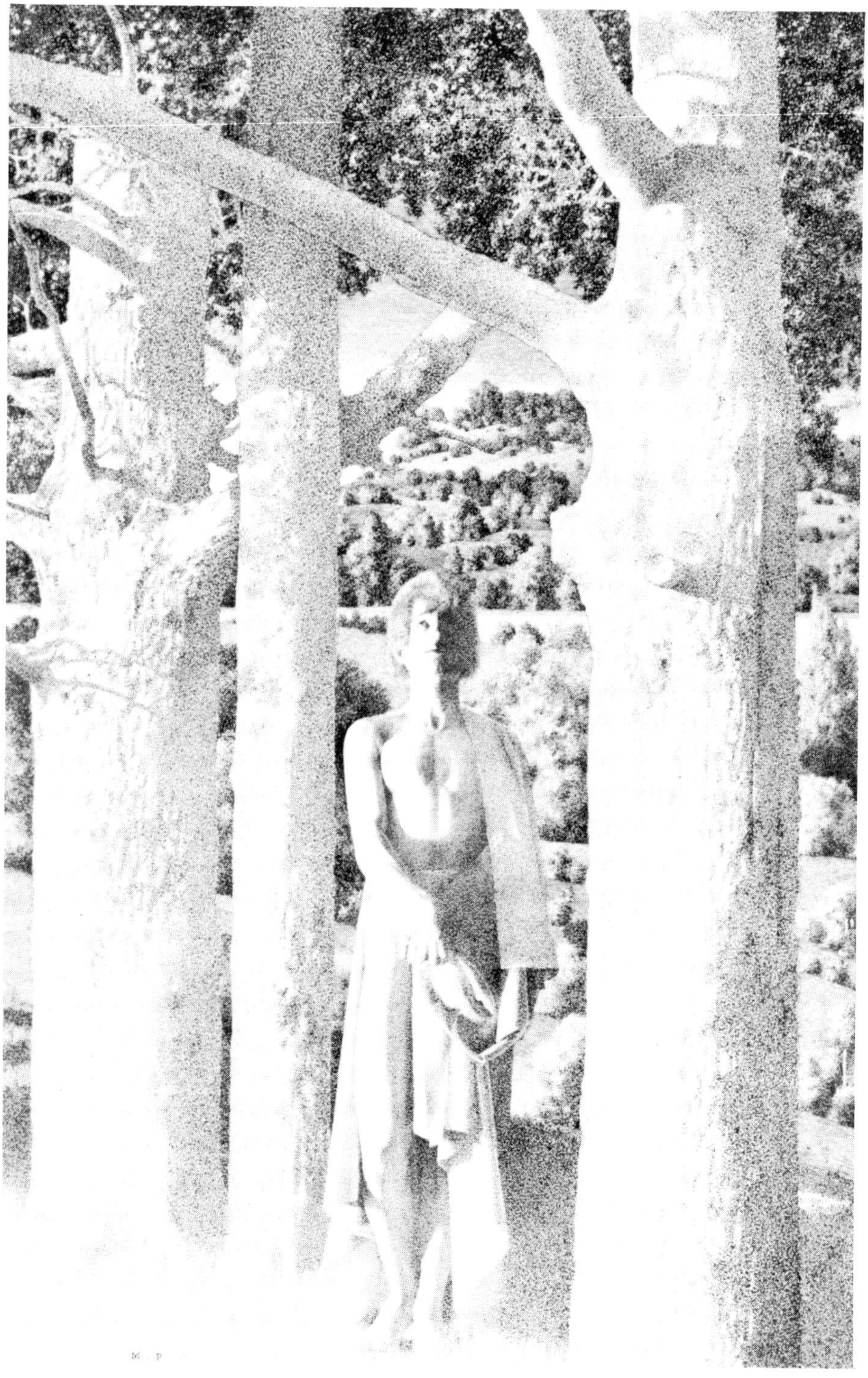

66. Parish: *A Hill Prayer.* This excellent drawing, done about 1895 for a collection of poems, shows us the almost photographic eye for detail of this artist, who sadly was later to turn to commercial art.

from the earth. Rops gives us commonplace pictures of masks under which death's-heads can be glimpsed, while Ensor harks back nostalgically to the village fairs of old. He is a marvellously gifted painter, even if the clumsiness of his draughtsmanship is not always deliberate. Here is Jean Lorrain's evocation of the visions Ensor reveals to us, sometimes borrowed from Bruegel or Gilray: 'Under the artist's etching-needle, the very wallpaper of the room becomes a sinister, purulent tapestry. This room is inhabited by tadpoles and gnomes with writhing bodies; grimaces and sardonic grins, blind dead eyes and slavering mouths float across the walls and over the bed-hangings.' Ensor's hell is a carnival. In 1883, he began painting his *Masques Scandalisés*, and then produced *Les Masques sur la Plage*, *L'Étonnement du Masque Wouse*, and a fine series of engravings entitled simply *Masques*, finishing up with the vast *Entrée du Christ à Bruxelles*, with its thousands of masks expressing stupid satisfaction. This last canvas carries a cruel and simple message, like the biblico-social pictures of Henry de Groux. One has the impression that Ensor's chimera was a malevolent, multicoloured parrot, fluttering round the ivory tower in which his Symbolist brothers were working on their esoteric pictures.

To all these different forms of nostalgia must be added what the English call *la nostalgie de la boue*, a nostalgia best exemplified by Dorian Gray seeking his pleasures in the slums of Whitechapel. This is a very *fin de siècle* feeling, an ephemeral personal decadence; but while the chimeras love blood and tears, mud is not greatly to their taste, and the artists who followed them remained impervious to this penchant, powerful though it was in their world. They left this type of nostalgia to Toulouse-Lautrec or Steinlen.

67. Khnopff: *Memories*. This very large pastel is one of the most typical of Belgian Symbolism. Photographs of the artist's sister have been used for each of the seven figures depicted.

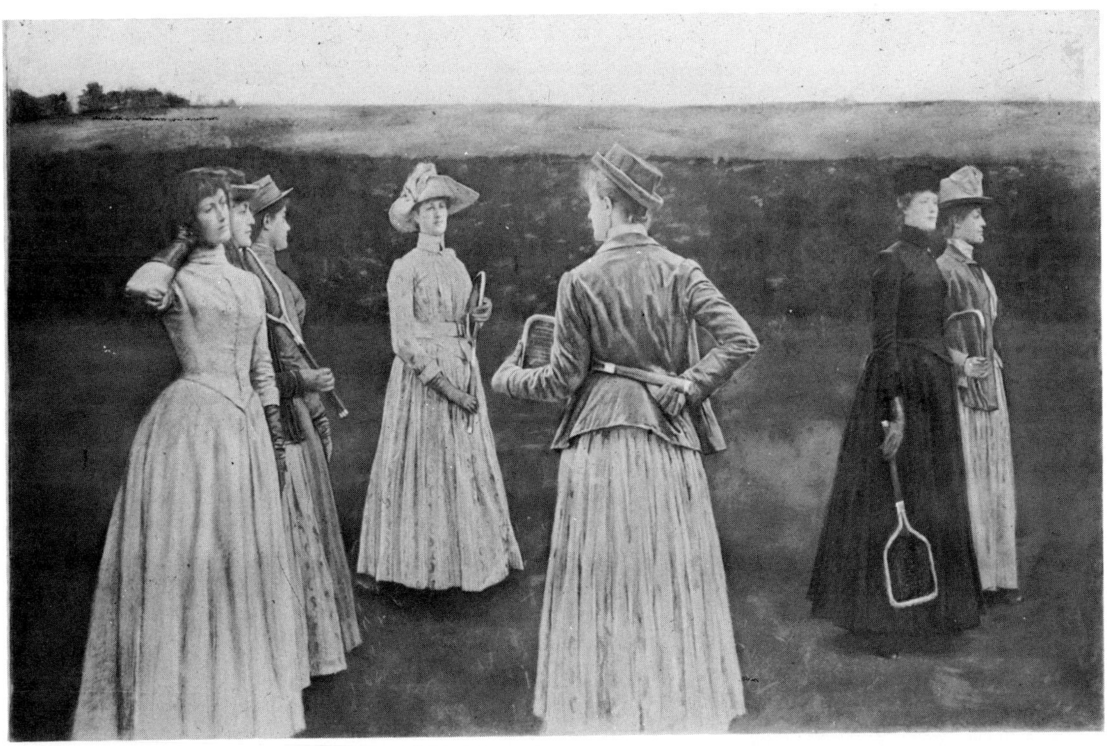

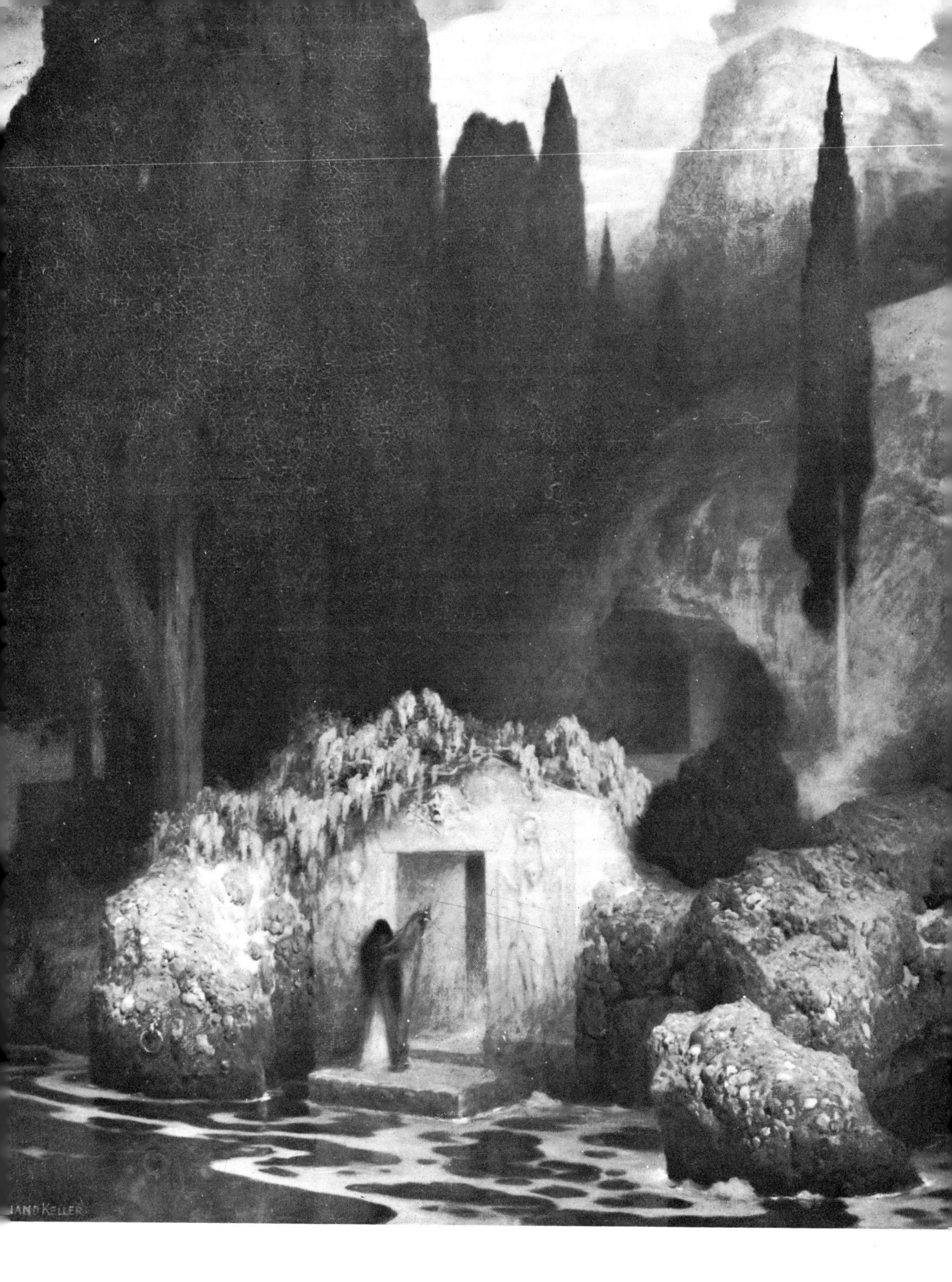

68. Ferdinand Keller: *The Tomb of Böcklin.* This tribute to the painter of the *Island of the Dead* adds the sentimental note of wistaria to the drama of classical fatalism.

8 From Benares to Bruges

INDIA. Exoticism in Moreau and in Flaubert is experienced at two removes. Their India is that of Alexander's conquests, their Africa that of the Carthaginians, for the Chimeras travel in both time and space. Similarly the Italy of the Pre-Raphaelites is that of Dante. For the aesthete-artists who saw the world through books and pictures, Romantic Orientalism was no longer enough; they therefore left minarets and dancing-girls to the academic Salon painters, and turned to Delacroix's *Sardanapalus* to take them out of their times. Baudelaire loved that picture more than any other, for in it, mingled in a massacre worthy of Sade's most frenzied inventions, he found splendid nudes, treasures scattered over silk draperies, black slaves, and beautiful horses. To paint *Sardanapalus*, Delacroix had studied Indian miniatures, so that the satrap is a turbanned Maharajah and the massacre a *suttee*, the ritual funeral pyre on which Hindu widows sacrificed themselves.

Moreau too had dreams of India, and one of his notes defines the mystical exoticism which transfigures the most hackneyed myths: 'How can anyone love and understand or dream of India, of the forests of the New World, of the fantastic archipelagoes of the East Indies, or of the antediluvian flora of Central Africa, with a mind that is incredulous or sceptical, or, worst of all, inclined to pretentious paradox?' But he needed a great many pictures to feed his dreams, and he found those pictures in an admirably illustrated periodical entitled *Le Tour du Monde* (Around the World) which began publication towards the end of the Second Empire; a series of articles on the India of the Rajahs, for example, provided him with details of costumes and architecture, as well as pictures of bejewelled elephants and lascivious goddesses. Apart from the collection of *Le Tour du Monde*, Moreau also possessed a work on India by Gustave Lebon, also lavishly illustrated, but more philosophical in tone. These documents were used for *Le Triomphe d'Alexandre* and for the richly esoteric settings in which the painter placed his mythological scenes; thus the flowers and figures on the columns surrounding Jupiter and Selene recall the polychrome

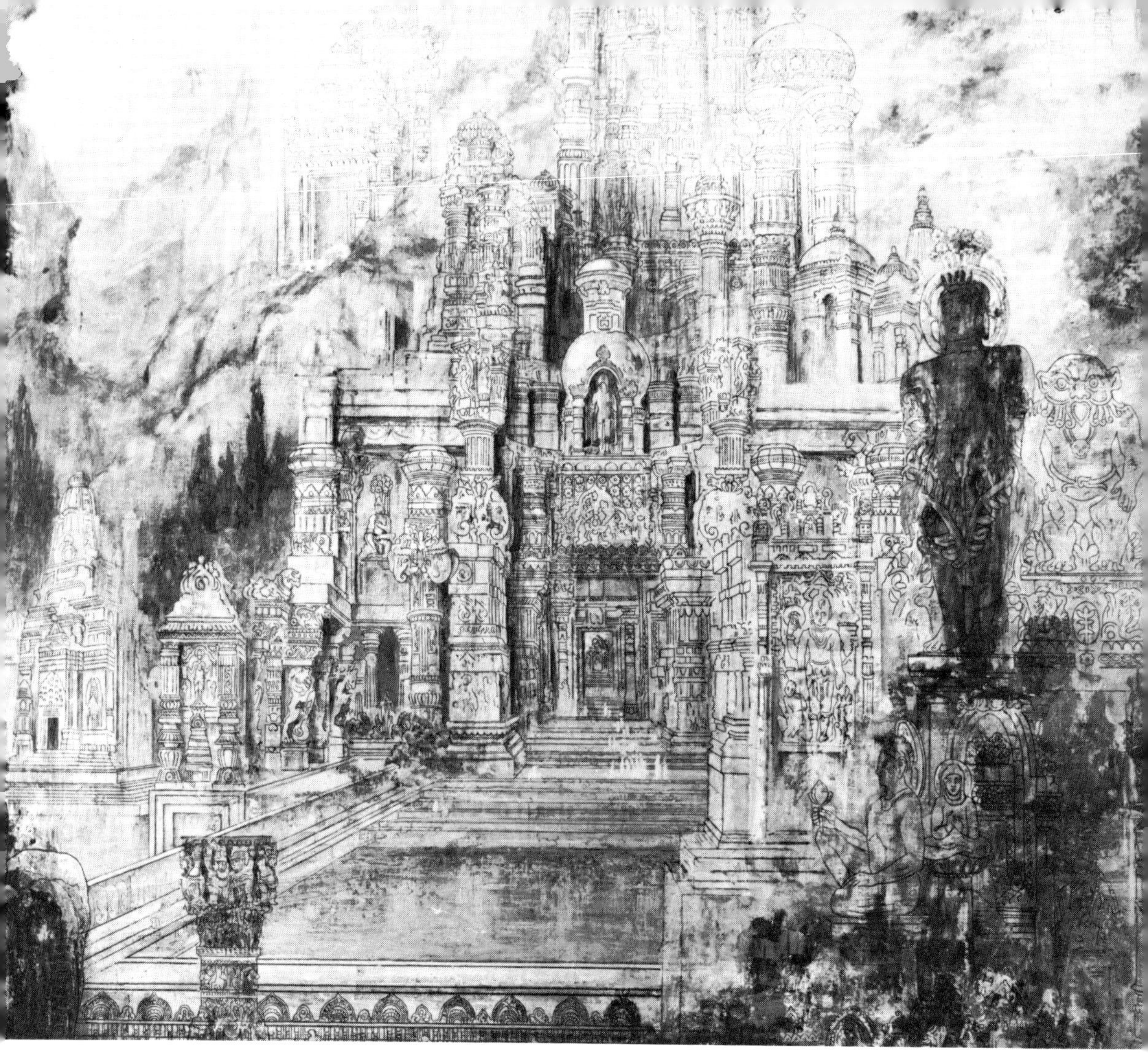

69. Moreau: *Le Triomphe d'Alexandre* (detail). The scrupulous attention to historical detail is more reminiscent of the Universal Exhibition of 1889 than of Benares. Here Moreau is close to Leconte de Lisle and Villiers de l'Isle-Adam. The blue-and-gold Oriental city is a pendant to the accursed medieval city of the chimeras.

motifs on the temples of Madurai, while Jupiter himself, impassive beneath his lotus-blossoms and pearls, is a Vishnu to whom a sacrificial victim is being offered. Thanks to the discovery of its myths and monuments, India had become the mystical centre of European intellectuals (22). Asia had taken the place of Greece, frozen by academic art. In *La Tentation de Saint Antoine* Flaubert shows us 'gymnosophist' fakirs who are both picturesque and supernatural. His Vedic gods recall Moreau's princes. These two great imaginations were never closer than they are here:

> He is young and beardless, more beautiful than any maiden, and covered with diaphanous veils. The pearls of his tiara shine softly like so many moons; a chain of stars is wound several times round his chest; and with one hand under his head and the other arm stretched out, he rests there with a dreamy, intoxicated air . . . Straddling birds, rocked in palanquins, sitting on golden thrones and standing in niches, they dream, travel, give orders, drink wine, breathe the scent of flowers.

In Redon's works there are visions which are just as colourful, but devoid of any picturesque element. His India has a Buddhist serenity rather than a Hindu exuberance. Redon is inspired where Moreau is mannered. Laforgue is therefore closer to Redon than Flaubert when he writes in his *Complainte des voix sous le figuier bouddhique: Les Voluptuantes*:

La lune en son halo ravagé n'est qu'un œil
Mangé de mouches, tout rayonnant de grands deuils,
Vitraux, murs déshérités, flagellés d'aurore,
Les yeux promis sont dans les plus grands deuils encore.
The moon in its ravaged halo is but an eye
Eaten up by flies, radiant with deep mourning,
Stained-glass windows, disinherited walls, flagellated by the dawn,
The promised eyes are in deeper mourning still.

The same rich melancholy is to be found in Villiers de l'Isle-Adam's story *Akdysseril*, the tale of a very young betrothed couple, the prisoners of a queen, who die of joy when she allows them to come together. The story is set in Benares.

India inspired poems by Verhaeren, Moréas, and Cazalis, that great friend of Redon and Moréas who took the Indian name of Lahor. One of Cazalis's poems, *Kali* (after the Indian Goddess of that name), recalls a picture by Ranson which shows a temple with red columns streaked with black, with some sinister vegetation in the foreground:

Déesse de la mort, reine des voluptés,
Âme des nuits d'amour, âme des nuits sanglantes,
Déesse au corps livide, aux regards redoutés
Comme l'âcre poison des serpents et des plantes.
Goddess of death, queen of pleasure,
Spirit of nights of love and nights of blood,
Goddess of the pale body, with a gaze feared
Like the bitter poison of snakes and plants.

Ranson had a predilection for Buddhas and lotus-blossoms: for him as well as for Schuffenecker, the road from Pont-Aven led to Benares.

Mucha's illustrations for Paul Verola's *Le Rama*, which obtained considerable success when published in *La Plume*, are similar in taste; and Kupka's watercolour triptych, *L'Âme du Lotus* (1898), shows the same inspiration. This fellow countryman of Mucha's who was to become one of the pioneers of abstract art, offers us an ethereal spirit, a cruel prince covered in jewels, nautch-girls, gigantic lotus-blossoms, and slender minarets.

The Americans too fell under the influence of India's magic; thus Elihu Vedder, at the end of his life, not content with illustrating Omar Khayyam in the Indian style, painted a picture entitled *The Cup of Death* which might have been the work of a Watts converted by Madame Blavatsky. Blashfield, likewise fascinated by India, painted *The Keeper of the Threshold.* But it is interesting to note that Indian esoterism had very little influence on English artists of the period.

Mention must be made here of Jean Lorrain's splendid pages on Benares in *Monsieur de Phocas.* For the Decadents, the idea of half-charred corpses, their smoke mingling with the scent of flowers, was irresistible, but the breviary of morbid exoticism was to be, not Lorrain's book, but Mirbeau's *Le Jardin des Supplices.* Gauguin's Oceanic Orient failed to inspire any writers, except perhaps for Victor Ségalen. But Mirbeau insisted on linking the painter with India: 'In this work of his there is a disturbing, attractive mixture of barbaric splendour, Catholic liturgy, Hindu reverie, Gothic imagery, and subtle, obscure Symbolism.'

The China and Japan of Loti and Lafcadio Hearn are merely travellers' watercolours. Judith Gautier alone, in novels which have fallen into unmerited oblivion, gives those countries the historical dimension which makes them interesting. The lack of interest in the Far East shown by the Symbolists and their painters can also be explained by the fact that the Impressionists had been enthusiastic admirers of Japanese engravings, and that collectors such as the Goncourt brothers had discovered the Chinese *objet d'art.* True, Whistler, who often bridged the gap between the Symbolists and the Impressionists, adapted certain Japanese compositions in a poetic fashion, but with de Feure we are back to mere colour-prints.

THE ORIENT OF LEGEND. Poetic inspiration used to follow hard on the heels of archaeological discovery, so that the Orient of the Decadents was derived not from the Romantics' Turkish creations, but from Bactria or Cappadocia with their polychrome temples dedicated to gods with exotic names, lands which the Parnassians had just explored. Their dazzling trophies suggested strange visions to the poets and painters of the *fin de siècle,* who began to outdo the bizarre Flaubertian vocabulary. Witness in particular Villiers de l'Isle-Adam, whose story *L'Annonciateur* is set in the great temple of 'Hierouschalaïm'. This tale describes a Moreau vision without sparing us a single candelabrum or a single ruby. Salome, the sacred nautch-girl, appears before an apse which recalls Byzantium with its mosaics and the Alhambra with its columns, and, of course, India with its stifling luxury and delirious

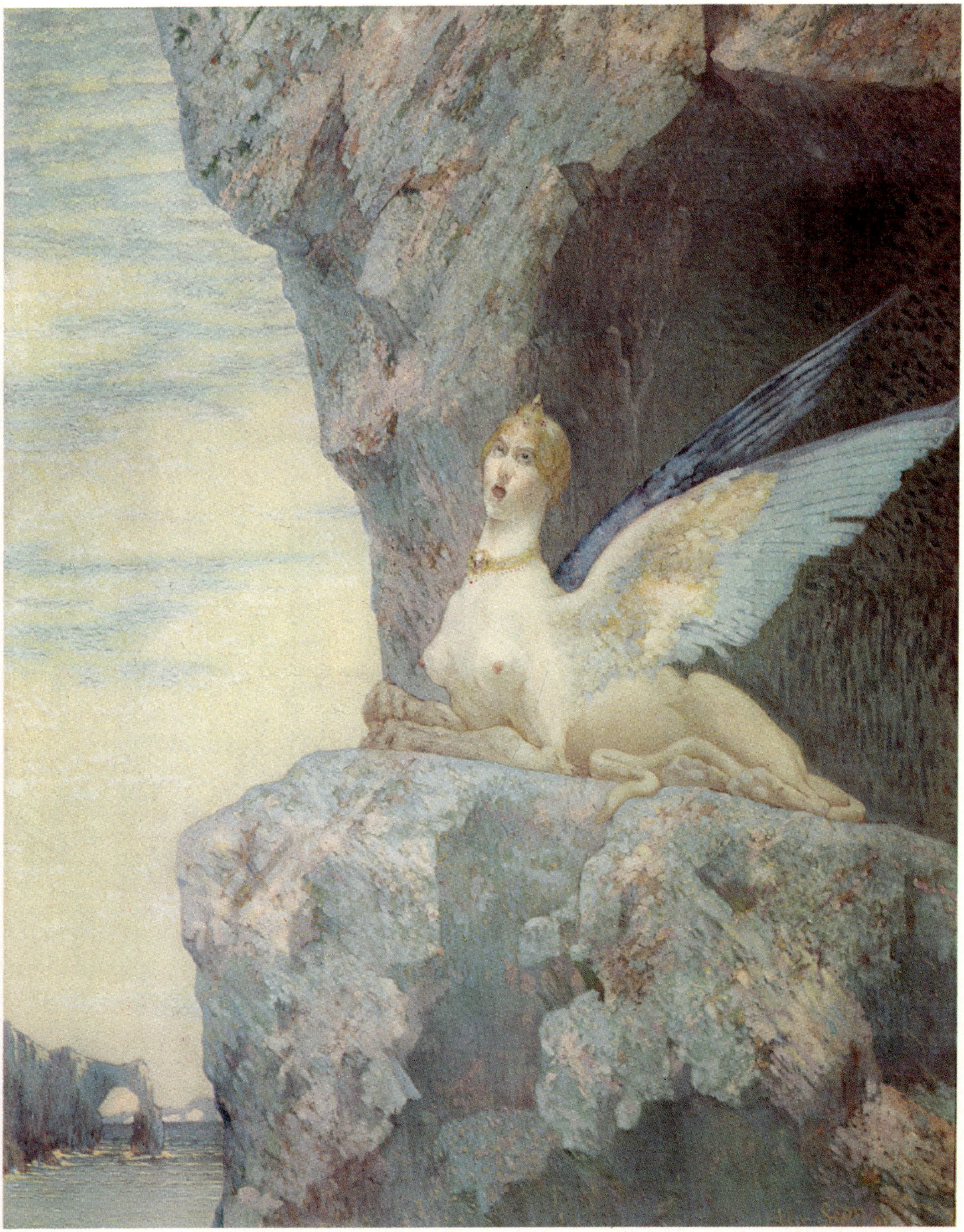

70. Séon: *Le Désespoir de la Chimère*. This picture had an immense success when it was first exhibited at the *Salon des Rose+Croix*. The subject and the drawing are derived from Moreau but the blue colouring places the Chimera in a dream landscape which belongs entirely to the Symbolists. The face and hairstyle are those of a *femme fatale* like Cléo de Mérode.

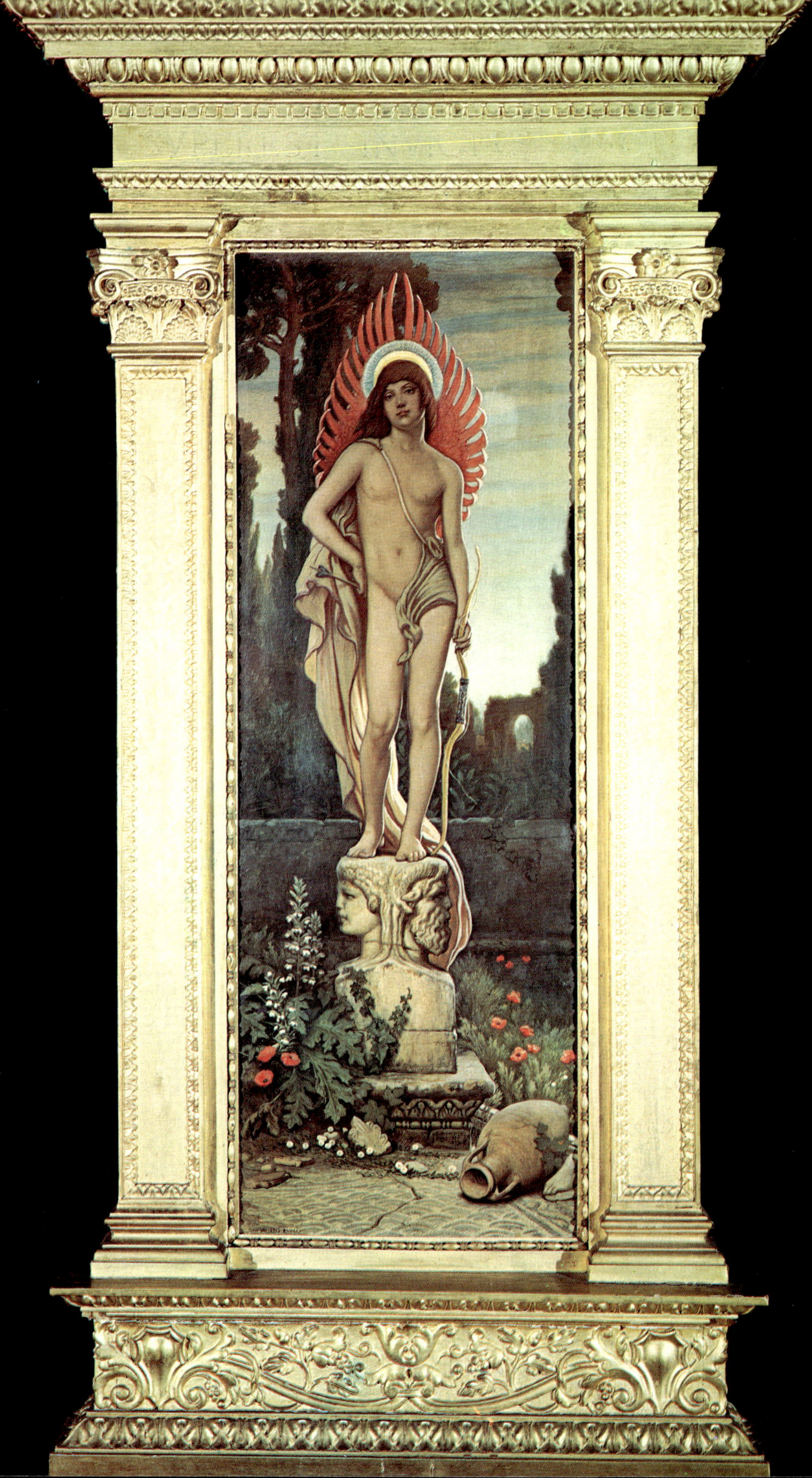

decoration. The best guide-book to this Orient of the gods is Wilde's *The Sphinx*; Hammon, Antinous, Baal, Cleopatra, Astarte, and all the gods and all the queens visit the Sphinx and propose strange pleasures to her (51). This scandalous Baedeker of the esoteric Middle East ends up with the evocation of Christ. There is a close link between the reveries of the poet and the works which Rossetti painted towards the end of his life, under the combined influence of opium and his last love, a magnificently vulgar woman who aroused the painter's latent masochism. He depicted her as a sensual, despotic creature, in turn Venus, Astarte, Circe, and Lilith. Wilde's imagination made this kind of Oriental vision a success in spite of everything. Rossetti's late works, on the other hand, were best described by Montesquiou when he called them 'bizarre Bouguereaus'. (Long before the publication of *The Sphinx*, Rossetti's paintings and the Swinburne poems which had grown out of them had stirred up a violent reaction in the public and in 1871 the critic Buchanan attacked what he called 'the Fleshly School', denouncing the influence of Baudelaire and even of Sade.)

Another Pre-Raphaelite, Holman Hunt, who was much more austere than Rossetti and not at all a sensualist, had settled in Jerusalem in order to get closer to Biblical truth. Even Tissot, later on the fashionable painter of actresses and *cocottes*, had taken refuge in mysticism after an unhappy love-affair, and after deciding to illustrate the Bible, also travelled to Judea. Finally, Ary Renan, one of Moreau's favourite pupils, painted *Les Filles de Jephté* for the 1886 Salon. Jules Laforgue gave this impression of the picture: 'The daughters walking in procession, draped in blue, with an epic gaze in their eyes and fatalistic attitudes: it is motionless, mysterious, and immortally precious, in a little corner of the future.'

Jerusalem, after appearing in the background of a Bresdin engraving, bristling with towers, fascinated both artists and poets in this period of religious revival. The wind blowing over Jerusalem, Benares, and Alexandria reached as far as Moreau's studio, stirring his heroines' veils, and as far as Samain's study, making his queens quiver with emotion. It even blew on the other side of the Atlantic, thanks to the most gifted but least spiritual of American painters, John Singer Sargent; for when he was commissioned in 1890 to paint a mural at Boston depicting the history of religion, he travelled to the Middle East and painted an Astarte endowed with all the attributes of the goddesses described by Flaubert – a tiara, a cloak embroidered with moons, and jewels in the shape of flowers. But when he came to depict the religions of the West, Sargent turned for inspiration to Puvis de Chavannes.

71. Elihu Vedder: *Superest Invictus Amor.* In the academic style of a Bouguereau or a Leighton, this American artist provides a morbid version of a Gustave Moreau. The dark forest in the background recalls Böcklin. The picture is encased in a gilded Renaissance frame, as though it were a Mantegna in an architectural setting.

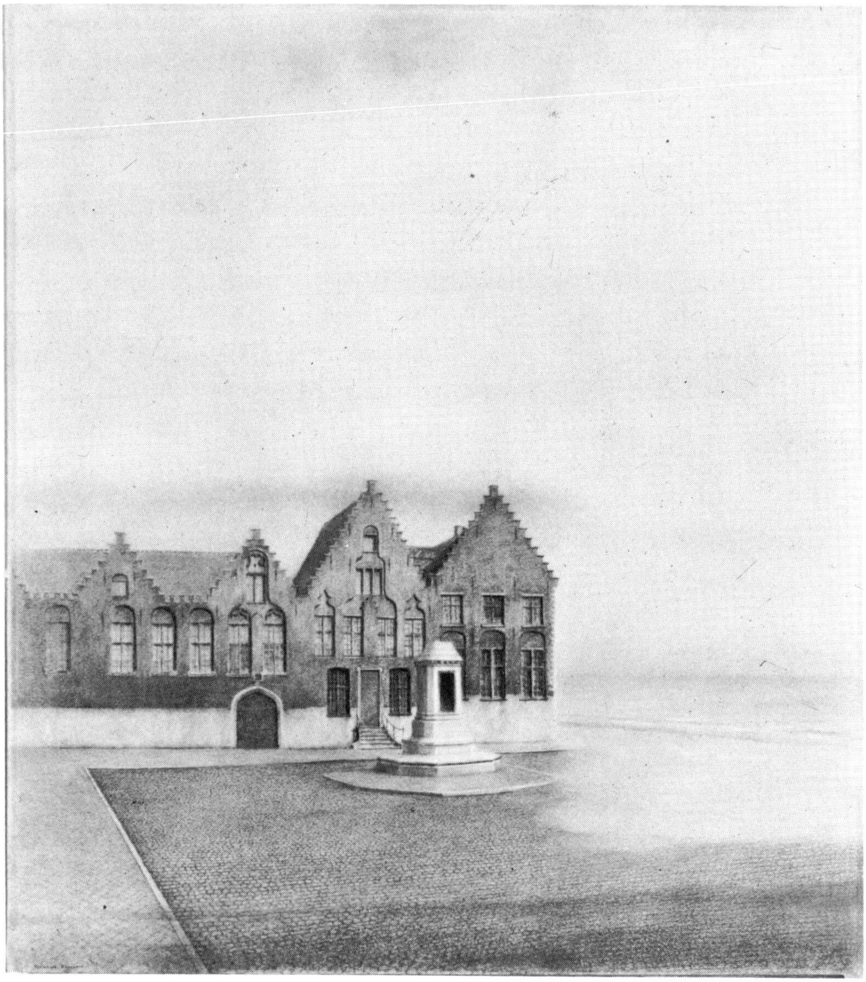

72. Khnopff: *The Abandoned City*. This large drawing, one of the most remarkable works of Symbolist art, provides a sort of mixture between Bruges and the city of Ys sinking beneath the waters. The grey tones and the water which gently laps against closed doors symbolize silence and forgetfulness.

ATHENS. Puvis de Chavannes depicted a grey, distinguished Greece whose heroes seem to be perpetually wandering along a Champs-Élysées planted at regular intervals with statues and columns. Though a less attractive master than Moreau, he exerted a considerable influence, not so much through these very academic subjects as through poetic pictures such as *Le Pauvre Pêcheur* or *Le Fils Prodigue*; the Symbolists loved his figures, for they are 'souls' far removed from any carnal contingencies. A large painting by Delville, entitled *L'École de Platon* and relegated for the past sixty years to the storeroom of a French museum, is the best example of Puvis's art as imitated by a disciple in 1902. It shows a white peacock on a wistaria, some temples on the horizon beside an opal sea, and a group of pale-faced ephebes on a marble bench listening to a Plato who looks more like a sort of Leonardo da Vinci dressed as Christ. Although a disciple of Moreau, Ary Renan comes closer to Puvis in an ambiguous idyllic scene entitled *Ischia*. Puvis's influence can also be discerned in the works of Osbert, of his pupil Séon, and of Henri Martin, the only Symbolist to become an official painter and to depict Third Republic personalities being crowned with laurels on the Champs-Élysées by ladies in night-dresses. Very close to Henri Martin were the American painters who, about 1890, began covering public buildings with vast murals. To please the benefactors who had founded these libraries and museums, painters such as John LaFarge and E. E. Blashfield created an image of a Greece seen through puritanical eyes. Blashfield himself, who was more a symbol than a symbolist, was praised on one occasion for 'his peculiar talent for clarifying abstract ideas'. And Maxfield Parish continued this tradition right into the Thirties. But the best of Puvis's American imitators was, of course, Sargent in the second part of his murals for the Boston Library. The Chicago Exhibition of 1893 also offered vast surfaces to these painters who rapidly became academic artists in Europe.

Some painters were tempted to follow the example of the Parnassians and to daub academic plaster figures with bright colours. This extract from a review which appeared in *Le Décadent* in 1888 shows us what was expected of Olympus at that time: 'What an orgy of Prussian blue in Lagarde's *Orphée*! I love this artificial art with its clever imitation of the primitives. You must admit that these mysterious things which one is tempted to attribute to Apollodoros of Athens, nicknamed the Skiograph, are calculated to charm the subtle dilettantism of a Decadent critic.' These lines could also be applied to Rochegrosse, whose influence was so considerable that one of the most perspicacious of the Symbolist critics, Camille Mauclair, allowed himself to be swept away by the enthusiasm which his mythological massacres aroused during every Salon:

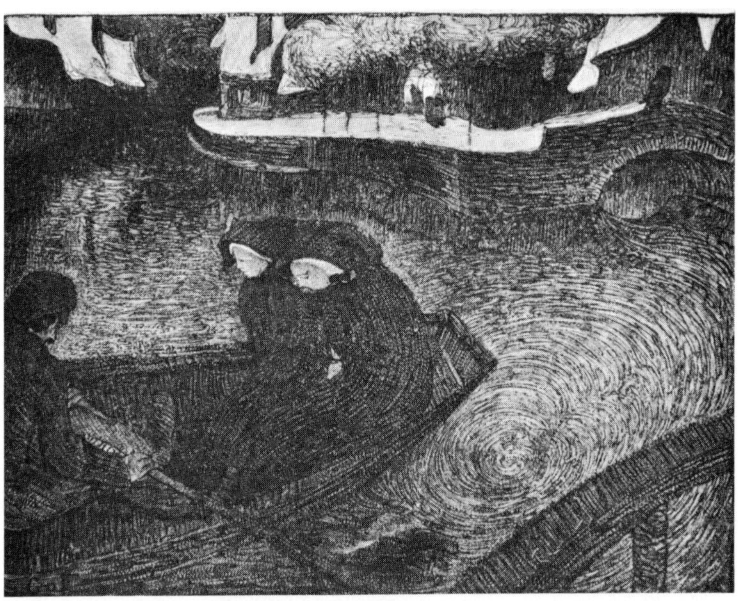

73. De Feure: *Petit Nocturne de Bruges*. This woodcut for a work by Rodenbach formed part of one of the greatest successes of art publishing of about 1895.

> He has shattered the narrow conventions of historical painting by flooding it with his violent imagination, his intuitive knowledge of the barbarian races, his understanding of the tragic theatre of the Orient, his vast and astonishing erudition which has made him familiar with all the Mediterranean civilizations and the ancient traditions of Asia, mingling like the Orientals themselves the taste for subtle symbolism with the taste for blood and pleasure . . .

Rochegrosse is above all else the painter of Flaubert's *Salammbô*, which he illustrated in great detail with absolute accuracy but a complete lack of understanding.

The antique pictures which the artists of the *fin de siècle* offer us are more often than not laborious reconstructions and pretexts to depict nudes. Alma-Tadema, an English painter born in Holland, gives us a curiously ambiguous vision of a Hellenic Orient, and his picture *Octave cendrée* actually found favour in Huysmans's eyes. He was also d'Annunzio's favourite painter, and he had almost as much influence as Puvis de Chavannes on the mural painters of America: witness Robert Blum's murals for the Brooklyn Museum. Feuerbach, who was to have a great influence on Klimt, painted some Antigones and Circes who are rather Baudelairean in character. This ambiguous sexuality has saved these two painters from the oblivion into which Lord Leighton and Bouguereau have fallen, and it lends an added charm to the works of Böcklin.

To obtain some idea of Greece as it appeared to the artists of the *fin de siècle*, one has only to walk through the Empress of Austria's villa on Corfu, the Achilleion; it is the perfect setting for Böcklin's paintings and the Baron de Gloeben's homosexual photographs. At the very end of the *fin de siècle*, Klimt would delight in raising up hieratic Athenas in the face of agitated allegories, but his goddess would be more Byzantine than Hellenic. We shall meet him again, in any case, when we reach Byzantium, that spiritual capital of the Decadence. France, after the decline of Symbolism, was to return to a purer concept of Greece, with Bourdelle's statues and Ménard's landscapes.

FLORENCE. Ever since the middle of the nineteenth century, the city of the Medicis had been the capital of aestheticism. In the name of Walter Pater, a despotic lesbian called Vernon Lee reigned there over a court of more or less Botticellian characters in a neo-Platonic atmosphere. In 1881, when still a young woman, Vernon Lee had written *Euphorion and Belcarro*. Two of her female friends, an aunt and niece who called themselves 'Michael Field', devoted their time to putting the Primitives into sonnets. These ladies had countless imitators who hung around the Ponte Vecchio looking for some Beatrice, or else for a page, preferably disguised as a character from Rossetti. As we have already seen, Dante Gabriel Rossetti's talent was to be spoilt by his taste for Levantine lushness; but he produced his masterpieces by conjuring up on canvas the city of Florence which he knew through his parents, who were political refugees, and through the reading of Dante. As early as 1848 the young man painted Dante's meeting with Beatrice. From his paintings, his poems and his sister's poems, there arose a mystical city which owed as much to Oxford as to Florence, a dark medieval city lit by lilies and radiant faces. Ruskin's admiration lent added fire to these visions, and Rossetti's meeting with Elizabeth Siddal enabled the painter, in 1851, to create the ideal Beatrice, whose beauty he was to impose on several generations: a delightful creature who, renouncing corsets, crinolines, heels, and false chignons, became the 'New Woman'. Her simplicity offered a deliberate contrast to vulgar Victorian overdressing, while her casual stance, her full neck and her flowing hair showed the way towards the line of an *Art Nouveau* arabesque. As we have seen, his young wife's death cheated Dante Gabriel of his genius, and his admirers then turned to Botticelli to find a model who was possibly younger and certainly more ambiguous than Elizabeth.

From 1880 onwards, Florence was seen through the blue-tinted spectacles of certain lady aesthetes, whom Anatole France gently caricatured in the person of 'Miss Bell' in *Le Lys Rouge*, for the French flocked to Florence in almost as great numbers as the English, though far fewer settled there. The result for France was

74. Walter Crane: *The Horses of Neptune*. One of the best-known compositions of this artist, who aimed at adapting Greek themes to the precepts of William Morris.

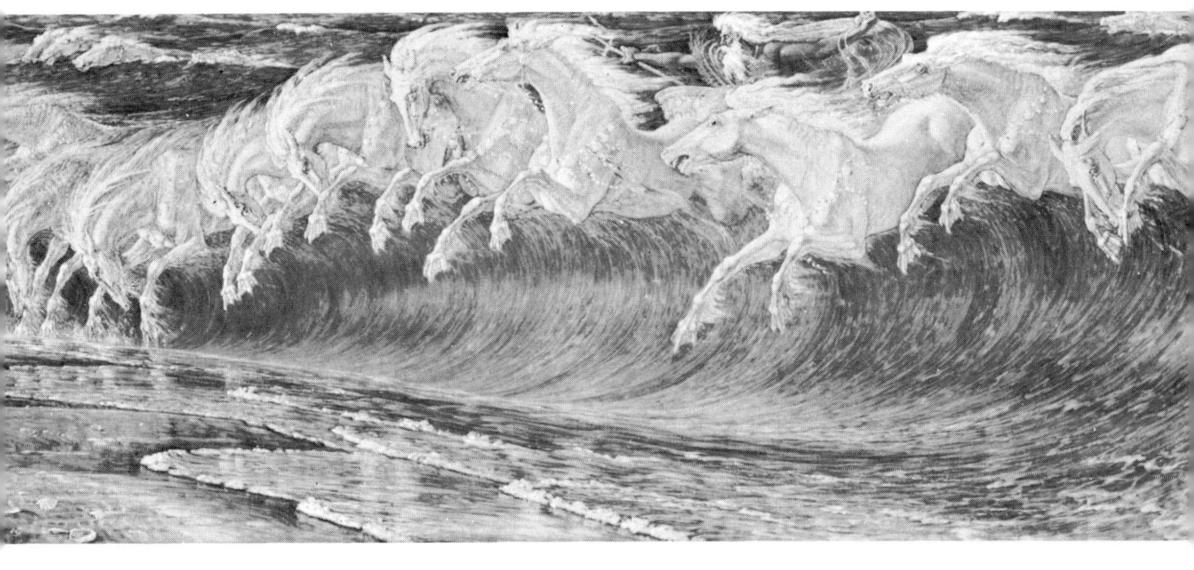

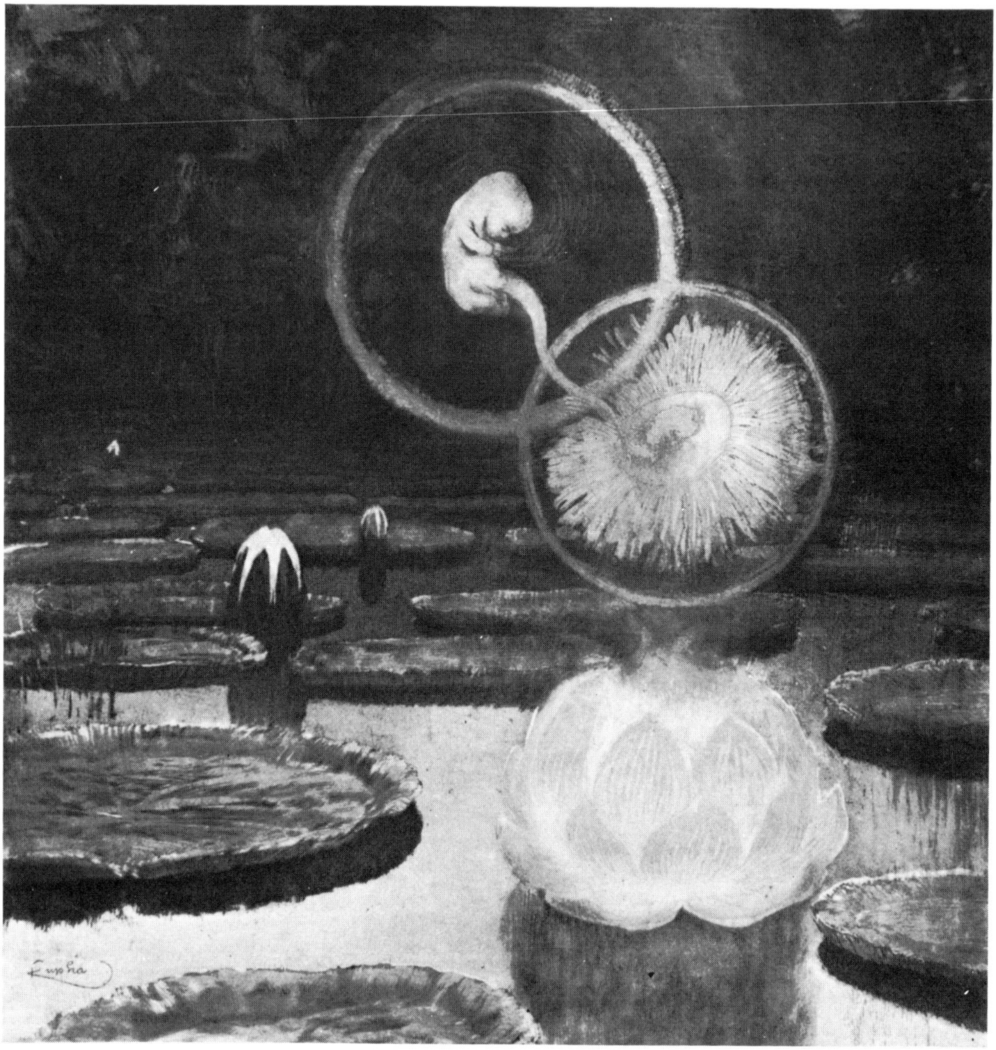

75. Kupka: *The Beginning of Life.* This Czech artist, who was to become a painter of abstracts in his later years, was originally much influenced by Odilon Redon and oriental exoticism. The lotus is, of course, the flower of Buddha.

a great many paintings by Maurice Denis, the poems of the Abbé Le Cardonnel, and the poetic prose of Francis Poictevin, a great friend of Moreau's. The atmosphere in Florence was one 'in which one feels a certain regret at not dying suddenly', and in which Schuré met 'a woman of superhuman beauty, with a mysterious force in her eyes', who inspired him to write *Les Grands Initiés.* But if Schuré was a man of virtue, Lorrain visited the banks of the Arno in search of 'the Leonardesque head of the Medusa' (14). We find the Medusa, that fatal beauty, in many novels of 1900, and in Péladan's works, as we have seen, we also find the disquieting Mona Lisa: 'In the Mona Lisa, the cerebral authority of the man of genius is combined with the sensual charms of the woman of beauty in a moral hermaphroditism.' His stay in Florence, together with his subsequent visit to Bayreuth, exerted a decisive influence on Péladan's thought. His ideal and Pater's theory about the Mona Lisa were to be developed by Merejkovsky, and it was from the works of that writer that Freud derived the main elements of his essay *Leonardo's Childhood Memories*. During the same period also, Böcklin was painting his robust allegories at the gates of Florence, using a rich palette more reminiscent of the Venetians than of the sober Tuscans.

VENICE. Venice, for her part, had had painters who were too much in love with life to appeal to the Decadents, with the possible exception of the strange, angular Crivelli. What they loved was the decrepitude of the palaces, the vapours rising from the lagoons, in short all the things that inspired the finest pages in Barrès's *Amori et Dolori Sacrum*: 'Those who feel the need to hurt themselves, to tear themselves on their thoughts, are happy in a city where no beauty is entirely flawless.' Proust adorned his Albertine with the splendour of the city: 'The dress Albertine was wearing that evening seemed to me like the tempting shadow of that invisible Venice. It was covered with Arab motifs like Venice, like the columns whose Oriental birds alternately signifying life and death were reflected in the shimmering deep blue material.' (This was a blue which Proust had perhaps discovered in John Addington Symonds's *In the Key of Blue*.) It was not subjects that Venice gave the *fin de siècle* painters – Delacroix had taken all too many, fifty years before – but colours used in a symbolic palette of alternately bright and dull hues, of all those shades of mildew which we find again in d'Annunzio's *Fire* and in Thomas Mann's *Death in Venice*, that cruel satire of *fin de siècle* pretensions.

So though Venice had many writers, it had few painters. True, Moreau, who in his youth had spent several weeks in Venice copying Carpaccio, occasionally revived his memories of the city in allegorical watercolours (55). And mention must be made of that curious work of art which transmitted the strange and dazzling message of the Decadence down to the Second World War: the Marchesa Casati. Whether she posed for Boldini, Van Dongen, or Augustus John, she remained first and foremost the *femme fatale* of the Nineties. A Medusa covered in Lalique jewellery, with a dead-white face and eyes ringed with black, a Circe who used to take out leopards on a leash, her legend is still alive in Venice, where she gave entertainments worthy of Moreau, at which she appeared in Tiepolo costumes re-created by Beardsley and wigs which might have been created by Klimt.

BRUGES. It was in another dead city, crisscrossed by canals, that the dreamers of the North set their chimeras free (5). Rodenbach's novel, *Bruges-la-Morte*, which was to inspire de Feure's finest lithographs, did for Bruges what Rossetti's poems had done for

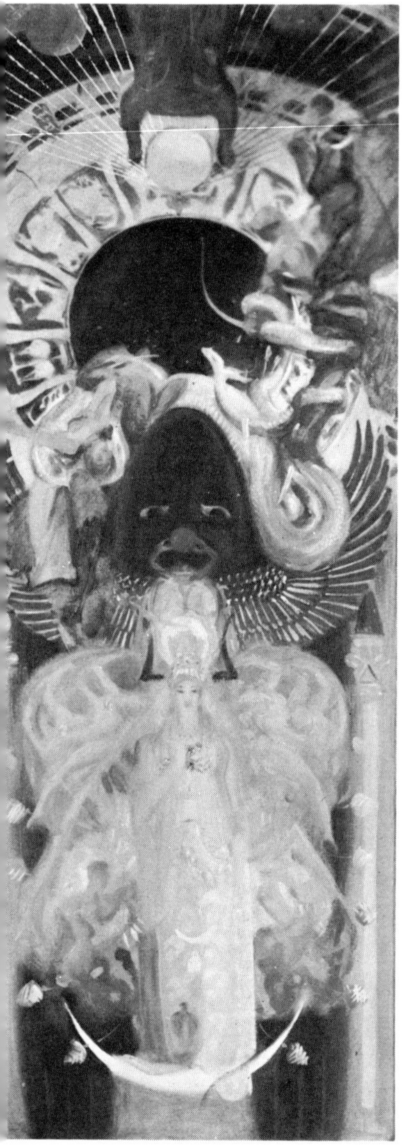

76. John Singer Sargent: *Astarte*. This sketch for the fresco in the library at Boston could be an illustration for *Salammbô*. After studying the history of religion, Sargent created this strange divinity in pale moonlight colours surrounded by the esoteric symbols dear to the Rosicrucians, with vague souls and *Art Nouveau* dragons. This was his only incursion into this type of painting.

Florence, but with the difference that in Belgium a national school developed around the chosen city. This sudden artistic flowering in a profoundly bourgeois country can be explained as much by a reaction against the conformity denounced by Baudelaire as by a new self-awareness on the part of the artists who were to represent a national culture. Some of these artists, such as Carlos Schwabe or the illustrator Van Offel, took Memling as their inspiration, as some English artists had taken Botticelli, but he was a less disquieting source and therefore less effective. What Bruges contributed was an atmosphere: 'And above everything, silence, the crystallization of the soul sleeping in some distant age, in peace, the holy silence of the angels, the quiet which allows the inner melody to be heard' (Camille Mauclair).

Nobody has evoked this atmosphere better than de Feure in his illustrations for *Petit Nocturne de Bruges* when it appeared in *L'Image*:

Ah! il fait vraiment triste et d'un tel recul nostalgique,
C'est bien là qu'il faut aller quand on a le cœur veuf de tout.
Les mantes chantent ténèbres, les mantes sont des orgues aux tuyaux de plis.

Ah, it is really very sad and so full of nostalgia,
It is the place to go when one's heart is grieving for everything.
The cloaks sing darkness, the cloaks are organs with folds as pipes.

The author of these verses, Georges Rodenbach, is one of the most important and endearing figures in the history of Symbolism. He made Bruges a spiritual capital. 'He had very little interest in life, and was full of crepuscular dreams, religious images, sickness, and suffering; but he hid these deep-seated wounds beneath an elegant exterior . . . The walls of his soul were so thin that a strange light shone through them that was not of this world' (Camille Mauclair).

Around Bruges, a flat, watery countryside under a grey sky inspired artists such as the architect Van de Velde to paint delightful watercolours in pale, flat hues, and Leon Spilaert (1881–1946) to depict girls on the dunes in a somewhat Japanese style. A colony on the Pre-Raphaelite pattern was founded near Bruges, at Laethem-Saint-Martin, in which the foremost artist was the sculptor Georges Minne (1866–1944). His pencil drawings of poor people and rachitic boys have a sort of Gothic feeling which fits in with the mysticism of Bruges without any suggestion of historical pastiche, for the Bruges of the Symbolists was not an exotic city or even a place of pilgrimage like Florence, but the centre of a real artistic renaissance; and even a mediocre artist like Mellery gives his interiors a hint of the mystery of the place.

One of Khnopff's finest drawings has as its title a line from one of Rodenbach's poems: '*L'eau pâle qui s'en va en chemins de silence*' (The pale water which goes away along paths of silence). It is a picture of a medieval street being gently invaded by the sea. At the end of this 'path of silence' we shall find Ophelia with Maeterlinck's whispering Princesses, soon to become the queens of Symbolism, maidens already crowned by Rossetti in his illustrations to Tennyson's poems. Their hair, moistened by the rain, clings to their delicate shoulders. Mélisande is a cousin of Isolde, as also of the Little Mermaid and Ophelia. All belong to the realm of water; and Maeterlinck's pale heroines with their flowing hair spring naturally to mind when we consider the work of a painter who also belongs to the realm of water, since he was born in Java and lived in Amsterdam: Toorop. He was the most decadent of all the *fin de siècle* painters, so that he inevitably made a profound impression on Lorrain's Monsieur de Phocas:

> A sort of semi-monastic *diablerie* in a landscape inhabited by flowing, undulating, vomitory spectres, like a tidal wave of leeches, with three female figures shrouded in gauze like Spanish Madonnas – the three fiancées: the fiancée of Heaven, the fiancée of Earth, and the fiancée of Hell – and the fiancée of Hell, with her two snakes coiled around her head and holding her veil, has the most attractive face, the deepest eyes, and the most intoxicating smile anyone could imagine . . . There are

77. Federico Faruffini: *The Virgin of the Nile*. Somewhat prior to Symbolism, this picture had a great effect in Italy on account of its macabre eroticism.

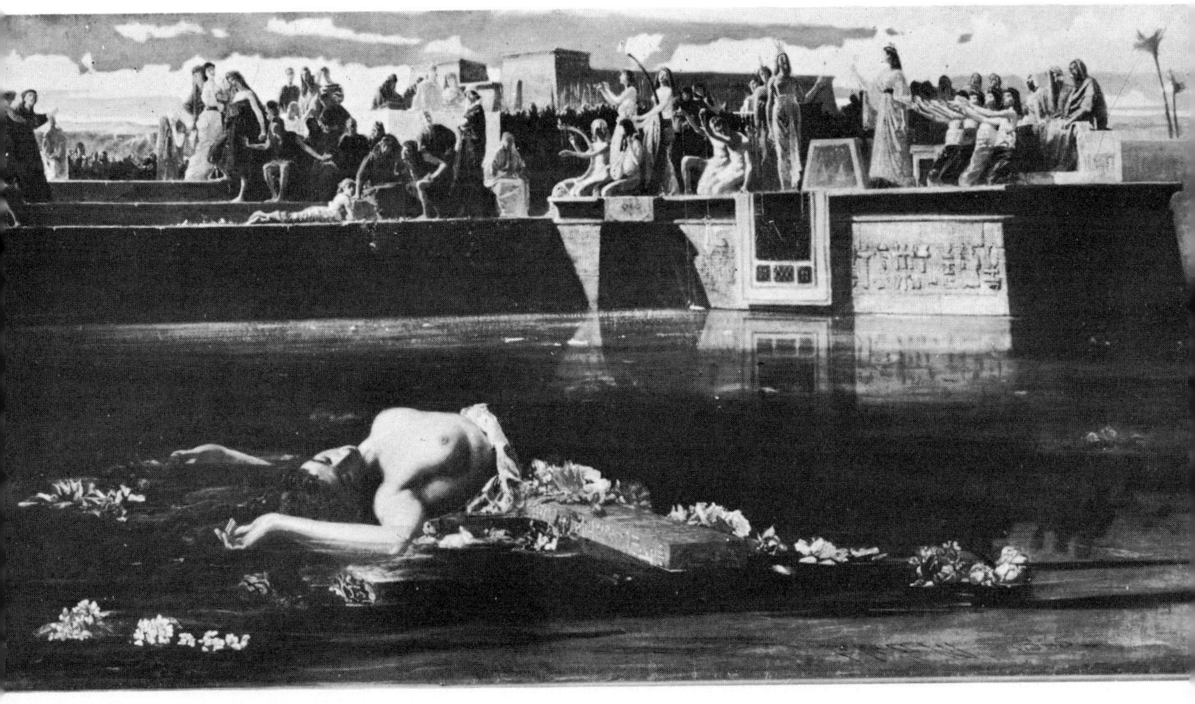

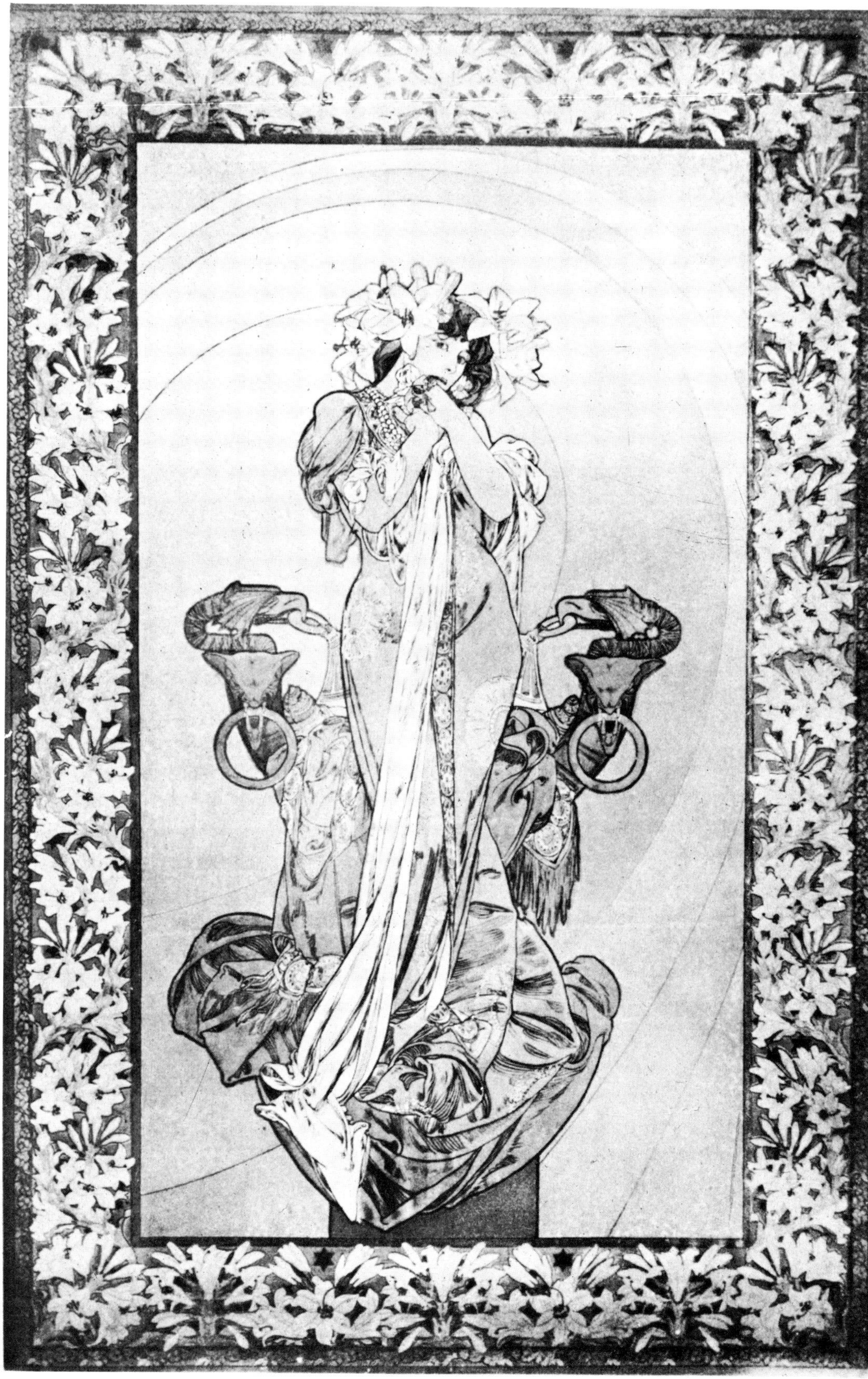

only three painters in the world who can paint eyes like that: Toorop himself, Burne-Jones and the great Khnopff.

Like Khnopff, Toorop studied painting in England and married an Englishwoman; his angels are the elongated, dislocated descendants of William Blake, with an additional element of Balinese art. Later on, this curious individual, very Oriental in appearance, was to become a fervent Catholic and paint some deplorable triptychs. Like most inspired artists whose art is linked to a literary school, his genius found expression only during the brief period in which that style flourished.

Just as Venice was a continuation of Byzantium, Bruges was a projection of the city of Ys, that Sodom of the North, condemned to water instead of the flames. All the Symbolists had heard the sound of its bells. Bruges was also a port of call on the way to that distant island of Thule from which the Viking ships had come, decorated with those interlaced designs dear to Munch and the sculptor Willumsen. The poets dreamed of it (53): Alphonse Retté sang of 'purple kisses' and 'moonlight spreading shrouds upon the ground' in his *Thulé des Brumes*. Later would come Renée Vivien's *Les Fjords* (1902) for which Lévy-Dhurmer was to design a cover in icy hues. Two mad artists who had both worked in Paris were the most representative figures in Scandinavian art: Fredrik Hill (1849–1911), whose drawings were between Symbolism and that 'crude art' which was to be so admired fifty years later, and Josefson (1851–1906), whose *Vision of the Virgin* was an exercise in folklore Symbolism. But the greatest influence was that of Strindberg, who also painted grey clouds and bleak landscapes.

For the English, Ireland was Thule, with its 'Celtic twilight' shrouding everything in green and purple shadows in which the fairies of Yeats's poems hid themselves. This was a twilight which spread over the Brittany of Pont-Aven, a rustic resting-place on a sublime route, but one where the most interesting painters made a halt – apart from Gauguin, these were Filiger, Sérusier, Émile Bernard, Séguin, and Maurice Denis. And between these spiritual capitals stretched the Symbolist forest, the forest of Dodon and Broceliande, the sacred wood of Puvis de Chavannes, the clearings of Maurice Denis and Séon, and the Black Forest inhabited by Wagnerian monsters.

The reader will have noticed that this route avoided the beaten tracks of the Romantics. Spain, Naples and the banks of the Rhine held no attraction for the artists of the *fin de siècle*: those places were too exuberant, too picturesque. The 'souls' preferred an 'atmosphere': the Romantic journey was an adventure, the Symbolist journey the first stage of a dream.

78. Alphonse Mucha: Decorative panel for *La Princesse Lointaine*, interpreted for the theatre by Sarah Bernhardt.

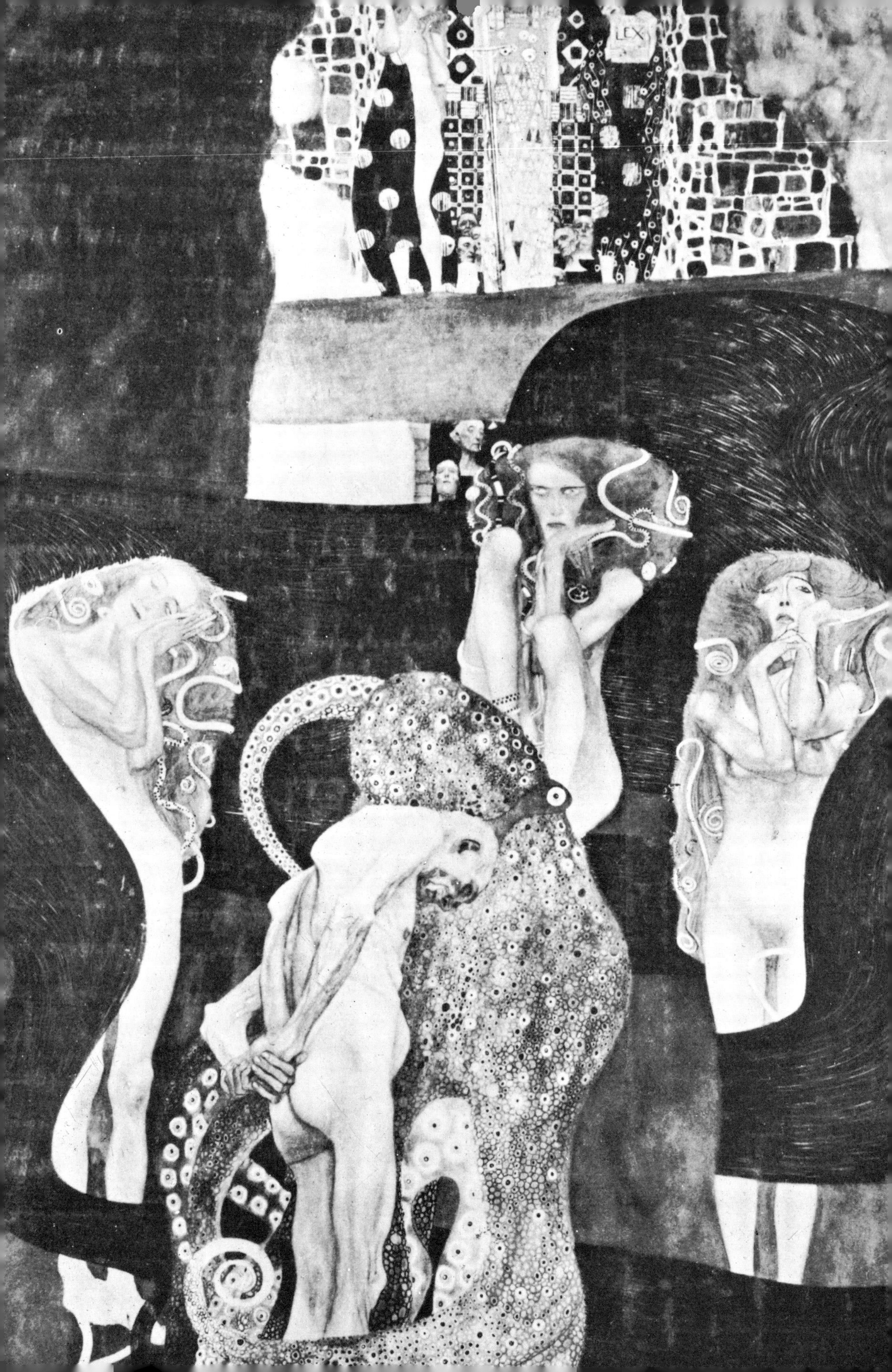
LEX

9 Byzantium

THE BYZANTINE EMPIRE

Je suis l'Empire à la fin de la décadence
Qui regarde passer les grands Barbares blancs
En composant des acrostiches indolents
D'un style d'or où la langueur du soleil danse.
I am the Empire at the end of the Decadence
Watching the tall white Barbarians go by
While composing indolent acrostics
In a golden style in which the languid sunshine dances.

In a commentary on these lines by Verlaine, Professor Praz writes:

> The period of antiquity with which the artists of the *fin de siècle* liked best to compare their own was the long Byzantine twilight, that gloomy apse gleaming with dull gold and gory purple, from which peer enigmatic faces, barbaric yet refined, with dilated neurasthenic pupils . . . The writers of the first part of the nineteenth century, filled with nostalgia, had evoked the Imperial orgies of the Orient and of Rome, dominated by some monstrous superhuman figure such as Sardanapalus, Semiramis, Cleopatra, Nero, and Heliogabalus; but on the threshold of the present century even this virile personal element seemed to disappear. The Byzantine period was a period of anonymous corruption, with nothing of the heroic about it; only there stand out against the monotonous background figures such as Theodora or Irene, who are static personifications of the female lust for power.

Heliogabalus, however, retained considerable prestige. Thus Stefan George devoted his most famous poem to that Emperor who stifled his guests under roses, a figure dear to the Decadents, whom d'Annunzio would also treat in later years (40). Perhaps that imperial dandy recalled Ludwig II of Bavaria, who is likewise said to have turned his languid gaze on a dying favourite. As

79. Klimt: *Jurisprudence*. This panel, which decorated a hall in the University of Vienna, was destroyed in 1945 by the S.S. as a scandalous symbol of decadence. The upper part of this extraordinary work is obviously based on the mosaics of Ravenna, but the naked figures draped in their hair are reminiscent of Celtic fairies. The octopus symbolizing evil is unique in European art.

for George's rich prosody, it makes one think of those mosaic cloaks in which Klimt was to drape his figures a few years later (17). Alfred Jarry's astonishing Messalina, who ends up by impaling herself on a sword, is closely related to this Heliogabalus.

The *fin de siècle*, which Wilhelm II tried to alarm with the spectre of the Yellow Peril, was obsessed with the decline of its own civilization. As Cioran writes in *Précis de décomposition*, 'the dazzling corruption of every historical autumn is darkened by the proximity of the Scythe . . . The connoisseur of sunsets contemplates the failure of every refinement and the impudent advance of vitality.' The word 'darkened' is not quite accurate, when one considers the splendid spasms which convulsed the Empire as it waited for the Barbarians, enjoying its last pleasures and impatient for the end. Jean Lorrain's very Byzantine hero, Prince Norontsoff, calls for 'all the hordes of the yellow races to kill, pillage, rob, and massacre the people of Nice, including himself and his mother'(4). Albert Aurier, the Symbolist critic, likewise foresaw a period of massacres. The poetry of these inspired *fin de siècle* writers is full

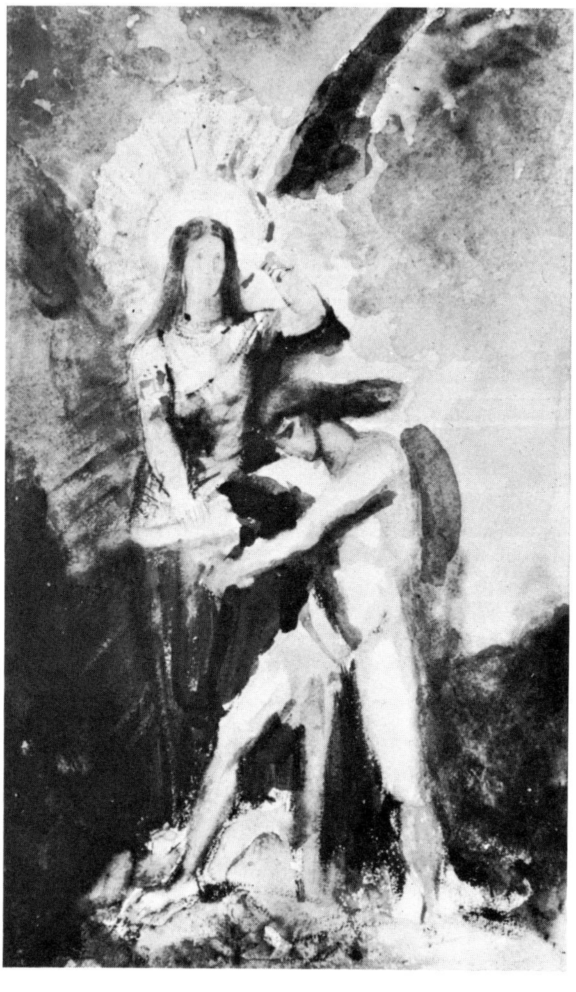

80. Moreau: *Jacob et l'Ange*. The angel's halo, dress and erect posture are completely Byzantine.

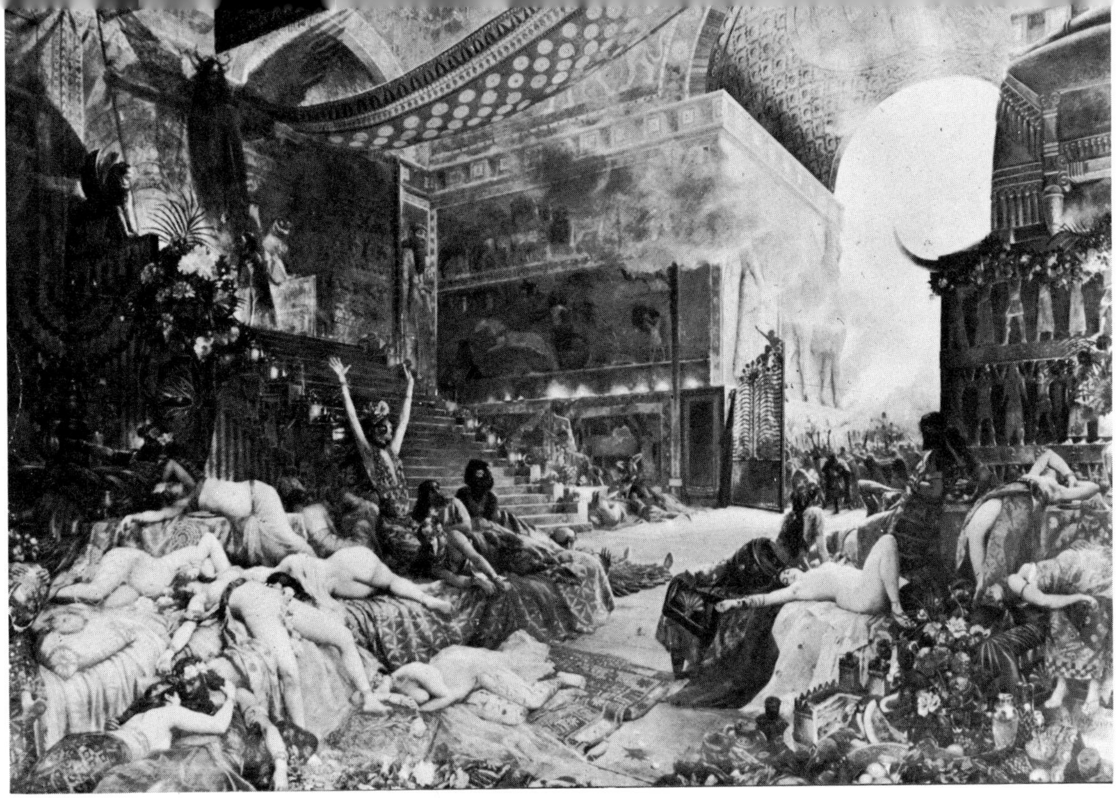

81. Rochegrosse: *Les derniers Jours de Babylone*. In this picture of the horrors of Babylon we can see the influence of Flaubert's *Salammbô* on a Decadent painter. The bourgeois of the *fin de siècle* saw this picture as a warning. Sarah Bernhardt acted her plays in a similar setting.

of premonitions: Milosz, before he died, had a detailed presentiment of the catastrophe of 1939. Several Decadents were to treat this theme, and none better than Kavafy, who shows us the disappointment of the Senators when the Barbarians' arrival is delayed, and the frenzied desire for destruction after frantic excesses which has led to comparison between Byzantium and Sodom.

Babylon, which had the Oriental splendour of the former and the misfortune of the latter, was also taken as a subject by many *fin de siècle* artists, but never treated more extravagantly than in Rochegrosse's great picture, *Les Derniers Jours de Babylone*, which according to Aurier was the main attraction of the 1891 Salon. Salammbôs and Salomes, swooning among the flowers in front of the idols, are about to fall prey to the Barbarians who can be seen already forcing the gates at the far end of the basilica. A moment from now, a civilization is going to collapse, and one woman is kneeling on the cushions, howling with terror or impatience. In its composition this picture is directly inspired by Delacroix's *Sardanapalus* – at the same 1891 Salon, incidentally, Chalom exhibited another *Sardanapalus* – but the theme is that of Thomas Couture's famous picture, *Les Romains de la Décadence*, painted fifty years earlier: the Decadence under Louis-Philippe, however, strikes us now as tame and philosophical compared with the Decadence under President Carnot.

The death-agony of Byzantium has one attraction which that of Babylon lacks – religion; for the Church offers a writer a sumptuous, often sacrilegious setting, and all the riches of the liturgical vocabulary. The most extravagant Byzantium of the *fin de siècle* is the one imagined by Jean Lombard, the Marseilles autodidact – who also created a Heliogabalus in *L'Agonie* – while Paul Adam's *Irène et les Eunuques* is a delirious pastiche of Flaubert. These interior decorators of the novel had a certain kinship with the theatrical designers who gaily imitated marble and onyx for Sardou's plays, and the wildest excesses were possible in the settings they created. Thus Rémy de Gourmont, in *L'Histoire Tragique de la Princesse Phénissa* (6), goes so far as to have the prince disembowel his pregnant wife, who exclaims: 'Oh, Phebor, glory and love be yours! You have delivered the world from the tyranny of hope!' This particular Byzantium surpasses even Péladan's tragedy *Babylone* in madness.

The prince of these writer-decorators was to be d'Annunzio, who set his play *La Nave* in a Byzantine Venice, with settings which inspired the architects of the Milan railway station. And *La Commenna*, the heroine of another d'Annunzio play, is descended from a line of emperors: 'Centuries of pomp, perfidy and pillage have nourished the blood which flows through your veins: the blood of traitors and usurpers. Everything you touch becomes a wound which can never heal. You feed your soul on the dreams of bygone crimes.' These sins, richly set in d'Annunzio's prose, are like the jewels with which Prince Norontsoff covers the young Pole he desires in Jean Lorrain's *Coins de Byzance* (17). All these follies had the same enormous success as Rochegrosse's picture. It was through Byzantium that the Decadent taste was imposed on the general public, thanks to writers and painters of the second rank who flattered that public's secret passion for pillage and sacrilege.

SPLENDOURS. Jean Lorrain's and d'Annunzio's heroes still manage to sparkle a little under the ashes of oblivion, like the gold and jewelled peacocks under the dust of Ravenna. For the Symbolists the peacock represents soulless splendour, while the swan expresses deathless aspirations in its final song. The nordic swan is a bird of the water, while the peacock hails from the Indies and represents the sun; it resembles the bird which accompanies the Queen of Sheba in *La Tentation de Saint Antoine*. There are some peacocks in Verlaine (36), but they are particularly Byzantine in this poem by Gilkin:

Et des paons merveilleux d'azur et d'émeraude,
Des fouras bleu de perle et de rouges ibis
Errent silencieux sur la terrasse chaude
Parmi les vases d'or tout meurtris de rubis.

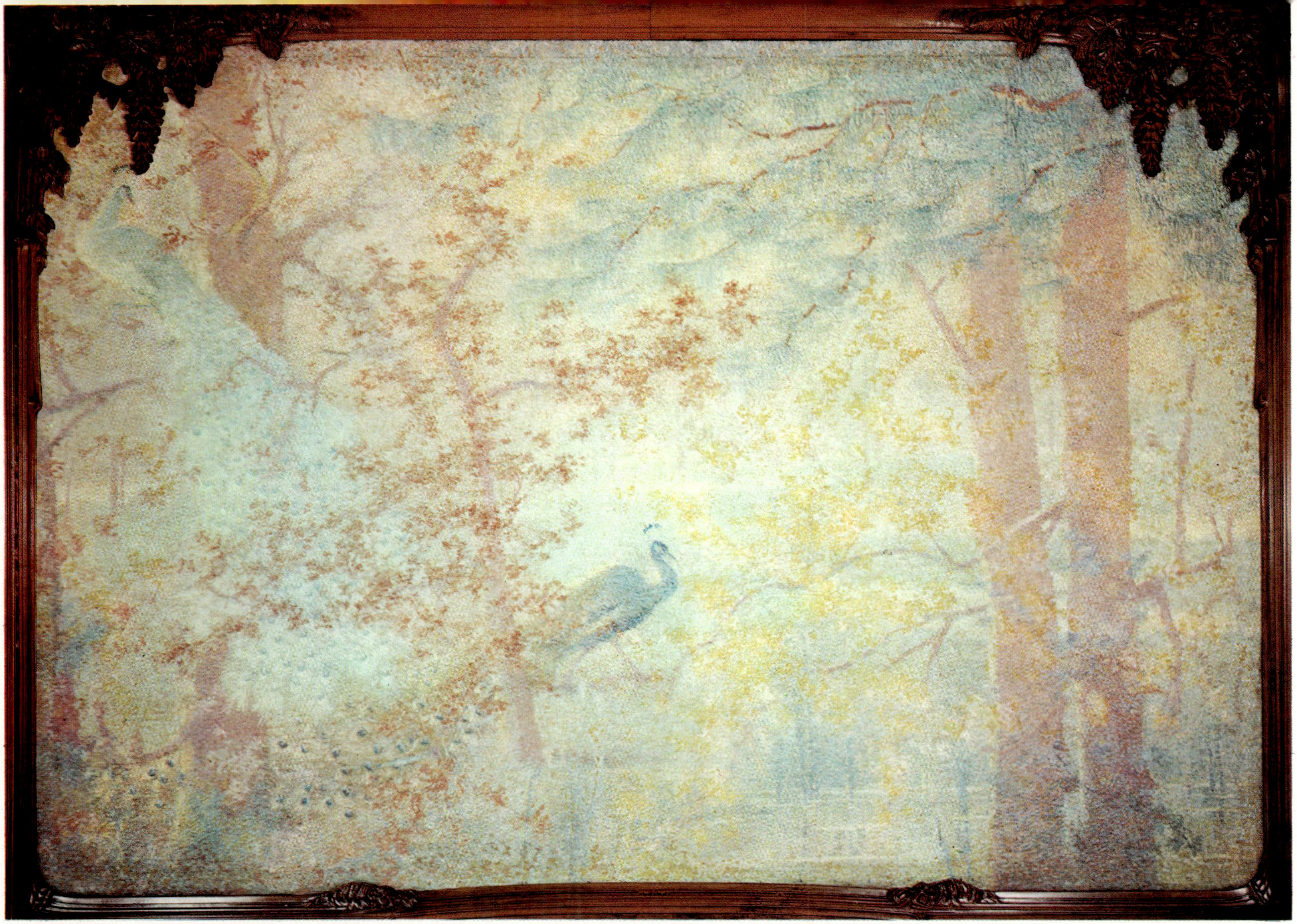

82. Lévy-Dhurmer: *Marsh Birds in Landscapes*. A section from a dining-room the wooden panels of which were designed by Majorelle. Painted by one of the most 'colourist' of the French Symbolists, the picture provides an echo of Whistler's Peacock Room set in a Wagnerian forest.

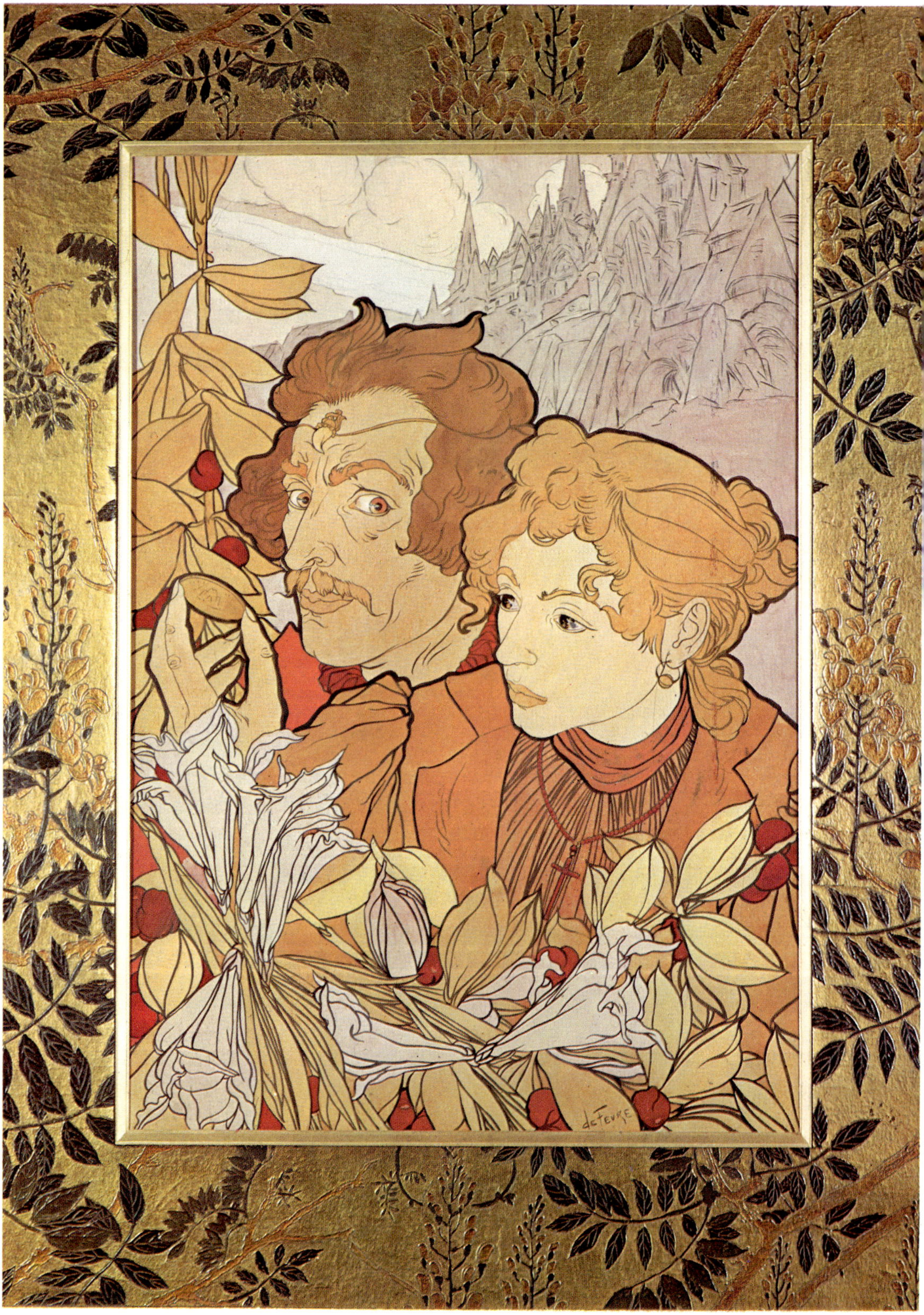

83. De Feure: *Les Fleurs du Mal.* Baudelairean characters visualized by the most elegant of the Decadents. The frame, in embossed and gilded leather, is also by the artist.

And marvellous blue and emerald peacocks,
Pearl-blue fouras and red ibises
Wander silently about the warm terrace
Among the golden vases spotted with rubies.

A whole collection of Montesquiou's poems is devoted to the peacock. Bresdin's peacocks perch clumsily on dead branches; Beardsley dresses Salome in ocellated robes, though perhaps only in memory of Whistler's Peacock Room; and Madeleine Lemaire installs a peacock on the back of a chair, behind a character in *Les Plaisirs et les Jours.* All these peacocks recall the splendours of the imperial religion, with its processions of dignitaries laden with gold and mysterious titles.

On mourait au fond des basiliques amples . . .
Les prodomes et les hypostases meurent au pied du roc crenelé . . .
People died at the back of vast basilicas . . .
Prodomes and hypostases die at the foot of the jagged rock . . .

These lines from Gustave Kahn's *Les Palais Nomades* stress the fact that Byzantium had the multiple attraction of death, lechery, and faith. Dominating all these splendours was the sombre figure of the Pantocrator, with his ascetic face and black cloak, against a background of golden mosaics. The *fin de siècle* Christ was an Oriental, almost a fakir, what Flaubert would have called a gymnosophist; in contrast with the spirituality of the body, the halo borrowed its brilliance and its shape from the peacock's tail. In the works of certain artists such as Odilon Redon, faithful in this respect to the spirit of Schuré's *Grands Initiés*, the iconography of Christ was almost indistinguishable from that of Buddha. The Virgin was often dressed in the black cloak of the Byzantine Madonnas, and even Bouguereau followed this fashion to the extent of installing his famous *Vierge de consolation* on the marble throne of the exarchs. After 1880, the City of God took on a decidedly Byzantine appearance: witness the neo-Byzantine basilica of Sacré-Cœur in Paris.

Moreau, alas, failed to depict a single Byzantine scene, but the mosaic-encrusted buildings in his paintings, the mages dressed like archimandrites, the stylized flowers and the whole Greco-Oriental décor are worthy of Byzantium. Moreau is likewise very close to Byzantium when he freezes his figures in hieratical postures. Here he is following the principle of the 'Beauty of Inertia', according to Professor Praz, who quotes these lines by Moreau himself: 'All these figures seem frozen in a sleepwalker's gesture; they are unaware of the movement they are executing, sunk in reverie to the extent of appearing to be carried away towards other worlds.'

The critic rightly comments on the contrast with Delacroix's dynamism, a contrast which is all the more striking when the two artists treat the same subject: the fight between Jacob and the Angel. Moreau's angel, motionless, his eyes fixed in a stare, his head encircled by a blazing halo, is completely Oriental, but the young wrestlers under the oak in the Saint-Sulpice fresco are pure Renaissance.

In the course of a long stay in Venice, where he copied Carpaccio and the mosaics in St. Mark's, Moreau worked out artistic principles and a pictorial mystique which he was to expound, many years later, to Ary Renan (73). But the sombre, implacable Pantocrator of the basilicas was too far removed from Moreau's vague deism for him to do more than evoke Byzantium in anything but a few watercolours depicting an allegorical Venice. Writers who needed to renew their inspiration went to the Salon to see Jean-Paul Laurens's *Théodora Insultée par Saint Jean Chrysostome*, or Benjamin Constant's *Justinien*, seated on a blue marble throne. Very few knew Filiger's mosaicized watercolours, reminiscent of the *mandaba*, or artistic meditations, recommended by the Hindus. Jung entered a certain number into a notebook in which he also sketched his visions in a Byzantine style. Filiger had a fate similar to that of his senior Simeon Solomon, who had also been influenced by the splendours of Byzantium, somewhat confused, incidentally, with the mysteries of Judaism. Like Solomon, Filiger was forced to disappear from the public eye, after a homosexual scandal.

THE SLAVS. It was not subtle, refined artists who popularized Byzantium, but Sarah Bernhardt in her various roles – Theodora, Gismonda, and the *Princesse Lointaine*. It was all these bejewelled, bedizened Sarahs who made people dream of that empire which historians such as Diehl and Schlumberger were busy reconstructing. And Jean Lorrain became Theodora's poet.

To spread the picture of Theodora across the walls of Paris, Sarah had discovered, in 1894, a young painter, a subject of the Austrian Emperor but a native of Moravia, in other words a true Slav. Thirty years old, with long hair and a bushy beard, and dressed like a character in Murger's *Vie de Bohème*, Mucha had undergone the influence of Makart in Munich and Jean-Paul Laurens in Paris. This helped him to recreate the glittering, intoxicating atmosphere of the spiritual home of the Slavs, the city of Constantine. Thus Sarah the Empress, or even Sarah the *Dame aux Camélias*, was depicted in a 'hieratic posture', against a background of mosaics, her head encircled by peacock-feather haloes. Stylized motifs around Mucha's posters recalled Ravenna and also the inter-

84. Filiger: *Notation chromatique.* The picture owes as much to stained-glass windows as to the Byzantine mosaics of Ravenna. It is most carefully composed according to the laws of the Golden Mean.

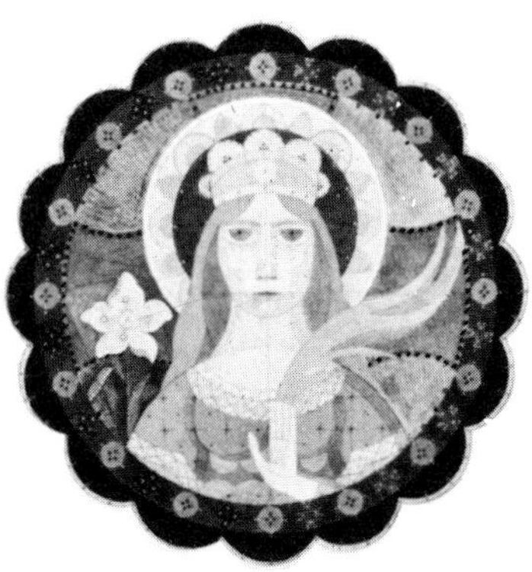

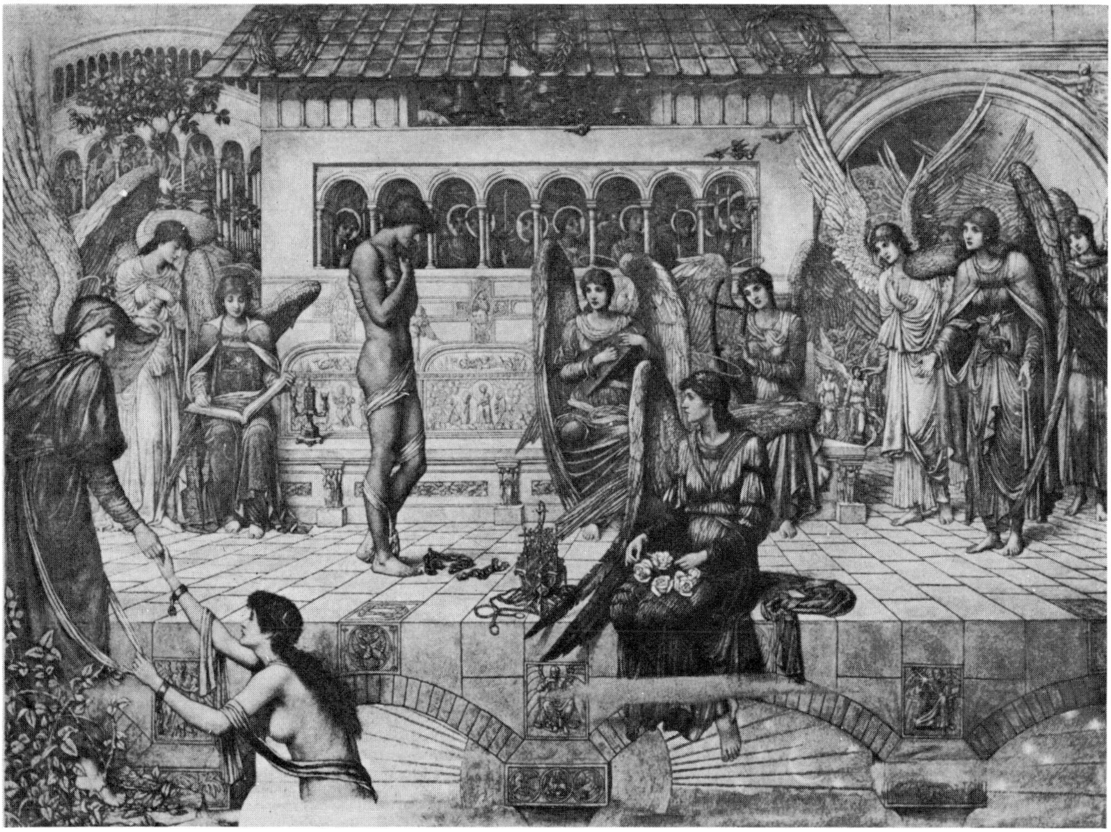

85. John Strudwick: *The Ramparts of God's House*. This imitator of Burne-Jones drew the inspiration for his Victorian Paradise from the Romanesque style, but encumbered his 'souls' with somewhat clumsy wings.

laced designs on the Barbarians' boats. Under wreaths in which flowers mingle with jewels, the actress's face has the haunted look of one who has seen the beauties of another world.

Mucha was in fact a convinced spiritualist. His mystical beliefs led him to illustrate a Paternoster with a curious picture of beautiful Viennese women between rose-windows and chrismas. Like many others, Mucha had greatly admired Makart's three Flemish nudes in his famous *Charles the Fifth's Entry into Antwerp,* and this taste for the nude often led Mucha away from Byzantium. He delighted in drawing full-bodied women whose hair mingled with the lilies in the background mosaics; but, oddly enough, these appetizing creatures have something lugubrious about them, for Mucha had all the melancholy of the true Slav. Ivanhoe Rambosson, the art critic on *La Plume*, admired his picture *Angoisse* at the 1898 Salon des Indépendants, describing it as 'a stampede of fantastic figures with terrified faces'. The colours of the posters are dimmed by the mists of the Beyond. On the other hand, in certain buildings in Prague where there has been no stinginess in the use of gold, Mucha's art strikes one as truly Byzantine.

Klimt too was inspired by Jewesses in his Oriental visions. Madame Meyer-Bloch, for example, in a famous portrait, wears her black hair like Theodora her diadem, and her dress is studded

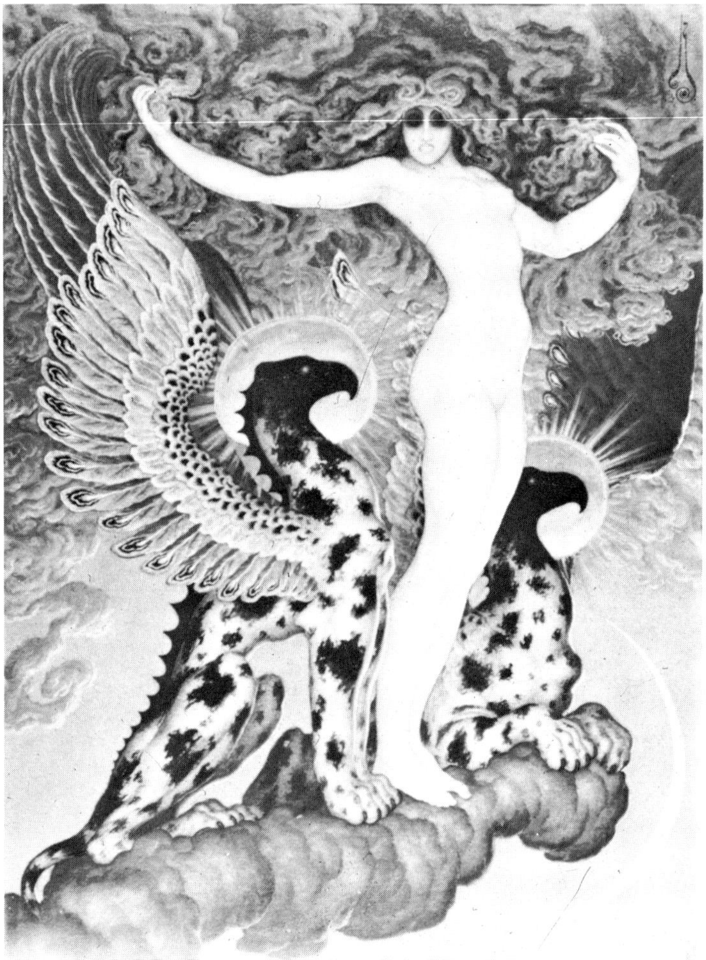

86. Nicholas Kalmakoff: *Chimera.* Done in 1926, this is a late work by a Russian émigré who was still sunk in the depths of Byzantine-inspired Decadence.

with cabochons. Whether he was painting a banker's wife, Salomé or an allegory of Jurisprudence, Klimt remained faithful to this type of woman, with rings under her eyes, quivering nostrils, and a sensual little mouth. The highly cultured Jews of Vienna dominated the capital's intellectual life, and Klimt unconsciously depicted the members of this society as courtiers of a Basileus. He was the first of the chimerical painters to regain his popularity with the public in recent years, because he was the strangest of them all and hence the most representative of a style. His technique, which at first recalled Makart's rich style, was soon influenced by Besnard's lighting effects and above all by Klinger's eroticism. It was around Klinger's polychrome statue of Beethoven, exhibited in 1902 at the *Sezession* Pavilion, that Klimt painted his murals. They caused a scandal at the time, but very soon became an inspiration to the whole of central Europe. As a very young man, Klimt had covered the staircases of the Kunsthistorisches Museum and the Burgtheater with scenes of antiquity reminiscent of Alma-Tadema, but when the Decadence reached

Vienna, his art developed until he finally created a sort of Byzantine music-hall, in which the strangest attraction was an elegantly speckled octopus embracing a convicted criminal under the worried eyes of Jurisprudence. This was a music-hall entitled *Jurisprudence* whose stars, Salome and Judith, presented to the public in frames of gilded metal, were cousins of Sarah Bernhardt. While he was working in Belgium for Monsieur Stoclet, Klimt, who was very easily influenced, started imitating the decorative compositions of Margaret MacDonald. He was also strongly attracted by the Ballets Russes, and his work came to serve as a link between the triumphant Decadence and the Decorative Art of 1925. It is hard to avoid the impression that his female models, hieratic in the murals and hedonistic in the drawings, were patients of Professor Freud's. Klimt's drawings are clearly superior to his paintings.

The Byzantine influence was often very obvious in interior décors, which clients wanted to be both luxurious and mysterious, and painters used to produce inexpensive imitations of mosaics. One of these painters, who was strongly influenced by Grasset and produced some extremely delicate panels, was the Swiss artist Augusto Giacometti (1877–1947), the father of the sculptor. The Venetian Vittorio Zecchin (1878–1947) was influenced by Klimt and the mosaics in St. Mark's, and his Salome, like his harpists, shows how close Byzantium was to the Ballets Russes.

The Russian painters, who always remained rather academic and realistic, were Byzantine in their choice of subjects. Their own

87. Carl Strahtmann: *Dante on his Deathbed.* This German painter evoked the atmosphere of Byzantium by the rigidity of his subjects and the mosaic pattern of his backgrounds.

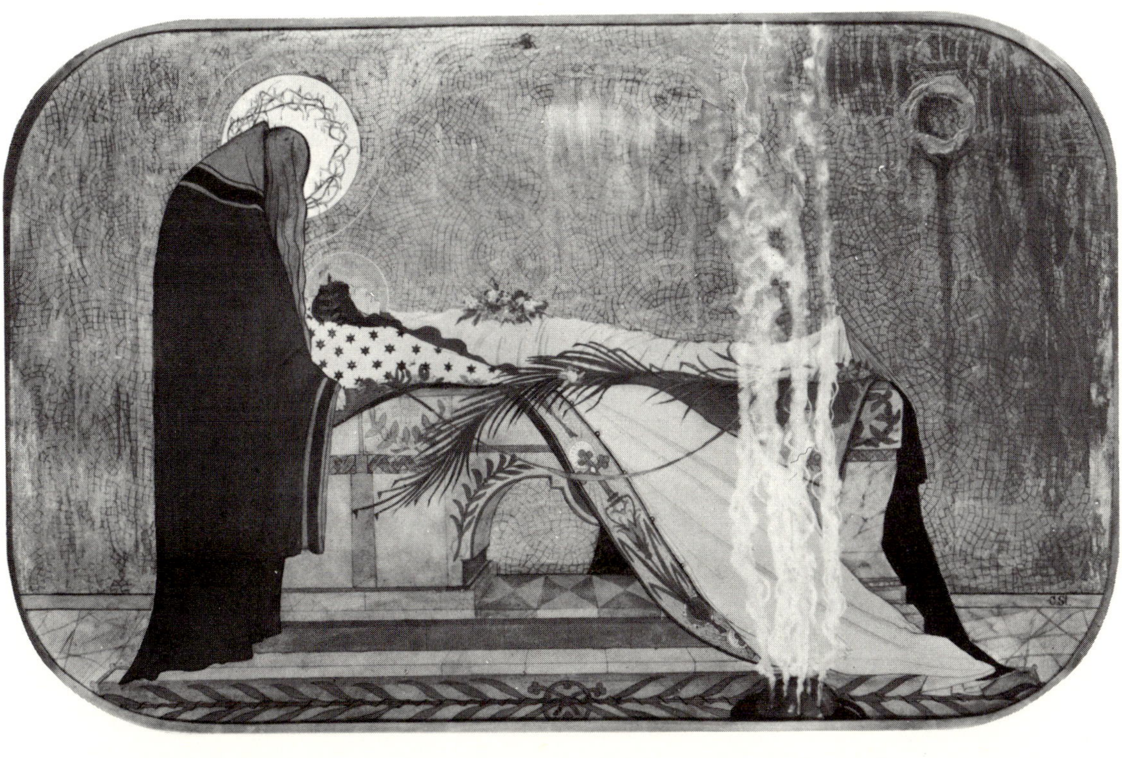

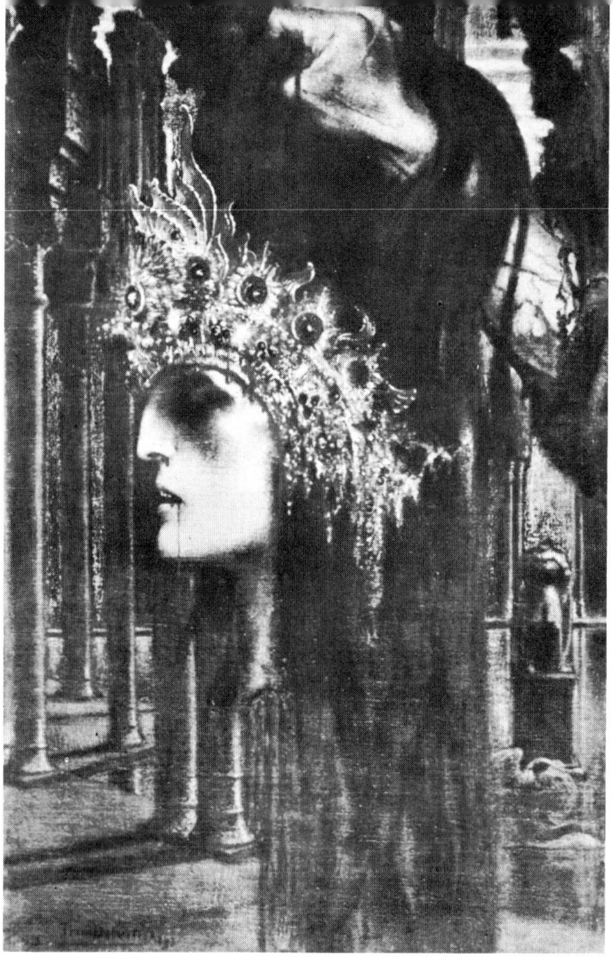

88. Delville: *La Fin d'un Règne.* The decapitated *basilissa* against a background of Oriental ruins recalls Moreau's *Salomé.*

history, savagely prolonging that of the Greek Empire, provided plenty of episodes full of incense, blood, furs, jewels scattered in the snow, naked women whipped by Cossacks, and coronations degenerating into massacres. Repin and Sukirov depicted incidents which foreshadowed that very Byzantine drama, the murder of Rasputin. In their works it is the atmosphere which is decadent, not the style. In the Russian museums one can also find huge pictures full of infinite sadness, showing purple clouds over the steppes, with sometimes a lone rider returning home, bent under the weight of a curse, and sometimes nothing but a few cranes and crows. Verechtchaguin's pictures impressed Tolstoy, and even the critical Félix Fénéon praised what he called these 'imperishable works'. Tolstoy's fundamentally Victorian ideas on art (104) still inspire the painters of Soviet Russia, and consequently Repin and Verechtchaguin have never known the decline in popularity suffered by such as Rochegrosse. Their pictures were sometimes sent abroad: Jules Laforgue saw a *Massacre* by Verechtchaguin exhibited in Berlin with an organ accompaniment, and was touched by this attempt to combine the arts. Munkacsy, a Hungarian painter well known in Paris, and close to these Russians in his choice of subjects and the size of his canvases, tried to inspire visitors in much the same way, by installing a pianist playing Liszt in front of his immense *Crucifixion*.

But these painters are taking us away from our subject: belated disciples of Delacroix, they interest us really only in that they prepared the general public, from 1870 onwards, to understand certain experiments carried out by the painters of the imagination. Two Russian writers encouraged an apocalyptic mysticism in works on the Devil: Soloviev, who recorded a great many visions, half-erotic and half-religious, and Merejkovsky, whose books on Julian the Apostate and Leonardo da Vinci were read all over Europe. These two writers asserted that the sacred mission of Russian art was to express ideas. As for Leontiev, he was the great aesthete of Byzantium and ended on Mount Athos. Much later, an *émigré* called Kalmakoff was to paint angels and Byzantine princesses, but in a style more suggestive of the Casino de Paris than of Santa Sophia.

Europe would have to wait for the Ballets Russes, with their golden draperies, processions, and incense-burners, to obtain, by way of Russia, some idea of the splendours of Byzantium. Bakst reconstructed the later Empire only for d'Annunzio's *Saint Sebastian*, in which Ida Rubinstein triumphed, looking sad and ambiguous, like one of Moreau's models.

Under the rule of monarchs who were Byzantine in several respects, such as King Ferdinand of Bulgaria and Queen Marie of Rumania (both of whom dreamed of being crowned in Santa Sophia), the Balkans witnessed the flowering of a neo-Byzantine style, of which the chief examples were Sofia Cathedral, decorated by Czech disciples of Mucha's, notably Mrkvicka, and Sinaia Palace (in Rumania), where the beautiful queen imagined herself to be the *princesse lointaine*.

Sargent too was influenced by Byzantium in his Boston murals depicting Christianity, but the most interesting example of Byzantium in America is to be found in Blashfield's decoration of St. Matthew's Church in Washington. However, the Byzantine influence was comparatively weak in the Protestant countries, and it left very little mark on English or American painting, except for a few stiff angels in the works of some late Pre-Raphaelites. It can be discerned very clearly, however, in the architecture of the Catholic Cathedral of Westminster, and also in a play by Wilde's women friends 'Michael Field', as well as in some of Yeats's poems. In Germany, Wagnerian mysticism brought the public back to the semi-Oriental splendour of the Hohenstaufen Empire and the Palermo mosaics; traces of the Byzantine influence can sometimes be seen in the great buildings of Kaiser Wilhelm's reign, for the new German Empire claimed to be the heir to Charlemagne.

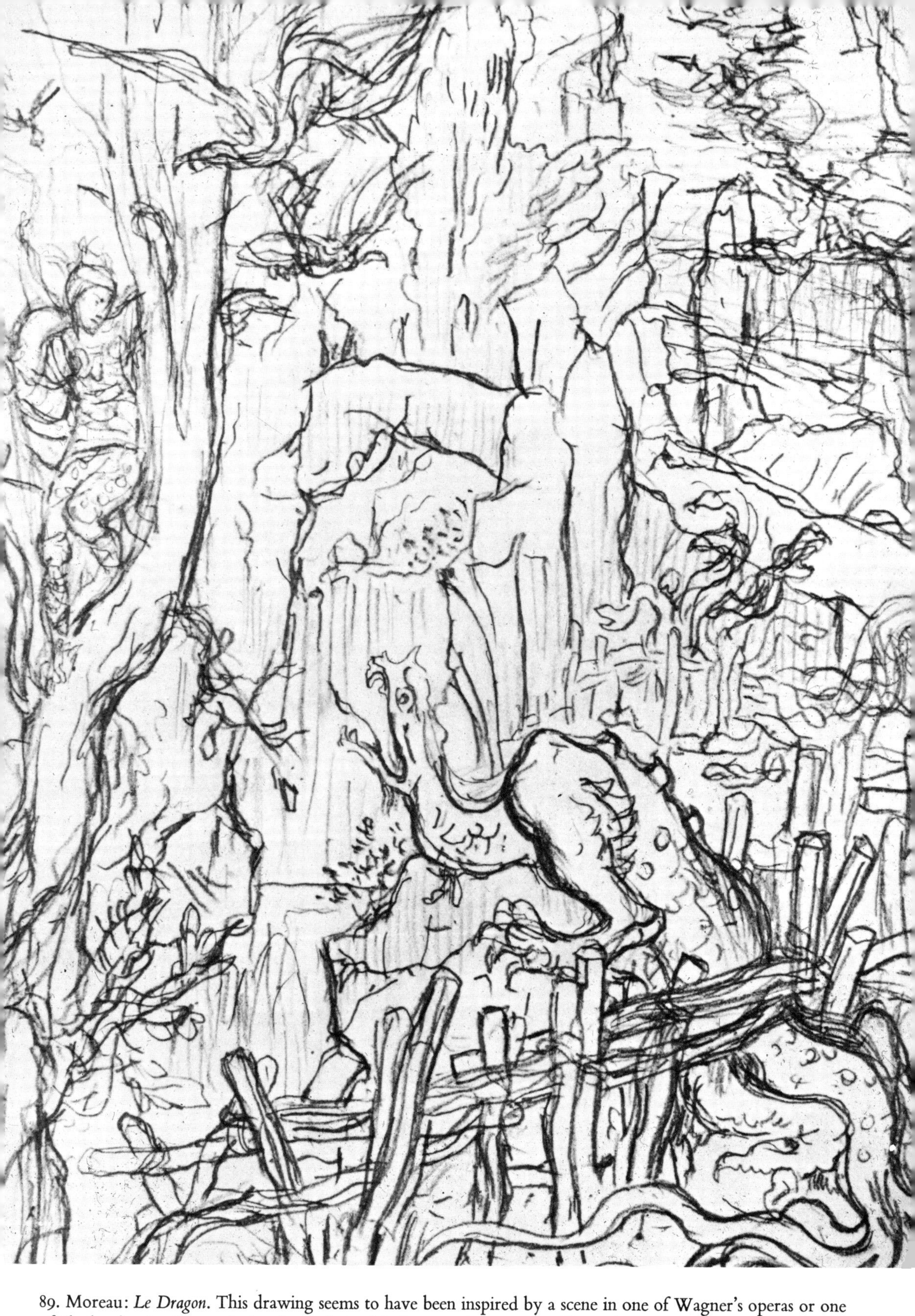

89. Moreau: *Le Dragon*. This drawing seems to have been inspired by a scene in one of Wagner's operas or one of Flaubert's tales. It reveals the close relationship between Moreau, Böcklin and Gustave Doré.

10 Decadent Mythology

THE DEAD GODS. The large numbers of fairies to be found in the art of the *fin de siècle* was only one sign of a widespread return to primitive gods: chiefly to the gods of Germany, thanks to Wagner, but also to those of classical antiquity, which Schliemann's discoveries had made it possible to endow with a less academic and more archaic and bizarre appearance than before.

The painter of these rediscovered gods was Böcklin (1827–1901) – a very great painter, who may be compared in some respects to Courbet, but whose taste and colours are often repellent. Thus his scarlet-faced tritons sometimes look as if they were wallowing in an ocean of beer, and his bacchantes come straight out of the Munich carnival. Similarly his bright blue skies and his combinations of red and green, which are traditional in German art, shock art-lovers of other countries for they are accustomed to seeing these subjects painted in more sober colours. Unfortunately the sirens of classicism kept Böcklin under Mediterranean skies. He lived in Florence, imitated the Venetians (especially Titian), and painted his finest pictures in Corfu. Wagner rightly regretted that he never devoted himself to the Nordic myths, or more precisely to the illustration of Wagner's own works.

Böcklin has several features in common with Moreau. Like him, he wanted to be master of the new Renaissance, and turned his back on his times, remaining at once academic and *avant-garde*. His influence on the writers of his period was enormous. Thus Hugo von Hofmannsthal, the poet of 'the tragic sense of life', wrote a *Funeral Hymn* for the anniversary of his death which was recited by a Florentine page dressed in black – a hymn expressing 'the pantheism of him who had given life to Nature'. Finally, like Moreau, Böcklin restored a dramatic meaning to the most hackneyed episodes in mythology. But there the similarities end. There is nothing ambiguous or precious about Böcklin, and his vitality prevents him from being classed with the Decadents, even though they imitated him. He has always been immensely popular in Germany, and his *Island of the Dead* has been reproduced so often

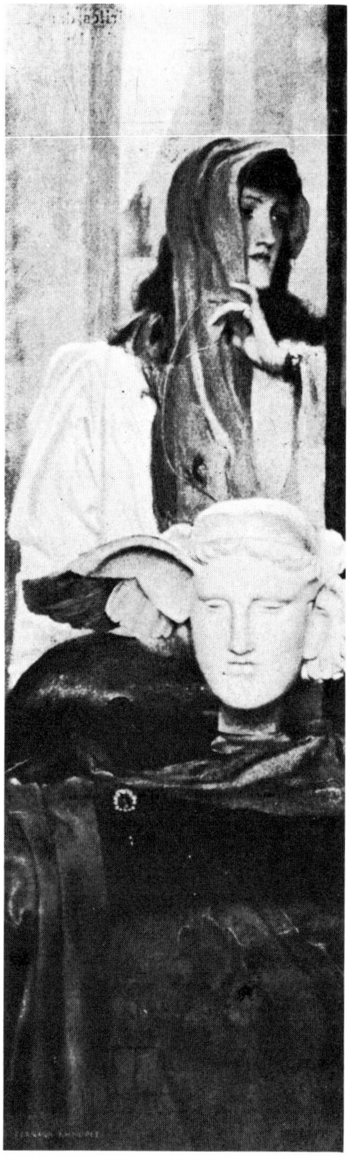

90. Khnopff: *A Blue Wing*. Casts such as this occupy an important place in the work of this Belgian painter.

that the German public has become immune to its aesthetic qualities. But it has lost none of its power to move the rest of us, and in that picture and other Böcklin evocations of a Nature ravaged by the wrath of the gods, we can see how dramatic his landscapes can be. In front of those palaces washed by a leaden sea, in those mountain passes guarded by dragons, and in the depths of those forests inhabited either by the satyrs of Greece or by the Unicorn of the Middle Ages, we are conscious of the approach of a terrible storm, an earthquake, or a plague.

The most important element in Böcklin's work which links him with Symbolism, in spite of academic draughtsmanship and a realistic style, is the constant presence of water – water which carries Ophelia, La Motte-Fouquet's Undine, Hans Andersen's Little Mermaid and Tennyson's Lady of Shalott to the depths where a destiny of cold innocence awaits them; water which is a symbol of oblivion rather than destruction, a mirror on its surface and a kingdom of death in its depths. It is water which distinguishes Moreau, the painter of fire which he expresses with golds and precious stones, from Böcklin, the painter of the Styx. The dead in Moreau's works end up on funeral pyres and, at best, are turned into phoenixes, while Böcklin's dead sink to the depths beneath Tristan's boat and guard the treasure of the gods.

But Böcklin's heroines like those of Moreau, however gauche they may appear, have an expression of curious melancholy which one might call Baudelairean if it had not appeared before Baudelaire's day in the paintings of Anselm Feuerbach, who was similarly obsessed by Medeas and Phaedras. Böcklin can also be compared to his friend Hans von Marées, who found his gods on the beach at Capri; this sort of homosexual Puvis de Chavannes had a considerable influence on literature. Neither von Marées nor Puvis can, however, lead us, as Böcklin does, into a world at once fantastic and accessible, a Black Forest which ends in a Scylla or Charybdis. In his landscapes Böcklin is close to Nietzsche – even closer than Wagner – and, like Nietzsche, fascinated by the Mediterranean.

Böcklin invented what the Germans call *Sinnbildcharakter*, in other words a realistic setting which evokes an irrational content. One of his disciples, Eugen Bracht, obtains a Symbolist effect by this means in his painting *Lieu d'oubli*, with its snow-covered peaks barely touched by a ray of pink sunlight. In Holman Hunt's work we find the same intensification of reality to the point of surrealism in landscapes in which a miracle is always imminent. That is why in spite of Böcklin's apparent realism, the critic Muther placed him in 1894 'in the great four-leafed clover of modern Idealism', with Moreau, Puvis de Chavannes, and Burne-Jones.

Böcklin was regarded as the Michelangelo of Bismarck's Germany, and had considerable influence on de Chirico, whose architecture is steeped in a tragic atmosphere; he even influenced Dali, who in a way fulfilled Wagner's wishes, by using *The Island of the Dead* in several pictures, and with greater success, in his ballet *Tristan Fou*. But the painter who was most influenced by Böcklin was von Stuck, who converted the old master's Medusas and Sirens into the *Jugendstil*. A visit to his house in Munich is essential for anybody wishing to understand the Neronian character of Wilhelm II's empire.

THE SPHINX. The Sphinx is even more awe-inspiring than the Medusa, for she possesses the faculty of thought. As is well known, Gustave Moreau obtained his first success, in the 1864 Salon, with a painting of the Sphinx; and a poem by Heine which the painter had in his library very probably inspired the monster's feminine cruelty: 'Delicious martyrdom, painful ecstasy, infinite suffering and pleasure; while I was kissing those ravishing lips, the nails of the claws were wounding me cruelly.' Théophile Gautier, another precursor of the Decadence, had called Oedipus the Hamlet of Greece. 'It is the earthy Chimera, as gross as matter and just as attractive, who is represented by this charming head of the winged woman. She is a promise of the Ideal, with the body of a carnivorous beast.' This comment by Moreau sums up all the symbolism of his works. Rossetti too had been tempted by the Sphinx: a

91. Luc Olivier Merson: *Pan et la Chimère*. A Decadent theme treated by an academic artist whose works were often reproduced in French periodicals of the time.

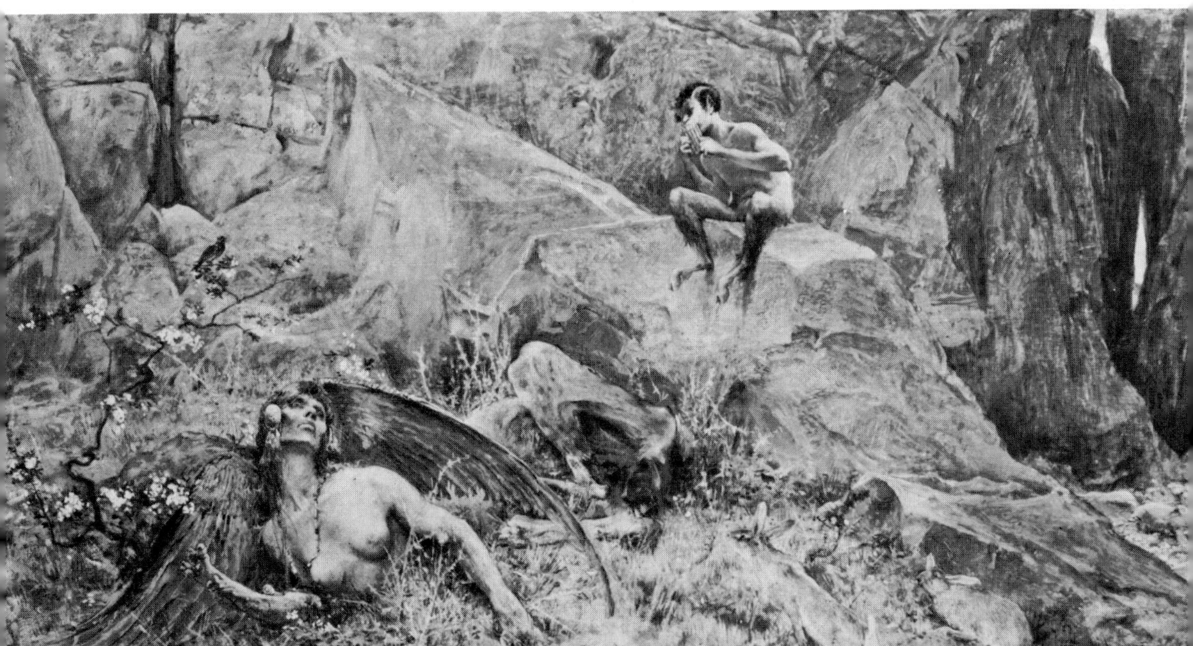

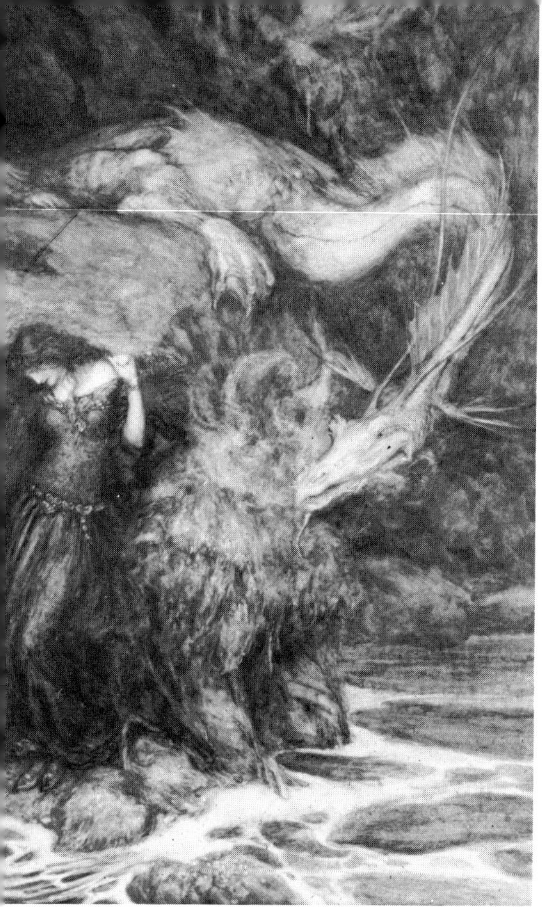

92. Arthur Rackham: *Andromeda*. In his pictures for children's books, this marvellous Wagnerian illustrator brought back to life all the monsters of Northern mythology and all the fairies and spirits of Celtic culture.

detailed but mediocre drawing of his, undoubtedly inspired by Ingres's famous picture, is accompanied by the commonplace dictum: 'The idea is that of a man questioning the unknown.' And then there is Wilde's poem *The Sphinx* which is too long to quote in full here – an extraordinary development of Flaubert's *Tentation*, which contains all the themes of the Decadence and which he took twenty years to write.

One of the strangest of all the Sphinxes is that painted by von Stuck, with the head and torso of a beautiful Jewess with rings under her eyes, lying in front of a bluish Abu Simbel. For many writers and artists of the *fin de siècle*, the Sphinx and the Mona Lisa were one: for ten years nearly every chimera, chosen maiden or *belle dame sans merci* smiled 'a sphinx-like smile'. And the Decadents, presumably in order to have a miniature sphinx within reach, followed Gautier, Baudelaire, and Poe in attributing occult powers to the cat. When he christened his tavern and review *Le Chat noir*, Rodolphe Salis was honouring a mysterious gutter-cat; and on Steinlen's poster a Byzantine halo surrounded the animal's head.

The great painter of the Sphinx-Woman was the Belgian Khnopff (1858–1921). His most famous picture is *L'Art des Caresses*, which shows the Sphinx, a panther with a woman's head, brushing with her paw the naked body of a poet, against the background of a pink landscape (51). Khnopff was born into a rich family in the Ardennes and was one of the few Decadents who managed to be both an artist and an aesthete. Verhaeren saw him as the epitome of artistic distinction: 'Two very sharp little steely eyes, a slightly pointed chin, a disdainful mouth, and a splendid head of wild red hair, falling in curls over the forehead in a sort of barbaric crown. A simple nature, a stiff bearing, correct behaviour. A horror of anything slovenly. A clergyman in the process of becoming a dandy . . .'

Khnopff had spent several years in England, and although the chief object of his admiration was Moreau, whose pupil he had been in 1879, he was even more influenced by the Pre-Raphaelites, especially Watts, whose portraits of haughty, icy ladies delighted him. He himself was infatuated with his own appearance – he looked like an unfeeling version of d'Annunzio – and had himself photographed in vast bare halls decorated with marble statues and hung with blue-grey draperies. Occasionally he unbent so far as to smile: 'If persistent stupidity drives one's patience to breaking-point, one may sometimes take pleasure in a little practical joke, brilliantly planned, cruelly executed, and terminated with a discreet laugh which is the expression of sublime and concentrated joy.'

Every year, at the *Salon des XX*, Khnopff created a scandal with pictures such as *Angoisse*, inspired by Flaubert, or a *Reine de Saba* very close to Moreau. The painter saw his pictures as inseparable from the works of the writers who had inspired them: hence titles

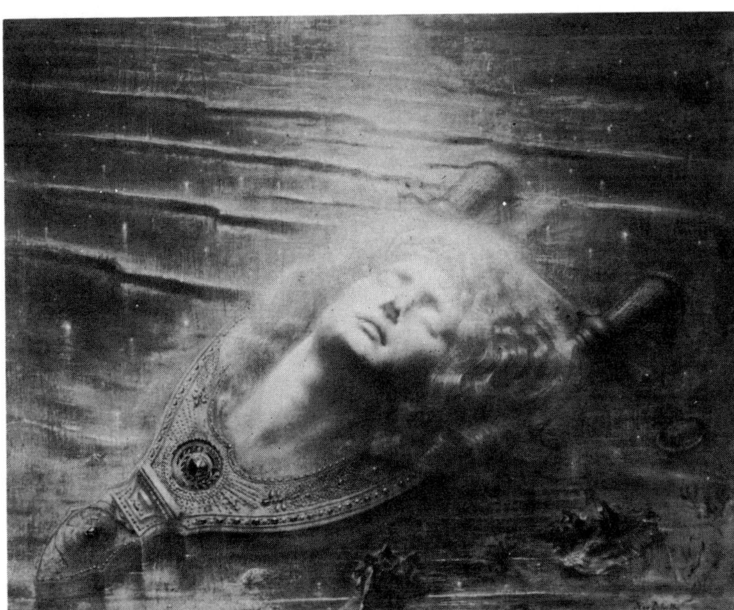

93. Delville: *Orphée*. Moreau's influence is obvious in this fine picture, and the closed eyes and the presence of water place it in the Symbolist world.

such as *Avec Émile Verhaeren: un Ange*, or *Avec Péladan: Istar*. Maeterlinck inspired his painting *Britomar, Tintagile et sa sœur Ygraine*; and he sent the review *Pan* a magnificent drawing illustrating a poem by Mallarmé. Shortly before his death, he produced a series of deplorable lithographs for *Pelléas*. He was the supreme exponent of a particular style; and once that style fell into discredit, he lost his talent. He must have realized this, for he spent his last years in complete retirement.

He is the painter of silence, of closed eyes, of curtains half-drawn over a solemn face, that of his beloved sister. The face is often also that of the Medusa; sometimes it is the face of a creature with a panther's body; and sometimes it can be discerned half-hidden behind locks of red hair, as in the masterpiece entitled *After a Poem by Christina Rossetti: I lock my door upon myself*. This line might have been the poet's own motto. The cave in which the Oedipus of Brussels solved the riddles of Sphinxes dressed like Queen Alexandra was in fact nothing more or less than a camera! After the painter's death, some excellent photographs were found which he used as the basis of his drawings of these mysterious grey figures. Sometimes he even developed them on drawing-paper and touched them up with a charcoal pencil. Perhaps Khnopff should really be ranked among the great photographers, next to Édouard Steichen.

If Khnopff, greatly admired at first, later disappointed the public, Lévy-Dhurmer on the contrary became a great artist, if one makes allowances for his concessions to fashion. He was a dazzling colourist, with a talent for using pastels. While Khnopff had an obsession for panther-women, Lévy-Dhurmer had a Baudelairean passion for hair. He used to ask Renée Vivien's most beautiful friends to pose for him with their hair down, as melancholy bacchantes or morphinomaniac Sapphos. He was not the greatest painter of his time, but he is among the most representative – the artist who reproduced the flora of Gallé and Tiffany on his canvases. The two great panels which the Metropolitan Museum bought recently are a poetic jungle which could be either Klingsor's Garden or the Garden of the Hesperides, and where one might expect to meet either Circe dressed as the Mona Lisa or those monsters which surround Carriès's ceramics.

THE MONSTERS. The legends of mankind are full of dragons, those web-winged creatures which come out of the mud, spitting fire, and are traditionally regarded as the counterpart of angels. In the popular subconscious they may be a memory of prehistoric monsters; and it is therefore not surprising that they should appear in the company of fairies and dead gods. A great illustrator of

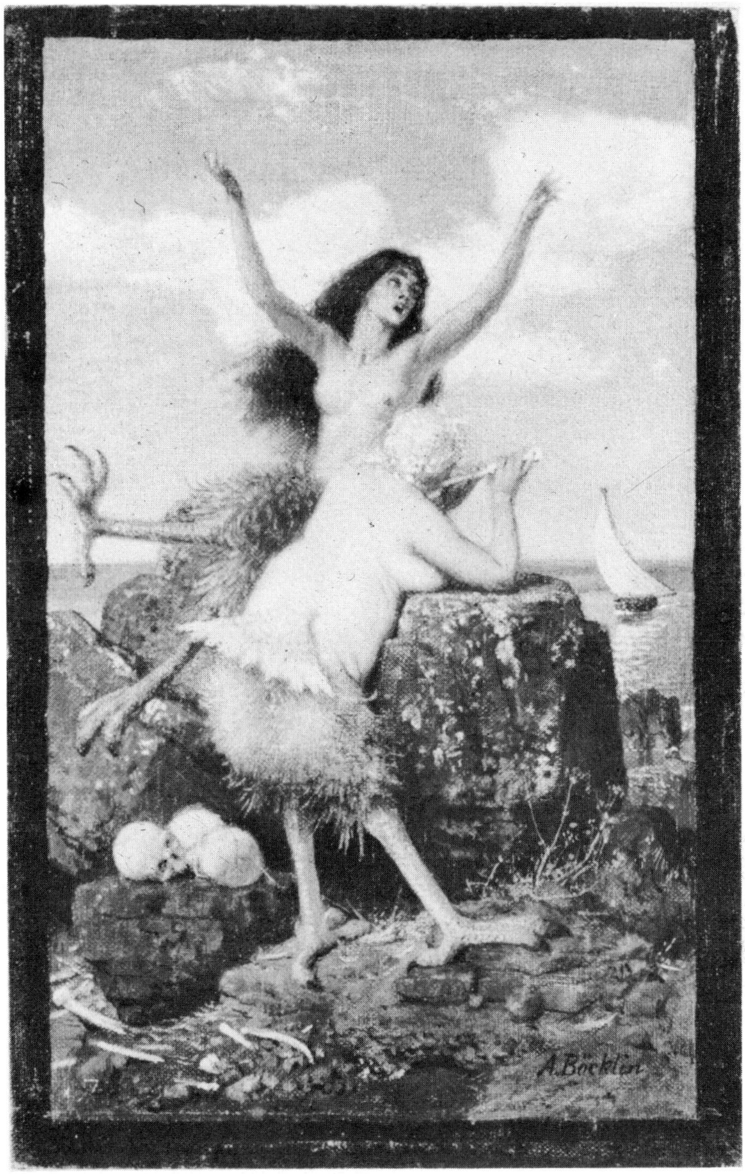

94. Arnold Böcklin: *The Sirens.* An example of the bad taste of which this great painter was all too often guilty.

legends, Gustave Doré, who died at the beginning of the period we are studying, drew a great many dragons, from the repulsive monsters in *Orlando Furioso* to the comical creatures in *Contes Drolatiques.*

Like Böcklin, Doré often tends to be vulgar; and like him, he is very much a man of his country: his fairies wear crinolines, and the Sleeping Beauty's palace is furnished like the Nautilus. Unlike Böcklin, however, Doré is not himself a poet, but when a great poet carries him off on his wings, he is capable of being sublime. Certain illustrations, like those he did for *The Raven*, did more to inspire poets than artists. In Doré, as in Hugo, the sublime rubs shoulders with the ridiculous: thus his angels are straight out of any shop selling devotional objects. What is more, unlike those perpetually weary artists we are considering, Doré has a vitality which still repels the more delicate art-lovers. His huge, sentimental pictures, which were very popular in England, have none of the bizarre features which we find attractive in even the least impressive of the Pre-Raphaelites. In short, if Doré was too normal to belong to the Decadence, he certainly provided it with images.

There is a connection between Doré's dragon-like monsters and two other kinds of monster which became very popular with the public: those created by Jarry and Méliè. The former are the more disquieting, for they represent infinite stupidity; the latter, which are every bit as picturesque as Doré's, drag their way through the early films, flying jerkily towards the moon or crawling through pools full of Gallé-like plants. As in the case of gargoyles, it is easy to recognize the elements which went to the making of these creatures. They are not, however, as disquieting as Odilon Redon's monsters, which have come from some mysterious world of psychology or the occult; Huysmans observed that they seemed to be derived from pictures of microbes, which had become familiar to the public through popular works on science. Since the monsters manufactured in accordance with the old recipes had lost their power to frighten, they were being replaced by scientific monsters. This is borne out by the present-day fear of microbes in the popular imagination.

Another inventor of modern monsters, this time not organic but psycho-analytic, was the German artist Klinger (1857–1920). He is the painter of nightmares. What is the meaning of those long empty gloves floating in the dark, their fingers parted to suggest a crocodile's jaws? What interpretation are we to place on those lobsters being ridden by naked women, or those exotic birds sadly gazing at a new-born child? Where does that tiger come from which we see bounding into a luxurious drawing-room? Why does that mountain look like Beethoven's head? All these are questions to which Freud's disciples must have been tempted to find answers in accordance with the new methods. Klinger's monsters, which are perhaps too skilfully drawn and too heavily loaded with picturesque details to be really frightening, are truly dream-like creations; his engravings foreshadow the collages Max Ernst was to produce forty years later in *La Semaine de Bonté*.

There is a great difference between the monsters in the Christian legends and the monsters of Antiquity. The former are just old dragons which the first knight who comes along can easily disembowel; but the latter have never lost their macabre power. As Charles Lamb wrote in *Witches and Other Night Fears*, 'Gorgons, and Hydras, and Chimeras may reproduce themselves in the brain

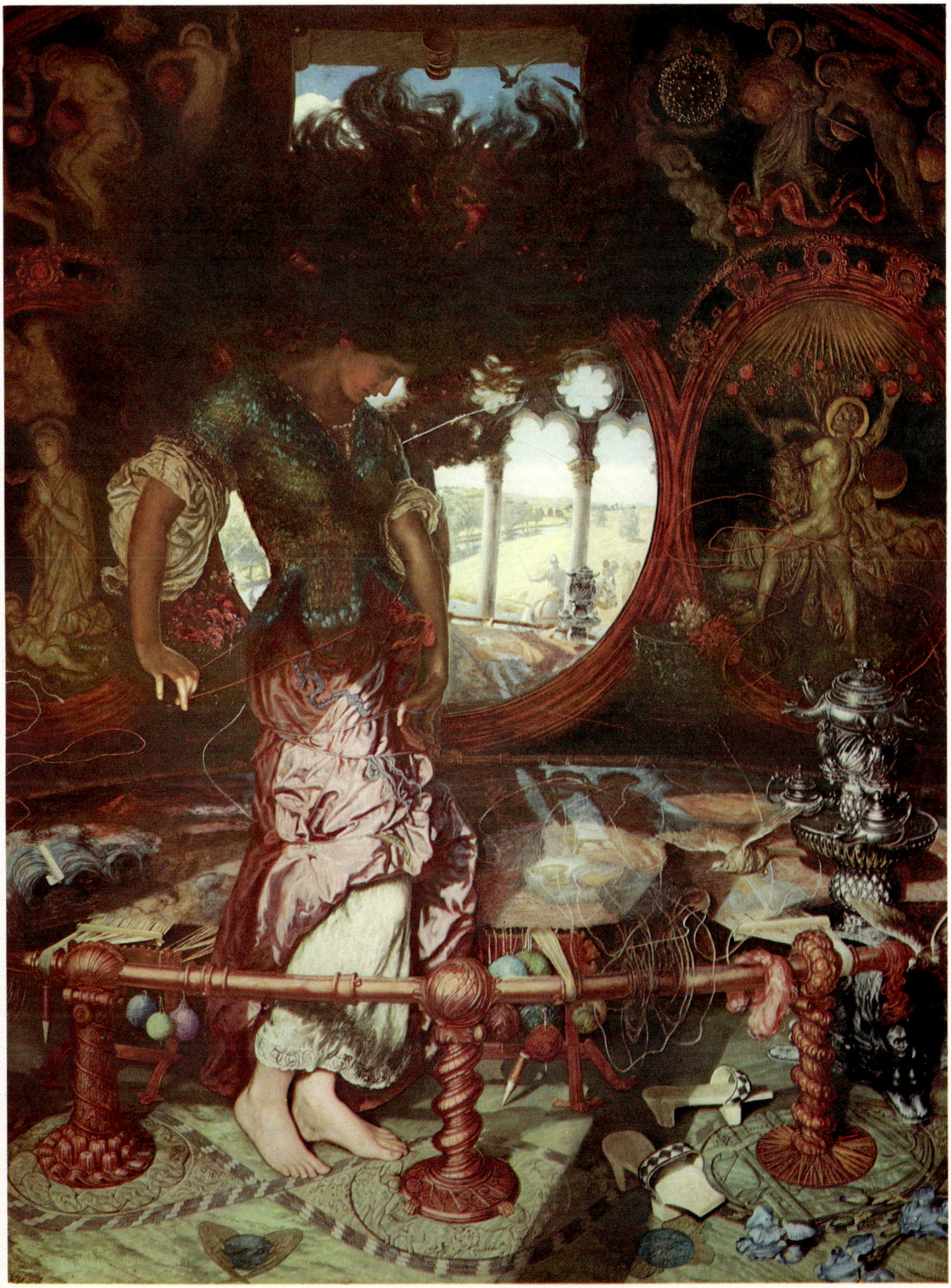

95. W. Holman Hunt: *The Lady of Shalott.* This masterpiece of Pre-Raphaelite painting brought together the themes of Symbolist art thirty years early. The heroine of Tennyson's poem is the mother of the Symbolists' Mélisande.

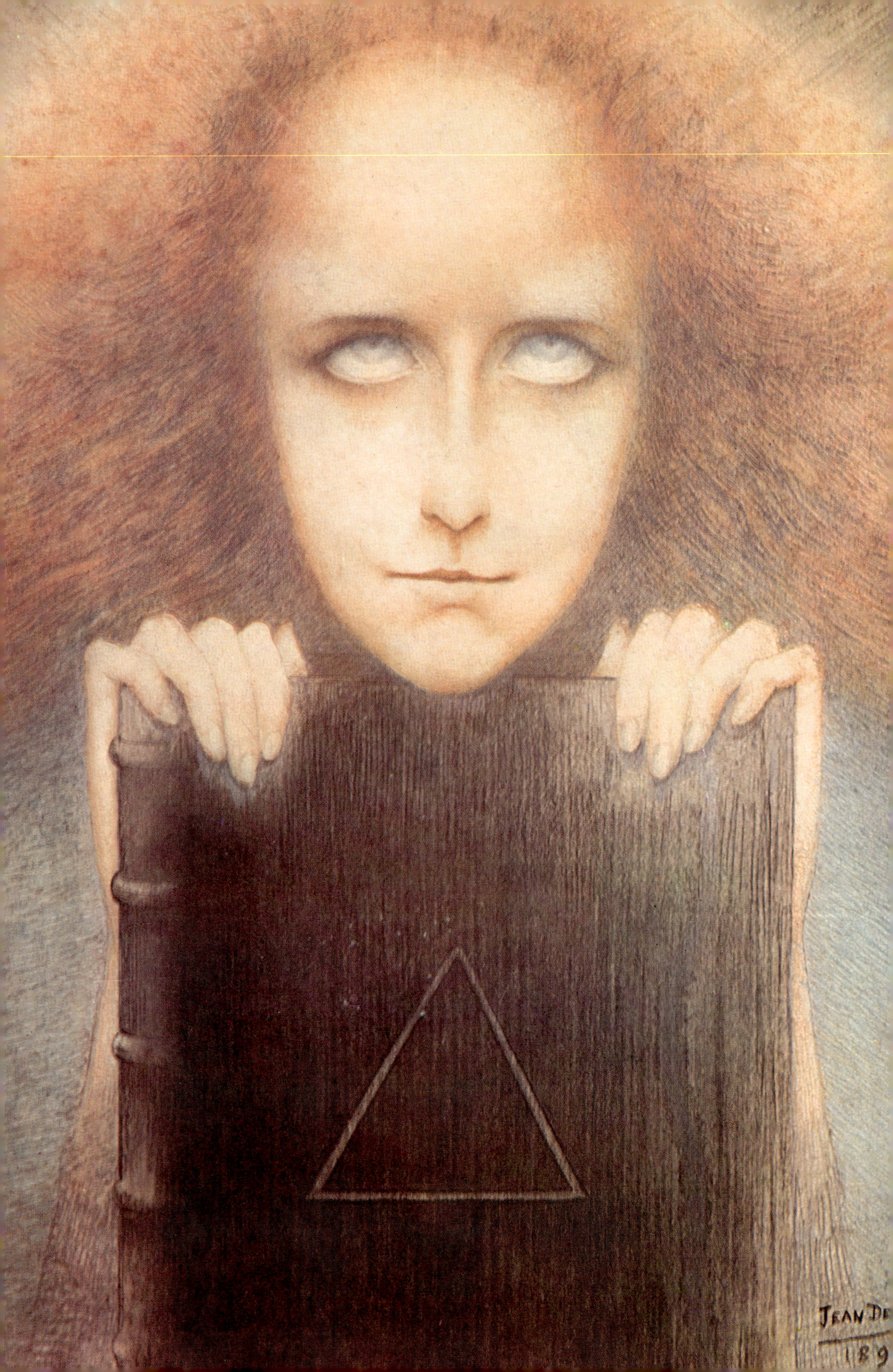
JEAN DE
189

of superstition – but they were there before. They are transcripts, types – the archetypes are in us, and eternal.' Monsters may become more decorative motifs when there is a decline in religious feeling, but their power is reasserted as soon as a society begins to break up. Such was the case at the end of the Gothic era, a great period of witchcraft. These chimeras reappeared in the shape of baroque monsters in the twilight of the Renaissance. Again at the end of the Enlightenment, they heralded a return of nameless fears, as Goethe showed in his *Walpurgisnacht*: the same ancient myths were to embody the phobias and fears of the last Romantics, phobias which we should probably call 'complexes' today. The Medusa, who ever since the Etruscans has been alternately a myth and a decorative object, inspired a large number of poets since Shelley (30); it is the Medusa who looks up at us from the canvases of Klimt, or less imposingly from the bottom of 1900 ashtrays. Linked with her is the octopus, and again there are countless octopus-women in *fin de siècle* art, the most lascivious of them among Carabin's statuettes.

LILIES AND SWANS. The lily, the antithesis of these monsters and one of the supreme symbols of Christianity, is to be found *ad nauseam* in the works of *fin de siècle* artists, whether they were Christians or not. The angels, saints, and dead women of the Pre-Raphaelites, Puvis de Chavannes, and the Rosicrucians all carry lilies, for the lily was the symbol of their soul. There are the white lilies of countless *Annunciations*, the red lily of Florence, the tiger lilies which Swinburne's heroines press to their bosoms. Moreau even perches the allegorical figure which dominates *Les Lyres Mortes* on a gigantic lily. There are Viélé-Griffin's suave lilies, Gilkin's frightening lilies, and Paul Valéry's lilies which so delighted Monsieur de Phocas, *alias* Jean Lorrain:

> *O frères, tristes lis, je languis de beauté*
> *Pour m'être désiré dans votre nudité.*
> O brothers, melancholy lilies, I am sick from beauty
> For having desired myself in your nudity.

Rimbaud, however, had not waited for this large-scale cultivation of the lily to make fun of it in a letter to Banville. Much more than the orchid, which only entered literature thanks to Odette de Crécy, the lily was the chosen flower of the aesthetes (25). Thus the Baronne Deslandes, Burne-Jones's model and the friend of Wilde and Barrès, used to receive her admirers lying on a bed of lilies. Sarah Bernhardt was frequently surrounded by lilies, an excellent choice incidentally for *La Dame aux Camélias*, since the lily stands for virginity rediscovered, the soul unsullied by the

96. Delville: *Portrait of Madame Stuart Merrill.* A positively magical vision of the wife of the excellent Symbolist poet, a great friend of both Wilde and Mallarmé.

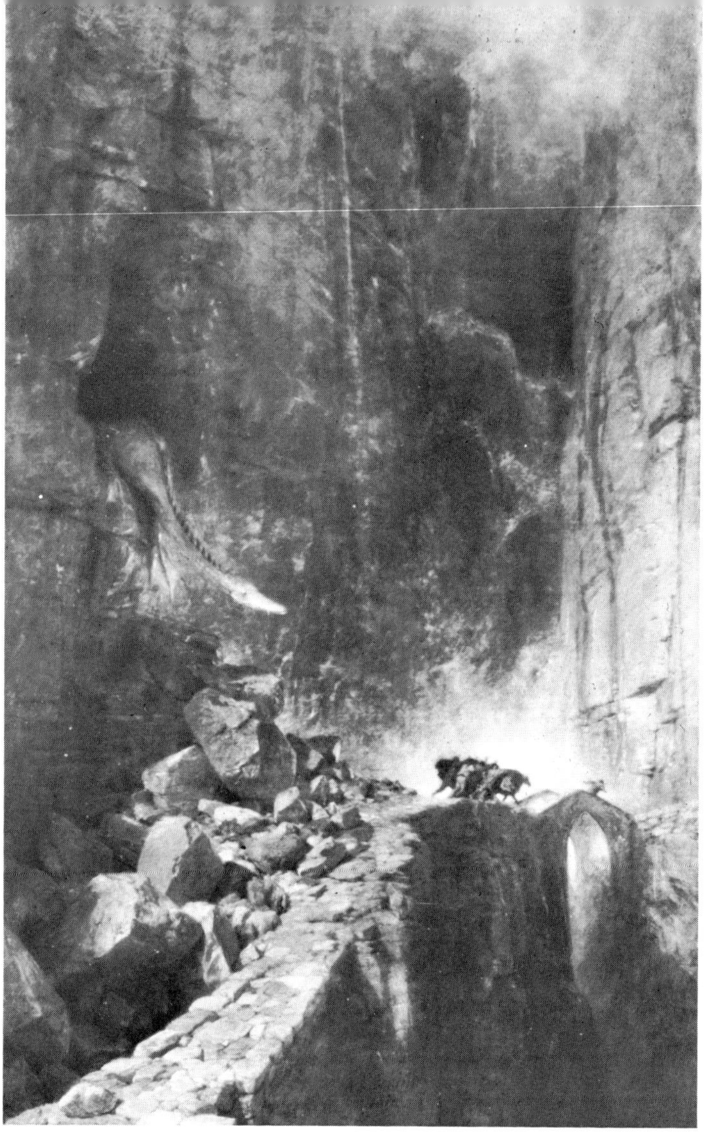

97. Böcklin: *Rocky Gorge*. One of the finest paintings of this great artist whom Wagner would have liked to commission to design the settings for his operas. It is very reminiscent of some of Gustave Doré's illustrations.

evils of the day. Hence too the countless lilies in Mucha's illustrations for Zola's *Le Rêve*. The symbolic significance of the lily was so well understood at the time that it is never to be found in any of the Impressionists' paintings.

The lily was the mystical flower, with the black lily as its sinister counterpart (23). But nostalgic artists preferred faded roses, losing their petals under the weight of their beauty (40); roses indeed became the symbol of overpowering beauty. Algabal's guests in George's poem are suffocated under a pile of roses, and later d'Annunzio's Pisanella suffers the same fate. Rose-petals are scattered about in Maurice Denis's lithographs, and there are rose-bushes in the purple parks where Clara d'Ellébeuse waits for the Grand Meaulnes.

In the parks there are also canals and lakes on which glides the swan, the Mallarméan bird (52), and in this typical atmosphere it recalls Wagner:

Par la nage et le vol de son cygne idéal,
Surgit sous la clarté que réfracte son casque
Lohengrin, le héros grave du Saint Graal.
Through the swimming and flying of his ideal swan,
There appears beneath the light glinting on his helmet
Lohengrin, the grave hero of the Holy Grail.

A macabre poet such as Gilkin allows the swans to carry him out of his nightmares:

Les cygnes blancs au clair de lune
Avec leurs plumages fluides,
Dans le brouillard blanc, sur l'eau brune
Glissent comme des nefs liquides.
The white swans in the moonlight
With their fluid plumage,
In the white fog, on the brown water
Glide like liquid ships.

This *Art Nouveau* bird is to be found in countless decorative compositions. It appears in Vallotton's woodcuts and even in Eckmann's wallpaper. It dots with white the black eddies of the fiords beside which Munch's figures take their anguished walks. The swan is the symbol of an innocent beauty as cold as the water on which it glides.

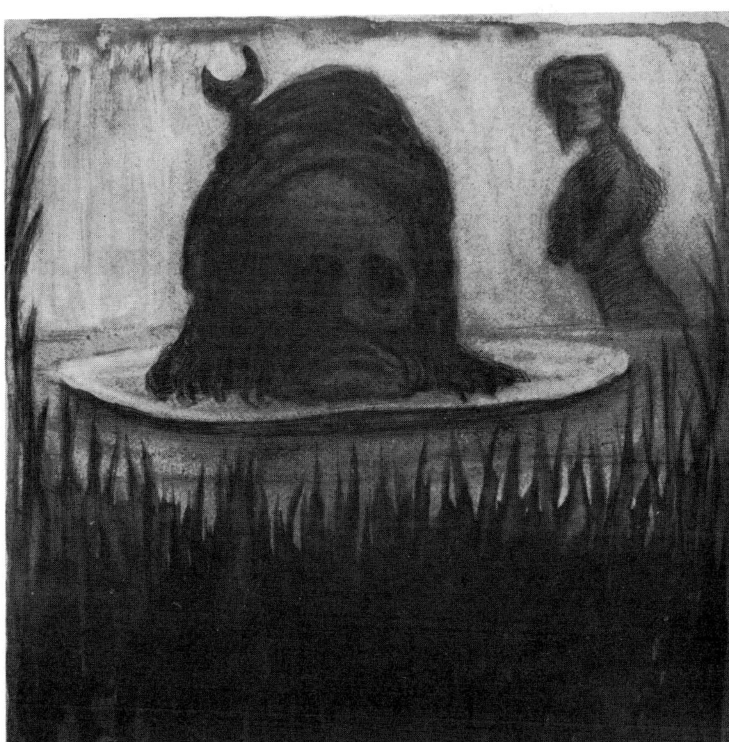

98. Kubin: *Black Flowers.* Redon's influence mingles with that of Mucha in the work of this artist, who became one of the pioneers of modern art.

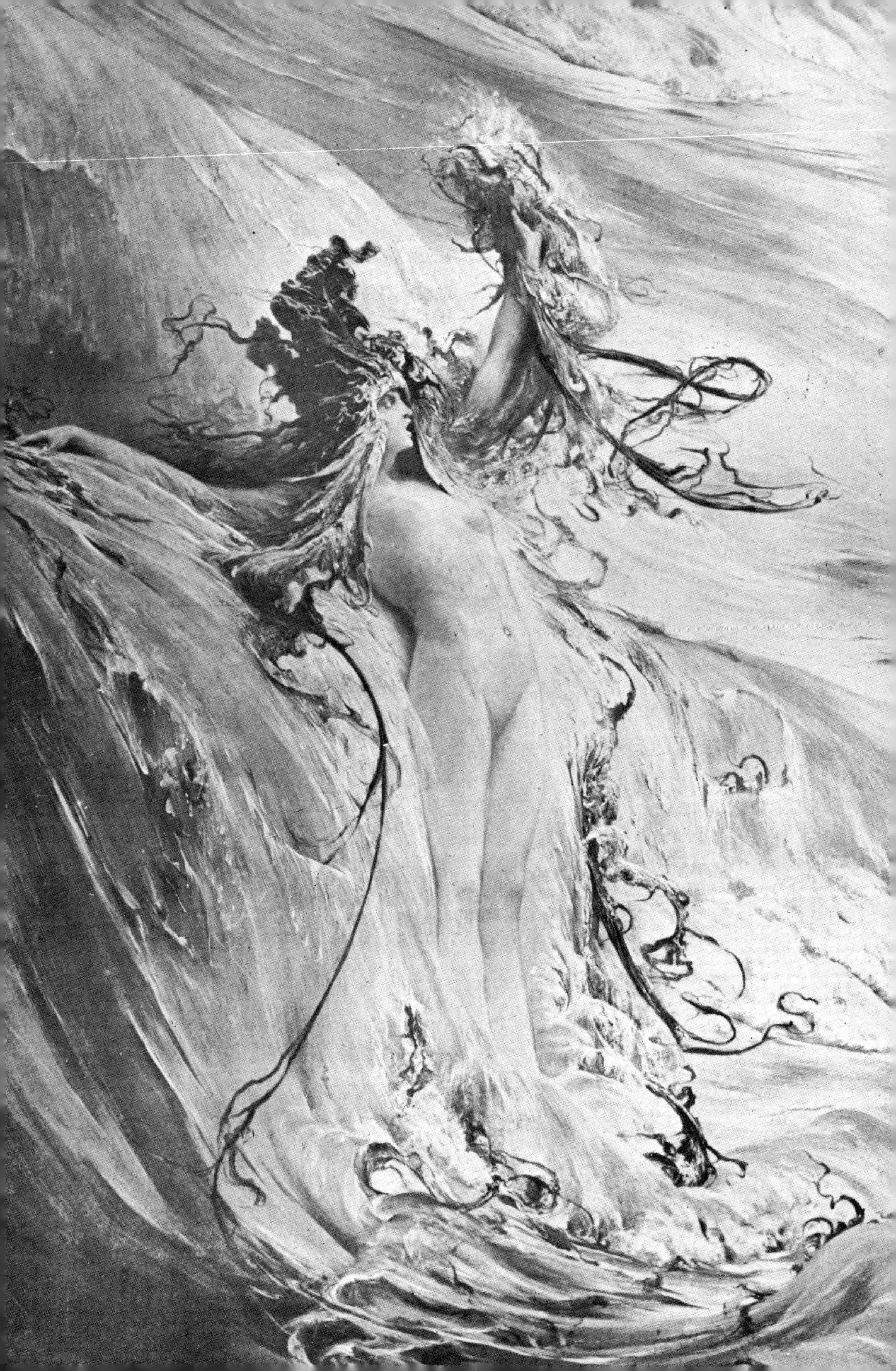

11 The Mediators

Ludwig II. In Zola's day, in a vulgar world divided by politics and with nothing to relieve its drabness but the childish gewgaws of nationalism, a few extraordinary personages remained to offer consolation to the poets. These individuals, by virtue of their position or their works, but above all by virtue of their follies, acted so to speak as mediators between the artists and the world they dreamed of, provided a justification for their pleasures, and served as guides to their dreams. They had allowed the chimeras to carry them further than anyone else, and if they fell in full flight, their fate was all the more beautiful for that.

Wagner, for one, did not fall. He was the magician whom countless artists visited to hear his oracular pronouncements. Villiers de l'Isle-Adam and Judith Gautier brought back to France a new concept of drama after listening to the master explaining his theory of art. According to Mallarmé, Wagner was 'the threatening peak of the absolute to be revealed after the disappearance of the clouds, glittering up there, naked and alone. A spectacle of the future . . . a monster which cannot be.'

The actual person of the god, on the other hand, had nothing inspiring about it, and if it disappointed the poets in their longing for the sublime, they transferred their fervour to the man who loved, served, and understood their 'god' with unexampled generosity: Ludwig II of Bavaria. Catulle Mendès's book *Le Roi Vierge* revealed the King's personality to a wide public, and Ludwig II reigned over every mind addicted to dreams. When he died, Banville's striking phrase – 'He and the shadows spoke to one another' – was a finer epitaph than Verlaine's clandestine poem:

L'Europe embourgeoisée et féminine tant
Néanmoins admira en Louis de Bavière,
Roi vierge au grand cœur pour l'homme seul battant . . .
Europe, which had grown so bourgeois and feminine,
Nonetheless admired in Ludwig of Bavaria,
That virgin king with the great heart beating for man alone . . .

99. Georges Clairin: *La Grande Vague*. This picture, by the great admirer of Sarah Bernhardt, was inspired by a visit he made to her in Brittany. Academic by training, Clairin was influenced by the actress to popularize *Art Nouveau*. The seaweed could have been designed by Lalique. The picture had a great success at the Paris Exhibition of 1900.

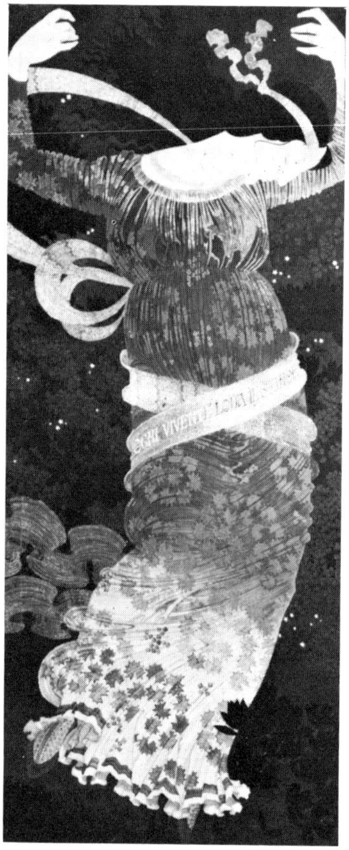

100. Augusto Giacometti: *Night*. This decorative panel in tones of dark blue and green shows the influence of Grasset on this Swiss artist, the father of the sculptor.

Robert de Montesquiou, who felt a positive veneration for the King, obtained an account from Ludwig's last favourite, the actor Kainz, of his arrival one night at Linderhof Castle:

> All of a sudden the rock moved; an opening appeared through which we entered a long corridor, brightly lit with a red light. Along the walls of the grotto the King's servants stood in line.
>
> Still following the servants who were leading the way, I walked to the end of the corridor, as far as what appeared to be a natural opening in the rock. Through this opening there poured a sea of blue light. The interior of the grotto looked like a huge, dazzling sapphire, whose flickering brilliance spread over the craggy walls, entered every tiny crack, and cast a sort of magic veil over every object. I had stopped on the threshold, behind an overhanging rock, dumbfounded by the grandiose splendour that surrounded me; I was breathless with amazement. The ceiling of the grotto was vaulted, like that of a cathedral. I was inside the Venusberg.
>
> I took a step forward and stopped again. The rock which had concealed me until then had prevented me from seeing on my right a lake of astonishingly limpid water, lit by a sky-blue light. On it there glided two snow-white swans, while on the shores stood a tall man, all alone, and apparently deep in thought: this was the King.
>
> For a moment I gazed at his fine head, his broad shoulders, his remarkably white hands which were casually tossing pieces of bread to the two swans; I also noticed the bright star made up of sapphires which was fastened to his hat.
>
> He shook me warmly by the hand, releasing me from the feeling of depression which had affected me till then. Then the King took me up a path leading to the top of a hill in front of us. On the top of this hill there was a table made of sea-shells which stood on a large conch supported by crystal feet. Near this table there was a seat made of the same materials, and the servants brought along another. The King invited me to sit down, and supper was served.
>
> Every quarter of an hour the King gave a signal and the lighting of the grotto changed; it turned red, then green, then blue, then gold, and into my imagination came memories of ancient legends and fabulous fairy-tales.

One might be reading the description of a palace by Villiers de l'Isle-Adam or Jules Verne. Unfortunately this wonderland was singularly deficient in works of art. If the idea of Ludwig II's castles, perched like fairy palaces on mountain peaks or the shores of lakes, is full of fantasy, their interior decoration offers some of the worst examples of Gothic pastiche. One has to realize, like Barrès (27), that these imperfect works are merely the symbols of a perfection which can only be attained in dreams. Besides, if one studies them closely, one can sense the presence of *Art Nouveau* everywhere, ready to appear in the stalactites of the grotto, in the roots spreading out from the feet of the pillars, in the bronze peacocks keeping watch around the empty thrones.

If Ludwig II had died fifteen years later than he did, he would certainly have provided palaces for the practitioners of *Art Nouveau*; the only palaces, however, in that style and worthy of the painter-magicians, were those built by Gaudí and the ephemeral hall erected for the 1900 Exhibition. One such remains to this day at Darmstadt, the capital of the *Jugendstil*, for Grand-Duke Ernest-Ludwig of Hesse, the brother of the last Empress of Russia, was almost as devoted to the cause of beauty as Ludwig II. Olbrich was his Wagner, and he lived in the presence of an admirable *St. George* by Burne-Jones. But his influence was more on the decorative arts than on painting.

Among his operatic *trompe-l'œil* settings, Ludwig II had recreated the character of Hamlet, who, according to Mallarmé,

101. Paul Gauguin: *Figure de Spectre*. This charcoal sketch was inspired by one of Rachilde's occultist dramas and offered to the writer, whose morbid works had great influence around 1890.

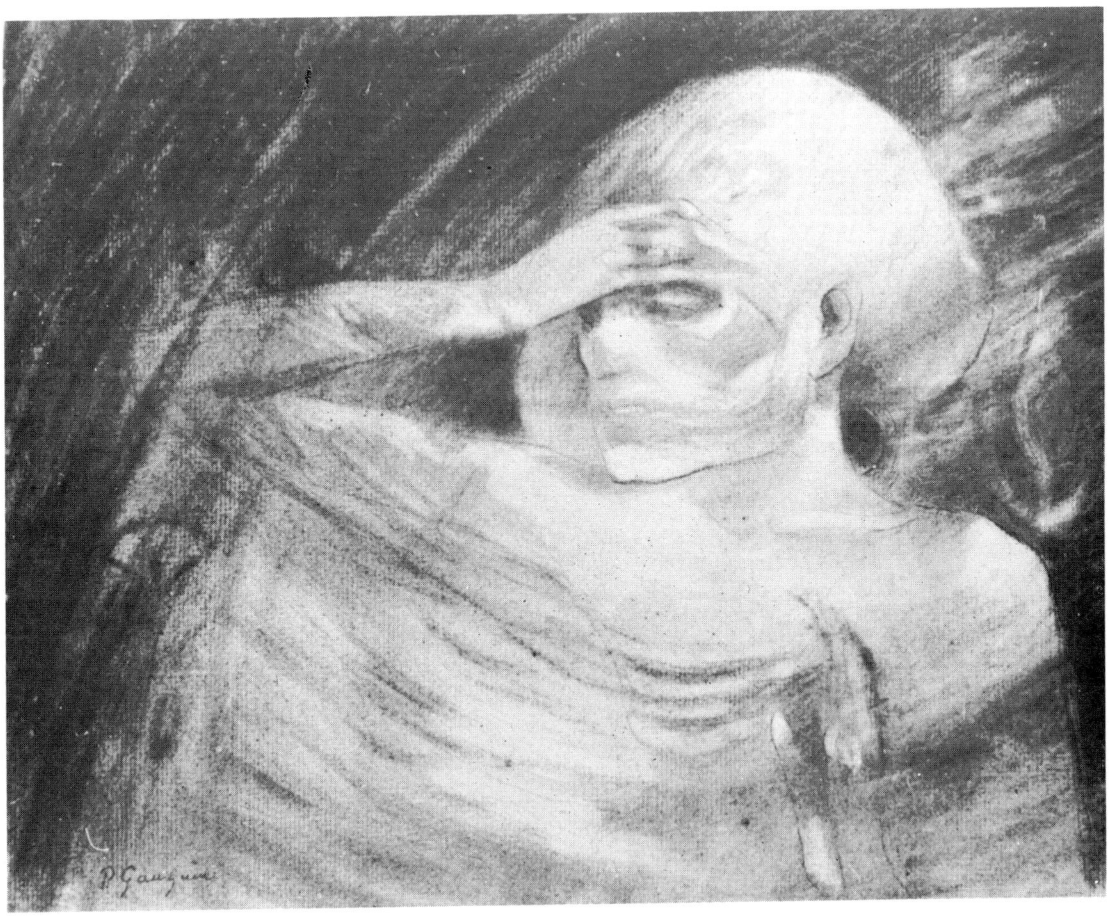

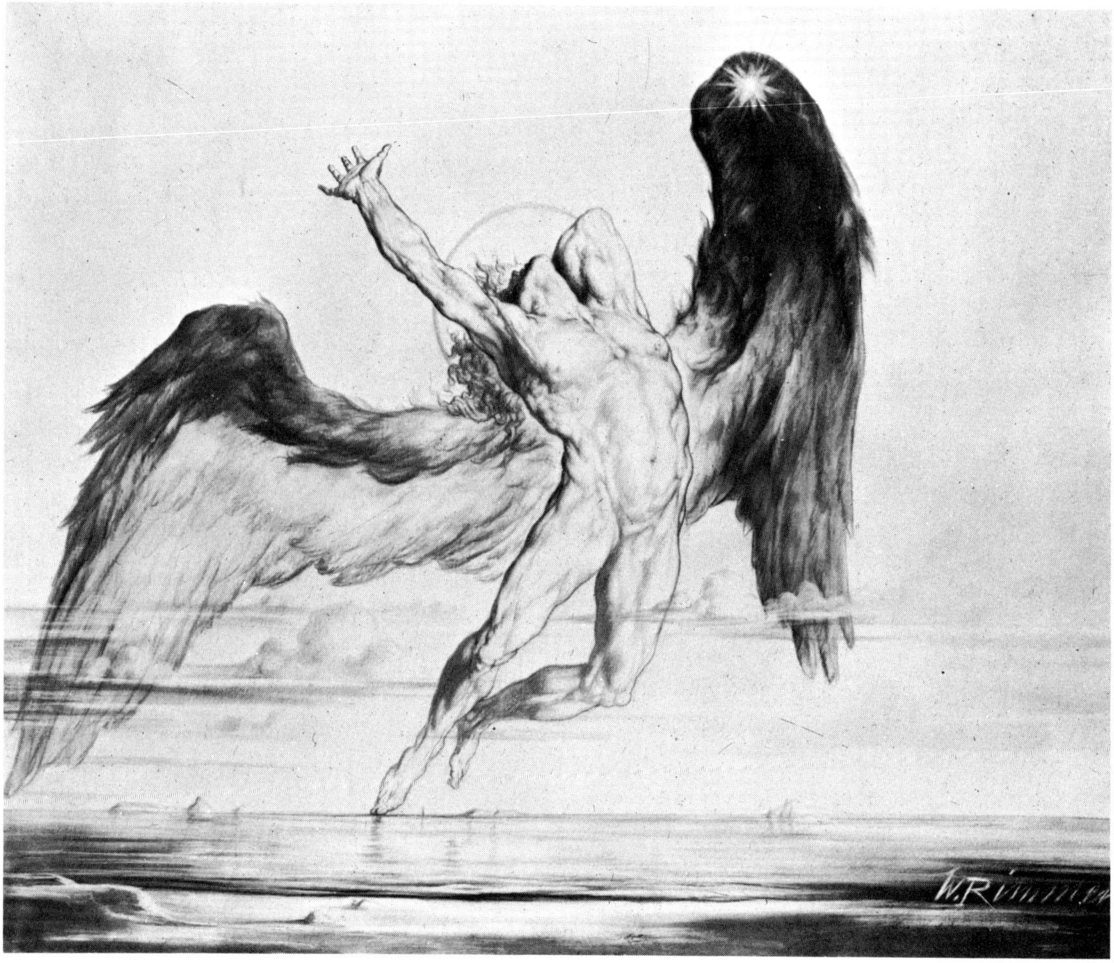

102. William Rimmer: *Evening: Fall of Day*. Nearer to Gustave Doré than William Blake, this asexual athlete naïvely reveals the metaphysical aspirations of an American artist who was a contemporary of Moreau.

'exists by virtue of heredity in all *fin de siècle* minds' – Hamlet, who was embodied by the shy visitor whose story we have read above, and who was to become Germany's greatest actor, Hofmannsthal's friend, Josef Kainz (19). Ludwig II, who excited the imagination of so many Frenchmen, did not arouse the same fervour in England, possibly because Rossetti and Swinburne, the disciples of William Morris, were democrats, and in any case had little admiration for Wagner. But in France, if we ignore Gustave Kahn's mediocre novel, the *fin de siècle* Hamlet was Grand-Duke Floris in Élémir Bourges's admirable work, *Les Oiseaux s'envolent et les Fleurs tombent*. This is a story of princely entertainments and bloody murders in castles worthy of Ludwig II and landscapes which might have been created by Böcklin. Nostalgic dreams of grandeur, passion, beauty, and mysticism, at once satisfied and disappointed, create situations which may have been copied from Shakespeare but are certainly worthy of him. As Ludwig II did, and as so many poets have tried to do, Élémir Bourges's hero, after clashing with society and rejecting everything that could console him, commits suicide. Aristocrats fare no better in the modern world than aesthetes; they become eccentric or unapproachable, and end up by disappearing as the dinosaurs disappeared, annihilated by a change in climatic conditions. During the last years of the nineteenth century, the monarchs of the world had a last chance to discharge an all-important function – that of giving the people poetry and fantasy. Bourges's two novels, and especially *Le Crépuscule des Dieux*, seem to be ablaze with the final glow of personal power, and rotten from contact with capitalism.

The cult of Ludwig II was inseparable from that of his cousin, 'the Empress of Solitude', Elizabeth of Austria, who inspired some of the finest pages in Barrès's *Amori et Dolori Sacrum*. But here again there were no pictorial masterpieces, merely a few portraits by Winterhalter. Yet how we should love to have a picture of Elizabeth by Romako, who painted so many Austro-Hungarian ladies on the verge of hysterics, against a background of purple lace; or else a portrait of the Empress by Böcklin trailing her veils like his Medea under the arcades of the Achilleion; or on the terrace with the distant view of the Island of the Dead. True, Khnopff did a pencil-drawing of Elizabeth from a photograph, but then she looked like all his usual heroines.

The entry of these potentates into the mythology of the *fin de siècle* owed as much to mystical reasons as to their romantic fascination and aesthetic appeal. Thanks to Péladan and Villiers de l'Isle-Adam, the old families came to be regarded as the repositories of strange secrets. The idea of aristocracy became linked with the idea of death: '*Absterben ist vornehm* (to die out is distinguished),' wrote Eduard von Keyserling in *Houses in the Evening*. Nearly all the women depicted by the painters we are studying are queens or princesses, unlike the women portrayed by the Impressionists or the official painters. The rank conferred on them by art makes them untouchable. D'Annunzio's *Virgins of the Rock* are the best examples of these women of too ancient a lineage to survive in the modern world. Poe's Ushers were already doomed: at the royal level the coronation ceremony endows them with a positive halo. There was thus a veritable cult of royalty in Europe at the very time when the last dynasties were being threatened by democracy or anarchy.

SARAH BERNHARDT. From sadness and inaccessibility let us turn now to vulgarity and self-advertisement. Yet the royal figures who shunned human society had certain features in common with the publicity-seeking actress: a fine contempt for good taste and moderation, a sincere love of Beauty, especially if it was new and unconventional, and a belief in their own divinity. Sarah Bernhardt, in Paris and on her travels round the world, used the crudest and hence the most effective methods to spread the message of *Art Nouveau*. The 'Princess of Gesture', she bent her very body into the arabesque of the new style, until she finally came to resemble a Gallé vase (44). And thanks to a belated Romantic, the dramatist Sardou, she embodied all the themes of the Decadence. In *Fédora*, as early as 1876, she personified the myth of the Slav woman, capricious and enigmatic, spreading despair around her: a new type of femininity which was to become familiar to the French through translations of Russian novels and then through Ibsen's plays. In *Gismonda* and *Théodora* Sarah embodied the crimes and splendours of Byzantium. Then Rostand offered her some plays which were like Symbolist flowers cultivated in an academic hothouse. With *La Samaritaine*, Sarah became the muse of mysticism, an apotheosis to which Péladan had also contributed, for a great many religious plays were produced in Paris about 1895. Then, with *La Princesse Lointaine*, she clothed herself in the gar-

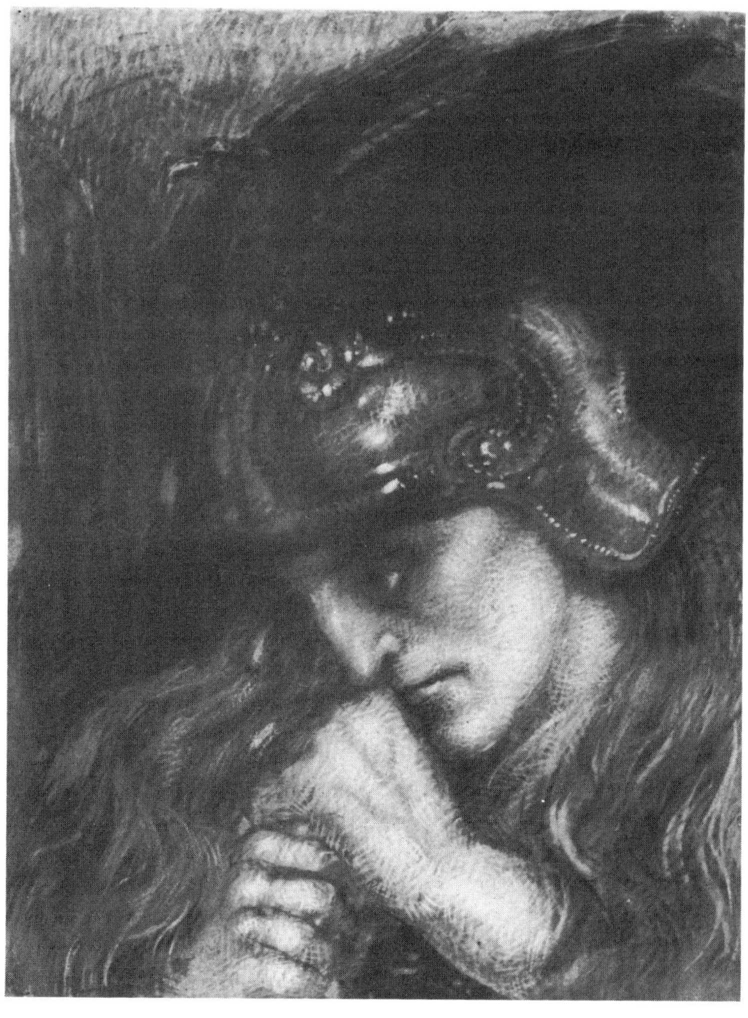

103. Henry de Groux: *Lohengrin*. It is hard to tell whether this is a Valkyrie or Lohengrin. All the characters in the works of this neurotic painter resembled him while he himself looked like Dante. His appearance and the dramatic subjects which he liked to depict constituted a large part of his success.

ments of Isolde and Mélisande. She discovered Mucha, encouraged Lalique, and fascinated Burne-Jones, who saw her as *La belle Dame sans Merci*. Lionized in England, she helped to popularize Pre-Raphaelite fashions in France, dressing in Paris as if she were living at Tintagel. One can recognize her tawny hair and casual stance in the pictures of many painters for whom she never posed, but above all in those of her admirer Clairin, who painted her almost a hundred times, as a fairy, as an empress, or as Pierrot.

Clairin lived for forty years in her shadow. 'One day I was painting a fresco,' he writes, 'when inspiration failed me. I jumped into a cab and drove to Sarah's. She was lying stretched out on her furs. Without saying a single word, I looked at her, and she returned my gaze just as silently. We remained like that for almost a quarter of an hour; then I went back to my fresco and started painting like a madman. Yesterday it was absinthe; today it's Sarah!'

Moreau was her master, as she told Jean Lorrain:

> Sarah is there, standing before me, with her delicate, irritating profile, and her cold, sparkling eyes, like a pair of precious stones. Seeing her like that, pale and languid beneath the glitter of her metal belt, I reflect that she too belongs to the family of that old King David and that young archangel with the woman's face; yes, the enigmatic Sarah is truly Gustave Moreau's daughter, the sister of the muses carrying decapitated heads, of Orpheus and the slim, bloodthirsty Salomes – the Salome of the famous watercolours praised by Huysmans, the Salome of *The Apparition*, whose triumphant, coruscating costume, incidentally, she wears in *Théodora*.

Legend portrayed the actress as 'a sphinx greedy for every sensual pleasure'. She was photographed in a coffin, drinking out of a skull. Pale and thin at a time when it was fashionable for women to be plump, Sarah used all the tricks of Romanticism to seem utterly up-to-date, and succeeded completely. Her love-affairs were stormy and eclectic: right to the end, her preference went to handsome young men, but her liaison with Louise Abbema (an artist who, alas, was not very *Art Nouveau*) was an open secret. A close friend too of Augusta Holmès, a lady who was Wagnerian in physique as well as musical taste, she used to recite her *Hymn to Love* at spiritualist seances; for naturally Sarah was in touch with the spirit world, like her fairy godfather Victor Hugo (whose last love she was), her artistic adviser Montesquiou, her favourite author Sardou, and her poster-painter Mucha. On one occasion the latter painted her looking like an ectoplasm, nestling at the feet of her beloved son.

In this period which rediscovered the hermaphrodite, her best parts were transvestite: the title roles of *Le Passant*, *Hamlet*, *Lorenzaccio*, and *L'Aiglon*. She encouraged anyone who could excite her ghoulish powers, such as Maurice Rollinat, for whom she gave a party in 1883 at which he appeared as the *Spectre de la Névrose* (the spectre of neurosis).

Sarah wanted to be Wilde's Salome, and the poet and the actress discussed sets for the play inspired by Gustave Moreau. Alas, the public was never destined to see Sarah in that part, her bare feet standing out like white doves on the black earth, beneath a purple sky obscured by perfume-braziers. The Lord Chamberlain banned the play, deciding that the follies of aestheticism had gone too far – a warning which the poet failed to heed.

WILDE AND OTHERS. The Irish writer must be recognized as one of the greatest figures of his time, for misfortune endowed him with an importance for the Decadence not entirely merited by most of his work, which owes much to pastiche and gratuitous paradox. Wilde was first of all the publicity agent of Aestheticism; then he embodied the triumphant Decadence; and finally, after disaster had overtaken him, he became the magician dispensing oracular wisdom to young poets on café terraces. Gide, Jarry, and Pierre Louÿs were lost in admiration for him. Estranged from the converted, dying Beardsley, Wilde had hoped that Khnopff would illustrate *The Ballad of Reading Gaol*, but the idea came to nothing. He is known to have greatly admired a young Dutch Rosicrucian, Sareluys, but for his beauty rather than his art: he made him stand on a table at a banquet in Verhaeren's honour and crowned him with flowers, like the figure in a Simeon Solomon drawing which unfortunately disappeared in the looting of his house. He also had some long conversations with Henry de Groux; but the only artist he admired in his later years was Rodin. He met the sculptor once or twice in the pavilion housing his works at the 1900 Exhibition: 'He showed me anew all his great dreams in marble. He is by far the greatest poet in France, and has, as I was glad to tell myself, completely outshone Victor Hugo.' But in 1900 *Art Nouveau*, popularized by the Exhibition, had lost its attraction for the artists of the soul. The Impressionists were triumphant, and the number of their imitators was growing. Wilde, who had once admired them, wrote from Sicily in the last year of his life:

> The lemon-groves and the orange-gardens were so entirely perfect that I became again a Pre-Raphaelite, and loathed the ordinary Impressionists, whose muddy souls and blurred intelligences would have rendered by mud and blur those 'golden lamps hung in a green night' that filled me with such joy.

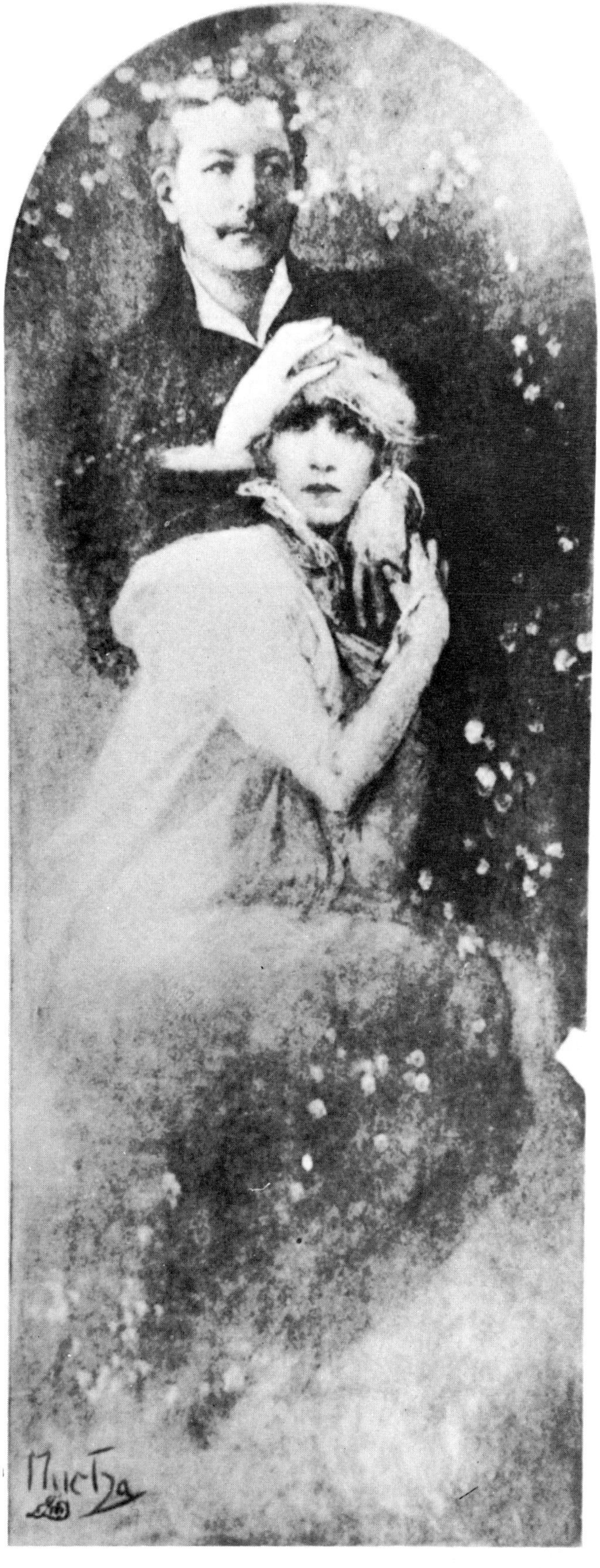

104. Mucha: *Sarah Bernhardt et son Fils*. Mucha, who was passionately interested in spiritualism, seems to have wished to present here a mystical vision of Sarah protected by her beloved son. The photograph of this lost picture was found among Robert de Montesquiou's papers.

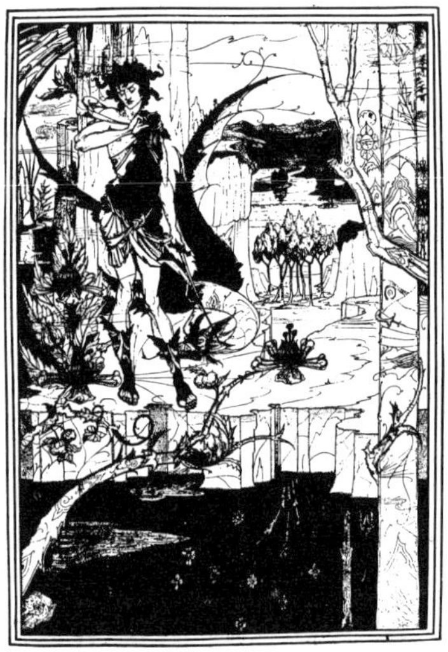

105. Beardsley: *Siegfried.* This Siegfried surrounded by poisonous flowers could be the hero of one of Wilde's tales.

For just under ten years, Wilde had been the theorist of imagination. He had propounded Ruskin's theories and Pater's more discreet messages in essays which had been widely read. But while expatiating on these ideas in the drawing-rooms of London, he had also amused himself by destroying them with impertinent witticisms. A pompous Wilde would have had more prestige and fewer readers, and we must be thankful for his insolence, because his style is marvellous even if his artistic taste was sometimes deplorable. How close *The Picture of Dorian Gray* is to Lorrain, for example: the same setting, the same vices! The principal difference lies in the style, and also in a personal charm which still lingers on, especially in the comedies, for the man who combined in himself every sort of bad taste could be irresistible:

> All, that he came to give,
> He gave, and went again:
> I have seen one man live,
> I have seen one man reign,
> With all the graces in his train.
>
> With a light word, he took
> The hearts of men in thrall:
> And, with a golden look,
> Welcomed them, at his call
> Giving their love, their strength, their all.
>
> (Lionel Johnson)

A man must be more serious to be a magician. That gravity which Wilde acquired only in misfortune was a quality which the German Stefan George had always assiduously cultivated; thus, instead of becoming infatuated with shallow young men, George had cherished a very noble, very painful passion for Hugo von Hofmannsthal. He appeared to the young poet rather in the guise of a magician in the *Tales of Hoffmann*:

> He received me in a gallery which I found strangely oppressive, full of sweet, suffocating smells. There were astonishing birds hanging in it, and snakes with speckled skins. His gentle voice has an intoxicating, seductive power. He can curdle the air with fear and kill you without even touching you.

Later George found a very young disciple of exquisite beauty called Maximin: 'His intelligence is godlike; he is the new Christ come to reconcile the poet with the world.' George used to read his poetry in a voice of liturgical monotony: 'That art which digs the furrows of the Mind.' Often dressed in classical garments, he was the Plato of an esoteric, homosexual academy. Unfortunately, some photographs have come down to us taken at the 1904 Munich Carnival which are more suggestive of a provincial Byzantium than of Greece. George sometimes took himself for a second Dante, to whom he bore a facial resemblance. In these fancy-dress parties nobody behaved more scandalously than Alfred Schuler, the inventor of Cosmism, who sometimes took himself for a maenad and went dancing in the woods, while at other times he posed as a sibyl. He plunged into Oriental esotericism, and finally emerged with the swastika.

The whole of this circle had a considerable influence on von Stuck, on the illustrator Fidus, and on the *Sezession* group generally. Painters like Klimt, the creators of the *Jugendstil*, were steeped in formulas such as George's: 'The dead space and being live again in the image.'

While Stefan George was handsome – an important attribute for a magician – Walter Pater was extremely ugly. He had a weakness for works of art depicting beautiful young men: 'He never allowed life to approach him without ceremony, remaining on his guard against the indiscretion of the event.' Consequently he played a more secret role than Mallarmé, who was always surrounded by people, and a more important role too, for the preciosity of his style never obscured his thought. He dreamed his life away among books and pictures, a hermit in the 'Palace of the Arts' which he had invented.

One hesitates to class Gabriele d'Annunzio with these great minds: he is much closer to Sarah Bernhardt. Like her, he excited generations and groups which had no part in Symbolism. He frantically revived all the themes of the Decadence, inspiring a bizarre style of painting which can be seen in the empty rooms of the Museum of Modern Art in Rome and which was admired at the first Venice Biennale. The work of Sartorio (1860–1932) offers the most imposing and the most ambiguous example of this style, but a great many minor painters imitated the Pre-Raphaelites when illustrating d'Annunzio's early poems. Like Rostand, d'Annunzio was a few years behind his times. He too exploited the chimeras; he copied Wilde's poses and Sarah's publicity, and when his models were dead or forgotten, he pursued his dreams in a strange, disquieting dwelling which he made his prison and which witnessed some horrific scenes. This villa on the shores of Lake Garda, the Vittoriale, remains one of the most bizarre creations of the heroic Decadence, a sort of porter's lodge for one of Ludwig II's castles.

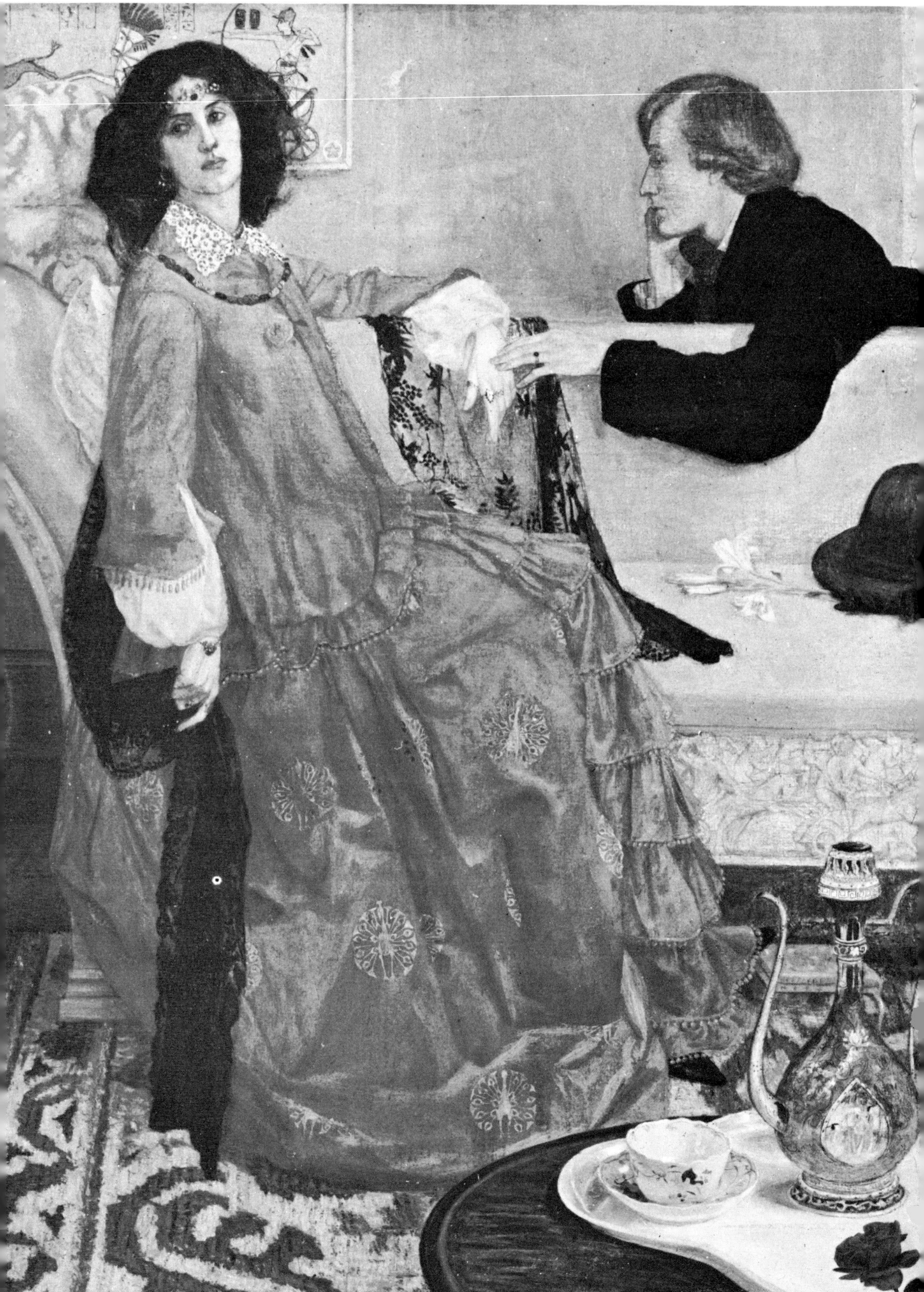

12 The Chimera-Catchers

THE RECLUSES. The two poets who have been frequently quoted in this study, because they too followed the chimeras at a distance, did not figure among the mediators in the previous chapter, each for a different reason. As Rossetti entered into a decline, Swinburne, suffering from alcoholism and threatened with madness, placed himself in the power of a solicitor who dabbled in poetry but basically acted as a male nurse, and who prolonged his life for some thirty years in a house in the London suburbs. The English Baudelaire there became a sort of monument which young men used to visit as they would a tomb.

Mallarmé, at the centre of the most brilliant intellectual circle in Europe, had too much taste to take any interest in a style of painting far removed from that of friends of his such as Manet or Whistler. The fact that he published a sonnet next to a drawing by Khnopff does not mean that he felt any great enthusiasm for the latter's art, although it was much closer to his own experimental work than that of the Impressionists. He took a benign interest in the eccentricities of the little reviews, but this very straightforward man, who loved boating and pretty women, must have felt a certain horror of the Decadent world which sang his praises.

Moreau felt no greater liking than Mallarmé for those who, by imitating him, brought out the weaknesses in his work. 'They are young men with a crazy belief in themselves, full of the impertinence of a boldness ignorant of danger and failure . . . But why is that innocence so irritating in its artistic enterprises?' Possibly Moreau, who placed his art far above mere fashion, rather regretted being so fashionable. Among his papers there was found the rough draft of a letter which reveals to the full his utter contempt for success: 'Dear Sir . . . Do as you please: put prose in the place of poetry, thistles in the place of lilies, dung in the place of scents. Do as you please: I don't give a damn. Make innovations, destroy everything, turn everything upside down: what does it matter? The laws and the immortal existence of Art will always and inevitably regain the upper hand.

106. Maxwell Armfield: *Faustine*. This homage to Swinburne, in which the furnishing and decoration of the room is allegorical down to the smallest detail, depicts the *fin-de-siècle* ideal of elegant corruption.

This letter, which seems to have been intended for a supporter of Naturalism, must have delighted the master's pupils. Moreau always goes further than any school; his chimeras leave the peacocks of this world to play the games of fashion: 'There is a fateful moment when an art changes in order to take on the qualities of other arts. It is at that moment that short-sighted people start complaining about decadence.'

Redon too showed a certain repugnance for the success fashion brought him, possibly because he shared that success with people for whom he felt no respect. It is interesting to note that, like Moreau, he had refused to exhibit any of his works at the Rosicrucian Salons. The following remarks were addressed to his admirers: 'What have I put in my works to give them the impression of so many subtleties? All I put in my works was a little door opening on to mystery. I invented fictions, and it is up to them to go further.' Another dictum, likewise taken from *À Soi-même*, shows clearly that Redon's visions were, so to speak, sent to him, and that he had done nothing to provoke them: 'A thought cannot become a work of art, except in literature.' This is the very negation of Symbolism. In the same way Delacroix had shown little enthusiasm for Romanticism.

Among these solitary artists who did not deign to mix with their Rosicrucian or Decadent admirers, the coldest was undoubtedly Puvis de Chavannes – Puvis whose influence on the pictorial arts was to be the most extensive of all, since traces of it can be found a long way from the painters of the imagination, in the works of Hodler and Picasso. Puvis is the Anti-Moreau: his chimera is a swan which never leaves the cold waters that are its natural habitat, and it was probably in connection with his academic colleague that Moreau wrote the following note: 'Nowadays our men about town, our collectors of Japanese curios, our admirers of exotic, esoteric art, are going mad about this austere art which is the direct continuation of the outdated poetical and rhetorical styles of the past, rejuvenated only in so far as they have the pretentious appearance of an ash-coloured hair-shirt in the middle of a drunken orgy.' At the Salon of 1881 the most ardent of Moreau's admirers, Huysmans, felt it incumbent on him to pay tribute to Puvis, but he did it with ill grace (38). Verlaine for his part was deeply affected by Puvis's paintings, but for reasons which the master certainly never intended.

If his art had been a little more disquieting, Puvis would have been the Burne-Jones of France. His German equivalent – an artist whose works possessed the disquieting element lacking in his own – was Hans von Marées. But for many years reproductions of Puvis's *Sainte Geneviève veillant sur Paris* – showing the patron saint of Paris watching over the city – hung in girls' bedrooms all over France. The walls of Péguy's paradise are almost certainly decorated with Puvis frescoes, and Claudel's *L'Annonce faite à Marie* also owes a great deal to this austere symbolism.

THE ZEALOTS. The zealots, frantically imitating the follies and eccentricities of Sarah or Wilde, tried to break down the doors of these recluses, while a small but noisy public gave ecstatic encouragement to the chimeras, only to abandon them a few years later to ridicule and oblivion. It is difficult to distinguish between affectation and sincerity in the stars of the *fin de siècle*, whose effigies have been respectfully retrieved in recent years from under the cobwebs of the Palace of Fantasy. Of all these minor figures, none had greater influence and none was more representative than Jean Lorrain, often quoted in this book either heralding a fashion or denouncing an absurdity. A hulking, flabby creature, painted and beringed like a tart, Lorrain was the Petronius of the Decadence. He haunted the private galleries and little theatres of Paris, launching a painter or slating a star in articles which he signed with a wide variety of names from Sentillama and Salterella to Mimosa

107. Thomas Theodore Heine: *The Caterpillar*. This Freudian nightmare by one of the best draughtsmen of the magazine *Simplicissimus* is highly characteristic of the black humour dear to the Decadents.

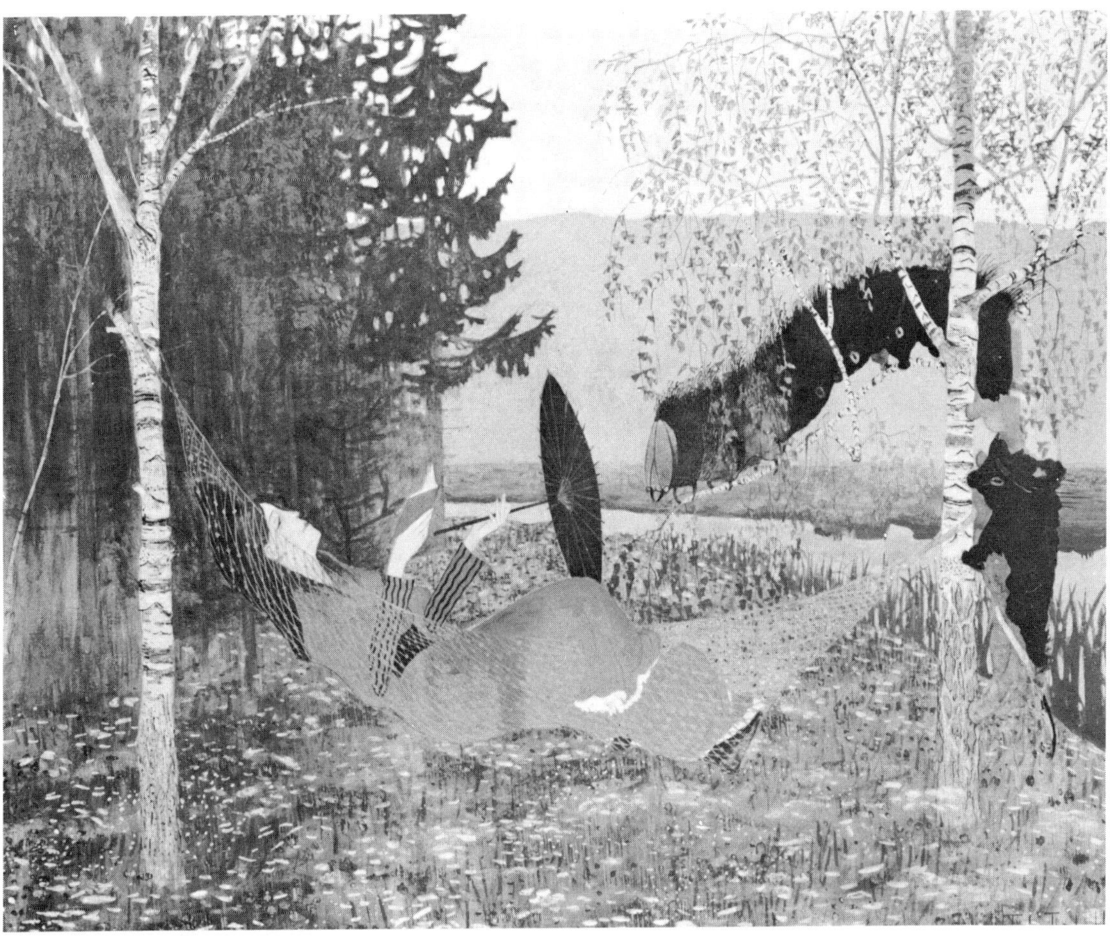

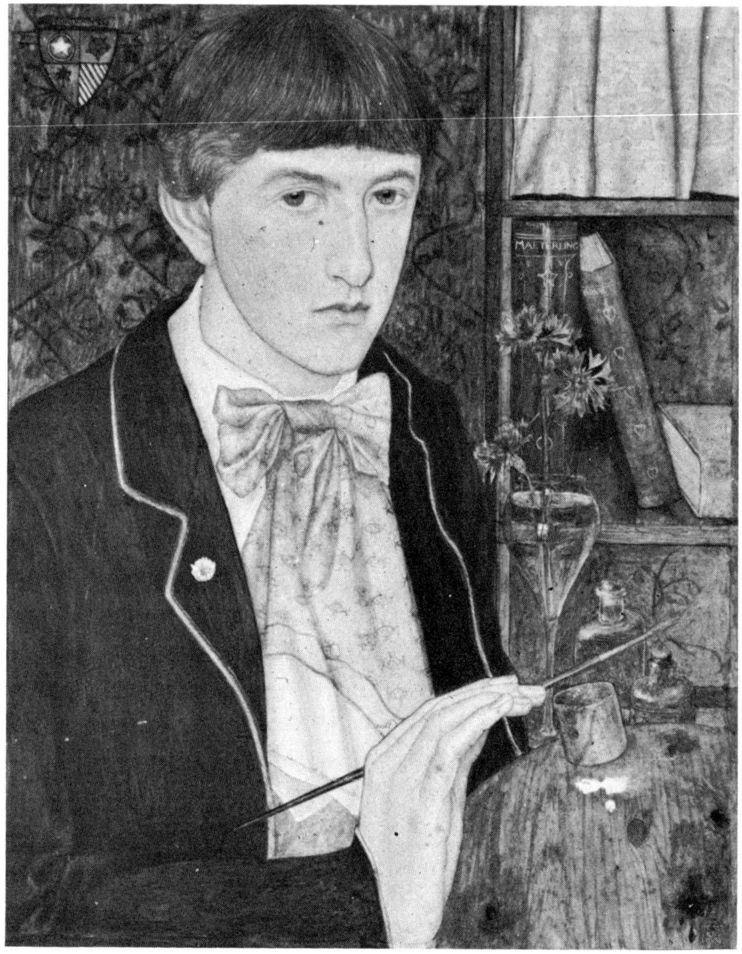

108. Armfield: *Self-Portrait.* Very much influenced by the Flemish Primitives, it represents the artist as a young man at the end of the 1890s.

and even Stendhaletta. Lorrain's strength lies in his unbounded bad taste: the reader begins by laughing, then stays to see how far he can go 'too far'. He exhumes all the sins in the Bible, all the perversions in the *Psychopathia Sexualis*, and even the smell of ether fails to mask entirely the stench of the grave. When literature leaves Zola's world to enter Maeterlinck's, only Lorrain's characters, thirsty for beauty, can explain to us the transition from Nana to Mélisande. But it is not every bird that can become a phoenix; chickens and turkeys who aspire to the blue heavens of aestheticism singe their wings in the sacred funeral-pyre, and then look to morphine or the whip, to little girls or fairground wrestlers, to plunge them into the delirium they had hoped to find in Art. Yet in the very depths of depravity and degradation, they still go on noting the exact colour of a sky, the 'exacerbated Botticellicism of a profile'. The Pelléastres put up with ridicule out of love of music, Monsieur de Phocas goes to his death searching for the wonderful shade of green he had once glimpsed in a pair of eyes, and that heroic dandy Monsieur de Bougrelon dies of hunger in his fine linen and laces.

This extraordinary longing for beauty in characters who are either mad or repellent, saves them from being mere puppets. It should not be forgotten that the same fervour found expression in Sarah's complaints and Montesquiou's yelps; that it inspired Gallé and Beardsley, Klimt and Horta. For some, perversity was a routine; for others, it was a form of asceticism which led to the creation of masterpieces. Lorrain stopped half-way along that road, but he had set off full of hope.

Next to the scandalously unbuttoned Lorrain, the tightly corseted Montesquiou tends to irritate us today, until we recognize that, like a Ludwig II lost among the Verdurins, he devoted his life to a certain ideal of beauty. The melancholy quality of a certain number of his poems has led to neglect of his all-too-rare pieces of art-criticism. He lives on, not only in the character of Baron Charlus, but in all the aesthetic passages in Proust, to whom he was as it were a Professor of Beauty.

A long way after Montesquiou one might mention a curious individual, torn between dreams and snobbery, whom Proust calls Legrandin and who was really Mallarmé's friend Cazalis. Under the name of Jean Lahor, he wrote a number of Buddhist-Florentine meditations and works of aesthetic Socialism. Tailhade once referred to him as 'Cazalis who puts nothingness into verse'. Saint-Pol-Roux (whose real name was Paul Roux) was a more interesting figure than Jean Lahor, a genuine *poète maudit.* After the failure of most of his works, he retired to a Breton castle to live for his dreams. However, his play in free verse, *La Dame à la Faux*, had obtained a certain success in 1899, as well as his collection *Limaires.* And before that, in 1893, his theory of Magnificism – a matter of 'conjugating the games of speech and light' and taking up a grandiose attitude to life – had aroused the enthusiasm of many young poets. The names he gave his children bear witness to his sincerity: Divine, Magnus, Loredan, Coecilian. Long after Symbolism had gone out of fashion, he continued to advocate a magical art in articles and poems. And before he died he had the satisfaction of being recognized as a prophet by the Surrealists.

In Paris, during the last quarter of the nineteenth century, and to a lesser degree up to 1914, two people lent their patronage to every eccentricity. One was a young woman, Rachilde, the author of *Monsieur Vénus* and *La Marquise de Sade*, whose bad taste and tortured imagination hid a heart of gold. The other was Catulle Mendès, who spent the whole of his life trying to live up to Baudelaire's remark: 'I like that young man – he has all the vices.' Mendès acted as a link between Baudelaire and Cocteau, whom he is said to have debauched. In his countless poems, imitating Hugo and Coppée in turn, we can find all the themes of the Decadence.

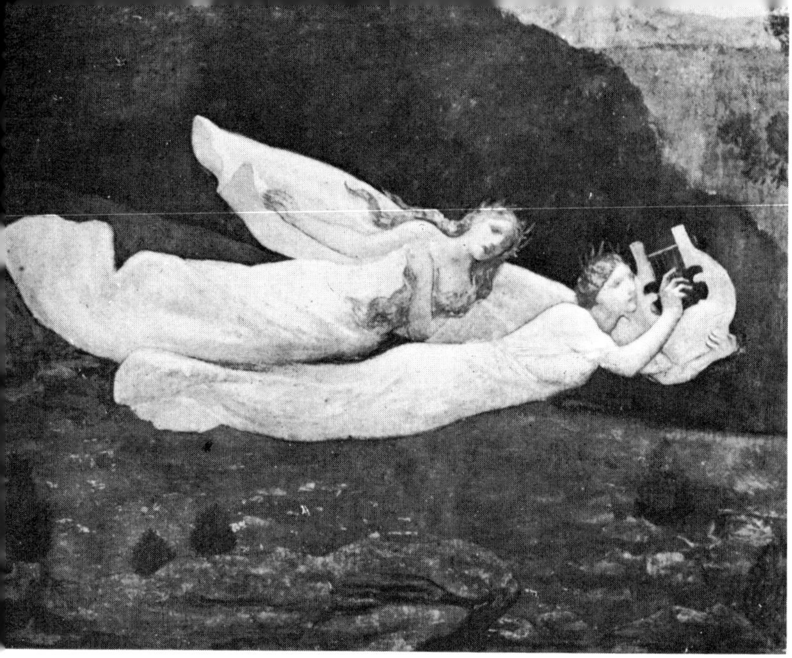

109. Puvis de Chavannes: *Le Bois sacré*. This poetic detail from a huge and very academic fresco explains Puvis's prestige with the Rosicrucians, Gauguin and Maurice Denis. The muses are spirits hovering in a grey-blue atmosphere.

These very bad writers enjoyed considerable prestige abroad: Mendès influenced d'Annunzio, and Wilde was impressed by Rachilde.

On the whole, the thinkers of the Aesthetic Movement in England were unimpressive, if we except Wilde himself. John Addington Symonds was to some extent Wilde's John the Baptist. His remarkable *History of the Italian Renaissance* was written entirely from the aesthetic point of view, and his book *In the Key of Blue* with its cover by Ricketts was to be found in countless libraries between *Intentions* and the works of Vernon Lee. It contains the subjects of nearly all the pictures painted by the Symbolists with a colour key *à la Whistler*. The last stanza expresses the discouragement felt by a writer in love with Beauty who has only words to render it.

Two of Wilde's disciples are now regarded as little more than literary curiosities: Richard Le Gallienne and Arthur Symons. Le Gallienne wrote *The Religion of the Literary Man* and a great many poems, some of which reveal his loyalty to the Medusa theme (30). As for Symons (1865–1945), he was so to speak the poor man's Wilde; lacking a taste for boys, he kept up with fashion by dabbling in satanism. Symons served as the model for the character Enoch Soames, Max Beerbohm's caricature of the English Decadent – an unfair caricature, for Symons, who was a fair poet and an excellent critic, was responsible for making Symbolism and the Symbolist artists known to the English public. To take one example, he wrote an excellent article on Odilon Redon in which he rightly described him as the William Blake of France. He played much the same role in this respect as George Moore had done for the Impressionists.

THE SNOBS. Rachilde and Mendès did not take much interest in painting, but Lorrain, Montesquiou, and Cazalis were aesthetes who saw the world through pictorial works. They were also snobs, who paid exaggerated respect to the judgement of a few elegant individuals well disposed to anything which came from London or Bayreuth. The most interesting fictional characters of the period come from this environment. The first of these characters, and the craziest, is Andrea Sperelli, in d'Annunzio's *Il Piacere*, closely followed by Dorian Gray: they live the same elegant life in the same settings. Then there was Proust's Swann, or the disillusioned aesthete, and finally Rilke's Malte Laurids Brigge, or the pathetic aesthete. The creators of these four characters had a marked weakness for the aristocracy, which they had dreamed about in their youth. Their weakness for titles is surpassed only by their love for works of art. They regarded women as beautiful *objets d'art*, and, incapable of artistic creation, modelled the beloved creature either on an ideal found in the art-galleries – Botticelli for Swann, the *Lady with the Unicorn* for Malte – or an ideal provided by the artists in fashion at the time. Thus d'Annunzio's women are Böcklins and Khnopffs, while Dorian Gray's victim, Sybil Vane, is a Burne-Jones. The world in which they live is the world of high society (except in the case of Malte Laurids Brigge), where everyone has a great deal of money and all the time in the world to devote to satisfying his caprices.

In the United States the Aesthetic Movement for which Wilde had conducted a crusade as early as 1883 became a sort of finishing school for well-bred souls. Artists such as Abbott Thayer, Arthur Davies, and Maxfield Parish painted maidens in long flowing dresses in contrast to the crisp and lusty Gibson girls. A spiritual snobbery came into being alongside the financial snobbery that already existed – a snobbery highlighted by the critic Royal Cortissoz in *Some Imaginative Types in American Art* (1895):

> Beauty, pure Beauty. It is that which brings their imaginative powers into play: the realities of life purged by artistic inspiration in the fullest sense of the term. These are the facts they raise to a higher and sweeter reality . . . The only ideal that is ultimately worth serving, the only leader who goes on unfaltering to the end, the only goddess whose feet are not of clay is she to whom you can say in Elia's perfect words: 'I have not found a whiter soul than thine.'

In the event these 'souls' could not stand the atmosphere of their country for long and went into voluntary exile. There was Nathalie Barney in Paris, Mabel Dodge in Florence, and countless others who pursued the chimeras from Capri to Chelsea.

In Vienna, on the other hand, aestheticism was cultivated at home as intensively as in London ten years before. The splendour of an empire in decline and a large Jewish community helped to create an environment whose importance can be judged by a few of the names which distinguished it: in music, Webern, Schoenberg and Berg; in the theatre, Hofmannsthal and Schnitzler; in theatrical production, Max Reinhardt and in literature, Rilke and Musil. Freud occupied only a lowly place in this dazzling world which, after Klimt, produced Schiele and Kokoschka. The leading Austrian spokesman for aestheticism was Peter Altenberg, 'the reporter of the soul', whose favourite words were 'Bohemia', 'Fate', and 'Decadence'. While some of the products of this environment were in the William Morris tradition, as, for example, the edition of Hugo von Hofmannsthal's poem *Der Kaiser und die Hexe* illustrated by Vogeler-Worpswede (1900), some on the contrary foreshadowed the *Arts Décoratifs* style of 1925 – the *Sezession* Pavilion (1898) was indeed twenty years ahead of its time. The Aesthetic Movement in Vienna continued to be brilliantly inventive right up to the outbreak of the First World War, in other words much longer than in other European countries.

A wealthy, worldly society wants distraction above all else, which explains above all the lack of enthusiasm felt by high society for Impressionism; that style of painting, linked to Naturalism in literature, was not considered *chic*, and what is more it did not offer much to the imagination. Towards the end of his life Manet observed with a certain bitterness in a letter to Antonin Proust: 'People in high society are going into ecstasies over *Jacob et l'Ange*. Moreau is having a deplorable influence, taking us back to the incomprehensible. But there's no denying that he's having the best of it just now.' A few elegant, intelligent women did in fact find their way to Moreau's hermitage. There was his neighbour, Mrs. Howland, Degas's close friend, then Montesquiou's relatives, the Princesse de Chimay and her daughter the Comtesse Greffulhe, a great friend of Wilde's, Lady Brooke, the Ranee of Sarawak, and many others, whose visiting cards are to be found among the master's papers.

Among these people who acted as catalysts between artists and public, none was more typical of her time than the Baronne Deslandes. Barrès's mistress and Wilde's intimate, painted by Burne-Jones and caricatured by Lorrain, this half-Jewish diminutive blonde with the big nose was the international lady aesthete *par excellence*, lionized in Bayreuth, Florence, and London. Péladan's feminine admirers were legion; one of the most prominent was Lady Caithness, the Duchess of Pomar, who believed that she was the reincarnation of Mary Queen of Scots. It is hard to say to what extent the various Madame Verdurins encouraged the painters of the time; some idea may be obtained from those novels which described artistic circles in the last years of the nineteenth century. Léon Daudet's novel *Les Kamchatka*, for example, tells of a rich woman who is 'mad about art'. She has two children, Morgane and Siegmund, who dabble respectively in drugs and anarchy. These people find Monet and Whistler distasteful, but like Trauguin (Gauguin) and Cardon (Redon): 'An arch of a white bridge in some asphalt, with a square eye above, and below, half a death's-head sliced through like cheese.' They rush to the exhibition of the Knights of Jerusalem to see 'spiritual conditions represented by a series of figures shaped like snakes asleep in the mist. A blue ball inside which a knight is strangling a nymph.' These feminine aesthetes are presumably acquainted with the heroine of Anatole France's Florentine novel *Le Lys Rouge*, for 'anyone who comes back from Florence is marked with a mysterious sign, like someone who has heard *Parsifal*.'

110. William Shackleton: *The Reliquary*. Characteristic of the style of picture popularized by *Studio*, it seems to have been painted after a photograph. Works of this kind were exhibited at the Royal Academy up to the beginning of the Second World War.

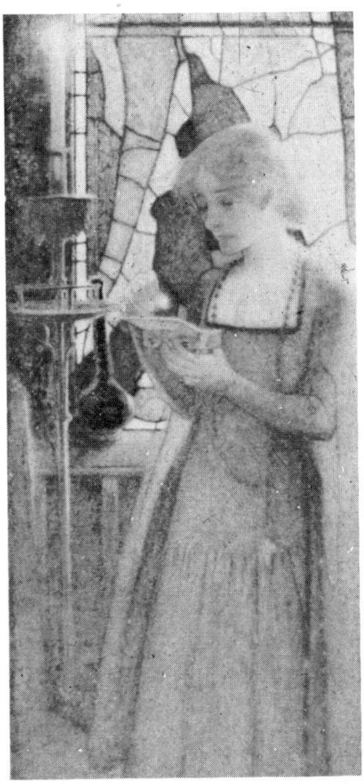

Another story, entitled *Chez les Snobs*, which appeared in *La Vie Parisienne* in 1895, shows us even better than Daudet's novel the energetic cultivation of spiritual values in an upper middle-class setting, where the art-mad 'Maissenes' foreshadow Proust's Verdurins. 'The Snob', states the anonymous author, 'is the *bourgeois gentilhomme* of aesthetics.' In an ultra-aesthetic drawing-room they put on a performance of *Genesis*, a symphony in nine movements by Rolf Maaden. The Maissenes are exploited by a young poet, Michel Cœurderoy, who speaks the language of Symbolism, and by a sinister occultist called Myriam Boréal. All these people come together at a performance of *The Lighthouse of Haparanda*, a play attributed to Ibsen:

> Myriam, in the Pentacle's box, is dressed in her magician's robes; huge rings, made of unknown metals and set with gems with sonorous-sounding names, adorn her fingers; she is surrounded by a crowd of beardless youths . . . Madame Maissene has removed the gloves from her famous arms, which poets have compared to the pistils of rare flowers, to jungle creepers, to alabaster columns; she is wearing a green dress the colour of evil eyes, with a necklace of huge dead turquoises set in platinum. In her hand she is casually holding an enormous water-lily.

These satires on aestheticism recall the much milder *Patience* in which Gilbert and Sullivan had poked fun at Wilde's eccentricities ten years before.

The favourite painter of the ladies in question was Lévy-Dhurmer, who used to depict his sitters in the oddest postures in an otherworldly atmosphere. The influence of these circles was particularly noticeable in the production of engravings. The 'Maissenes' and their friends could be called 'iconophiles': for their benefit, art publishers brought out some admirable periodicals containing prints accompanied by poems: Marty's *L'Estampe Originale*, Maurice Dumont's *L'Épreuve*, and finally Meir-Graefe's *Le Germinal*. Books illustrated by Carlos Schwabe or de Feure were published with luxurious bindings – though here we are encroaching on the sphere of decorative art. The early 1890s saw the appearance of a host of new images representing dreams, spiritual conditions and a wide variety of moods, and ranging from the delightful to the deplorable. On the popular level the same phenomenon occurred with the revival of poster art.

THE TWILIGHT OF THE CHIMERAS. An article by Mirbeau tolled the knell of these aesthetic affectations: 'Oh, what a lot of harm they did, those wretched aesthetes, when, in their honeyed voices, they preached a horror of nature and life, proclaimed the futility of draughtsmanship, and advocated the return of art to Papuan concepts, embryonic forms, a spectral existence; the extremes of ugliness, the depths of nothingness.'

So far this was simply what had been said about the first Impressionists, and what might have been said about many abstract painters if modern criticism did not lean heavily in favour of everything *avant-garde*. But Mirbeau went further than this, passing from aesthetics to morality, and accusing the Decadents of vices which at that time were regarded with considerable disapproval (49). His article, significantly enough, was written in May 1895, just after Wilde had been convicted. (It is ironic to remember that Mirbeau himself, three years later, was to bring out *Le Jardin des supplices*, a book which treats the most nauseating themes of the Decadence.)

At the same time Lorrain declared: 'After the Burne-Jones crash we now have the Botticelli crash.' All of a sudden people realized that the Mona Lisa's beauty had become a commonplace (31). The snobs took fright and the public waxed indignant. As a result, when the finest of all Symbolist works, Debussy's *Pelléas*, was produced in 1902, it arrived ten years too late and was given a hostile reception. Patriotism had something to do with its failure: the work was condemned as Belgian, the sets as German and the music as Wagnerian. As if to live up to his nickname of 'Jehanne ma bonne Lorraine', Jean Lorrain attacked the idols of his youth in a novel which illness prevented him from finishing, and savagely criticized the work of a painter for aesthetes (106). The snobs, who had kept the little reviews alive and financed the *avant-garde* theatres, took a rest pending the arrival of the Ballets Russes.

There were more serious reasons than a change in fashion for the death of the Decadence and the decline of Aestheticism – namely the Wilde scandal and the Dreyfus affair. In 1895, exasperated by the tickling of peacock feathers, Victorian England trampled like an old elephant over the aesthetic flower-beds. Wilde had exhausted the country's patience. In his fall the poet took with him Beardsley and all the others who were accused of having turned the 'Palace of the Arts' into a place of ill-repute. The Imperial sun dissipated the mists of the mauve Nineties, and Kipling and Conrad, the least aesthetic of writers, rose to rapid fame. Henceforth painters like Sargent or Brangwyn were to bear witness to the prosperity of the Edwardian era, and reproductions of Pre-Raphaelite paintings ceased to be seen anywhere except in Florentine boarding-houses. America reacted in the same way, even in the *Chap-Book*, a Decadent periodical (108).

True, the Decadents had had less influence in France than the Aesthetes in England, but the vogue for *Art Nouveau* – described by Mirbeau as 'the product of the depraved Englishman, the foxy Belgian and the morphinomaniac Jewess' – enabled the French nationalists to denounce snobs and aesthetes. The Panama scandal had already stirred up French public opinion against the international bankers who included many patrons of modern art. 'Hayem and Ephrussi monopolized Moreau and Redon,' wrote Lorrain; and it is true that snobbery and a solidly based – if Germanic – culture led many rich Jews to patronize the painters of the chimeras, whose opulent works may also have flattered in them an age-old nostalgia for the East. The nationalists on the other hand wanted a virile France, and therefore condemned the affectations of the Rosicrucians.

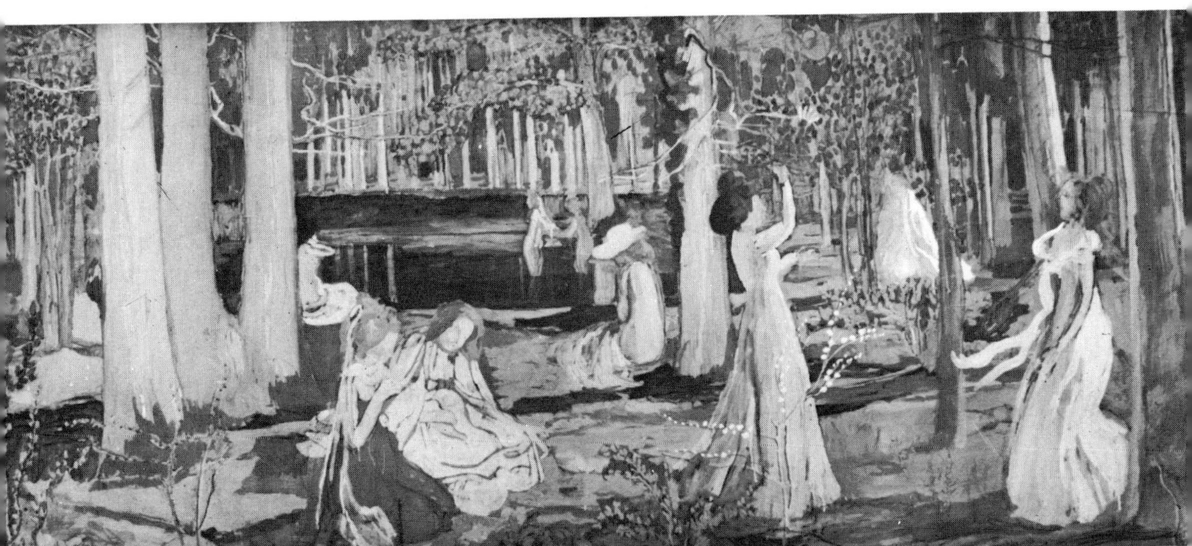

111. Maurice Denis: *Le Bois sacré*. The influence of Puvis de Chavannes' fresco of the same title is considerable in this panel, but the colours of pale yellow and green are plainly modern, and this Sacred Wood could easily be the Bois de Boulogne.

The leading aesthetes in France, Bourget and Barrès, both became nationalists: the former in order to eradicate the memory of his homosexual past and to enter the Academy, the latter because, after his novels on the *culte du moi*, he had nothing more to gain from aestheticism. On the anniversary of Verlaine's death, Barrès declared somewhat airily that 'these games' had lasted long enough.

As early as 1893 a book by a German called Max Nordau, which rapidly became famous all over Europe, set out to clip the chimeras' wings. 'We are in the midst of a mental epidemic,' wrote the author, 'a sort of Black Death of degeneration and hysteria.' Nordau, whose arguments would later be repeated by the Nazis, begged the élite to denounce this artistic insanity, which he blamed on tobacco, alcohol, and urbanization, before it spread to the common people. He described artists in much the same terms as Cesare Lombroso applied to criminals, and attacked Wilde and Mallarmé in particular. When the Dreyfus Affair exploded, nearly all the artists in France supported Dreyfus, admirers of Wagner were accused of working for Germany, and *L'Action Française* invoked the purifying virtues of war.

However, it is probable that, even without these scandals which accelerated the evolution of public taste, the artists we have been studying would have gone out of fashion fairly quickly, for the triumph of *Art Nouveau* at the 1900 Exhibition highlighted their weaknesses. *Le Rire* made fun of their affectations in Métivet's caricatures, just as *Punch* had made fun of the Aesthetes, twenty years earlier, in Du Maurier's cartoons. In Germany and Austria, on the other hand, the *Sezession*, from scandalous beginnings, became almost an official institution. Klimt was actually commissioned to decorate the University, possibly because under all his eccentricities he retained something of Mackart and Besnard. The review *Jugend* too did a great deal to spread the *fin de siècle* style and themes among the public. There was also an ethnic explanation for the implantation of *Art Nouveau* in the Germanic countries: its lines recall the fluidities of German Rococo. It is in fact a style of Nordic inspiration, rooted in ancient Slav or Celtic traditions; and themes emanating from a collective legendary dream are rarely acceptable to communities with a logical turn of mind. However, the great Böcklin fell into disfavour when the Impressionists were introduced to Germany by Meir-Graefe. A harsh article by the critic described that strange painter as an interior decorator of middle-class homes.

In the Latin countries *Art Nouveau*, in spite of a few great artists, was a foreign import. In France one of the consequences of the decline of aestheticism was the belated but suddenly accelerated

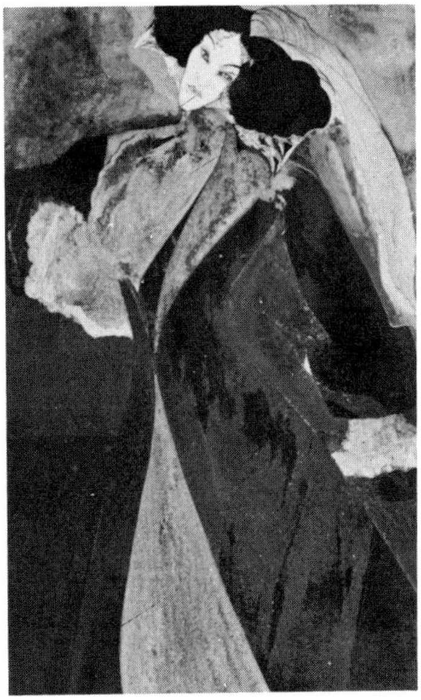

112. Christoph Tot Babberich: *Promeneuse*. A lady aesthete depicted by a young Dutch artist who was influenced by both Beardsley and de Feure.

triumph of Impressionism, which had all the qualities of simplicity and gaiety which the newly disgraced school was accused of lacking: in short, it was praised as a 'very French' style of painting. This change in taste is exemplified by Proust who in his references to *Art Nouveau* passed rapidly from affection to caricature. Describing the actress Rachel fifteen years later, he was to stress the ridiculous side of her aesthetic affectations, in contrast to his sympathetic portrait of the Botticelli-like Odette. Rather like Lorrain, alas, we find Ruskin's translator condemning Symbolism in the *Revue Blanche*: 'Loud, empty sea-shells; pieces of wood which have rotted or been thrown up on the shore, and which the first comer can take if he likes, if the ebbing generation has not carried them away.' But when he needed mysterious images, it was still from Moreau that he borrowed them (17). And it should not be forgotten that according to Saint-Loup the Duchesse de Guermantes, like Madame Greffulhe, possessed 'some moving paintings by Gustave Moreau'.

What became of 'the ebbing generation', the artists who had chosen to follow the chimeras? Some, such as Toorop, followed Beardsley's example and became ardent Catholics; Filiger disappeared; Khnopff withdrew from his age. Nearly all were regarded as failures. And these misunderstood painters had no other consolation than to tell themselves that they were *artistes maudits.* Moreau survived thanks to his Fauve pupils, but the public expressed surprise that such 'geniuses' should have been able to learn anything from that 'opera painter'. Only Redon's fame continued to grow, because his flower pictures led critics to class him among the Impressionists. From the ivory tower to which the Symbolist painters had withdrawn, they could see the successive waves of Fauvism and Cubism sweeping away their illusions; and, if they had lived long enough, they would have observed that, when their style eventually found favour once more with the public, it was not for their exquisite, melancholy images, but for the most vulgar products of their school.

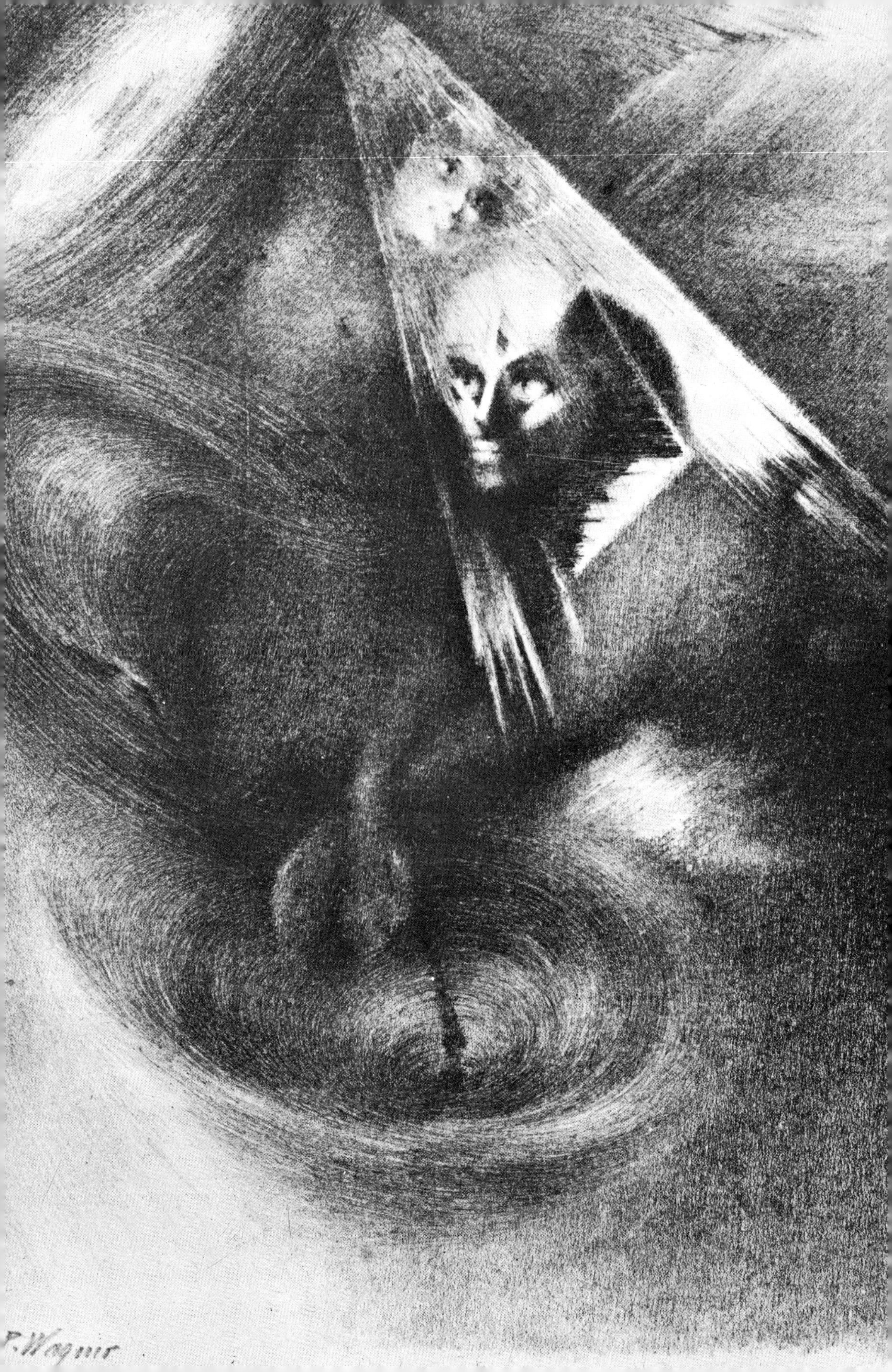

13 Breeding the Chimeras

113. J. F. Wagner: *Le Rêve*. This lithograph on an esoteric theme by one of Redon's imitators appeared in *L'Estampe originale*, a publication which did a great deal to interest collectors in *Art Nouveau*. Each picture was accompanied by a poem.

THE EXHIBITIONS. Now, after following the flight of the Chimeras towards very different realms, tracing their influence on at least two generations, and recording their rapid decline, let us see in what nests their eggs were hatched, how certain species succeeded in making their home in foreign lands, and by what affinities, at the end of tho last century, all the Chimeras' familiars came to form their artistic International. For they themselves were very conscious of belonging to an aristocracy of Beauty (whence their horror of democracy), to a secret order of chivalry which was sometimes cursed with ill-fate, as were the Knights Templar, and far above national differences. Although the poets and philosophers who prepared men's minds for creative dreams, showed their dreams, they lived far apart from one another; where did they find the forms which were to stimulate their fantasies?

The most important means of diffusion was photographic reproduction, from 1875 onwards. Thus Alinari sent photographs to Oxford of all the Botticellis in the Uffizi, to Burne-Jones of the Mantegnas at Padua, and to Péladan of Leonardo's drawings. Less expensive and more faithful than engraving, photography propagated the history of art: a similar phenomenon is taking place today in the sphere of music, as recording techniques are gradually improved. Thus we have a letter from Lorrain to Barrès, accompanying some framed reproductions of Burne-Jones and Rossetti, destined to be hung on the staircase of Barrès's home at Charmes. Robert de Montesquiou had albums full of similar photographs, reproducing pictures both ancient and modern.

While the Impressionists had nothing to gain from a process which could not render colour, the literary painters, to whom line was more important, benefited enormously from photography. Thus Moreau and Puvis were known in other countries long before their works were exhibited abroad, for reproductions of the most admired works on show were sold at every Salon.

The Paris Salon was an event of national importance, just like the Royal Academy Exhibition in London. Academic art reigned supreme there, and Moreau and Puvis were the only exhibitors to attract artists to the Salon. On the other hand, the Universal Exhibitions contained foreign sections where pictures from neighbouring countries could be seen. Monsieur Jacques Lethève, who has made a profound study of the Pre-Raphaelites' influence in France, tells us that at the 1855 Exhibition the French public could already see Millais's *Ophelia* and Hunt's *The Light of the World*, which incidentally they likened to coloured photographs. Taine taught the public to appreciate this unfamiliar art, and Burne-Jones's pictures at the 1878 Exhibition, *Love among the Ruins* and *Merlin and Vivian*, obtained an enormous success. Charles Blanc, an Academician and the doyen of French art historians, declared that these paintings were 'a quintessence of the ideal, a sublimated poetry'. Burne-Jones had another triumph at the 1889 Exhibition with *King Cophetua and the Beggar-Maid*.

It would be superfluous to recall the disagreements which led to the founding of the *Salon des Indépendants*, at which Redon and Carrière were among the exhibitors. The latter, it should be remembered, seemed to his contemporaries to be a very great figure in the art world, even in Redon's eyes. Cazin too impressed Redon with what the latter regarded as his simplicity, but which was later revealed to be mediocrity. It is not uncommon for critics to be blind or the public to be mistaken, but the errors of judgement committed by great artists have strange causes: artists often express envy of someone else's work which is successful, without in fact being as vulgar as they like to claim.

The Idealists began exhibiting at the 1889 Exhibition, next to the Impressionists and the Synthetists. Later on the Independents gave shelter to three Rosicrucian Salons. It is interesting to think what a superb museum of modern art could be made out of the best works in any single one of these exhibitions: Seurat, Van Gogh, Lautrec, the Douanier Rousseau with *La Guerre*, which was to win the praise of Gourmont and Jarry, and then Filiger, Osbert, and the most advanced artist of them all, the Dane Willumsen.

But the role played by the galleries was much more important than that of the Salons. The best gallery in Paris was that of Georges Petit, where a private view was a social event. The new painters were soon made welcome there, but found themselves in what strikes us as the astonishing company of Gervex, Roll, and Renoir. They felt more at home in the little Le Barc de Boutteville gallery in the Rue Le Peletier. The same artists were invited to the *Salon des XX* in Brussels.

Then came Bing, a German who had introduced Japanese art to Europe: his shop, *L'Art Nouveau*, at 22 Rue de Provence, crystallized the style to which it gave its name. The works exhibited

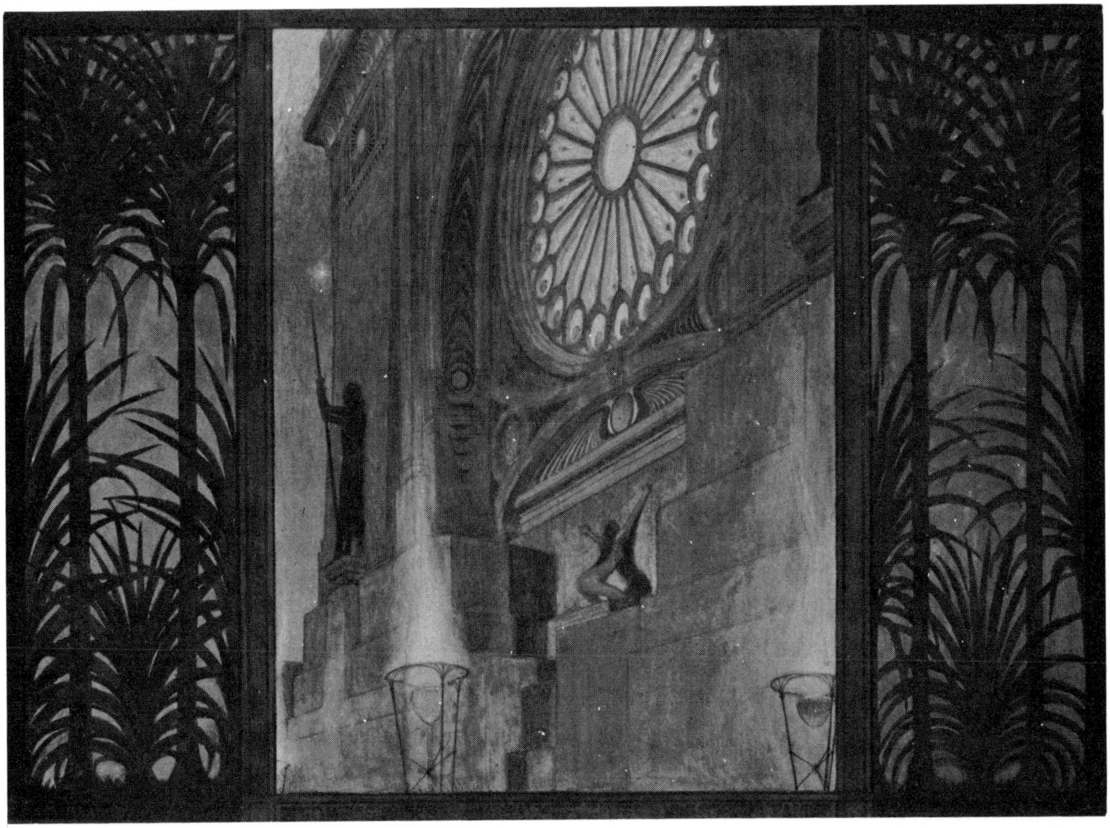

114. Fidus: *Orante*. The world of Stefan George is pictured for us here in this work by an artist who was very popular in Germany because of his equivocal subjects.

there were by Khnopff, Ibels, Walter Crane, and Maurice Denis, but also by Whistler and the Impressionists. That might surprise us today, if we were to forget that these artists were all 'modern' to their contemporaries, and shocked the general public to an equal degree. The picture-dealers were beginning to find their role: it was not as important yet as the role Vollard was going to play, but the Durand-Ruels did not hesitate to open their gallery to other painters besides the Impressionists, even though their name was henceforth to be inseparable from the latter. In 1894, for example, they put on the first Redon exhibition, and in 1891 they opened their doors to the Rosicrucians.

In their décor, and in the hospitality they showed to artists who were very different though never academic, all these galleries imitated the Grosvenor Gallery in London, where the Pre-Raphaelites and Whistler triumphed belatedly in the setting of a Florentine palace. Wilde was the central figure at these private views.

Although Germany was now politically united, she still lacked artistic unity. Munich, Böcklin's capital, was an important art centre, and so was Darmstadt later on, under the influence of the Grand Duke of Hesse, an enthusiastic admirer of *Art Nouveau*. Exhibitions of varying importance were organized in most of the big cities.

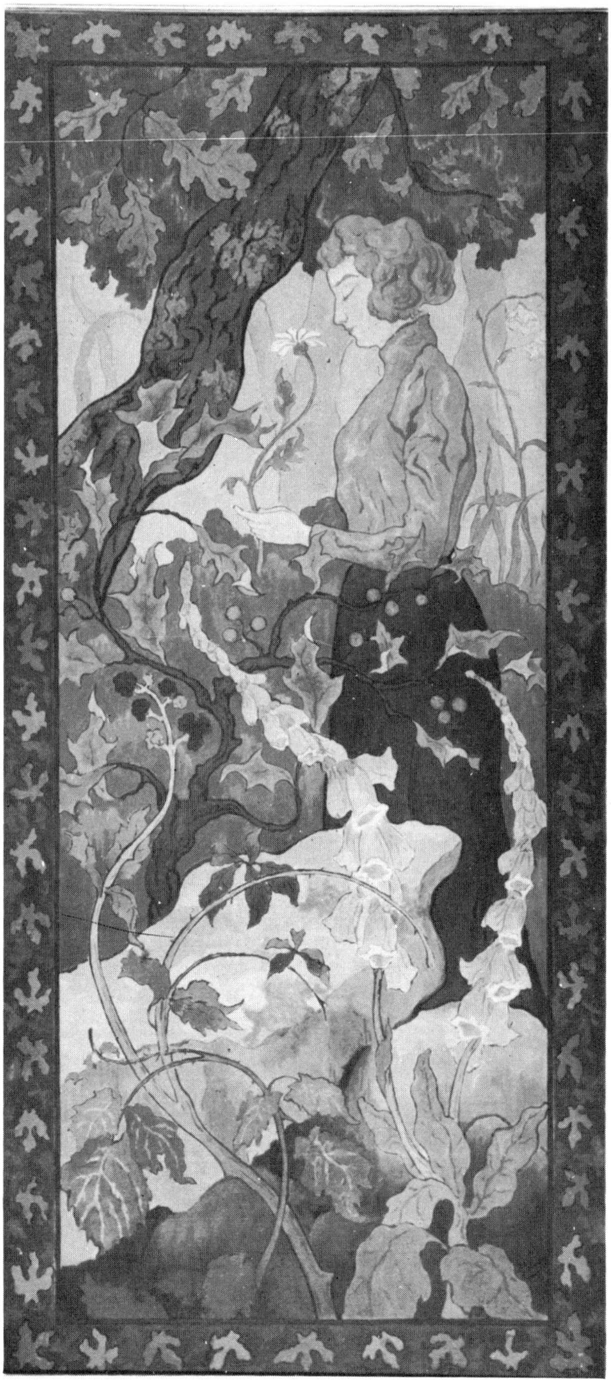

115. **Paul** Ranson: *Les Digitales.* In the same style as Grasset, but nearer modern painting, Ranson sometimes suggests a somewhat clumsy Matisse. His flat colours and curving lines are more those of an artisan image-maker than a painter.

Vienna, on the other hand, was the true artistic capital of a vast empire. Academic art was predominant, it is true, but the *Künstlerhaus* group put on exhibitions on the fringe of the official art world. In 1882 Puvis de Chavannes and Rodin sent some works to Vienna which had a considerable influence, especially on Klimt. The story of the *Sezession* group and the pavilion it opened in 1898 is too well-known to need repeating here.

THE REVIEWS. The reviews were of course one of the most effective means of propagating the new ideas. There were only a few of them before 1885, and the best was the *Gazette des Beaux-Arts*, founded twenty years earlier by Charles Blanc. Some of the most distinguished critics in France contributed to it; thus in 1863 Burty devoted a long article to Rossetti and Burne-Jones, in which he was the first to link their works with the *Fleurs du Mal*. The *Gazette* belonged at that time to Charles Ephrussi, a Russian Jew who was one of the greatest connoisseurs of his age. He was also a charming man who served as one of Proust's models for the character of Swann. Ephrussi's tastes were eclectic: he gave his patronage to Renoir, yet devoted long articles in his review to Moreau. In short, he seemed the ideal person to spread aesthetic ideas from one country to another, and this was precisely what he did. Thus he published several articles by Laforgue (for whom he had obtained a position as reader to the German Empress), in which the names of Böcklin and Klinger appeared for the first time. It was the *Gazette des Beaux-Arts* too which published Ary Renan's fine study of Gustave Moreau. However, destined as it was for a very rich or very learned clientele, the *Gazette* was obliged to devote itself more and more to either *objets d'art* or old masters. Desjardins's *Revue Wagnérienne* took the place of the *Gazette* after 1885 in supporting a new artistic style. The reproductions it contained were few in number but of excellent quality. They included some Wagnerian lithographs by Fantin-Latour, which were admittedly very restrained but showed a predilection for sinuous lines and flowing hair which had an undeniable influence; Redon's admirable *Parsifal*; and even a few paintings by Jacques-Émile Blanche, who had toyed with Impressionism and Idealism before deciding to paint for profit. The review also published a study of a typographical experiment aimed at translating music into visual form: the 'Catalogue of sixty-six aspects of the Leitmotif in "Parzifal".' Other contributors to the review were Swinburne, Verlaine, and Mallarmé (57). The latter, despite his admiration for Albert Besnard, declared: 'Today symphonic emotional painting must recognize Monsieur Puvis de Chavannes as a master.'

After 1890 an increasing number of art magazines came into being, adorned with original lithographs which made them collectors' items. *L'Image* contained texts by Decadent authors illustrated by Khnopff, Carlos Schwabe, the elegant de Feure, and Maurice Denis. Even more luxurious was *L'Ymagier*, a review founded by Rémy de Gourmont at the very end of the century, which published articles by Jarry, including a very interesting essay on monsters, reproductions of works by Filiger, and above all, Gothic or Indian woodcuts, printed on rare papers.

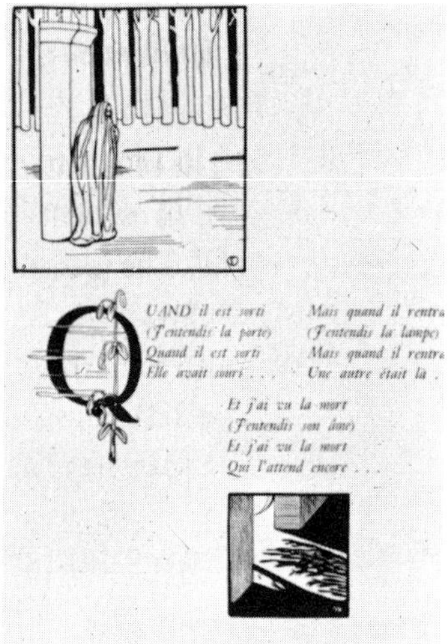

116. Doudelet: *Engravings for a Poem by Maeterlinck*. An illustration which appeared in the German review *Pan*, the most luxurious of all *fin-de-siècle* periodicals. Doudelet was one of the best illustrators of his time.

Very badly printed, on the other hand, with numerous but mediocre reproductions, *La Plume* aimed at a wide public for which it published, every now and then, a series of lithographs by Henry de Groux, Mucha, Ensor, Osbert, and Henry Rivière, and Moreau colour reproductions. *La Plume's* artistic tendencies ranged from the Rosicrucians to *Modern Style*, and in politics the magazine, published in the midst of the Dreyfus Affair, was on the left. One of its pictures, indeed, was a martyred *Zola* by Henry de Groux, an artist who according to his admirers combined Rubens's verve with Rembrandt's profundity. He was certainly one of the artists who helped to bring discredit upon the painting of ideas. As for his own huge canvases and confused lithographs, they allegedly had a Beethovian quality, and they may yet come to the surface again, as did the darkest Caravaggios, after sleeping for centuries in an attic. It is interesting to read the collected issues of *La Plume*, for to do so is to follow in the footsteps of the 'happy few', who were often more susceptible to the artificially eccentric than to the truly bizarre. But *La Revue blanche*, from its first appearance in 1891, succeeded in creating a more sober, more enduring style, by publishing the work of greater artists. The painters and engravers praised by *La Plume* found a home, this time with better reproductions, in *Art et Décoration*, which remains the best periodical of the more affluent Decadence.

The snobs of the *fin de siècle* were unlikely to have read *La Plume*, but all of them became subscribers to the London-based *Studio* as soon as it appeared, in 1893. This magazine continued the work of William Morris and adopted the Pre-Raphaelites' ideals as its own. The first issue, which contained a long article on Aubrey Beardsley, made him famous overnight all over Europe, thanks above all to the reproductions it published of his *Siegfried*. In the following issues there were articles on Toorop, on Chéret, who undoubtedly influenced Beardsley, on Khnopff, on Klinger, and on Voysey's wallpapers. However, *Studio* was not infallible: it praised a mediocre English painter, J. W. Waterhouse, on the grounds that he sometimes treated Pre-Raphaelite subjects. Nonetheless, the magazine was much more conversant than the French reviews with what was happening abroad, so that it obtained considerable international success, and its influence on the decorative arts was enormous. The magazine even gave its name to a new rectilinear style reminiscent of Mackintosh's buildings; it also devoted some articles to photography, and it is interesting to note that the photographers of the day busied themselves trying to produce Burne-Joneses and Alma-Tademas. Thus – admittedly before the Wilde scandal – *Studio* published some 'classical' photographs of Sicilian boys taken by Gloeben and that curious writer known to us as

Baron Corvo. At the same time *Studio* encouraged amateurs with competitions in poker-work, binding, and the design of book-plates, and the number of lady artists who followed its lead soon became considerable.

In contrast, the *Yellow Book* had nothing practical about it. Its thirteen volumes, publication of which began in 1894, were chiefly devoted to Beardsley – to such a degree that the *Westminster Gazette* called for Parliamentary action 'to make this sort of thing illegal'. However, next to the most provocative drawings, the

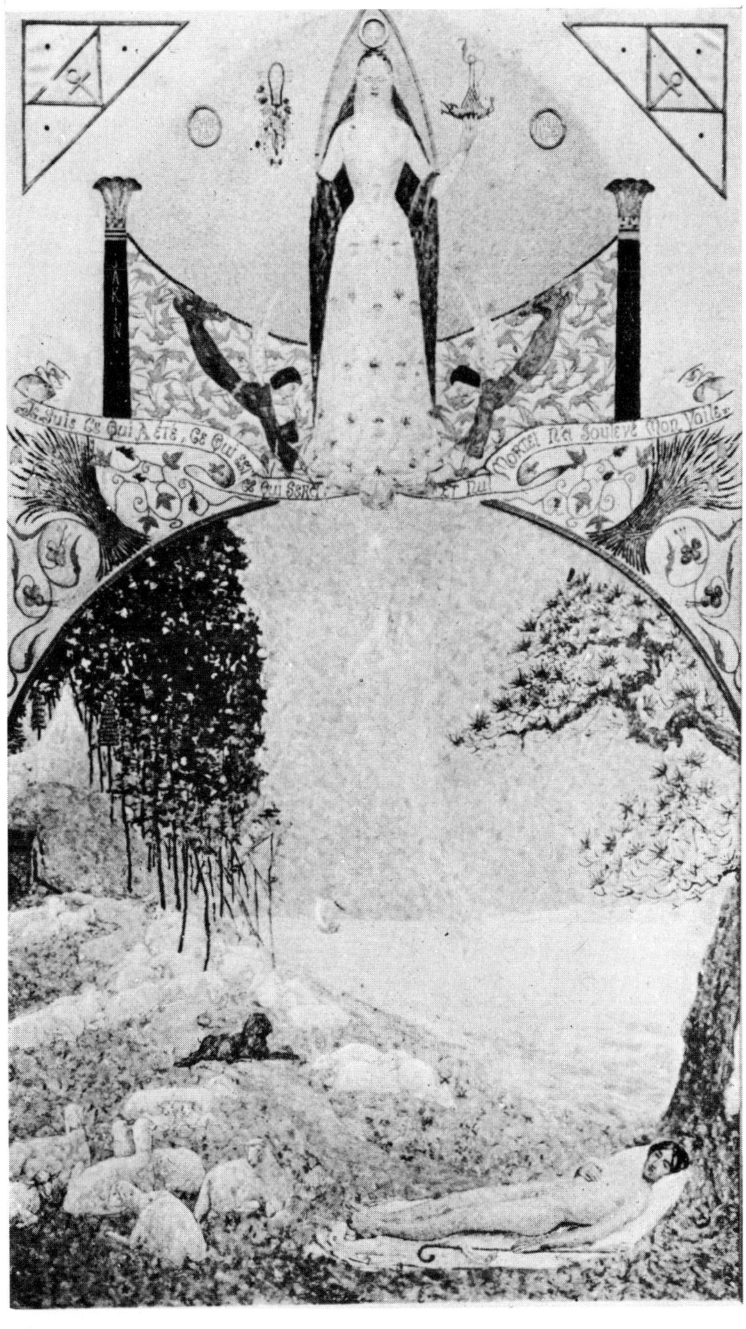

117. Antoine de La Rochefoucauld: *La bonne Déesse Isis initie le Berger*. This picture, exhibited at the *Salon des Rose+Croix* but since lost, is characteristic of the iconography advocated by Péladan. Antiquity, the Middle Ages and freemasonry are closely allied in it, but the actual style is really more pointillist.

Yellow Book offered reproductions of Conder, Sickert, and Wilson Steer, and a strange picture by a little-known imitator of Toorop, Herbert MacNaire. Its contributors also included artists who owed little to the inspiration of the chimeras, and writers as unchimerical as Henry James and Arnold Bennett. But everything else in the *Yellow Book* seems insipid compared to Beardsley. He even designed the vine-leaf motif on the cover of the elegantly bound yellow volumes. Besides, the spirit of the *Yellow Book* was more important than its contents. The magazine drew much of its inspiration from the Montmartre of the *Chat noir*; and the editor of the *Yellow Book*, Henry Harland, was a frequent visitor to Paris, as were his colleagues Symons and Le Gallienne, while Conder was a great friend of Toulouse-Lautrec. The role played by this review was an important one, since it was the *Yellow Book* that introduced the themes of the French Decadence into England. It had a successor, the *Savoy*, a more luxurious periodical which was also illustrated with a great many Beardsley drawings.

When the *Yellow Book* disappeared, a victim of the Wilde scandal even though it had never published so much as a single line of his, two of Wilde's friends, Ricketts and Shannon, launched the *Pageant*, a luxurious review with less dangerous tendencies. Ten years earlier they had already published a magazine, the *Dial*, noteworthy for the drawings of Ricketts himself, an innocent Beardsley who had provided pretty illustrations for Wilde's stories; Shannon was a more academic painter. In this ephemeral review we can find reproductions of Rossetti, Conder's *Blue Bird*, and a Byzantine play by Michael Field: nothing very novel, in fact, except for a decidedly homosexual drawing by Laurence Housman. For a few years Scotland had her own *Studio*, a magazine called *Evergreen*, which published the ghostliest creations of the Celtic Revival.

But it was Germany which, in 1895, was to give the period its most splendid and also its most interesting review: *Pan*. In this magazine we can find literary contributions by Mallarmé, Maeterlinck, Thomas Mann, Knut Hamsun, and Hugo von Hofmannsthal. Next to original lithographs by Toulouse-Lautrec and Signac, *Pan* contains Khnopffs, Segantinis, Willumsens, Klingers, decorative frames by von Hoffmann and Peter Behrens, Doudelets, and works by other artists responsible for the most elegant creations of *Art Nouveau*. At that time Germany had a few rich and cultured aristocrats, including such men as the Grand Duke of Hesse and Graf Kessler, which, together with the great Jewish families, was able to keep a magazine such as *Pan* alive.

In a more modest class, the review *Jugend* gave its name to a style as *Studio* did in England: a style as heavy and florid as the

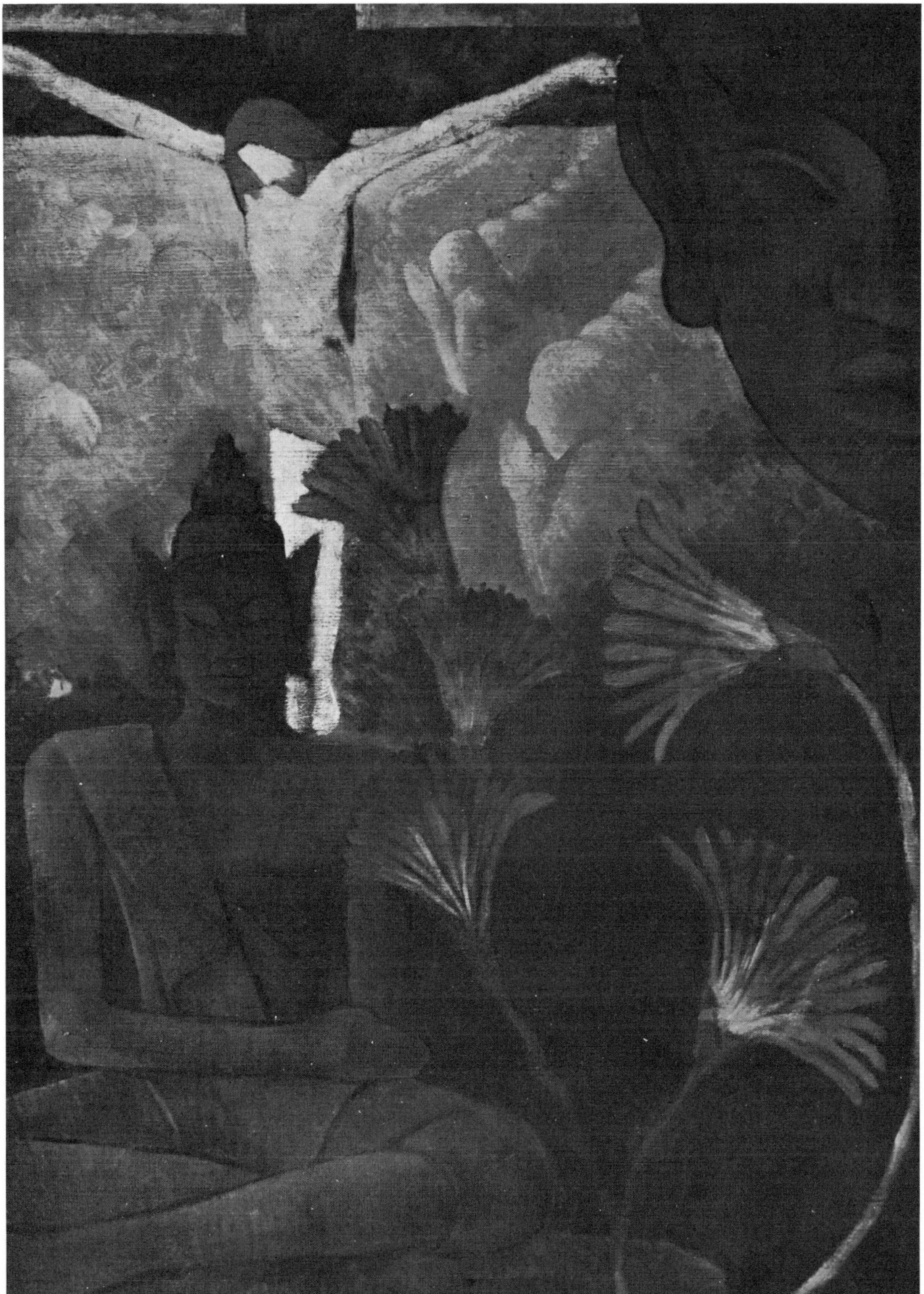

118. Paul Élie Ranson: *Christ and Buddha.* This is one of the most striking examples of the mystical reveries of the Pont-Aven school. It brings together Buddha and the Christ of a Breton Calvary, Oriental fantasy and praying figures. The large oriental mask at the top of the picture is close to Gauguin, who shared Ranson's views and ideas.

taste of *Studio* was sober. *Jugend*, which made *bourgeoises* out of Böcklin's chimeras, was published in Munich, like *Die Kunst*. Flanders too had a review of its own, which helped to propagate Van de Velde's work: *Van Nu en Straks*.

Vienna and St. Petersburg both took *Pan* as their model. In Vienna the organ of the *Sezession* was *Ver Sacrum*, which brought together the names of Gerhard Hauptmann, Rilke, Klimt, and Khnopff. With its typographical innovations and illustrators such as Klimt, Kolo Moser, Ludwig von Hoffman, and Anton Moser, *Ver Sacrum* was the most remarkable periodical of its time (1898–1903). In Russia Diaghilev founded his splendid review *The World of Art*, in which he reproduced drawings by Beardsley: this review formed a bridge between the *fin de siècle* and the Fauve art of the Ballets Russes. The *Studio* style flourished in Poland, exemplified in such works as Maleycrosk's *Tobias and the Angel*.

America had only a very small review, the *Chap-Book*, illustrated with Beardsley-type woodcuts by an artist from Chicago (then a much more *avant-garde* city than New York) called Bradley. But magazines such as *Harper's Bazaar* soon had Grasset covers and de Feure designs, in the same way as the *Figaro Illustré* in France.

THE THEATRE. Europe had to wait for the Ballets Russes to dissipate the Wagnerian influence which weighed so heavily on the theatre. Truth to tell, the aesthetes found that any theatrical performance, however well done, impeded their imagination; the Symbolists preferred concerts to operas, reading to the theatre. Consequently, in spite of a few very fine works such as *Axel* and *Pelléas*, both staged for the first time in 1893 by Lugné-Poe, the chimeras rarely took flight from a stage. No theatrical designer could match Moreau's fabulous architecture, and their very limited funds prevented the Théâtre de l'Art, and later the Théâtre de l'Œuvre, from using anything more elaborate than simple backcloths by Sérusier or the young Nabis. Unfortunately Redon did not design the sets for *Axel*, nor Burne-Jones those for *Pelléas*. Gauguin published a drawing in *La Plume* based on Rachilde's *Madame La Mort*: it shows a scene in a garden featuring the principal character's brain. As for the Théâtre de l'Œuvre productions of Ibsen, little remains of them but the programmes adorned with lithographs by Munch and Vuillard.

In England, in spite of some admirable actors, the theatre was very conservative. Gordon Craig's reforms only came later, but it should perhaps be mentioned that Craig was influenced by a remarkable aesthete, Lady Archibald Campbell, who organized outdoor performances of Shakespeare's plays. The great theatrical production of the *fin de siècle* was to have been Wilde's *Salome*,

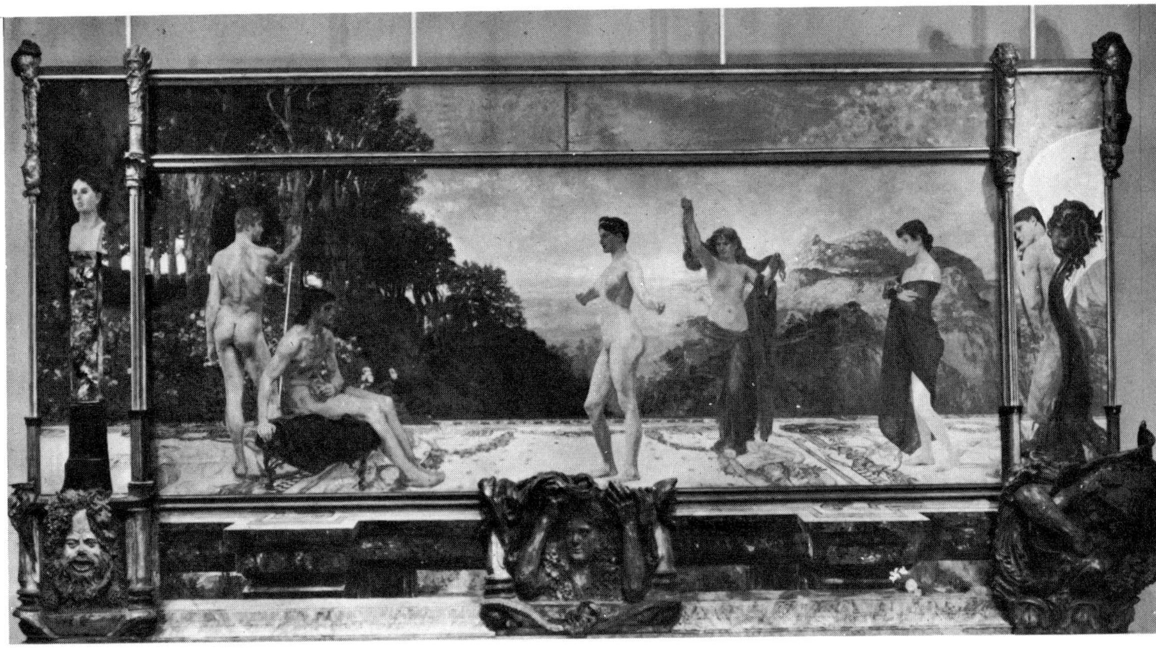

119. Klinger: *The Judgement of Paris*. There is a curious contrast between the very academic drawing of the figures, and the frame, moulded by the artist himself in gilt bronze, which was one of the highlights of the *Sezession* exhibition in Vienna.

with Sarah Bernhardt in the title role and sets inspired by Moreau's paintings. Unfortunately, as we have already seen, the Lord Chamberlain took fright and Europe had to make do with the brave but unpretentious production at the Théâtre de l'Œuvre.

However a few artistes took on the appearance of chimeras and tempted the dreamers of the day away from imperfect stage-sets towards the heights where the poets wished to carry them. First and foremost, of course, there was Sarah Bernhardt. In England there was Ellen Terry, who appeared as a Burne-Jones figure in her Shakespearian roles. In France a fair-haired beauty, less remarkable than Ellen Terry, but still 'madly artistic', was the feminine ideal of the Symbolists. This was Georgette Leblanc, who lived with Maeterlinck for many years and was an incomparable Mélisande in a production of *Pelléas* in the ruins of Saint-Wandrille Abbey. An unpublished letter from Mallarmé to Robert de Montesquiou, found among the latter's papers, gives us some idea of the young woman's achievement:

> My dear friend: I thought of you the other day, more particularly while I was watching a performance of infinitely rare and wonderful artistry, and I could not help saying so aloud. Mlle. Georgette Leblanc, who was miming and singing the part of a musical statue, did not fail for a moment. She seems very properly obsessed with the desire for your appreciation, and combining my friendship for you with my admiration for her, begs me to ask you to attend a private audition she wishes to give, between friends and without ceremony, for your benefit.

We can imagine Rachel, the actress in *A la recherche du temps perdu*, adopting Georgette Leblanc poses when, in the midst of the Guermantes' sniggering, she recites *Les Sept Princesses*. Saint-Loup's dark mistress, with her sharp profile and her Cléo de Mérode bandeaux, looked like Marthe Mellot. And finally, there was Loïe Fuller, that wonderful electric butterfly, who danced for only a few seasons, but put her imprint on a whole style (26).

AESTHETICS. These actresses lent their features to a great many heroines, and also to some ideas, if we try to see them through Rémy de Gourmont's eyes:

> The eternal truths are of all types. Some are fair-haired with a milky skin which tempts us with the nubility of a virgin; some have the four feet of an animal and an angular brow which contains all the anxiety of mankind in its geometry. Some have wings wider than the wings of condors and shelter beneath their feathers a host of thoughts . . . The eternal truths: the irony in their unchanging eyes turns towards the sky . . .

In another passage Gourmont writes: 'Personal Art – and that is the only art – is always almost incomprehensible. If it is understood, it ceases to be pure Art to become a subject for new artistic expressions.' These lines show quite clearly the impossibility of controlling the flight of the chimeras or of stipulating the colour of their plumage. The entire philosophy of Albert Aurier, the recognized critic of the Symbolist Movement, is summed up in these words: 'The artist must have that transcendental emotivity, so great and so precious, which makes the soul quiver before the changing drama of abstractions.'

In the space of twenty years the painter-poets succeeded in 'discrediting the facts', to adapt Wilde's expression, opening the way to painters who might be superior to them but could not be more intellectually daring. They helped to create a style and witnessed its decline; but when that style became fashionable once more, the world misjudged their ideal. Often, too, they failed in their enterprises. Remarkably successful in poster-art and book-illustration, they were less so in such fields as polychrome sculpture. Willumsen's huge creations in marble and gilded bronze are as pathetically unsuccessful as Klinger's coloured statues or Frampton's frescoes – such as his *Mysteriach* which was so greatly admired by subscribers to *Studio*. More modest but partly successful are the chimeras cast in bronze by Crabin or Dampt. And we should not forget to mention the enormous ceramic tabernacle commissioned from Carriès by Princess Edmond de Polignac to contain a Wagner manuscript.

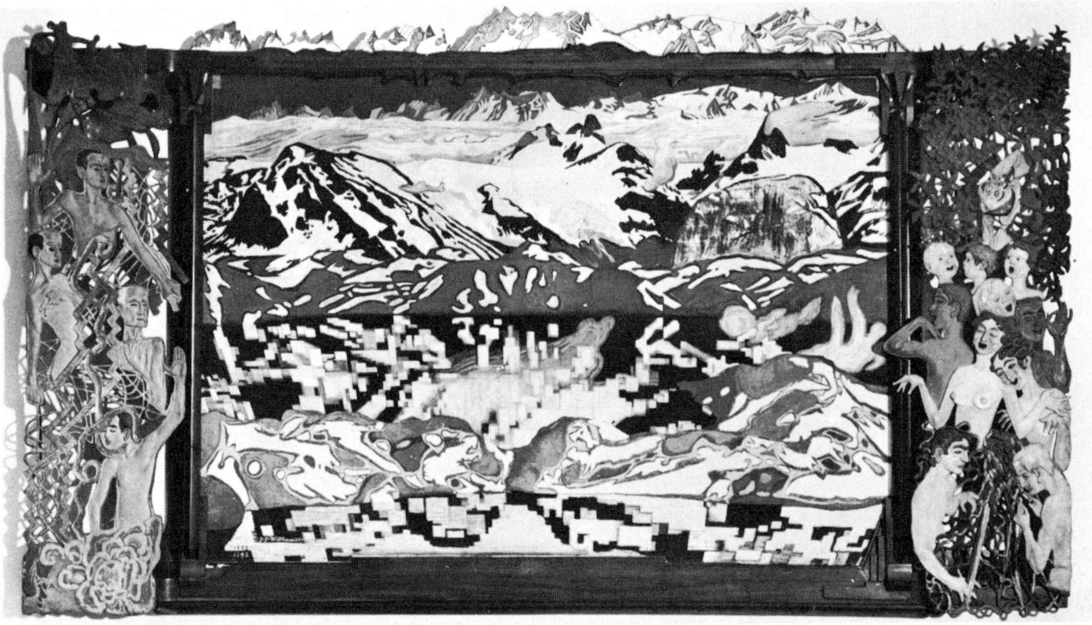

120. J. F. Willumsen: *Jotunheim*. This Danish painter and sculptor always attributed considerable importance to his frames. His gilded and polychrome groups were very famous in Scandinavia.

The attraction of novelty doubtless led critics to overlook a great many mistakes. Thus Jules Laforgue, a man of extreme sensitivity, actually wrote: 'I rate more highly than any bust in bronze or marble these wax busts, for example, with blue or black eyes, red or bloodless lips, hair and jewellery.' Was his judgement any better when he expressed fulsome admiration for certain frames? Perhaps it was, when the painting itself was mediocre, for then the picture became an object: 'The *Salons des Indépendants* have substituted an intelligent, refined variety of unusual frames for the perpetual gilded frame with the ornamental mouldings. A sunny green landscape, a wintry yellow beach, an interior sparkling with chandeliers require frames which only their respective creators know how to make. And so we have seen plain frames in white, pale pink, or daffodil yellow, or streaked in a variety of colours.' The Pre-Raphaelites had begun the fashion of decorating their frames themselves, and this fashion was carried to greater lengths by Toorop and particularly by Willumsen, the Danish painter and sculptor. In the catalogue of the 1893 *Salon des Indépendants* we read: 'The frame is carved in such a way as to be a continuation of the ornamental form, the contours gradually becoming parallel with the straight lines of the outer edges of the frame.' Willumsen eventually came to give his frames, with their stalactites and entwined sirens, greater importance than his pictures.

Laforgue, it will be remembered, countered Taine's dictum, 'Beauty is health' with the aphorism: 'Beauty is what is bizarre.' With this concept of painting as an object, one sees again how the painters of the imagination prepared the way for the Surrealists.

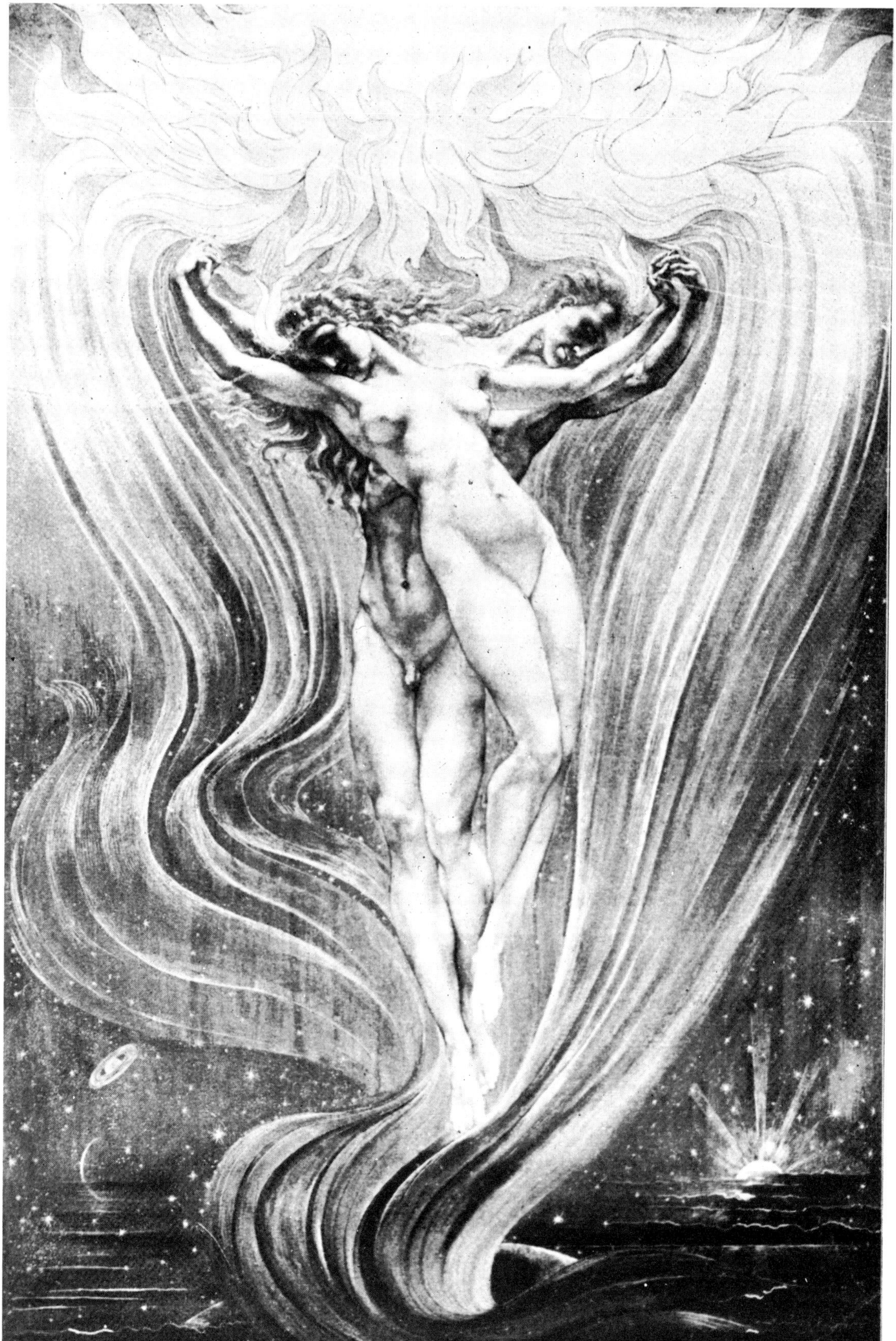

14 Conclusion

THE PICTURES and poems discussed in this book even more than the theories described in it, make it clear that the last quarter of the nineteenth century developed a style peculiar to itself, a style which can rightly be called Symbolist, so close are the links between the literary school of Symbolism and those artists who rejected both academic art and Impressionism. For the painters, the name of 'Symbolist' is more suitable than the terms '*Art Nouveau*' or '*Modern Style*', which are more applicable to the decorative arts than to intellectual painting. To appreciate the unity of this style, after studying its aspects in different countries, it may be useful to compare it with two other styles which are very close to it, one a long way away in time – Mannerism – and the other so near that at times it seems a continuation of Symbolism – Surrealism.

There are many similarities between mid-sixteenth-century Italy and post-1870 France. As the Italian States declined, the Papacy was ruined by the Reformation, and Renaissance art became academic, aesthetes began to appear in the courts of the Italian princes, who wanted to be amused with strange experiments. The Mannerists' works, which were produced at this time and seem artificial unless one knows of their links with the ballet and with allusive poetry such as Bembo's, were for a long time relegated to museum store-rooms. It was only after about 1920 that critics and art historians began to realize that this despised style had produced a few masterpieces and a great many curiosities. The latter more than the former reveal the analogies between Mannerism and Symbolism: in both styles artists elongate the human body and impose on it the artificial poses of the ballet, even in the most solemn scenes. The *figura serpentinata* which the aged Michelangelo recommended to his pupils is reminiscent of Sarah Bernhardt's 'Imaginary intertwinings'. There are resemblances too between the northern mannerist Bellange and de Feure, and, on a less frivolous level, between Duvet and Redon, both of them illustrators of the Apocalypse. There is a curious kinship between

121. Delville: *L'Amour des Ames*. This picture painted by Delville in his esoteric period shows the similarities between Symbolism and Mannerism, revealed in arabesques, the elongation of bodies, and the choice of strange subjects.

Pontormo's characters, always disquieting and melancholy in spite of the bright colours of their clothes, and Moreau's, between Rosso's indulgent angels and angelic fauns and Burne-Jones's knights. And there are many links, though more psychological this time, between Michelangelo and Moreau, whose *Chimères* were a nineteenth-century *Last Judgement*.

The Mannerists, as it happened, were as devoted to the Chimeras as were the nineteenth-century Symbolists. Rosso decorated the fireplaces of Fontainebleau with them, and they can be seen too in the Boboli Gardens and in ewers designed by Cellini – incidentally, the most representative artist of his time, as Gallé was of his, for in Decadent periods decorative art is more revealing than great art. Again, both periods show a pronounced taste for monsters: on the one hand, the statues of Bomanzo and Rosso's imaginary masquerades, and on the other, Böcklin's sirens and Beardsley's transvestites. Mention should be made of one final analogy: Mannerism adapted itself much more easily to the Nordic countries, with artists such as Spranger and Goltzius, than to France; and Cornelius Van Haarlem's *Massacre of the Innocents* bears a curious resemblance to Baron Frédéric's *Torrents*. It was also an art associated with courts – the court of the Medicis in Florence, or the court of Fontainebleau – just as Symbolism was the art of an aesthetic coterie.

The links between Symbolism and Surrealism are much less artistic than intellectual. Surrealists and Symbolists had two attitudes in common, both inspired by Baudelaire: the attitude of the *poète maudit* and the desire to shock the bourgeois. The Surrealists, in their childhood, had been fascinated by the pictures of certain poetic painters which were used as illustrations in children's books, almanacs and magazines. Rackham, Mucha, and Beardsley's imitators reached a wide public which had never heard of Moreau or Redon. In Germany Böcklin always remained a leading national painter, while the Pre-Raphaelites continued to delight a broad section of the English public for many years. And then there were the latecomers who followed the Chimeras far

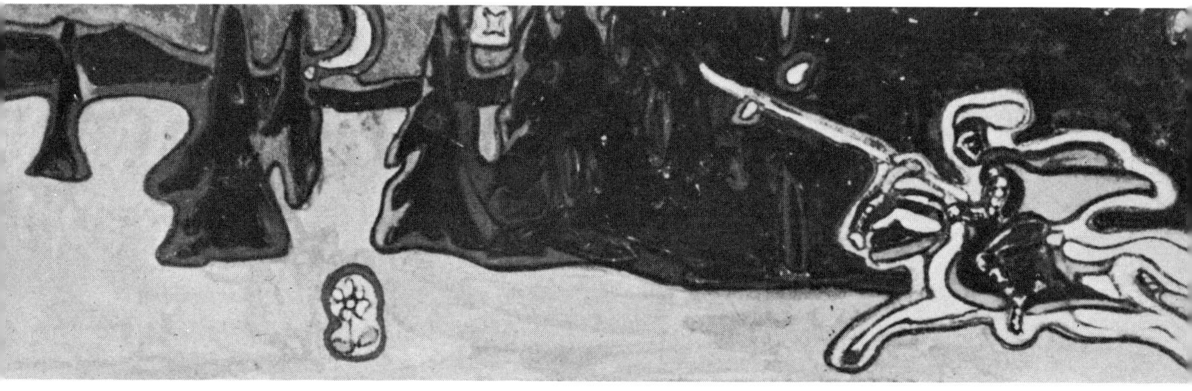

122. Kandinsky: *Evening*. The knight in this picture pre-figures the Blue Rider and goes back as much to the legend dear to the Pre-Raphaelites as it does to the illustrators who had been inspired by Russian folk-lore like Bilibine. Of all the masters of 'modern painting' Kandinsky was the most influenced by the Symbolist atmosphere.

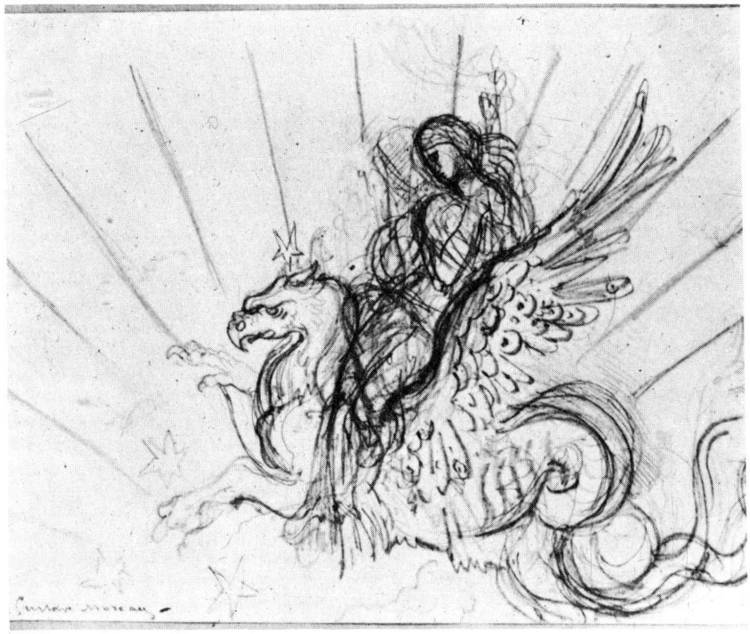

123. Moreau: *La Chimère*. Inspired by a miniature figure representing the Peri, an oriental spirit or fairy.

into this century, winning a wider audience than is generally realized, possibly because they satisfied fetishist longings which Cubism was incapable of fulfilling. These painters now strike us, in fact, as very like aged prostitutes, repulsive to everyone except those whose desires they know exactly how to satisfy. We have already met the disquieting Alastair and the Byzantine Kalmakoff; mention must also be made of a strange Dutchman, Christoph Tot Babberich, who resembled Beardsley even in his tubercular condition, and who turned Toorop's women into elegant spectres; and in Nice, an artist called Motta who drew fashion-plate chimeras clutching poets between their claws.

In Italy, where Symbolism enjoyed a considerable vogue thanks to d'Annunzio, monuments were put up (until the Fascist-Classical style became predominant) decorated with groups of twisted figures, in the *Salammbô* style which also inspired the architect of Milan Station and the director of the film *Cabiria*. In Norway, on the eve of the Second World War, the sculptor Vigeland was still populating a park with statues symbolizing the different stages of life. And at the same period England was coming to admire Stanley Spencer's naïve symbolism.

However, it is the cinema rather than painting which has done most to prolong the dreams of the *fin de siècle* down to our own times. Bergman, who owes so much to Maeterlinck in his allegorical films, and to Strindberg in his social films, recreates the atmosphere of both Klinger and Munch. Another Nordic director, Murnau, produced a film some fifty years ago which is strangely evocative of the Symbolist dream: *Nosferatu*, which might have

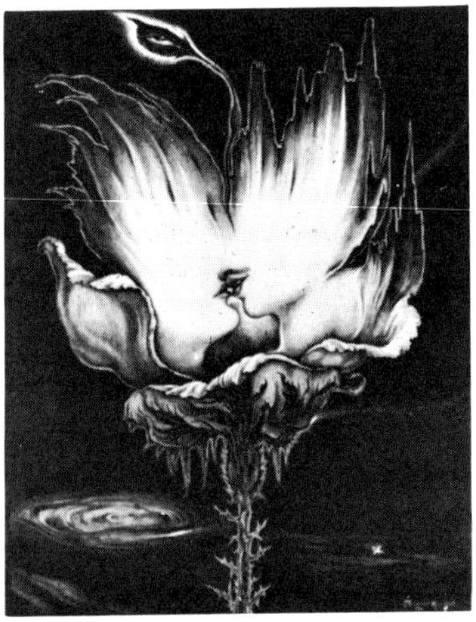

124. Alberto Martini: *Love*. This Italian artist, very much influenced by the work of Edgar Allan Poe, whom he illustrated in 1914, was a link between Symbolism and Surrealism. His French equivalent was Valentine Hugo.

been born in Poe's imagination, revives themes one had thought to be utterly hackneyed – redeeming love, lost castles, and ghost ships with dead crews – recalling Gilkin's poems and certain faces by Khnopff. In the same vein, though with less attractive images, Dreyer's *Vampire* and nearly all the films starring Conrad Veidt continued to exploit the Decadent myths, sometimes in an Expressionist setting. While making certain concessions to vulgarity, the first great film directors therefore worked as Symbolists, long before the artists whose images they borrowed were rediscovered by the public. Sometimes the cinema can contribute something which painting was incapable of giving: thus Wagner, who had never found a painter worthy of him, found in Fritz Lang the perfect director of the *Nibelungen*. Fritz Lang again, in *Metropolis*, evokes Gustave Moreau's settings and Henry de Groux's crowds. Monsters like Frankenstein may have been born in the Gothic novel, but the films of which they are the heroes are reminiscent in certain respects of Villiers de l'Isle-Adam. There is more Symbolism, this time belated and deliberate, in Cocteau's *L'Éternel Retour*, with its Ophelian heroine, Wagnerian landscapes, and Schopenhauerian theme.

The screen also revived the Pre-Raphaelite beauty: Lillian Gish was the 'flower beneath the foot' in countless Hollywood melodramas; and Georgette Leblanc, beautifully photographed by Marcel L'Herbier, brought Mélisande's features to a succession of adventure films. The Sphinx lived again in vamps such as Pola Negri and Theda Bara; while Salome was reincarnated by Nazimova in costumes worthy of Beardsley. In Hollywood, a new Sodom dreaming of the glories of Byzantium, Erich von Stroheim perpetuated the erotic and costume eccentricities of the Vienna – Klimt's Vienna – in which he had been raised. And *Atlantis* would have been an animated Gustave Moreau, if only the producer had found actors for it as beautiful as the master's models, for the heroine of the film is the younger sister of Moreau's Helens and Herodiades.

Thus the cinema gave an increasingly mechanized world the images of which Symbolism had dreamt thirty years before. Surrealism, which, unlike the cinema, was addressed to an élite, thought it was carrying out a revolution when in fact, in many respects, it was simply continuing the poetic movement begun two generations earlier. The similarities with the circumstances which had given rise to Symbolism, or rather to the Decadence, are numerous: confusion after the First World War; rebellion against society, but this time supported by the Russian example; the influence of German philosophy; and the power of dreams, this time interpreted by Freud. The public too was the same, with

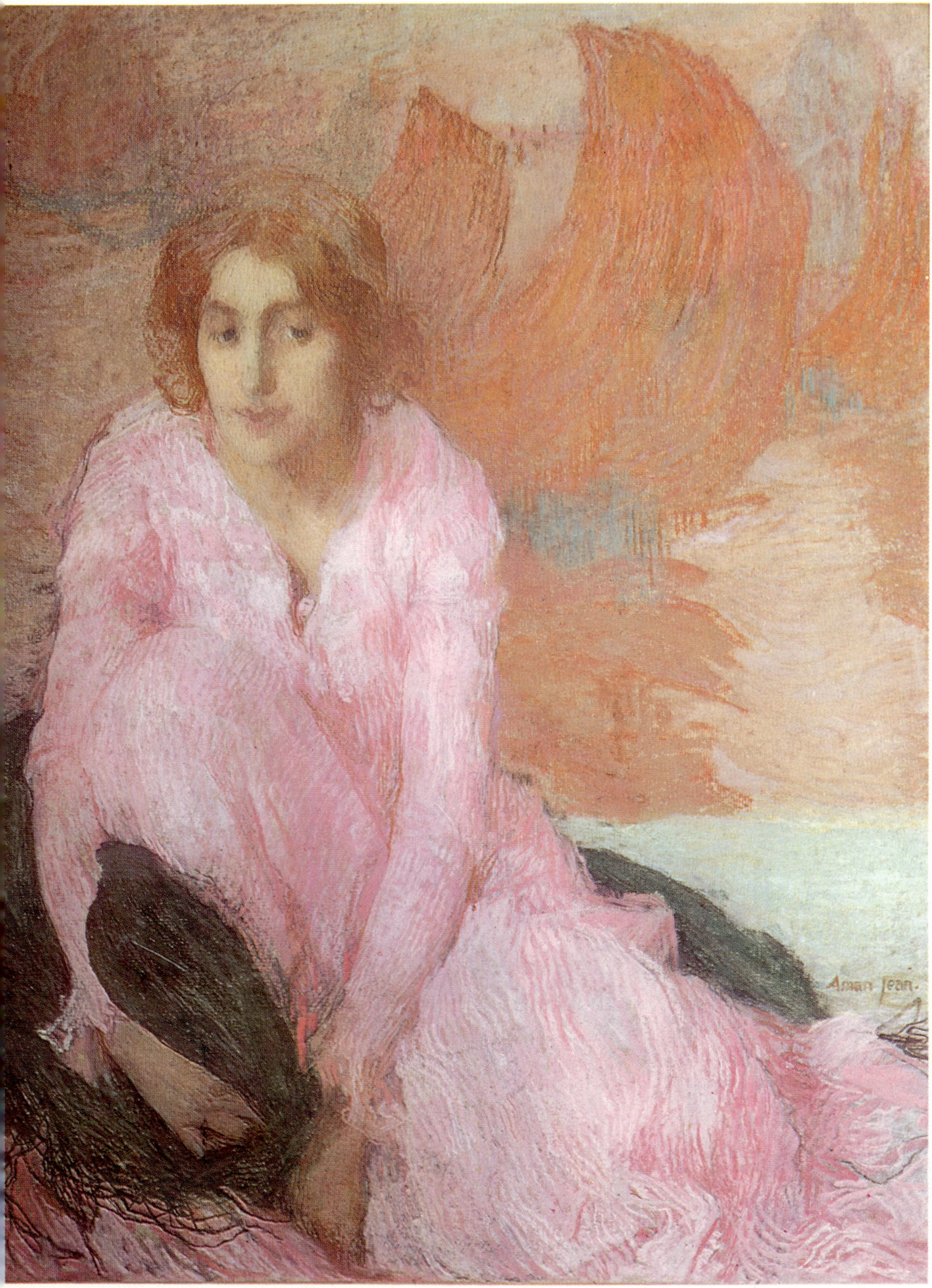

125. Aman-Jean: *Dame en rose*. Painted about 1898, when this rather pallid painter discovered colour in the course of a stay at Sorrento.

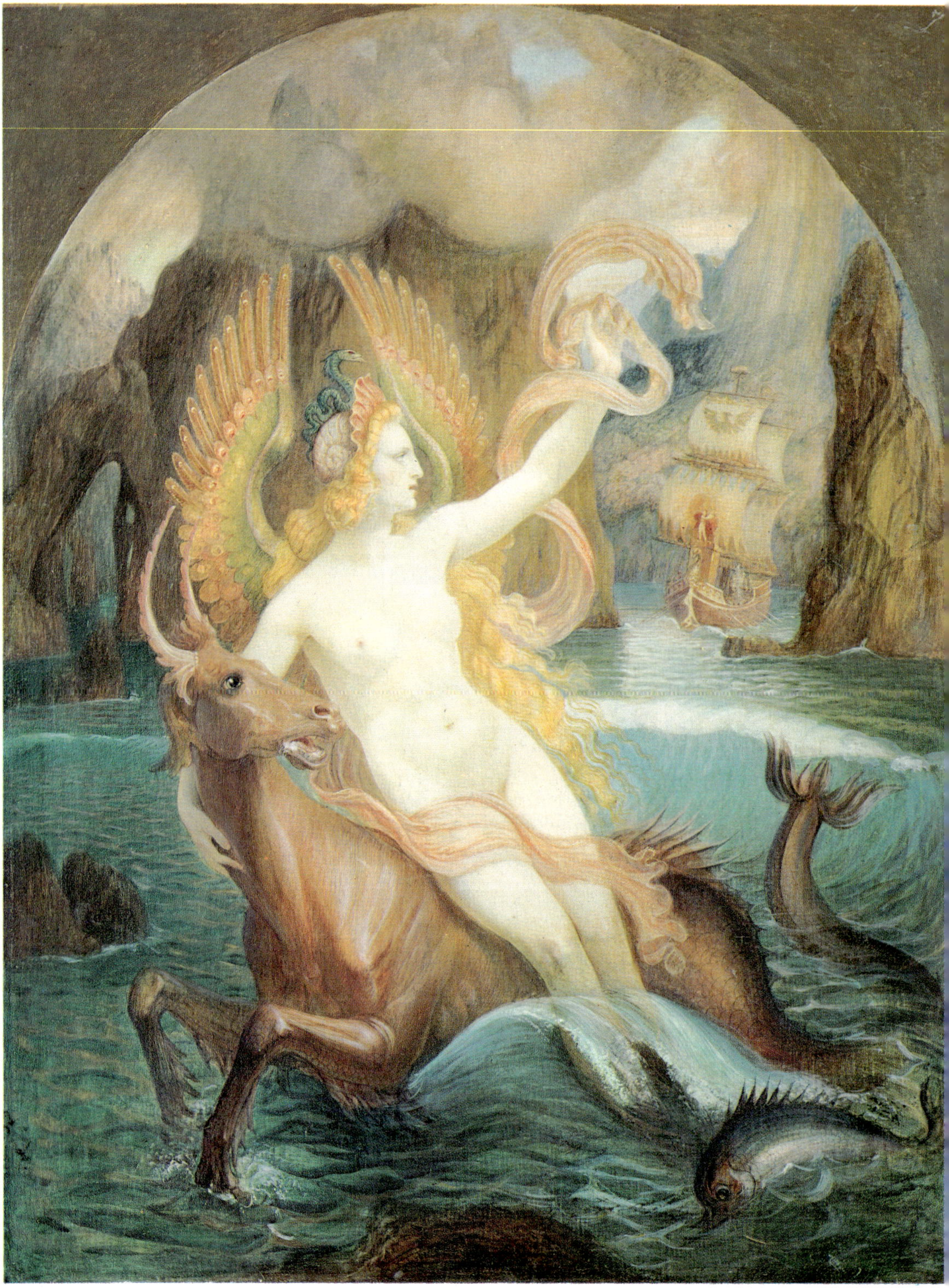

126. Point: *La Chimère*. A work by an excellent draughtsman who was a cold imitator of Gustave Moreau, and who was acclaimed for a brief period as a new Leonardo.

anarchy rubbing shoulders with *avant-garde* snobbery. Taking over from the Baronne Deslandes and Lady Archibald Campbell, strange women like Lise Deharme and Nancy Cunard surrounded themselves with artists: they too had a fatal beauty which we can see in Alastair's drawings and Man Ray's photographs. André Breton's *Nadja* could have been painted by Rossetti and praised by Swinburne.

As is well known, there were many cases of madness and suicide among the members of both movements; there were many conversions too, though it was chiefly to Communism that the Surrealists turned, in a desperate longing for order, when they felt their dreams giving way beneath them. To both Decadents and Surrealists one could apply the magnificent observation of Arthur Symons, who after describing the failures of the visionaries, Coleridge's opium, Villiers's pretensions to the throne of Jerusalem, and Blake's madness, wrote of the last: 'For he who half lives in eternity endures a rending of the structures of the mind, a crucifixion of the intellectual body.'

If there are considerable resemblances between the two movements they differ completely in the ways in which they express themselves. Surrealism is aggressive: its Baudelairean penchant for shocking the bourgeois has turned into a feeling of positive hatred, or else, as in the case of Salvador Dali, has become a systematic exploitation of snobbery. There is more vitality too in the Surrealists; they may be precious, but they are never languid. What is more, they adore women, and that constitutes another great difference. In the matter of inspiration, Freud has turned everything topsy-turvy: the analysis of dreams gives rise to a very different aesthetic from one based on aspirations towards a world of dreams. Vagueness in the Decadents is replaced by irony in the Surrealists, but both movements adopt a symbolism which, in the long run, produces clichés, such as lilies and peacocks. Freud wrote his great work in the middle of the Symbolist period; it is based on equivalents, but not, like Swedenborg's work, on celestial equivalents.

With heroes like Sade and Lautréamont, Surrealism becomes a black Symbolism. The grey period is over, and the Mona Lisa has given place to the vulture which, according to Freud, represents the libido of the child Leonardo. These equivalents, and above all a common stock of images enable us to link a large number of Surrealist painters with the chimerical artists. This is particularly true of Belgium, where the two schools offer some remarkable examples. How can one fail to think of Khnopff when one discovers the world of statues created by Delvaux? And are not some of Magritte's landscapes suburbs of Bruges-la-Morte? But there is

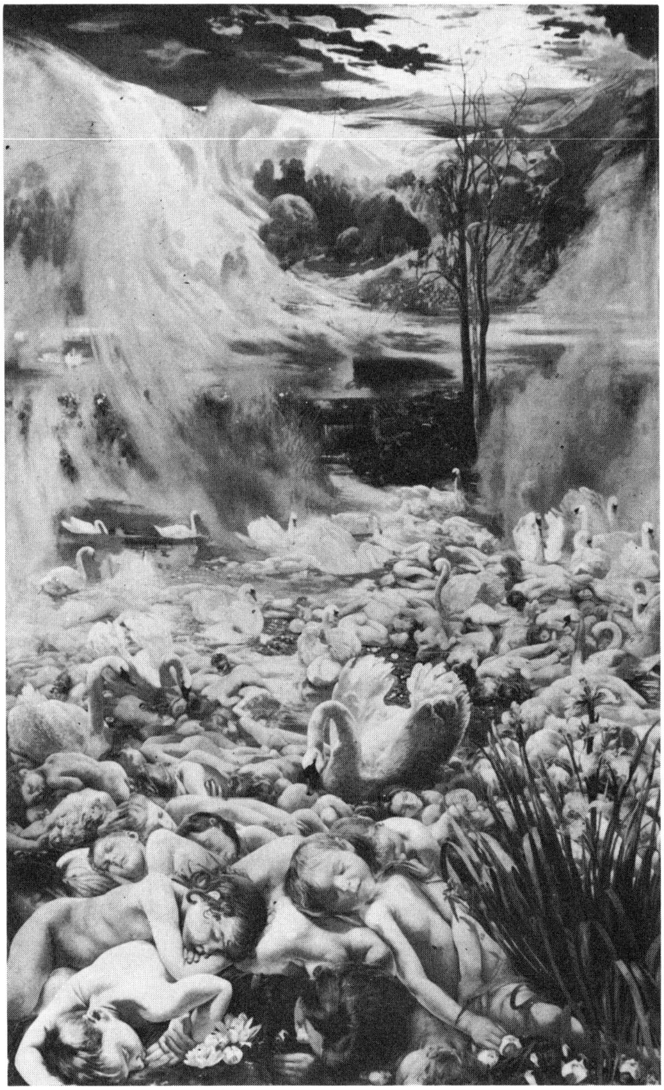

127. Léon Frédéric: *Le Torrent*. This pink-and-blue painting forms part of the triptych *Tout est mort*. The swans probably represent the survival of the animal world after the death of mankind.

no lack of links in other countries too, even if they are fortuitous; between Toorop, for example, and the vague, disquieting worlds of Wilfredo Lam or Matta. De Chirico's antiquity owes a great deal to Böcklin's, and it is well known that the Island of the Dead has been used more than once by Dali. This last artist, who, Breton declared, had 'died in 1938', should not be overlooked: he brought the *Modern Style* back into fashion and amusingly publicized the discoveries of his elders. It must be admitted that Dali showed a certain audacity in writing in 1933: '*Art Nouveau* objects reveal to us in the most concrete fashion the persistence of dreams in the face of reality.' We find no Dali among the other artists discussed in this book, for none of them, good or bad, ever thought of establishing a precise relationship between his art and money; none of them would ever have allowed one of his works to become a publicity gimmick.

Some minor artists – called 'minor' because they have devoted themselves to the art of illustration – have been and still are great Decadents; and none is more admirable than Valentine Hugo, who forms a remarkable link between German Romanticism and Surrealism. Some of Valentine Hugo's portraits, and his well-known illustrations of Rimbaud, suggest a Burne-Jones who has read Freud. Fuchs, while imitating sixteenth-century German engravings, resembles the strangest of the Rosicrucians; indeed, under the cover of Surrealism, the fantastic tradition is still very much alive in Germany. As for the sphinxes, they have always been in fashion since the eighteenth century, painted yesterday by von Stuck and Khnopff, and today by Leonor Fini. This last artist is herself a character out of Jean Lorrain, and her sphinxes would have inspired many Decadents to commit wild eccentricities. Bellmer's dolls, those rejuvenated, dislocated versions of Rops's old whores, also belong to the world of Symbolism. In the case of Max Ernst, who dominates his period as Moreau dominated his, his collages, as we have seen, have the same inspiration as Klinger's canvases, and the trees of his great petrified forests, with fearsome birds flying out of them, have the same roots as Böcklin's. Finally, Tchelichev's work *Cache-Cache* is full of esoteric symbols: the admirable draughtsmanship of that New York Russian, in the service of a philosophical art, would have won him a surer fame in the last century than in our own day.

Naturally, the differences between Symbolism and Surrealism are just as great as the resemblances. The latter movement is still very much alive after fifty years, and has not suffered the sudden disgrace of the former. This longevity cannot be explained solely by the talents of the respective artists. Surrealism is in fact an enter-

128. Klinger: *Nightmare*. This Surrealist of 1885 was greatly influenced at the time by Goya.

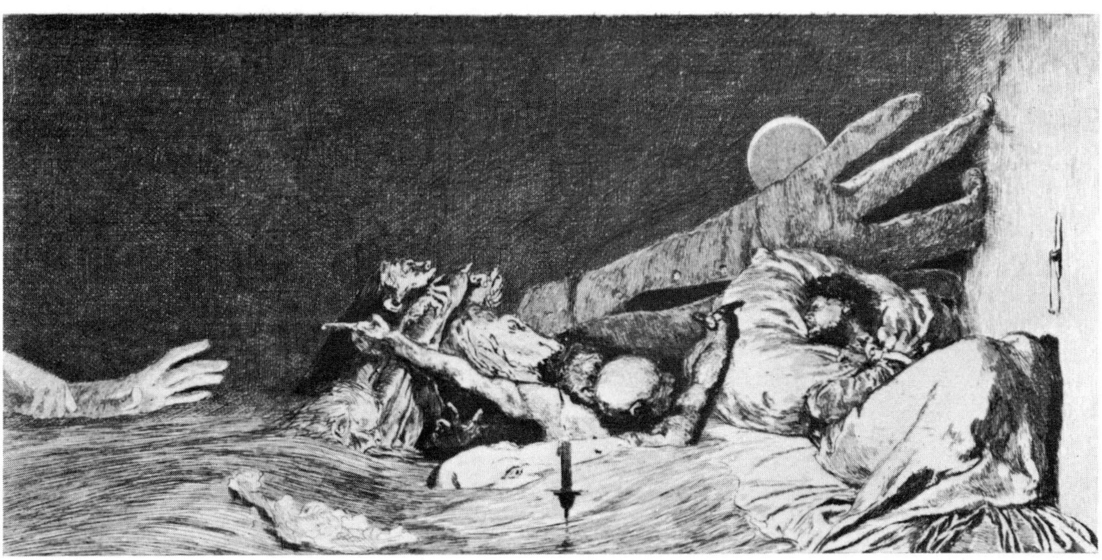

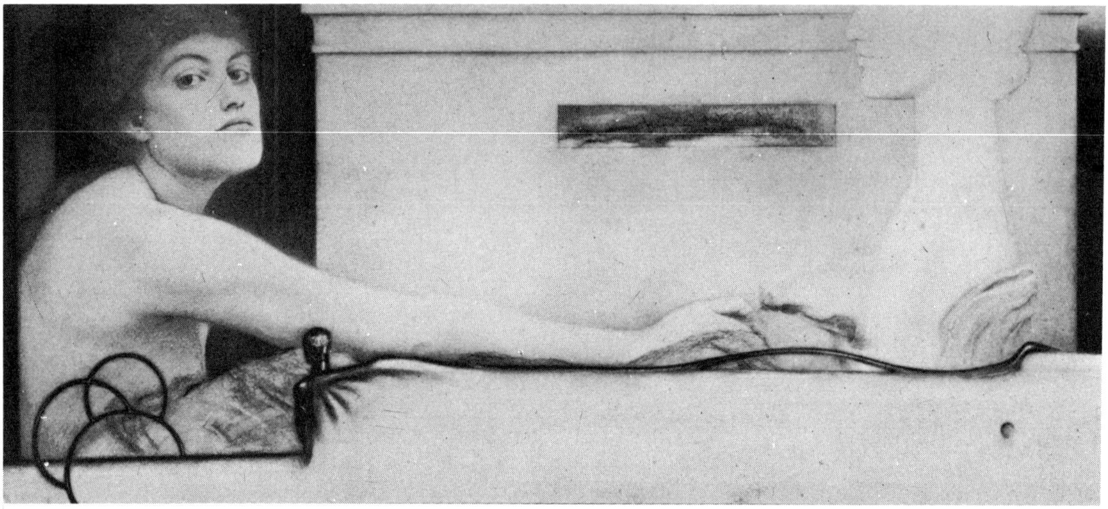

129. Khnopff: *The Offering*. This picture suggests the strangeness of a Magritte or a Delvaux. A plaster antique seen by a photographer of genius.

taining art, which was sorely needed during the boring reign of Abstract painting. We must be grateful to the painters and writers of that school for remaining aloof from Sartre's world, just as the Symbolists shunned that of Zola. The Surrealists could indeed have echoed Schuré's words: 'The abysses of the unconscious open up within ourselves, showing us the gulf from which we have emerged and the dizzy heights to which we aspire.' Thus Breton repeatedly paid homage to the Symbolist painters, writing with the serene insolence of a Magus, of a Villiers or a Baudelaire: 'Moreau, planning shortly before he died to paint that "Argo whose mast was made from a Dordona oak", consoles me for the existence of Renoir, exulting over his last dish of fruit to the extent of believing – and declaring – that he was still making progress.' And it was Moreau once again whom the best critic of contemporary painting, Lucien Alvard, quoted approvingly a few years ago in his preface to the catalogue of the *Antagonisme* exhibition: 'Art is the strenuous attempt to express inner feelings in plastic form.'

Perhaps it is already time for us to look back nostalgically to Messagier and Sam Francis, faced as we are with the offensive of Pop Art. Among those amusing creations, still in the process of becoming an art, the collages recall the images of the *fin de siècle*; the psychedelic artists, having found their way to dreamland by artificial means, cut de Feure's or Toorop's chimeras out of books and surround them with scrolls and whorls in the Mucha style, for they are no longer capable of creating the marvellous faces they glimpsed under the influence of drugs. Thus the Rosicrucian phenomenon has its connections with the hippy scene, not only in the external signs of spirituality – beards, long hair, flowing garments – but also in the attraction to Oriental wisdom. There are several features in common between the art advocated by Péladan and certain psychedelic formulas. Greenwich Village and the hippy communities offer constant analogies with the milieux we have been studying. There is even a revival of interest in magic, reflected in an 'erotico-religious' art and in esoteric 'comics' which instruct their quasi-illiterate readers in the myths evoked by Villiers de l'Isle-Adam or Toorop. Mythological monsters are quite at home in science fiction, and the use of hallucinatory drugs, like the habit of poetry, lends a new reality to the most hackneyed myths. A place as bizarre as the Electric Circus and a film as poetic as *The Yellow Submarine* are the continuation, eighty years later, of the Decadents' dream.

Today, as in the days of the silent film, it is the cinema rather than painting which is recreating the world of yesterday's poets, or rather which is giving life to their images, although without trying to give them a significance likely to strain the understanding of a child of twelve. Thus Vadim's *Barbarella*, an essay in infantile science fiction, revives all the themes of the *fin de siècle*: Barbarella is Ophelia lost among a host of Salomes; the Black Queen is the eternal Medusa; and the Angel is Péladan's chaste hermaphrodite. Many of his ideas are worthy of Villiers de l'Isle-Adam's *L'Ève Future*, and may well have been borrowed from that work; and the *Art Nouveau* sets, particularly the harem, in which the girls wear the most fantastic costumes, would have delighted the poet. The Angel's flight above a dead planet is pure Moreau, and some of the luminous shapes are reminiscent of Redon. Again, in Fellini's admirable *Satyricon* there is a deliberate imitation of Beardsley and Klimt, and sequences which reproduce pictures by Böcklin, Rochegrosse, and Alma-Tadema. The theme of the Byzantine Empire with all the perversions and superstitions of the Decadence has been revived with telling effect in a society which is growing increasingly aware of its own decline.

130. Redon: *Crowned Head.* The crown of laurels shows that Redon wished to represent here one of those poet-heroes so dear to Gustave Moreau – but without any sense of the picturesque in this case. The world of Moreau is always historical while the world of Redon comes from the subconscious and attempts to show anguish or yearning.

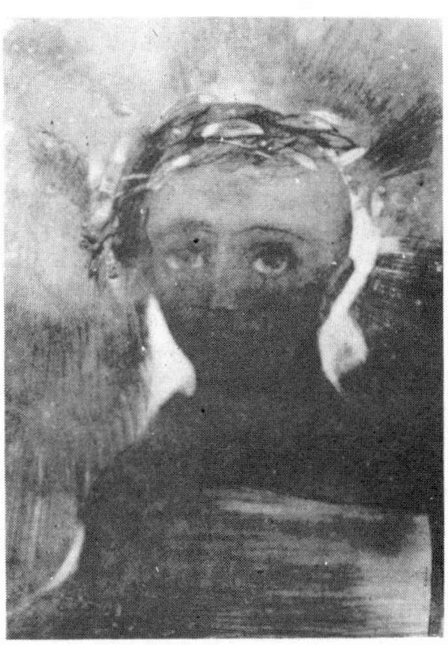

When the young artists of today, attracted by these images, start drawing, they adopt the style of either Beardsley or Mucha. Beardsley's admirers use stippling and blots to express a sort of naïve perversity; gentler natures prefer Mucha's elongations and soft colours. Beardsley and Mucha: these two names already enjoy greater prestige with the young than those of Pollock or Dubuffet, Monet or Renoir. 'The evocatory witchcraft of chance gives rise to similarities,' wrote Gustave Kahn (84). It matters little whether these repetitions of poetic themes are conscious or not, whether they are projected on a screen or a canvas, or even whether they delight a roomful of mental defectives or a theatre sparsely dotted with aesthetes. These dreams remain a living rejection of everyday life.

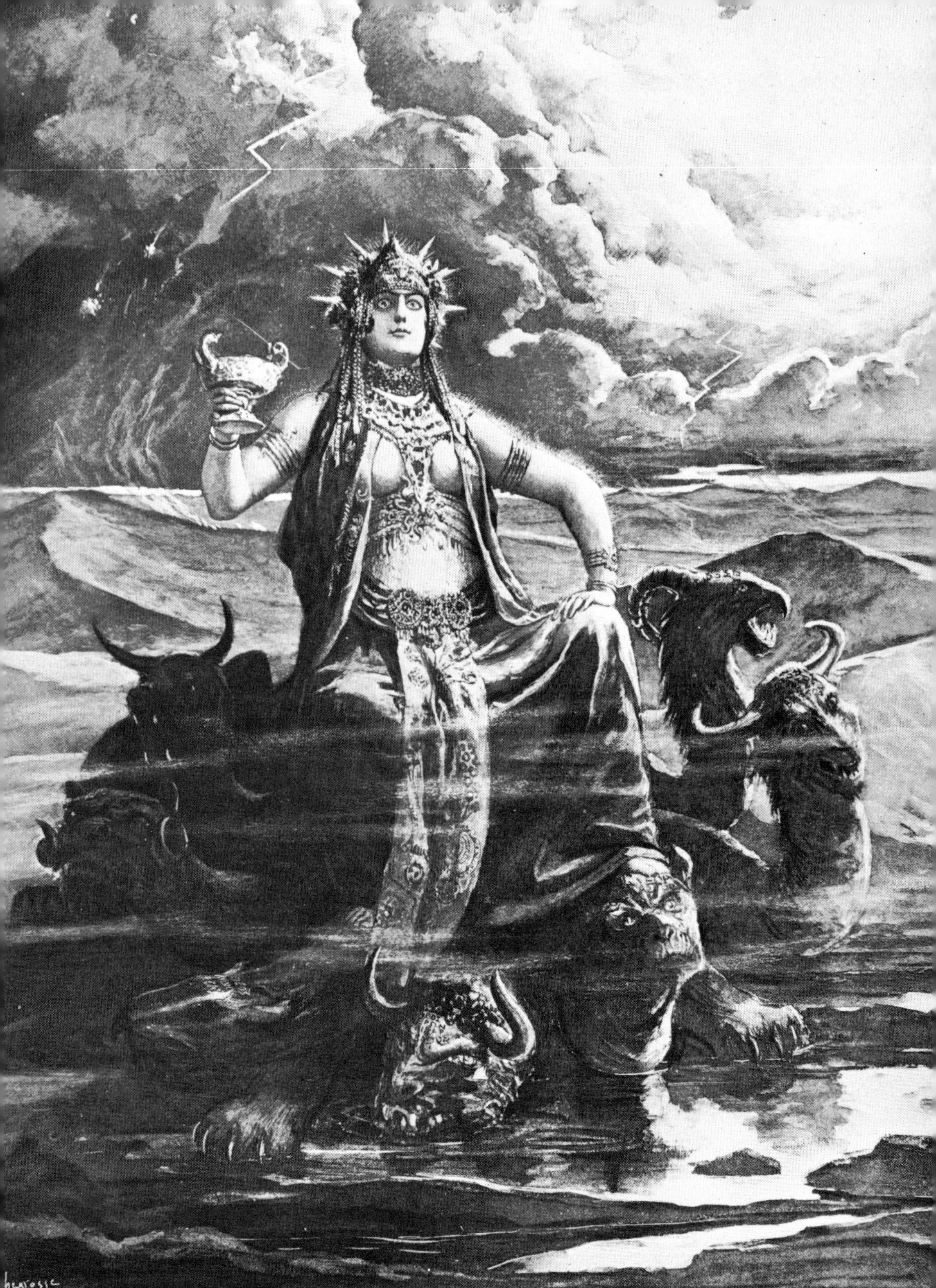

131. Rochegrosse: *Déesse et Chimère*. The Apocalypse as derived from Flaubert.

15 A Short Anthology of Symbolist Themes

1 ANGELS

Lo! 'tis a gala night
Within the lonesome latter years!
An angel throng, bewinged, bedight
In veils, and drowned in tears,
Sit in a theatre, to see
A play of hopes and fears,
While the orchestra breathes fitfully
The music of the spheres.

Edgar Allan Poe

Et j'étais là, debout parmi les marjolaines,
Virginal, et l'archet des blanches cantilènes
A mes doigts effilés d'ange immatériel.

Albert Samain (*Les Jardins de l'Infante*)

[And I was there, standing among the marjorams,
Virginal, with the bow of white cantilenas
Between the tapering fingers of an immaterial angel.]

Dark Angel, with thine aching lust
To rid the world of penitence:
Malicious Angel, who still dost
My soul such subtle violence!

Because of thee, no thought, no thing,
Abides for me undesecrate:
Dark Angel, ever on the wing,
Who never reaches me too late!

Lionel Johnson

2 ANIMALITY

A flabby woman, slumped heavily beneath her golden hair. A passive bosom, staring eyes. Twin pillars with architectural details in clusters, reminiscent of sexual emblems. And then two mysterious, motionless, haloed, illuminated skulls, lighthouses of death above the ebb and flow of naked flesh . . . The nocturnal eyes with a weary purple stain around their dull glow have exhausted themselves in concupiscent glances. The gold of the belly sounds the fanfares of unsatisfied lust.

Verhaeren (on Khnopff)

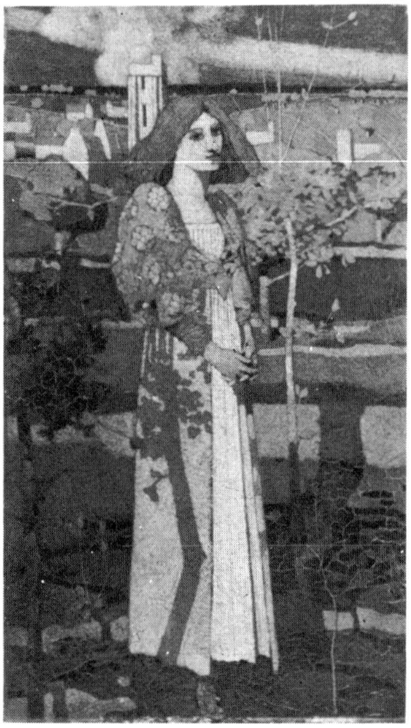

132. David Gauld: *Saint Agnes.* The subject is taken from a poem by Tennyson and was often treated by the Pre-Raphaelites. This version is much closer to the mystical schools of the continent like Pont-Aven or Beuron; it was exhibited at Munich in 1860.

3 AZURE

Art is the Azure.

Victor Hugo

I am haunted! The Azure! the Azure! the Azure! the Azure!

Mallarmé (*L'Azur*)

A symphony of blues and brown –
We were together in the town;
A grimy tavern with blurred walls,
Where dingy lamplight floats and falls
On working men and women, clad
In sober watchet, umber sad.
Two viols and one 'cello scream
Waltz music through the smoke and steam:
You rise, you clasp a comrade, who
Is clothed in triple blues like you:
Sunk in some dream voluptuously
Circle those azures richly blent,
Swim through the dusk, the melody;
Languidly breathing, you and he,
Uplifting the environment;
Ivory face and swart face laid
Cheek unto cheek, like man, like maid.

John Addington Symonds (*In the Key of Blue*, 1893)

4 BARBARIANS

Couchons-nous là;
Mourons dans les rires et les larmes;
Appelons à grands cris les barbares libérateurs;
Les mains des patriciens sont trop belles pour les armes;
Couchons-nous là, mourons dans les rires et les pleurs.

O. W. Milosz (*Le Coup de Grâce*)

[Let us lie down there;
Let us die in laughter and tears;
Let us call loudly for the liberating barbarians;
The hands of patricians are too fair to bear arms;
Let us lie down there and die in laughter and tears.]

'Yes, let them come, let them burn everything here, let them empty my caskets, let them crush my pearls, let them crucify the steward, let them rape my mother.'

And, in a final hiccough, he spat out at last the ancient soul of Byzantium which had lingered too long within him.

Jean Lorrain (*Coins de Byzance*)

5 BRUGES

Ames dont le songe à présent sur l'eau pâle s'en va,
L'eau pâle qui s'en va en chemins de silence.

Georges Rodenbach (*Vies encloses*)

[Souls whose dream now goes away over the pale water,
The pale water which goes away along paths of silence.]

In the solitude of that autumn evening in which the wind was sweeping away the last leaves, he felt more keenly than ever the desire to have done with his life and an impatience for the grave. It seemed as if a dead woman were stretching out on his soul, as if a whispering voice were rising from the water, the water coming to meet him as it came to meet Ophelia.

Rodenbach (*Bruges-la-morte*)

6 BYZANTIUM

Along the mosaic walls can be seen generals offering the Emperor the conquered cities in the palms of their hands. And everywhere there are basalt columns, gates in silver filigree, ivory seats and tapestries embroidered with pearls. The light falls from the ceiling. Ancient vapours are wafted about. Stationed in the ante-rooms, the guards, who look like automata, hold silver-gilt sticks on their shoulders . . . The Emperor is seated on his throne, wearing a purple tunic and red boots with black bands . . . A pearl diadem rests on his hair, which is arranged in symmetrical rolls. He has drooping eyelids, a straight nose, and sly, heavy features.

Flaubert (*La Tentation de Saint Antoine*)

Hernieder steig ich eine Marmortreppe,
Ein Leichnam ohne Haupt inmitten ruht,
Dort sickert meines teuren Bruders Blut,
Ich raffe leise nur die Purpurschleppe.

[I go down the steps of a marble staircase.
There in the middle lies a decapitated body,
My beloved brother's blood flows–
Lightly I merely draw aside my purple train.]

Stefan George (*Algabal*)

Our world is very small beside the ancient world; our feasts are paltry affairs compared with the terrifying banquets of Roman patricians and Asiatic princes. With our petty habits, we find it hard to conceive of those enormous existences which made reality of all the strangest, boldest, most monstrously impossible inventions of the imagination.

Théophile Gautier (*La Nuit de Cléopâtre*)

Phebor: Imperial succubus, what do you want with me? What have you come to ask of me? What have you come to offer me?
Phena: All the past and all the present.
Phebor: Ah, you at least are true. You are the now and not the tomorrow, the certainty and not the perhaps. You are the motionless eternity.
Phena: I am the shame of what is possible.

Rémy de Gourmont (*Histoire tragique de la Princesse Phénissa*)

7 CHIMERAS

La Chimère vit un Chevalier
Terrible adolescent j'ai peur de ton courage
Le Temple noir est bien ouvert à ton désir
Mais avant d'épouser l'ivresse de mourir
Rappelle-toi mon cri de pardon qui t'outrage

[The Chimera saw a Knight
Awesome youth I fear your courage
The Black Temple is wide open to your desire
But before espousing the lust for death
Remember my cry of forgiveness which offends you]

Jules Bois (after an engraving by Redon)

La Chimère indomptable aux yeux profonds et bleus,
Abîmes rayonnants dans un visage d'homme.

[The unconquerable Chimera with deep blue eyes,
Shining abysses in a man's face.]

Jean Lorrain (*Le Sang des Dieux*)

8 CHRIST

Surgit un nouveau Christ en lumière sculpté
Qui soulève vers lui l'Humanité
Et la bâtit aux feux de nouvelles Étoiles.

[There arises a new Christ carved in light
Who lifts up Mankind towards Him
And fashions it in the fires of new Stars.]

Verhaeren (*Là-bas*)

Jesu, no more! It is full tide;
From Thy head and from Thy feet,
From Thy hands, and from Thy side,
All the Purple rivers meet

But, O Thy side! Thy deep-digg'd side!
That hath a double Nilus going:
Nor ever was the Pharoan tide
Half so fruitful, half so flowing.

Richard Crashaw (*On a Bleeding Crucifix*)

About the crucifix,
Borne slow for all ye slow to follow,
Amyclaean scents of Hyacinthus hung,
And from the dead eyes of the Christ was flung,
Swiftly, the live glance of Apollo.

Edmund John (*The Flute of Sardonyx*, 1913)

9 DEAD GODS

Then there file past them idols of all nations and all ages, in wood, in metal, in granite, in feathers, in skins stitched together. The oldest of them, older than the Flood, are almost hidden by seaweed hanging down like manes. A few, too long for their bases, creak at the joints and break their backs as they walk . . . They become horrifying – with tall plumes, globular eyes, arms terminating in claws, and the jaws of sharks.

Flaubert (*La Tentation de Saint Antoine*)

Then through the monkish hymn
A strange note and a piercing sweetness ran;
And a young priest, who saw thee, clutched his beads,
And grew all pale as from the organ reeds
Pealed once the poignant pipes of Pan.

Edmund John (*The Flute of Sardonyx*)

10 DEAD WOMEN

Très douce, elle mourait ses petits pieds en croix
Et quand elle chantait, le cristal de sa voix
Faisait saigner au cœur ses blessures natales . . .
Et c'était comme une musique qui se fane . . .

Albert Samain (*Les Jardins de l'Infante*)

[She was meekly dying with her little feet crossed
And when she sang, the crystal of her voice
Made the wounds of birth bleed in her heart . . .
And it was like music withering away . . .]

C'est le moment où les cadavres introuvés,
Les blancs noyés, flottant, songeurs, entre deux eaux,
Saisis eux-mêmes aux premiers froids soulevés
Descendent s'abriter dans les vases profondes.

Henry Bataille (*La Chambre blanche*)

[It is the moment when the undiscovered corpses,
The white drowned bodies floating dreamily,
Themselves chilled by the first cold breeze
Go down to shelter in the deepest mud.]

Lointainement et si mystiquement pareils
De grands masques d'argent que la brume recule
Voguent au jour tombant sur les tombants soleils

Verhaeren (*Soir*)

[Distantly, mystically alike
Great masks of silver harried by the mist
Drift in the failing light across the setting suns.]

11 DEATH

. . . and near the deserted graves. Death is there . . . I have seen her, divine refuge, happy ending to the misery of life . . . O unknown goddess with the silent face, nameless fear, august immobility, how beautiful you are.

Odilon Redon (*A Soi-même*)

She loved the games men played with death,
Where death must win;
As though the slain man's blood and breath
Revived Faustine.

She drank the steaming drift and dust
Blown off the scene;
Blood could not ease the bitter lust
That galled Faustine.

Swinburne (*Ave Faustina Imperatrix*)

A ship sails over to the clouds
And now her sails are bathed in red;
A strange ship! – for her sails are shrouds,
Her hull the four planks of the dead.

Vincent O'Sullivan (*Brain Fever*)

Yea, but I dreamed: and lo! my feet were led
Down the slow spirals of those deadly stairs:
And I too in my inmost spirit bred

Desire of that fell fruit; and through the lairs
Of poison-fretted charnels crept, and came,
With quivering flesh and horror-stiffened hairs,

Beneath those dismal branches. There a flame
Burned the blue about the blossoms; and I stood,
And caught the falling juices; and, though shame

Shook my shivering pulse, I sniffed the lewd
Scent of those corpse-cold clusters; and I fell
Amid the dying, dead, delirious brood . . .

How can I teach you by what fearful fate
Foredoomed, dogged downward by what pangs, enticed
By what pale cravings, lured alike by hate

And love, these guilty things, of God despised,
Of man rejected, moaning crept beneath
The treacherous tree, and fed, and cursing Christ

Dragged the slow torture of plague-stricken breath
Onward through days or weeks or months or years
To fade at last in horror-shrouded death?

John Addington Symonds (*The Valley of Vain Desires*)

The improbable landscape bristles with trees, coppices, and thickets in the shape of demons or phantoms and full of birds with rats' heads and vegetable tails. From the ground, which is littered with vertebrae, ribs, and skulls, there spring gnarled and shaky willow-trees, in which skeletons are perched, waving bouquets and chanting songs of victory, while a Christ flies away into a mackerel sky; a hermit meditates, with his head in his hands, at the back of a grotto; and a beggar dies of privation and hunger, stretched out on his back, his feet pointing to a stagnant pool.

J.-K. Huysmans (*A Rebours*)

Yes, close your eyes, lie still . . . as death . . .
My lips hold yet the memory of your breath . . .
The feverish yellow moon is on the wane;
Closer it comes, silent, and mad, and vast,
With blackness round and dead shapes stealing past,
And splashed with one wild blood-red line of pain.

Edmund John (*The Flute of Sardonyx*)

12 EYES

Ah les yeux! Tous les yeux! Tant de reflets posthumes
Reliquaires du sang de tous les soirs tombants
Chaires où toute noce a promulgué ses bans
Sites où chaque automne a laissé de ses brumes . . .
[Ah the eyes! All eyes! So many posthumous reflections
Reliquaries of the blood of all falling dusks
Pulpits in which every marriage has published its banns
Sites in which each autumn has left its mists . . .]

Rodenbach (*Le Voyage dans les Yeux*)

If I had been able to put in a goblet the purity of your eyes, the softness of your breasts, and drink them, and die . . . with my soul all scented with you.

Jean Lahor (*Le Livre du Néant*)

13 FAIRIES

By a maze of gossamer dew
Measured, lay the pasture leas
Ruddy grey the sunlight glanced
Through the rippling poplar trees,
On the airy webs, where chanced
Dainty faery feet had danced
Without noise, the soft night through.

Lionel Johnson

C'était un soir de féeries
De vapeurs enrubannées
De mauves tendres aux prairies
En la plus belle de tes années.

Viélé-Griffin (*Joies*)

[It was an evening of faery joys
Of mists swirling in ribbons
Of soft mauves in the meadows
In the fairest of your years.]

133. Gauguin: *D'où venons-nous? Que sommes-nous? Où allons-nous?* Gauguin's masterpiece is also the masterpiece of all Symbolist painting. The composition is very close to Puvis de Chavannes. The title shows the anguish of an entire generation of poets.

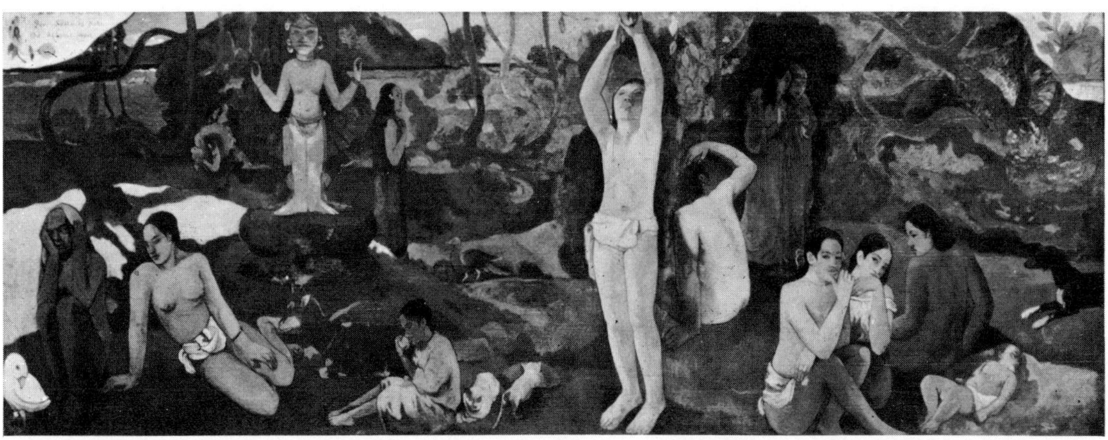

Morgane la fée était l'effroi du pâtre.
Vaguement entrevus dans son âtre bleuâtre
Dormaient las et charmés les preux casqués d'or froid
Et Morgane accoudée au milieu des nuages
Berce au-dessus des mers la ville des mirages.

[Morgan le Fay was the terror of the shepherd.
Vaguely glimpsed on her bluish heath
The warriors in their cold gold helmets slept weary and enchanted.
And Morgan lying in the midst of the clouds
Cradles the city of mirages above the seas.]

Jean Lorrain (*La Forêt bleue*)

14 FLORENCE

At eventide a mortal charm is exhaled by this Florentine atmosphere, with its poetic melancholy. And this ecstatic kiss of the darkness streaked with green tears is symbolized in the Medusa's head in the Uffizi . . . In these Florentine twilights one feels a certain regret at not dying suddenly.

Jean Lorrain (*Loïe Fuller*)

The city of the soul.

Ruskin (*The Seven Lamps of Architecture*)

134. Jessie M. King: *Pelléas and Mélisande*. The drawings of this artist of the Glasgow School look like lace; they were popularized by *Studio*. Their naïve style influenced many illustrators of children's books, and indeed Maeterlinck's characters have become children. The drawing is also a fine example of the importance of hair in Symbolist art – here it has become a sort of fantastic plant.

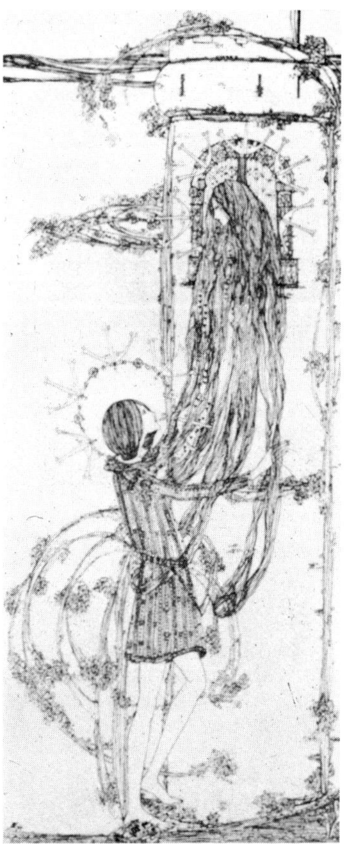

15 FURNISHINGS

Old chests, rare tapestries, two Carpaccios, three Botticellis; studies by Rossetti and Burne-Jones; a sedan-chair which carried the Marquise de Polignac beneath the fretted foliage of Versailles; a prodigious number of Byzantine Madonnas and Italian pots; pewter with matt blue tones next to Japanese porcelain; an aquarium in which, among the seaweed, there swim fish caught off the coast of Orissa. Then there are wide divans covered with the skins of black bears and stillborn tigers. Between two vases holding crimson flowers, on a table strewn with golden knives, stands a large goblet in the shape of a winged sexual organ containing Kanaka comfits. Hung from the ceiling by invisible threads, peacock feathers sway in the air to the plaintive lament of viols and the ecstatic sound of harmonicas.

Anon (*Gil Blas*, 1886)

These are the symbols. On that cloth of red
I' the centre is the Tripoint, perfect each
Except the second of its points, to teach
That Christ is not yet born. The books (whose head
Is golden Charity, as Paul hath said)
Those virtues are wherein the soul is rich;
Therefore on them the lily standeth, which
Is Innocence, being interpreted.

Dante Gabriel Rossetti
(verses on the frame of *The Childhood of the Virgin Mary*)

16 GANYMEDE

Toi seul, posthume enfant des époques sereines
Tu portes fièrement la honte d'être beau.

[You alone, posthumous child of serene times,
Bear proudly the stigma of beauty.]

Catulle Mendès

Autant le jeune homme profite
Dans l'intérêt de sa beauté,
Prêtre d'Éros ou néophyte
D'aimer en toute nudité.

[So does the young man benefit
In the interest of his beauty,
Priest of Eros or neophyte,
From loving completely naked.]

Verlaine (*Hombres*)

Le front étroit et bas et les larges prunelles
Qu'ont les êtres passifs aimés des dieux pervers.

[The low, narrow forehead and wide pupils
Of passive creatures loved by depraved gods.]

Jean Lorrain (*Le Sang des Dieux*)

17 GEMS

Vers le palais d'onyx pavé de malachites

[Towards the onyx palace paved with malachites]

Henri de Régnier (*Medailles d'Argile*)

He looks as if he were clad in ashes, but ashes gleaming with drops of water and gems; into the material of his robe are woven moonstones, opals and sards; a breast-plate studded with amethysts grips his torso and he wears a huge crown of enormous purplish poppies: dark poppies with rubies as pistils . . .

Jean Lorrain (*Le Vice errant: Coins de Byzance*)

O, beauté de la chair, toi qui marche drapée
Dans l'incendie aveugle et froid des pierreries

[O, beauty of the flesh, you who walk draped
In the blind cold fire of precious stones]

O. W. Milosz (*Poèmes de la Décadence*)

The kept woman, a chatoyant amalgam of mysterious, diabolical elements, set like a Gustave Moreau apparition in poisonous flowers intertwined with precious jewels.

Marcel Proust (Swann thinking of Odette)

Nun aber soll sie also sein:
Wie eine grosse fremde Dolde
Geformt aus feuerrotem Golde
Und reichem blitzendem Gestein.

[This is how she should be:
Like a great strange flower
Moulded in the glow of gold
And the rich brilliance of gems.]

Stefan George (*Die Spange*)

18 HAIR

That moment she was mine, mine, fair,
Perfectly pure and good: I found
A thing to do, and all her hair
In one long yellow string I wound
Three times her little throat around,

And strangled her. No pain felt she;
I am quite sure she felt no pain.
As a shut bud that holds a bee
I warily opened her lids; again
Laughed the blue eyes without a stain.

Robert Browning

Fasten your hair with a golden pin
And bind up every wandering tress . . .
You need but lift a pearl-pale hand
And bind up your long hair and sigh.

Yeats

Déesse qui descend dans le lac des péchés
Et dans l'ombre sur l'eau de ses cheveux penchée
Parmi tous les iris cueille la rouge vulve

[Goddess who descends into the lake of sins
And bending over the water in the shadow of her hair
Among all the irises picks the red vulva]

Pierre Louÿs

19 HAMLET

It does not displease us to find a little of Hamlet in Oedipus.

Théophile Gautier (on Moreau's picture)

Hamlet exists by virtue of heredity in *fin de siècle* minds.

Mallarmé

20 HELEN

She stands out against a sinister horizon, drenched in blood, and clad in a dress encrusted with gems like a shrine. Her eyes are wide-open in a cataleptic stare. At her feet lie piles of corpses. She is like an evil goddess who poisons all that approaches her.

Huysmans (on Gustave Moreau)

Possessed by all men, from the beggar to the Lord, covered with immemorial kisses, you are the last descendant, Helen, still surrounded by the ancient mystery.

D'Annunzio (*Poema paradisiaco*)

21 HERMAPHRODITE

The Gynander. Individual Parisian phenomenism. Individual Parisian ethic phenomenism. Tanmuz orphic ionian protagonist, reformer of love, victory over the lunary. Erotic: sentimental usurpation of women; great gynanders, Rose de Faventine, Lilith de Vonivre, Luce de Goulaine, Aschtoret, recurring characters of the sentimental initiation. The *habitorelle* and the Marquise de Nolay reappear too. In this book, all the distortions of nervous attraction, perversities and sexual psychopathy . . .

Péladan (*Le Vice suprême*)

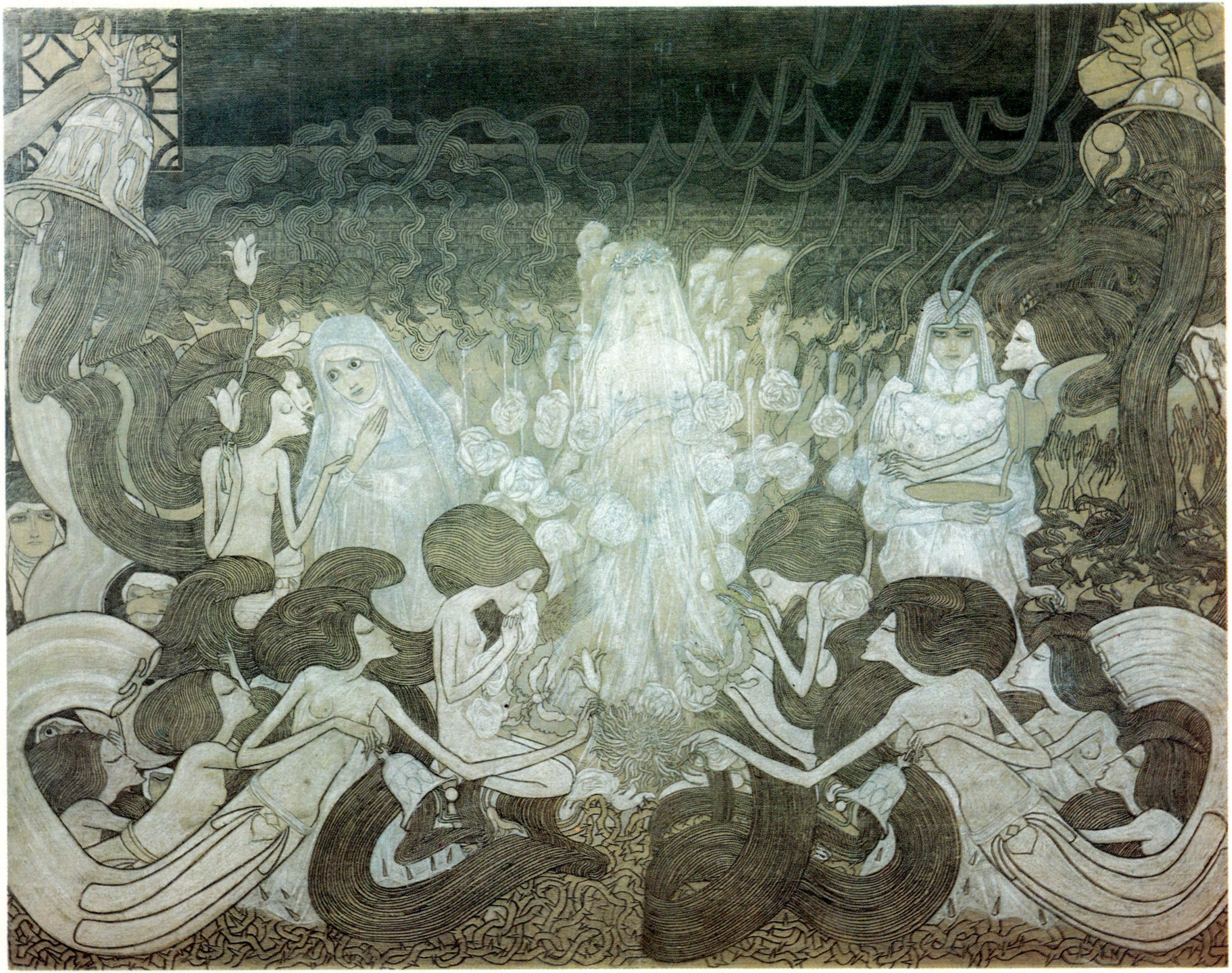

135. Toorop: *The Three Brides*. This picture caused a sensation at the Rosicrucian Exhibition. Poe's influence can be seen in the dead girls, the hair, and the bells. The bride of heaven is on the left, the bride of hell on the right. The angular gestures, reminiscent of those of Javanese puppets, are a reminder of the painter's Indonesian origins.

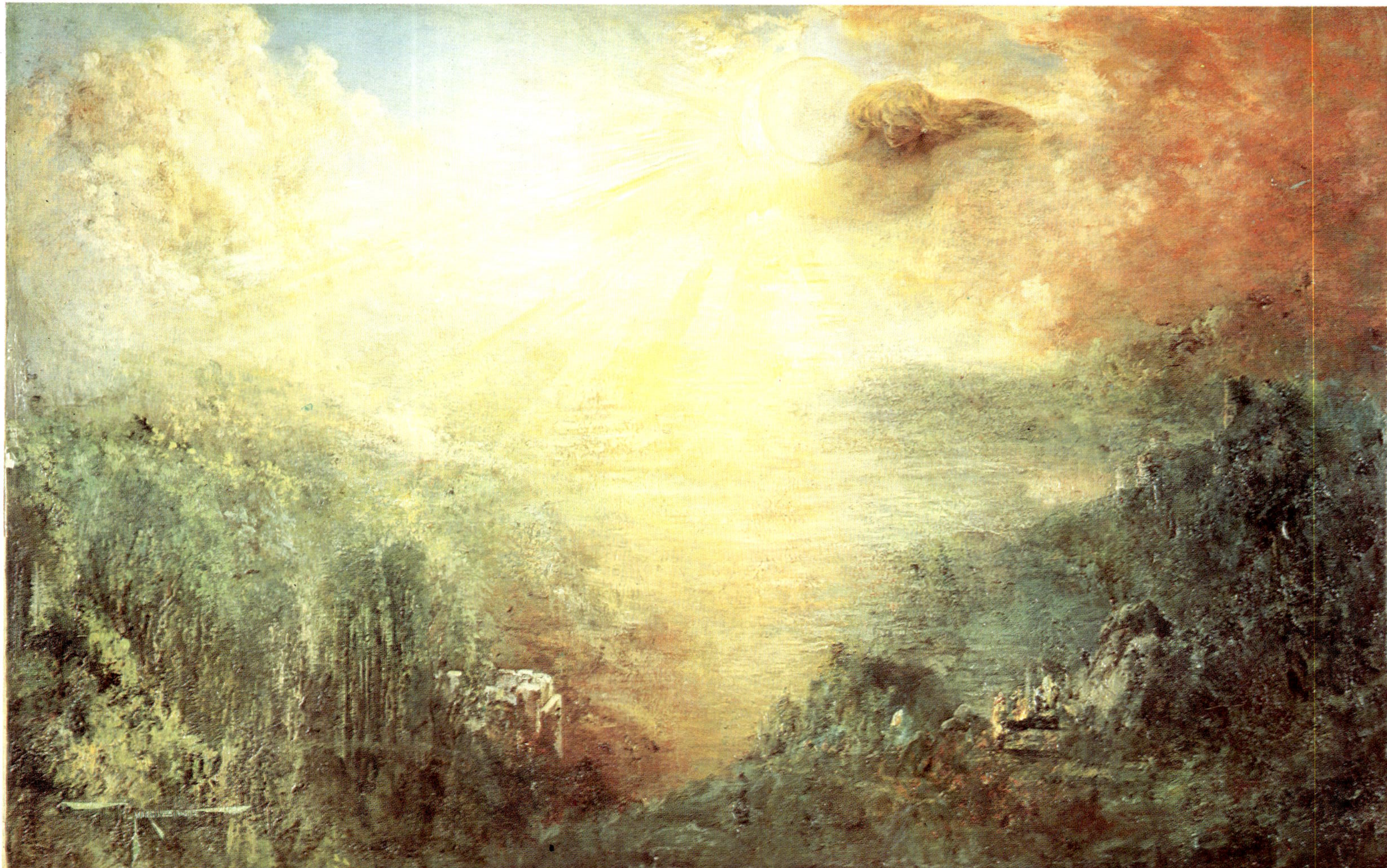

136. Pinky Marcius-Simmons: *The Clouds*. This very talented young American who exhibited at the *Salon des Rose+Croix* had probably been influenced by the imaginary landscapes of Point. This is one of the best expressions of the need for the infinite and a world of dreams that the Decadents felt so strongly.

Est-ce un jeune homme? Est-ce une femme?
Une déesse ou bien un dieu?
L'amour ayant peur d'être infâme
Hésite et suspend son aveu.

[Is it a young man? Is it a woman?
A goddess or a god?
Love being afraid of being infamous
Hesitates and suspends its declaration.]

Théophile Gautier (*Contralto*)

22 INDIA

Alors Maya, Maya l'astucieuse et la belle,
Pose ses doigts doux sur notre front qui se rebelle
Et câline susurre: Espérez toujours, c'est pour
Votre sacre que vont gronder les timbales vierges
Et vous aurez l'or et la pourpre de Bedjapour,
Esclave dont le sang teint la corde et les verges.

[Then Maya, Maya the astute and beautiful,
Places her gentle fingers on our rebellious brow
And whispers coaxingly: Go on hoping, it is for
Your coronation that the virgin drums will beat
And you shall have the gold and purple of Bijapur,
Slave whose blood stains the rope and the rods.]

Moréas (*Pur Concept*)

Désir d'être soudain la bête hiératique
D'un éclat noir sous les portiques
Escarboulés d'un temple à Bénarès

[A desire to be suddenly the hieratical beast
Black and brilliant beneath the
Jewelled porticoes of a temple in Benares.]

Verhaeren (*Là-bas*)

23 IRIS

Et les larges lis noirs, fleurs d'ombre et de ténèbres
Sur la bouche entrouvrant leurs calices funèbres
M'ont appris mon infâme et chaste déshonneur
Et descendue hélas dans l'horreur de mon être
J'ai savouré l'étrange et suave bonheur
De savoir m'adorer ayant cru me connaître.

[And the huge black lilies, flowers of shade and darkness,
Opening their mournful calyxes against my mouth,
Revealed to me my infamous and chaste dishonour,
And descending alas into the horror of my being,
I savoured the strange, sweet happiness
Of adoring myself after thinking I knew myself.]

Jean Lorrain (*La Forêt bleue*)

24 KNIGHT

This womanly figure with the full hips, this girlish body with flesh as white as elder pith, this mouth with the greedy lips, this slender waist, these prying fingers toying with a weapon, this swelling of the breastplate over the bosom which conceals the curve of the breasts, this glimpse of linen under the armpit between the shoulderpiece and the gorget, even this girlish blue ribbon tied under the chin – all this preys upon the mind. All the frenzied assimilations of Sodom seem to have been accepted by this hermaphrodite whose insinuating and now sorrowful beauty is already growing purer, as if transfigured by the slow approach of a god . . . This is a knight who, after hungering for lewd exploits, is dying under the weight of his sorrows.

J.-K. Huysmans (*Antiquités*, 1887)

25 LILIES

Lily, O Lily of the valley!
Lily, O Lily of Calvary Hill!
White with the glory of all graces,
Earth with the breath of thy pure soul fill:
Lily, O Lily of the Valley,
Lily, O Lily of Calvary Hill!

Lionel Johnson

J'ai fleuri mon royaume de lis frêles
Comme les vierges et comme les joies.

[I have decorated my kingdom with lilies
As frail as virgins or as joys.]

Viélé-Griffin (*Joies*)

Boire des lis d'eau froide au bord d'un pur oubli.
[To drink lilies of cold water on the edge of pure oblivion.]

Paul Valéry (*Narcisse*)

Et vous fleurs fixes mandragores à visage
Cactus obéliscals aux fruits en sarcophages
Forêts de cierges massifs forêts de polypiers
Palmiers de corail blanc aux résines d'acier
Lis marmoréen à sourires hystériques

And you, still mandrake flowers with faces,
Obeliscal cacti with sarcophagus fruits,
Forests of massive tapers, forests of polyparies,
White coral palm-trees with resin of steel,
Marmorean lily with hysterical smiles.

Jules Laforgue (*Climat, Faune et Flore de la Lune*)

26 LOIE FULLER

A frenzied dancer: the floor, avoided by leaps and bounds or hard to the toes, acquires the virginity of an undreamt-of city . . . The setting lies latent in the orchestra treasure of the imagination . . .

Mallarmé (*Revue franco-américaine*)

Déchirant l'ombre, et brusque, elle est là: c'est aurore!
D'un mauve de prélude enflé jusqu'au lilas
S'étant taillé des nuages en falbalas
Elle se décolore, elle se recolore . . .
. . . Sa robe est un bûcher de lis qui sont en feu
Dans ses chiffons en fleur du clair de lune infuse . . .

[Tearing the darkness, she is suddenly there: it is dawn!
Mauve at first, then swelling up to lilac,
After creating clouds out of her flounces,
She sheds her colour, then dons it again . . .
. . . Her dress is a pyre of lilies on fire,
Her floral garb infused with moonlight . . .]

Rodenbach (*Les Vierges*)

27 LUDWIG II

Roi, seul vrai Roi de ce siècle, salut Sire
Qui voulut mourir vengeant votre raison

[King, the only true King of this century, hail, Sire,
Who decided to die avenging your reason]

Verlaine (*Revue Wagnérienne*, 1886)

Ludwig II was a pure idealist and not an artistic voluptuary. The beauty or rather the very meaning of the things around him was perceptible to him alone. His castles and their furnishings were abstract signs for him. The paintings he amassed there had no other purpose than to maintain before his eyes the rules and exemplars which inspired him until the dawn.

Maurice Barrès (*Amori et Dolori Sacrum*)

28 MADONNAS

O Flower of flowers, our Lady of the May!
Thou leftest lilies rising from thy tomb:
They shone in stately and serene array,
Immaculate amid death's house of gloom.

Lionel Johnson

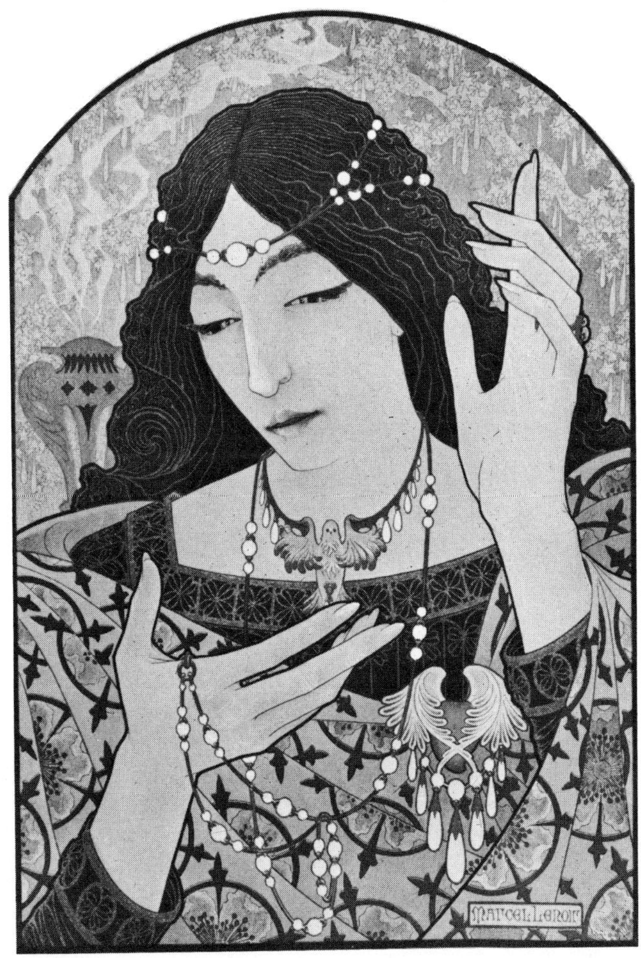

137. Lenoir: *Invocation à la Madone d'onyx vert*. This purple and bright green lithograph shows a *fin-de-siècle* witch wearing Lalique jewels.

And there was the divine de Mérode with her slim, natural and yet artificial elegance, her little, straight face, so virginal and yet so aware under the Madonna-like placidity of those smooth coils of hair, drawn over the ears and curved along the forehead.

Arthur Symons (on Aubrey Beardsley)

O mystical rose of the mire,
O house not of gold but of gain,
O house of unquenchable fire,
Our Lady of Pain.

Swinburne (*Dolores*)

An evening came since when I have done nothing but weep, grinding my teeth with insatiable longing, an evening of unforeseen madness . . . the crime of stealing the Madonna's garter.

Albert Aurier (*Le Symbolisme*)

29 MASKS

The women, the clowns and the priests had unchanging faces of silver, iron, copper, wood or cloth. And the clowns' masks were open in laughter, while the priests' masks were black with care.

Marcel Schwob (*La Porte des Rêves*)

What marvellous insight he has into the invisible and into the atmosphere created by our vices . . . our vices which turn our faces into masks . . .

Jean Lorrain (on Ensor)

30 MEDUSA

J'ai vu. Les autres n'ont point d'yeux, que verraient-ils?

Sorcière empoisonneuse aux rampantes manœuvres
J'ai vu tous tes pensers, tes désirs et tes œuvres
Sourdre dans tes cheveux en reptiles subtils.

Ivan Gilkin

[I have seen. The others have no eyes, so what should they see?
Poisonous witch with creeping movements,
I have seen all your thoughts, desires and deeds
Stealing forth in your hair in subtle reptiles.]

Pendue au pied du lit la tête aux lèvres peintes
Calme et blême égouttait ses lourds caillots de sang
Au-dessus d'un bassin de cuivre éblouissant
Et gorgé jusqu'au bord de lis et de jacinthes.

Jean Lorrain (*Pour Oscar Wilde*)

[Hanging at the foot of the bed, the head with the painted lips,
Calm and pale let drip its heavy clots of blood
Above a bowl of dazzling copper
Filled to the brim with lilies and hyacinths.]

31 MONA LISA

These fake Primaveras, these cut-price Mona Lisas of the painters' studios and the aesthetes' cafés, these artificial flowers of Montparnasse or Levallois-Perret.

Jean Lorrain (*Gil Blas*, 1899)

Spread over her face was that poor pallor I adore; on her lips was the cruel smile which the divine Leonardo pursued throughout his work. That smile contrasted with the gentle gaze of the long eyes and lent a superhuman charm to the beauty of those women whom the great Leonardo loved. Her mouth was a sorrowful flower.

D'Annunzio (*Il Piacere*)

32 OPHELIA

Les cheveux d'Ophélie envahissent l'eau grise
Tumulte inextricable où sa tête s'est prise;
Est-ce le lin d'un champ, est-ce sa chevelure?
L'embrouillamini vert qui rouit autour d'elle

[Ophelia's hair invades the grey water,
An inextricable tangle in which her head is caught;
Is it flax from a field, or is it her hair?
The green disorder steeping about her]

Rodenbach (*Les Vierges*)

La tête douloureuse, ardente et maladive,
A, dans le morne attrait de sa grâce native,
Le charme d'une vierge et d'un garçon pervers
Favori de prélat ou savante Ophélie
Son énigme est souffrance, entraînement, folie
Et comme un philtre noir coule dans ses yeux verts.

[The sorrowful head, ardent and sickly,
Has, in the bleak attraction of its native grace,
The charm of a virgin and of a depraved boy,
Prelate's favourite or learned Ophelia.
Its enigma is suffering, temptation, folly,
And a black philtre flows in the green eyes.]

Jean Lorrain (*Sur un Portrait de Botticelli*)

33 ORIENT

Pale and bent, drinking nothing, his sword across his knees, the Sar of the guard, Ben Jehu, sits on a cedar seat at the foot of the Throne, surrounded by his rough soldiers. This man, the Master's brother, the favourite of Abishag the Shulamite, and the executor of the rebel Adonia, is the great military servant, the murderer of Ebyatharet, of the Sar Simei and of Joab, the old Pontiff! He is the King's living herreb, he who strikes down the chosen victims, even as they cling with pleading hands to the Altar . . .

Villiers de l'Isle-Adam (*L'Annonciateur*)

Oh! peindre tes cheveux du bleu de la fumée.
Ta peau dorée est d'un ton tel qu'on croit voir presque
Une rose brûlée: Et ta chair embaumée
Dans les grands linges d'ange ainsi qu'en une fresque
Qui font plus brun ton corps gras et fin de Mauresque.

[Oh, to paint your smoke-blue hair.
Your skin is so golden it almost seems
A burnt rose. And your perfumed flesh
In the angelic fresco draperies
Which make even browner your plump Moorish body.]

Germain Nouveau (*Katchoum*)

34 PARKS

Je suis l'antique nymphe aux yeux de vétusté
Notre-Dame des Parcs errante sur les marches;
Aux vasques de jadis tremblaient des voluptés.

[I am the ancient nymph with the age-old eyes,
Our Lady of the Parks wandering along the steps;
Pleasure trembled in the fountains of yore.]

André Ibels (*Album des Légendes*)

Le parc malade de lune était profond comme une âme
La couleur de la nuit était belle comme la douleur
(Toutes ces choses sont si loin, si loin)

O. W. Milosz (*Lalie*)

[The moon-sick park was profound as a soul
The colour of the night was beautiful as pain
(All these things are so far away, so far away)]

35 PARSIFAL

Kundry meurt pardonné aux pieds de Parsifal
Son héros puéril qui sourit et bénit
Le sang miraculeux brille dans le cristal
Et les tours de Klingsor s'écroulent vers la nuit

Adolphe Retté (*Thulé des Brumes*)

[Kundry dies forgiven at the feet of Parsifal,
His childlike hero who smiles and blesses him.
The miraculous blood shines in the crystal
And Klingsor's towers crumble towards the night.]

36 PEACOCKS

Cependant que persiste
La splendeur, à côté,
Du plumage bleuté
De l'orgueil qui s'attriste
D'un paon jadis vainqueur
Au jardin du cœur

Verlaine (*Sur la Mona Rosa de Rossetti*)

[Meanwhile let there remain
The nearby splendour
Of the bluish plumage
And the melancholy pride
Of a peacock once victorious
In the garden of the heart.]

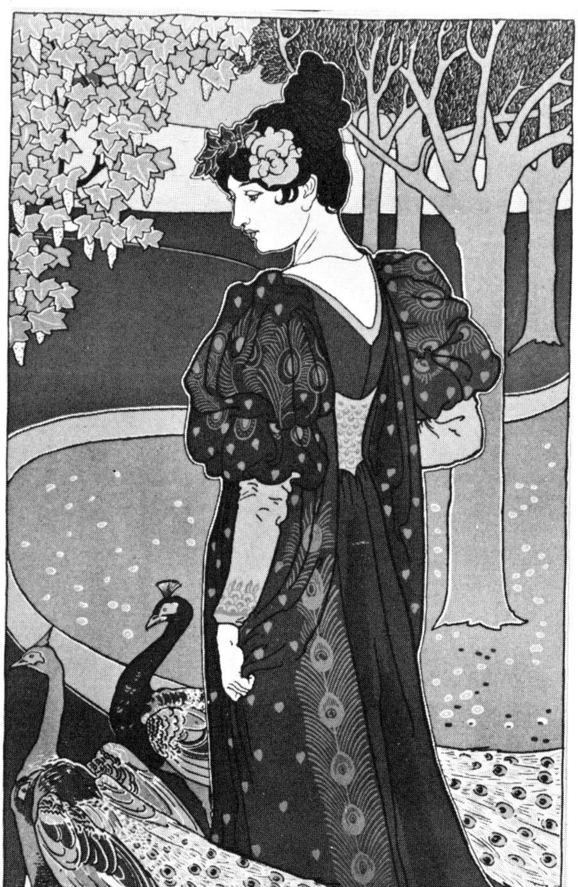

138. Louis Rhead: *Lady with Peacocks*. A coloured lithograph influenced by Alma-Tadema.

C'est un grand paon à l'œil rose
Dessiné sur un fond gris
Qui ne vole qu'à nuit close
Comme les chauves-souris.

[It is a large pink-eyed peacock
Drawn on a grey background
Which only flies after nightfall
Like bats.]

Gérard de Nerval (*Poèmes*)

37 PIERROT

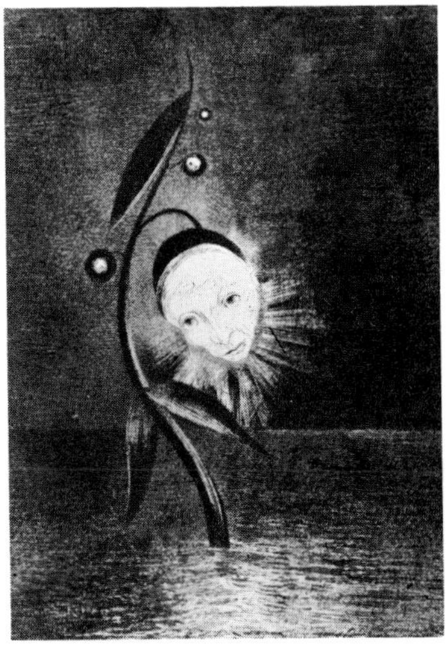

139. Redon: *La Fleur de Marécage.* In the Decadent setting of the swamp, this sad Pierrot's head, and the seeds, which are really death's-heads, call to mind the fantastic plants drawn by Edward Lear.

Sa gaîté comme sa chandelle est morte
Et son spectre aujourd'hui nous hante, mince et clair.
Ses yeux sont deux grands trous où rampe du phosphore
Et la farine rend plus effroyable encore
Sa face exsangue au nez pointu de moribond.
[His gaiety, like his candle, is dead
And today his ghost haunts us, slim and bright.
His eyes are two big holes in which phosphorus crawls
And the flour makes still more horrible
His bloodless face with the pointed nose of a dying man.]

Verlaine (*Jadis et Naguère*, 1883)

Pierrot is passionate; but he does not believe in great passions. He feels himself to be sickening with a fever, or else perilously convalescent; for love is a disease, which he is too weak to resist or endure . . . He knows that his face is powdered, and if he sobs, it is without tears; and it is hard to distinguish, under the chalk, if the grimace which twists his mouth away is more laughter or mockery . . . And so he becomes exquisitely false, dreading above all things that 'one touch of nature' which would ruffle his disguise, and leave him defenceless . . . His mournful contemplation of things becoming a kind of grotesque joy . . .

Arthur Symons (on Beardsley)

38 PUVIS DE CHAVANNES

Race blonde aux corps blancs brunis par le grand air,
Ludus pro patria, beaux éphèbes, sang fier,
Chair forte et deux yeux où rit la mort songeuse.
[Fair-haired race with white bodies bronzed by the open air,
Ludus pro patria, handsome ephebes, proud blood,
Strong flesh and eyes in which laughs pensive death.]

Verlaine (on a work by Puvis de Chavannes)

A crepuscular picture, suggestive of an old fresco dappled with moonlight and drenched with rain. It is painted in a lilac tinged with white and a lettuce-green mixed with milk . . . In spite of the revulsion this painting arouses in me when I am in front of it, I cannot help feeling a certain attraction towards it when I am far away.

Huysmans (*Salon de 1883*)

39 QUEENS

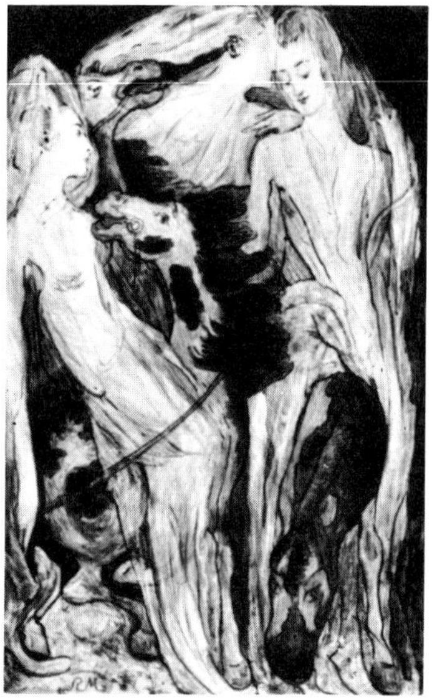

140. Robert de Montesquiou: *La Reine de Saba.* In his watercolours, done in the last years of his life, the aesthete rediscovered themes which he, more than anyone, had helped to make fashionable.

I know what queen at first you were
As though I had seen
Red gold and black imperious hair
Twice crown Faustine.

As if your fed sarcophagus
Spared flesh and skin,
You come back face to face with us,
The same Faustine.

Swinburne (*Ave Faustina Imperatrix*)

Là-bas Médée en feu dans le jardin lascif
Sent sa chair se dissoudre aux tièdes vents d'Asie . . .
[Yonder Medea on fire in the lascivious garden
Feels her flesh melting in the warm winds from Asia . . .]

Albert Samain (*Le Chariot d'Or*)

Le menton étranglé dans l'or brillant des gazes
Jaunes, le diadème au ras du sourcil peint,
L'Augusta se raidit dans l'argyrose éteint
D'un grand manteau brodé de paons de chrysoprases.
Dédaignant les affronts, méprisant les extases,
Elle tient à la main un grand lis byzantin
Un lis au cœur de perle, et sous son front hautain
Ses yeux, striés d'or fauve, ont l'air de deux topazes.
[Her chin caught in the bright gold of yellow gauze,
The diadem level with her painted eyebrows,
Augusta stands stiffly in the dull argentite
Of a great cloak embroidered with peacocks of chrysoprase.
Scorning all affronts, despising all ecstasies,
She holds in her hand a great Byzantine lily
With a pearly heart, and beneath her haughty brow
Her eyes, streaked with tawny gold, look like two topazes.]

Jean Lorrain (*Théodora*)

40 ROSES

J'ai trempé dans mon esprit bleu
Les roses des essences mortes.

[I have steeped in my blue mind
The roses of dead essences.]

Maeterlinck (*Serres chaudes*)

Auf die Schleusen!
Und aus Reusen
Regnen Rosen,
Güsse Flüsse
Die begraben.

[Open the lock gates
And let the roses
Of the rivers, of the waves
Which will be graves
Pour out in basketfuls.]

Stefan George (*Algabal*)

41 SAINTLY WOMEN

Elles sont quatre à me parler avec des
voix d'ailleurs
Toutes frêles d'entre leurs lèvres lentes
De belles voix douces et consolantes
Comme leurs robes et leurs mantes
Long-tombant et longuement calmantes . . .

[There are four of them talking to me
In far-away, faint voices between their
slow lips,
Beautiful voices, gentle and consoling,
Like their habits and their cloaks,
Slow-falling and soothing . . .]

Verhaeren (*Les Saintes*)

After offering the magic mirrors of her lonely room the worthless joy of her angel body, Elade put on the purple dress imposed upon her by the order of things and by the particular rules of her destiny . . . In order to free herself she wished she could be androgynous and bisexual, having repudiated the opposite sex as she had already repudiated her own; in unity she would inevitably have found intellectual peace and in sensual poverty the unheard-of richness of transcendental lust.

Rémy de Gourmont (*Histoire tragique de la Princesse Phénissa*)

42 SALOME

Comme c'est votre joie, ô fragiles poupées!
Car vous avez toujours aimé naïvement
Les joujoux flamboyantes et les têtes coupées

[Such is your joy, fragile dolls!
For you have always taken a naïve delight
In dazzling playthings and cut-off heads]

Théodore de Banville (*Rimes dorées*)

There on a cushion, among the debris of the ebony lyre, shone John's head – like Orpheus's once – coated with phosphorus, washed, painted and curled, grinning at those twenty-four million stars.

Laforgue (*Moralités légendaires*)

141. Wilhelm Volz: *Salomé.*

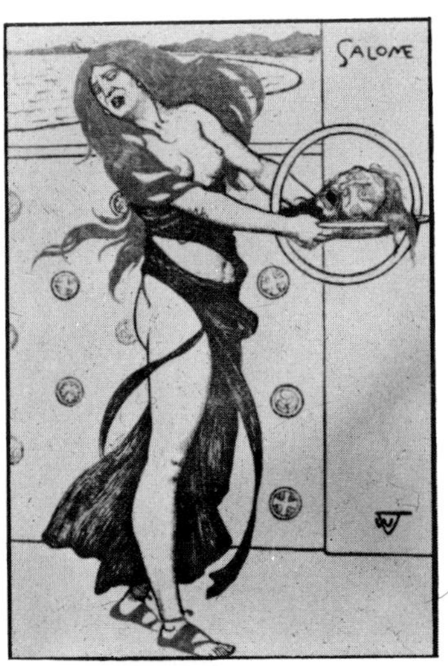

La vie d'un sage ne vaut pas, ma Salomé,
Ta danse d'orient sauvage comme la chair,
Et ta bouche couleur de meurtre,
Et tes sens couleur de désert,
O Salomé de mes Hontes,
Salomé!
[A sage's life is not to be compared, my Salome,
With your eastern dance, wild as the flesh,
And your mouth the colour of murder,
And your senses the colour of the desert,
O Salome of my Shame,
Salome!]

Milosz (*Poèmes de la Décadence*)

43 SAPPHO

Furieuse, les yeux caves et les seins roides,
Sapho que la langueur de son désir irrite
Comme une louve court le long des grèves froides.

Verlaine (*Parallèlement*)

[In a frenzy, her eyes hollow and her breasts stiff,
Sappho, exasperated by the languor of her desire,
Runs like a she-wolf along the cold shore.]

The last flower of that strange and ancient line whose origins go back to that evening of love when, in the mysterious parks of Mytilene, proud Sappho, driven mad by male songs she had not heard before, abandoned herself to the caresses of Orpheus, disguised as a priestess of Aphrodite.

Albert Aurier (*Irénée*)

44 SARAH BERNHARDT

Quand elle errait pareille aux jeunes immortelles,
De son rire sonore exaspérant Paris,
De vagues chaînes d'or sortaient de ses prunelles
Et ses pieds nus foulaient des corps d'amants meurtris.

Jean Lorrain (*Le Sang des Dieux*)

[When she roamed abroad like a young goddess,
Irritating Paris with her loud laugh,
Golden chains flashed from her eyes
And her bare feet trampled the bruised bodies of her lovers.]

45 SATAN

Dans un palais soie et or, dans Ecbatane,
De beaux démons, des satans adolescents
Au son d'une musique mahométane,
Font litière aux Sept Péchés de leurs cinq sens

Verlaine (*Poèmes saturniens*)

[In a silk and gold palace in Echbatan,
Beautiful demons, youthful Satans,
To the sound of Mohammedan music
Dedicate their five senses to the Seven Sins.]

46 SERPENTS

Les serpents violets des rêves
Qui s'enlacent dans mon sommeil
Mes désirs couronnés de glaives
Des lions noyés au soleil
Et des mains closes sans retour
Et les tiges rouges des haines
Entre les deuils verts de l'amour.

Maeterlinck (*Serres chaudes*)

[The purple serpents of dreams
Which intertwine in my sleep,
My desires crowned with swords,
Lions drowned in the sunshine,
And hands closed for ever,
And the red stems of hatred
Between the green sorrows of love.]

47 SILENCE

Silence où toute l'âme assombrie est encline
A se sentir de plus en plus comme orpheline,
Toute seule parmi le soir endolori,
A revoir son passé comme un tombeau fleuri

Rodenbach (*Petits Poèmes de Bruges*)

[Silence in which the saddened soul is inclined
To feel more and more like an orphan,
All alone in the melancholy evening,
Looking back at the past as at a flower-covered grave]

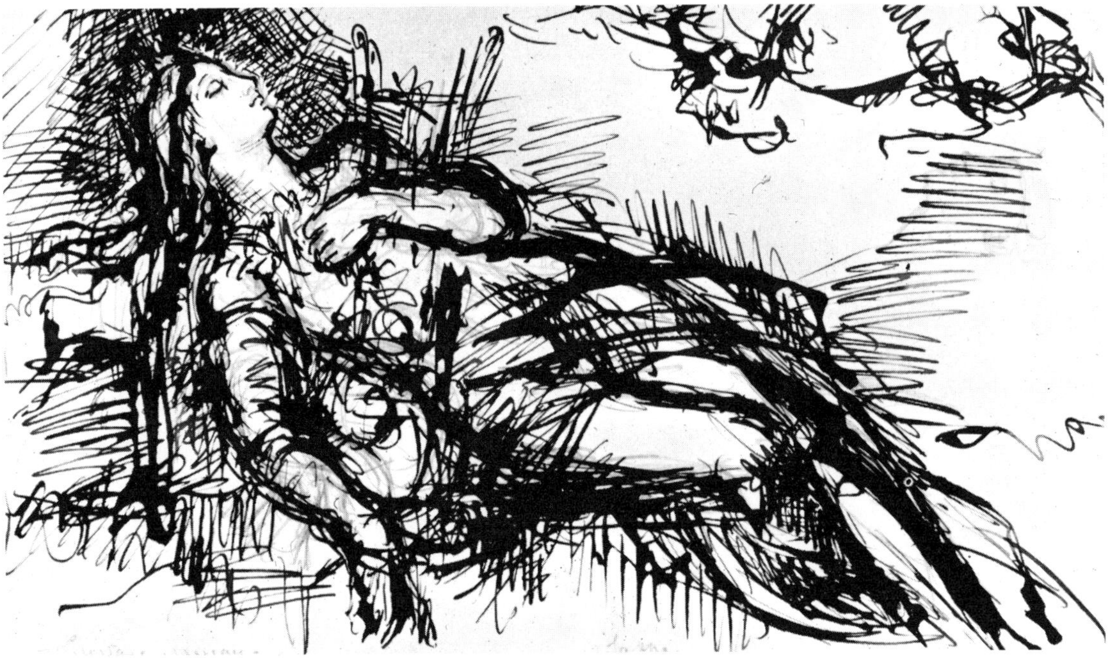

142. Moreau: *Sappho*. One of the great myths of Symbolism treated in a drawing worthy of Delacroix.

Above all else, silence, the crystallization of the soul sleeping in peace far from the present; sacred silence, father of dreams; sweet taciturnity which allows us to hear the inner melody.

Camille Mauclair (*L'Art en Silence*)

48 SIRENS

Des Lyres se mouraient dans l'air harmonieux
Suprêmes, une langueur s'exhalait des calices
Et les marins pâmés sentaient, lentes délices,
Les velours de baisers se poser sur leurs yeux

[Lyres were dying in the harmonious air,
Languorous exhalations came from the calyxes
And the swooning sailors felt the slow delight
Of velvet kisses settling on their eyes]

Albert Samain (*Le Chariot d'Or*)

J'arrachai mes yeux qui sombrèrent au fond des flots
Donne-moi ton âme afin que tu deviennes pareille aux noyés, aux amants,
Qui ne se souviennent d'aucune tendresse humaine
Et mon âme s'abîma dans les flots
[I tore out my eyes which sank to the bottom of the waves
Give me your soul so that you become like the drowned, like the lovers,
Who can remember no human affection
And my soul plunged into the waves]

Renée Vivien (*Ondines*)

49 SODOM

Glory to Cain! Glory to Sodom! Glory to Judas! Cain founded the race of strong men. Sodom terrified the world with its punishment. It was through Judas that God saved the world.

Flaubert (*La Tentation de Saint Antoine*)

Ah, their mistresses who walk without legs and who see without eyes, who love without genitals, and who, under mechanically-cut foliage, hold up hands broken at the wrist by the same eternal flexion! . . . Ah, their heroes who stink of sodomy, neurosis and syphilis!

Octave Mirbeau (*Critique*, 1895)

50 SOULS

And the Raven never flitting, still is sitting, still is sitting,
On the pallid bust of Pallas, just above my chamber door:
And his eyes have all the seeming of a demon's that is dreaming,
And the lamp-light o'er him streaming throws his shadow on
the floor;
And my soul from out that shadow that lies floating on the floor
Shall be lifted – nevermore!

Edgar Allan Poe (*The Raven*)

Ames d'enfants morts avant la rosée baptismale.
L'aile poussive, elles ne purent, les frêles, gagner le
paradis et les voici, non loin du sol, figés.
Tasses de larmes . . .
[Souls of children who died before the baptismal dew.
Weak-winged, the frail things could not reach Paradise and
here they are, close to the earth, frozen into immobility.
Cups of tears . . .]

Saint-Pol-Roux (*De la Colombe au Corbeau par le Paon*)

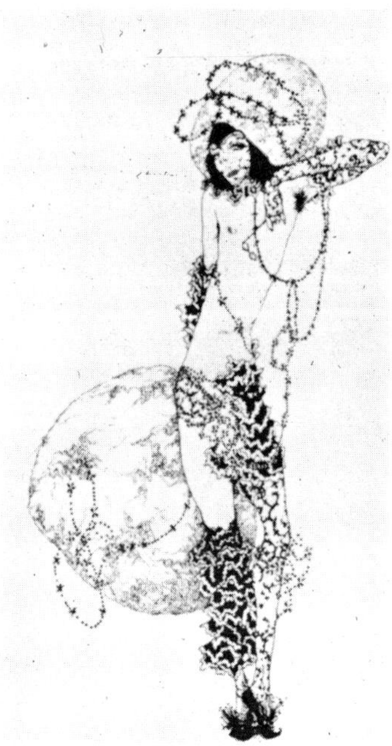

143. Alastair: Drawing for Oscar Wilde's *Sphinx*. During the 1920s Alastair continued Beardsley's follies with an even greater degree of perversity.

51 SPHINX

It is the earthly Chimera, base as matter, and likewise represented by this charming woman's head with wings, and the body of a carnivorous beast.

Gustave Moreau (unpublished notes)

The immateriality of a hieratical woman's body, girded with jewels and enveloped in metallic mists, at the neck, at the belly, it is a dream made flesh, tempting the mind to set off on a journey towards mystery. Female sphinxes for complicated perversities, female sphinxes for the jaded and bored, female sphinxes for the Sphinx himself.

Verhaeren (on Khnopff's *Sphinx*)

Great Ammon was your bedfellow! . . .
With blood of goats and blood of steers you taught him
monstrous miracles,
White Ammon was your bedfellow! Your chamber was the
steaming Nile,
And with your curved archaic smile you watched his passion
come and go.

Oscar Wilde (*The Sphinx*)

144. A. Vroubel: *The Swan Princess.* Russian folk-lore idealized in a symbolic myth. Vroubel deserves to be compared with Khnopff for his elegant evocations.

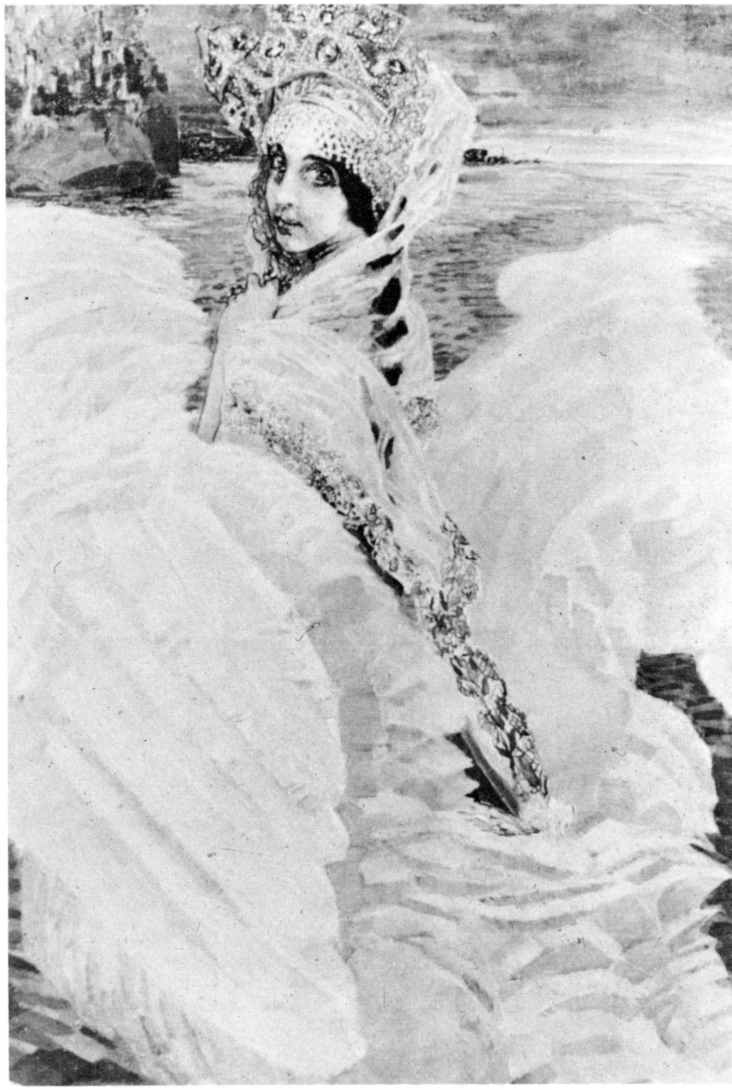

All those tormented by the desire for God, I have devoured.

Flaubert (*La Tentation de Saint Antoine*)

52 SWANS

Par la nage et le vol de son cygne idéal
Surgit sous la clarté que réfracte son casque
Lohengrin, le Héros grave du Saint Graal.

Stuart Merrill (*Fastes*)

[Through the swimming and flying of his ideal swan,
There appears beneath the light glinting on his helmet
Lohengrin, the grave hero of the Holy Grail.]

Les cygnes, en rochets plissés de séminaires,
Semaient dans l'eau, des lis et de blanches azalées
Pour l'élévation de la lune agrandie.

Rodenbach (*Paysages de Ville*)

[The swans, in pleated seminary surplices,
Were sowing lilies and white azaleas in the water,
For the elevation of the swollen moon.]

53 THULE

Vous les Nixes, là-bas, aux ceintures de givre,
De glaçons bleus coiffées
Qui réservez pour vous ce don de vivre
Claires dans la stérilité; reines et fées
Des lointaines et lucides Baltiques.

Verhaeren (*Les Apparues dans mes Chemins*)

[You the Nixies, over there, girded with hoar-frost,
Your heads wreathed in blue icicles,
You who keep for yourselves the gift of living
Bright in sterility, queens and fairies
Of the distant, lucid Baltic lands.]

54 VAMPIRES

She is older than the rocks among which she sits; like the vampire, she has been dead many times, and learned the secrets of the grave; and has been a diver in deep seas, and keeps their fallen day about her; and trafficked for strange webs with Eastern merchants; and, as Leda, was the mother of Helen of Troy, and, as Saint Anne, the mother of Mary.

Walter Pater (on the *Mona Lisa*)

55 VENICE

Oh, that beautiful, pensive woman's face, laid bare as befits a princess of the sea, like a royal cloak on the heraldic cruppers of the old lion of St. Mark. The eternal dreaminess of those huge eyes with the distant pupils . . . The imperial calm of that crowned head rising like a lily between the lion's two black wings.

Jean Lorrain (on a watercolour by Gustave Moreau entitled *Venise*)

56 VENUS

'Beneath the horizontal immobility of the long eyebrows, two dark blue eyes under languid Hindu lids, two magnificent eyes laden with dreams, spread about her a transfiguring magic over all things in heaven and on earth. He saturated with unknown charms the fateful features of that face whose beauty was unforgettable . . . the cruel flared nostrils which quivered at the scent of danger, the mouth tinged with a gleam of blood, the chin of a silent despoiler.'

'I shall endow that shadow with all the songs of Hoffmann's Antonia, with all the mystical passion of Edgar Allan Poe's Ligeias, with all the seductive ardour of the Venus of that great musician Richard Wagner.'

Villiers de l'Isle-Adam (*L'Ève future*)

57 WAGNER

The threatening peak of the absolute to be revealed after the disappearance of the clouds, glittering up there, naked and alone. A spectacle of the future . . . a monster which cannot be.

Mallarmé (*Revue Wagnérienne*)

It is as if he had unconsciously illustrated Wagner's gigantic work, the dense Germanic forest; and in the chiaroscuro of that Broceliande, Odilon Redon conjures up – half alive, half inanimate – enchanting girl-flowers . . . They all seem lapidified and yet one can feel that they are alive with the awesome life of ideas and idols; ghostly as they are, they all have the set profiles of Poe's sublime entities.

Jean Lorrain (on Redon)

58 WALTER PATER

Gracious God rest him! he who toiled so well
Secrets of grace to tell
Graciously; as the awed rejoicing priest
Officiates at the feast,
Knowing how deep within the liturgies
Lie hid the mysteries.
Half of a passionately pensive soul
He showed us, not the whole.
Who loved him best, they best, they only, knew
The deeps they might not view;
That which was private between God and him,
To others, justly dim.
Calm Oxford autumns and preluding springs!
To me your memory brings
Delight upon delight, but chiefest one:
The thought of Oxford's son,
Who gave me of his welcome and his praise
When white were still my days.

Lionel Johnson

59 WATER-LILIES (Nenuphars)

A little volume, bound in the same Nile green skin that has been powdered with gilded nenuphars . . .

Oscar Wilde (*The Critic as Artist*)

60 WITCHES

And the more I gazed at that passionate witch's silhouette, the more her white eucharistic flesh under plaited viper tresses seemed to me to be marked with the irreparable kiss . . . It was to a Black Mass that the exotic creature was wending her way.

Jean Lorrain (on a picture by Jeanne Jacquemin)

Vous boirez le vertige obscène
L'élixir des ruts monstrueux,
Le sang du stupre et de la haine
Et des grands viols incestueux.

Ivan Gilkin (*Ténèbres*)

[You will drink the obscene vertigo,
The elixir of monstrous ruts,
The blood of debauchery and hate
And of great incestuous rapes.]

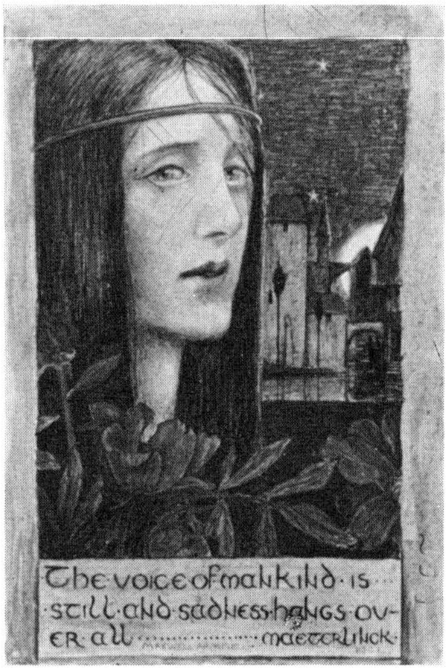

145\. Armfield: *The Voice of Mankind is Still and Sadness Hangs over All.* The influence of Belgian Symbolism on a late Pre-Raphaelite, who is still alive.

61

The mysterious road which leads to the interior.

Novalis

62

The road of excess leads to the palace of wisdom.

William Blake

63

Natural things exist only a little; reality lies only in dreams.

Baudelaire (*Paradis artificiels*)

64

In matters artistic I am a Supernaturalist. I believe that the artist cannot find all his models in Nature, but that the most remarkable are revealed to him in his soul.

Heine

65

Sinuous as water or as light, flexible and penetrative, delicate and rapid.

Swinburne (on Rossetti's poetry)

66

To grasp at any exquisite passions or any stirring of the senses, strange eyes, strange colours and curious odours, or the work of the artist's hands or the face of one's friend.

Walter Pater (on the *Mona Lisa*)

67

When I was composing my *Tristan* I immersed myself with utter confidence in the depths of the soul and its mysteries, and from that intimate centre of the world I saw its external form blossom forth . . . Life and death, the importance and the existence of the external world, all depend solely on the internal movements of the soul. The action which has just been performed depends on a single cause, on the soul which provokes it, and that action appears to the world in the form whose image the soul has fashioned in its dreams.

Wagner, 1861

68

Car nous voulons la nuance encor
Pas la couleur, rien que la nuance!
Or la nuance seule fiance
Le rêve au rêve et la flûte au cor.

Verlaine (*Art poétique*, 1874)

[For we want nuances,
Not colours, nothing but nuances!
For only nuances marry
Dream to dream and flute to horn.]

69

J'adore l'indécis, les sons, les couleurs frêles,
Tout ce qui tremble, ondule et frissonne et chatoie,
Les cheveux et les yeux, l'eau, les feuilles, la soie,
Et la spiritualité des formes grêles.

Albert Samain (*Les Jardins de l'Infante*)

[I worship what is vague, delicate sounds and colours,
Whatever trembles, ripples, shivers and shimmers,
Hair and eyes, water, leaves and silk,
And the spiritualty of slender shapes.]

70

One thing is dominant in me, the ardent attraction of the abstract. The expression of human feelings, of the passions, interests me no doubt, but I am less inclined to express these movements of the soul than to make visible, so to speak, the inner flashes of illumination which we cannot explain, which have something divine about them, and which, translated by the marvellous effects of pure plastic art, open up magical perspectives.

Gustave Moreau (unpublished notes)

71

Art died the day when, in composition, the rational combination of intelligence and common sense took the place in the artist of the almost purely plastic imaginative concept, in short: love of the arabesque.

Gustave Moreau (unpublished notes)

72

What does Nature matter in itself? For the artist it is only an opportunity to express himself . . . Art is the strenuous attempt to express inner feeling in plastic form.

Gustave Moreau (unpublished notes)

73

Just as a dream is situated in a suitably coloured atmosphere, so a concept, when it becomes a composition, needs to move in a fittingly coloured setting. There is obviously one particular colour attributed to some part of the picture which becomes a key and governs the other parts . . . All the figures, their arrangement in relation to one another, the landscape or interior which serves them as a background or horizon, their clothes, everything about them in fact must serve to illuminate the general idea and wear its original colour, its livery so to speak.

Gustave Moreau (unpublished notes)

74

Beauty and Good are in Heaven. Science is on earth, crawling on the ground.

Odilon Redon (*A Soi-même*)

75

Subjective art is as it were the radiation of things towards the dream, towards which the mind is travelling too. Decadence or not, that is what it is. Let us call it rather the growth and evolution of art for the ultimate advancement of our own life . . . All the critics' mistakes about me were committed because they failed to see that nothing must be defined, nothing must be understood, nothing must be limited and nothing must be made explicit, because everything that is sincerely and humbly new – like Beauty itself, indeed – carries its meaning in itself.

Odilon Redon (*A Soi-même*)

76

The essence of mystery is to remain perpetually ambiguous, to have two or three aspects or possible aspects.

Odilon Redon (*A Soi-même*)

77

All art is at once surface and symbol.

Oscar Wilde

78

All concrete phenomena cannot manifest themselves of their own accord. They are mere perceptible appearances intended to represent their esoteric affinities with the primordial Ideas.

Moréas (*Manifeste du Symbolisme*)

79

Never has the aspiration to the spiritual life or to the invisible world – an aspiration opposed by the materialistic theories of the scientists and by fashionable opinion – been more serious and more genuine. That aspiration can be found in the regrets and doubts, the black despair and even the blasphemies of our Naturalist novelists and our Decadent poets. Never has the human spirit had a more profound awareness of the inadequacy, the poverty, the unreality of this life. Never has it aspired more ardently to an invisible Beyond without managing to believe in it.

Schuré (Preface to *Les grands Initiés*)

80

Séguin is not a master. His faults are not yet sufficiently obvious to earn him that title. But he knows how to read the Book of Mystery and he knows how to speak the language of the Book . . . He expresses not what he sees but what he thinks through an original harmony of lines, through a curious use of arabesques.

Gauguin (*Letters*)

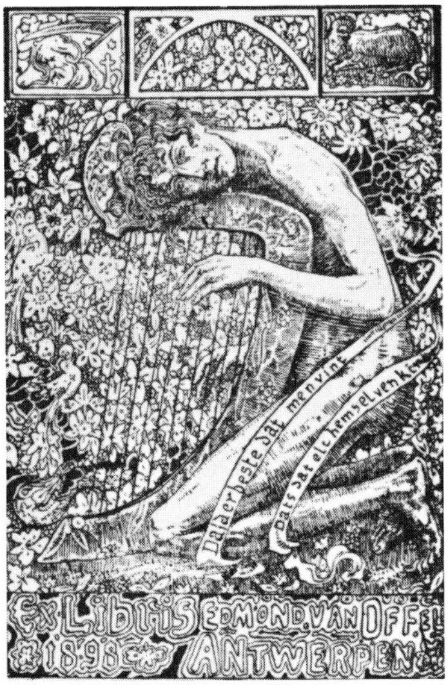

146. Edmond van Offel: *Ex-libris.* A little etching by a charming Belgian illustrator.

81
In aesthetic criticism attitude is everything. For in art there is no such thing as a universal truth. A truth in art is that whose contradictory is also true. And just as it is only in art-criticism, and through it, that we can apprehend the platonic theory of ideas, so it is only in art-criticism, and through it, that we can realize Hegel's system of contraries. The truths of metaphysics are the truths of masks.

Oscar Wilde (*The Truth of Masks*)

82
In landscape, space must be tinged with passionalism.

Péladan (on Manet)

83
To arms, citizens! Reason is dead.

Jules Laforgue

84
Remembrance vibrates, feathered with sorrows. The sufferings of memory are exacerbated by similarities. The present desire murmurs vaguely towards the past, towards the distance; the Chimeras weep in the taverns . . . And without looking for the way out of the labyrinth, the poor soul will relive perpetual rebirths, perpetual reawakenings.

Gustave Kahn

85
My dramas are deeds of prowess made visible by music.

Wagner

86
The future belongs to Decadism. Born of the world-weariness of a Schopenhauerian civilization, the Decadents are not a literary school. Their mission is not to found but to destroy, to demolish the old order and prepare the embryonic elements of the great national literature of the twentieth century.

Le Décadent, 1890

87
The work of art must be *Ideaist* since its unique ideal will be the expression of the idea, *Symbolist* since it will express that idea through forms, *Synthetic* since it will compose those forms in a universally comprehensible manner, and finally (as a natural consequence) *Decorative*.

The artist must have that transcendental emotivity, so great and precious, which makes the soul quiver before the changing drama of the abstract.

The aim of painting is to express ideas, by translating them into a special language . . . The symbols emerge from the darkness and begin to live with a life which is no longer our contingent life, but a life which is the essential life, the life of Art, the being of Being.

In the history of Art there exist two great contradictory tendencies which depend, the one on blindness, the other on clairvoyance, 'that man within man' as Swedenborg called it, the Realist tendency and the Ideaist tendency . . . Supreme Art cannot but be Ideaist, Art being simply the representational materialization of what is really divine in the world, and in the last analysis the only reality: the Idea. Those who cannot see the Idea are surely deserving of our pity, as were, for free men, the prisoners of Plato's symbolic cave.

Albert Aurier (*Le Symbolisme*)

88

We believe in neither progress nor salvation; for the moribund Latin race we are preparing a final explosion of splendour to dazzle and mollify the barbarians who are approaching. The last enthusiasts of this world, we come among the tavern crowds braying the *Marseillaise* to intone a final hymn to the Beauty which is God, and thus earn the right to gaze one day upon the mystic rose.

My lust for the ideals of the past has violated the tombs in which the miracles lay sleeping, and my debauchery has had knowledge of some very young ideas which will not develop for another century.

Péladan (*La Décadence latine*)

89

We must embody a symbol *through lines* in an amplified model of the archetype; we must homogenize that symbol *by means of colours* with the character of a living creature, or better still with its substratum. We must measure figure and form, enshrine the composition in a framework of decorative arabesques, choose colours and luminosity to match the subject to be treated, and combine their infinite tone values (for have they not a soul?) with some aesthetic emotion. We must take the Idea evoked by a gesture and *expletivize* it by means of a concordance of *expressive* linear directions, a dominant of *pertinent* symbolic colouration.

Alexandre Séon (*L'Art et l'Idée*, 1892)

90

In my concept of décor there begin to dawn some fuliginous phantoms, symbols of empiricism, of the incomprehension of causality, monstrous shapes of chimerical doctrines. Then the paper is activated with notes of curious shapes, bizarre adaptations of certain creatures to their vital condition, strange faces of night animals, a Cyclops eye, ghostly white glances, pteriopes wrapped in procinian cloaks, spectres and lemurs, vampires and notules.

Émile Gallé (letter to Montesquiou)

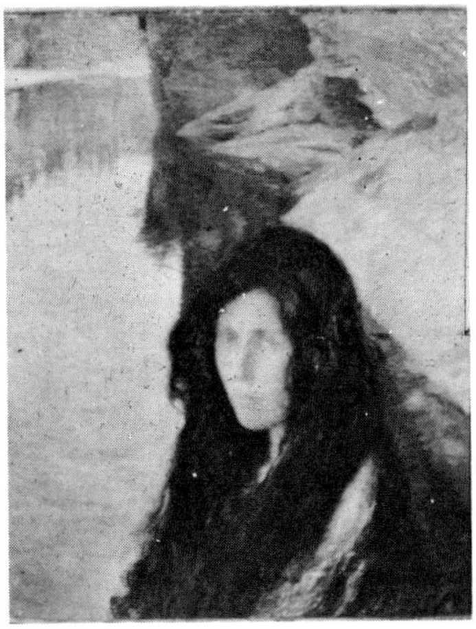

147. Henri Martin: *L'Abandonnée.* Martin was responsible for enormous decorations which recall both Puvis and the Pointillists. Around 1900 he had great success in the world of official exhibitions.

91

It is true (very) that the Eternal is concealed in each individual, that each individual is the epidermis with some mummer's epidermis, and that I prefer the artist who, instead of the eternal abstract, is content with accentuating – however little – the eternal soul poured down from heaven and the memory into the transparent bodies of contingencies. Filiger has our approval because he is a *deformer*, if that is the conventional name for a painter who does what *is* and not what is conventional.

Alfred Jarry (on Filiger)

92

What could one think of an artist who did not love suffering, who was even incapable of loving it for itself? Would he be anything but a compass without a needle, a needle without a magnet?

Artistic creation is an awe-inspiring commitment, a sort of silent, solemn duel in which the mind has to be concentrated in a fearless discipline.

Henry de Groux (*Notes sur l'Art*)

93

The effect of the art of our Art is a vague attraction towards a melancholy, grave ideal. – Art must objectivize the subjective. – My soul is alone and nothing influences it. It is like glass enclosed in silence, completely devoted to its interior spectacle.

Meditations by Khnopff, recorded by Verhaeren

94

If a poet conjures up the direct, evocative vision of Paris at night, and says: 'An immense algebra to which we have lost the key,' that bare phrase will recreate without the aid of any description or factual record a luminous, shadowy, awe-inspiring Paris.

Verhaeren (on Khnopff)

95

Testifying to their supremacy, harps are white; and blue are violins to surmount our passion; in the plenitude of ovations the brass is red; the flutes yellow, modulating the young girl astonished at the colour of her lips; and muffled by Earth and the Flesh, a simple synthesis of the only simple instruments, the black organs complain.

René Ghill (*Instrumentations poétiques*)

96

The Rosicrucians wish to destroy Realism. They reject all military, patriotic, anecdotal, Oriental, rustic or sporting scenes. On the other hand the Order encourages subjects drawn from Catholic dogma, the interpretation of Oriental theogonies, decorative allegories, and the sublimated nude. In respect of architecture, as that art was killed in 1789, the Salon accepts only restoration projects or plans for faery palaces. Finally, the ultimate 'magic rule' is that no woman shall ever exhibit among the Rosicrucians.

Rules of the Rosicrucian Exhibition

97

The Universe is, as it were, a huge manuscript in which each object is a letter and the totality of which recounts the Divine . . . Human beings endowed with thought can become aware of this symbolic script through Science, Art and Religion; they can decipher Divinity itself and gradually create it.

Camille Mauclair (*Esthétique de Mallarmé*)

98

Faces frozen in ecstasy, in which the soul murders the flesh, sexless virgins, an incredibly depraved and arrogant religion. Maurice Denis makes much use of soft colours; his languid, almost expiring *Dormeuse* is very poignant. How disquieting is the strange ugliness of these angel or demon faces weeping in the melancholy of fiery bluey-green landscapes in which greenish purples fulgurate – in a singing gamut – among the bleeding, brassy reds of hair and sunsets.

L'Académie française, 1893 (*L'Exposition Symboliste*)

99

My soul, by means of seraphically nimble sleight-of-hand, by means of tricks performed as it were with zephyr limbs, translates itself, defines itself, reveals itself to the eyes of the ingenuous, panting in front of the adamantine exaltation as if they had suddenly been confronted with a treasure-chest. It is (to use the hereditary and common device of a symbol comprehensible to mediocre minds) a kaleidoscope in which, according to a faithful interpretation, the essence is formulated, the transcendence is accessibilized, the abyss is practicabilized, and the ideas are figurativated. Every pirouette, every huge arabesque is the esoteric equivalent of a translated esotericism; every gesture, as if traced in white chalk on a black slate, is the adequate and spontaneous depiction of an abstraction; and this brings to the mind the First Idea which the alphabet of the intermediary stars will divulge when, sooner or later, it is deciphered.

To mirror itself: the perpetual occupation of Beauty.

Its mirrors: men.

Beauty remains the same, but the mirrors differ.

As varied as its conscious or unconscious mirrors, the one Beauty is consequently several, since a single idea of Beauty haunts each man.

The emotion of the mirror is the cry of the new-born work.

The work consists of rendering the reflection in plastic form.

The domain of these individual beauties, different expressions of the original Beauty, is called Art: the superiority of one of them is called a masterpiece.

Saint-Pol-Roux (*L'Ame saisissable*)

100
Art is the reverse of general ideas in that it describes only the particular, wants only the unique. It does not classify, it declassifies.

Marcel Schwob

101
Art digs in Matter the furrows of the Mind.

Stefan George

102
Personal Art – and that is the only art – is always almost incomprehensible. If it is understood it ceases to be Art to become a subject for new artistic expressions.

Rémy de Gourmont

103
We have seen enough of red coral: let it be blue. One of the elements of Art is Novelty. Without that element, like a vertebrate without vertebrae, Art collapses and liquefies into the gelatine of a jellyfish which the ebb-tide has left behind on the sand. Now, of all the artistic theories born in these penultimate days, only one seems novel, with an unheard-of, unprecedented novelty, and that is Symbolism, which, cleansed of the insulting interpretations put on it by shortsighted incompetents, can be literally translated by the word Liberty, and, for those of a violent temperament, by the word Anarchy.

Revue blanche, 1892

THE ENEMIES OF THE DREAM

104
Refined art has only been able to come into being thanks to the slavery of the masses; it will only be able to go on developing if that slavery continues to exist. Those men are stupid and immoral who proclaim with utter impudence that only superior intellects, the élite or Nietzsche's 'supermen' are to be allowed to share in the pleasures of art. Whatever new idiocy appears in art, the upper classes have no sooner accepted it than somebody promptly invents a theory to explain and sanction it.

Tolstoy (*What is Art?*)

105

Monsieur Odilon Redon draws you an eye roaming about an amorphous landscape on the end of a stem. And some commentators will tell you that this eye represents the eye of conscience, while others will say that it signifies the eye of uncertainty. One critic will explain that this eye synthetizes a sunset in the Hyperborean Seas, another that it symbolizes universal suffering.

Octave Mirbeau (*Le Gaulois*, 1886)

106

The incoherence of the mythologies represented was equalled only by the platitude of the representation; all the princesses of the Arthurian Legend followed on, corseted in gold-embroidered costumes and haloed in heraldic flowers, princesses and costumes looking as if they had been cut out of painted zinc; and then came the obligatory procession of witches and devils, Scandinavian heroes in helmets and sorceress-princesses in hennins.

Jean Lorrain (*Les Pelléastres*)

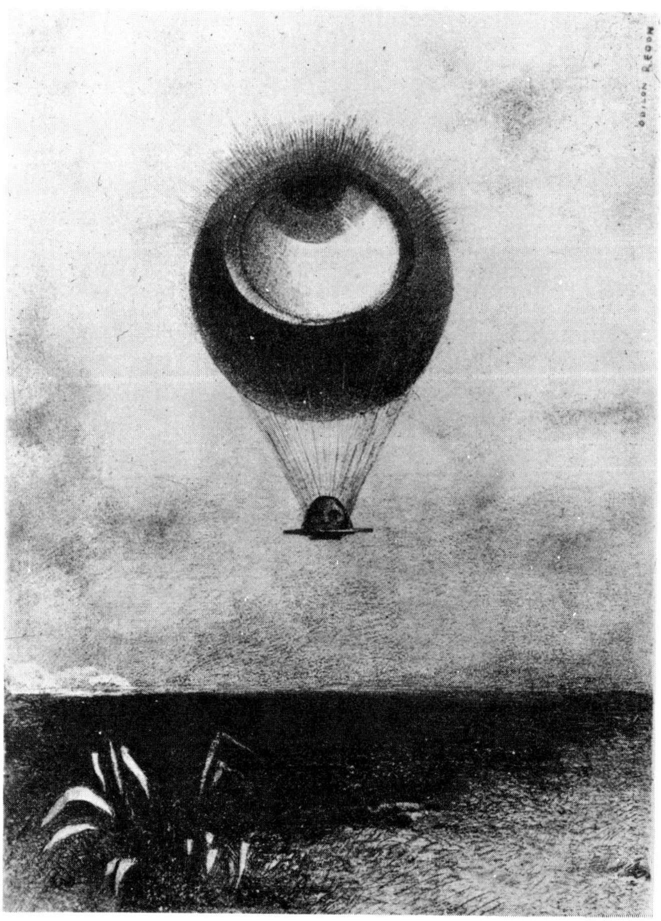

148. Redon: *L'Oeil comme un Ballon bizarre se dirige vers l'Infini*. The theme of the eye as the symbol of universal knowledge and of conscience often recurs in Redon's work. This lithograph was inspired by Edgar Allan Poe.

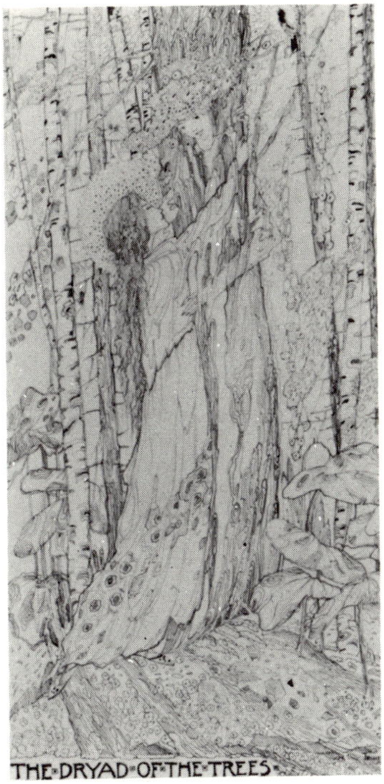

149. Jessie M. King: *The Dryad of the Trees*. This is a delightful confection by a favourite artist of *Studio* readers.

107
Nobody will ever be able to make Monsieur Fernand Khnopff or many of the other Rosicrucian exhibitors understand that a picture must first of all attract us with its rhythms, that a painter is really showing excessive humility when he chooses subjects already rich in literary meanings, that three pears depicted on a tablecloth by Paul Cézanne are moving and sometimes mystical, and that the whole Wagnerian Valhalla, when they paint it, is as uninteresting as the Chamber of Deputies.

Félix Fénéon

108
Idealism is our perversion, and the Soul depraves us. We are drinking the dregs of the immaterial and have touched the dingiest bottoms of purity.

The Chap-Book, 1895

109
Courbet was not wrong to laugh whenever anyone spoke to him of the soul; but there is still more soul in a square centimetre of the most materialist of Courbet's paintings than in all the combined works of the English Pre-Raphaelites, Gustave Moreau and Böcklin.

Élie Faure

110
Art begins when a man wishes to immortalize the most vivid moment he has ever lived. Life has already, to one not an artist, become art in that moment. And the making of one's life into art is after all the first duty and privilege of every man.

Arthur Symons

111
To fix the last fine shade, the quintessence of things; to fix it fleetingly; to be a disembodied soul, and yet the voice of a human soul; that is the ideal of Decadence.

Arthur Symons

112
A line is a force, filled with the energy of him who drew it.

Henry Van de Velde

113

Der Zeit ihre Kunst	[To each time its art
Der Kunst ihre Freiheit	To that art, its freedom]

Inscription on Olbrich's *Sezession* Building, Vienna

114
A is for Art of the age-end variety
We Decadents simply can't get a satiety.

Gelett Burgess (American)

List of Illustrations

The publishers wish to acknowledge the following sources of photographic material:
A.C.L., Brussels: plates 67, 72, 127; Alinari, Florence: 45; Paul Bijtebier, Brussels: 8; R. Bonnefoy, Paris: 20; Bulloz, Paris: 48, 109, 111; Françoise Foliot, Paris: 54, 103, 115; J. Guillot, Paris: 32; Peter Heilmann, Darmstadt: 17; P. Hinous, Paris: 142; Per Kruse, Copenhagen: 120; Gilbert Mangin, Nancy: 57; Musées Nationaux, Paris: 4, 41, 101, 106, 140; Photo. Rampazzi: 2, 63, 75, 118, 122, 124, 130; Steinkopf, Berlin: 47, 50.

47 Max Klinger: *Death is there* (etching). Berlin, Staatliche Museen.

48 Pablo Picasso: *Evocation*. Paris, Musée National d'Art Moderne.

49 Klinger: *Dead Mother* (etching). Berlin, Staatliche Museen.

50 Klinger: *Death of the Lovers* (etching). Berlin, Staatliche Museen.

51 Félicien Rops: *L'Amante du Christ* (etching). Paris, Bibliothèque Nationale.

52 Hubert de La Rochefoucauld: *Promeneuse* (print). Paris, Bibliothèque d'Art et d'Archéologie.

53 Marcel Lenoir: *Le Monstre* (drawing). Paris, Bibliothèque d'Art et d'Archéologie.

54 Stuck: *Eve* (pastel). Paris, Coll. Manoukian.

55 Eugène Carrière: Lithograph for the Rodin Exhibition. Paris, Bibliothèque Nationale.

56 Kupka: *The Conqueror Worm* (print). Paris, Bibliothèque Nationale.

57 Victor Prouvé: *L'Automne*. Nancy, Musée Corbin.

58 (*Colour*) Jean Delville: *Trésor de Satan*. Brussels, Musées Royaux des Beaux-Arts de Belgique.

59 (*Colour*) Odilon Redon: *L'Ange du Destin*. Paris, Coll. Mme. Gassart.

60 Georges de Feure: *Sous-Bois*. London, Ferrers Gallery.

61 De Feure: *Lac des Cygnes* (watercolour). London, Private Collection (ex Piccadilly Gallery).

62 E. Aman-Jean: *La jeune Fille au Paon* (lithograph). London, Fine Art Society Ltd.

63 Wassily Kandinsky: *Night*. Munich, Stadtische Galerie im Lenbachhaus.

64 Aman-Jean: *Tête de Femme* (lithograph). Paris, Archives Photographiques.

65 Ernest Laurent: Study for *Au Concert Colonne* (charcoal sketch). Paris, Louvre (Cabinet des Dessins).

66 Parish: *A Hill Prayer* (drawing). Cambridge, Mass., Fogg Art Museum (Grenville L. Winthrop Bequest).

67 Khnopff: *Memories* (pastel). Brussels, Musées Royaux des Beaux-Arts de Belgique.

68 Ferdinand Keller: *The Tomb of Böcklin*. Karlsruhe, Staatliche Kunsthalle.

69 Moreau: *Le Triomphe d'Alexandre* (detail). Paris, Musée Gustave Moreau.

70 (*Colour*) Alexandre Séon: *Le Désespoir de la Chimère*. Paris, Coll. Pierre Élie Flamand.

71 (*Colour*) Elihu Vedder: *Superest Invictus Amor*. New York, Brooklyn Museum (James Ricau Coll.).

72 Khnopff: *The Abandoned City* (drawing). Brussels, Galerie de l'Art Moderne.

73 De Feure: *Petit Nocturne de Bruges* (woodcut). Paris, Bibliothèque Nationale.

74 Walter Crane: *The Horses of Neptune*. Munich, Neue Pinakothek.

75 Kupka: *The Beginning of Life* (aquatint). Prague, Narodní Gallery.

76 John Singer Sargent: *Astarte* (drawing). Boston, Isabella Stewart Gardner Museum.

77 Federico Faruffini: *The Virgin of the Nile*. Rome, Galleria d'Arte Moderna.

78 Alphonse Mucha: Decorative panel for *La Princesse Lointaine*. Paris, Bibliothèque Nationale.

79 Klimt: *Jurisprudence*. Vienna, University.

80 Moreau: *Jacob et l'Ange*. Paris, Musée Gustave Moreau.

81 Rochegrosse: *Les derniers Jours de Babylone*. *Salon* of 1900; now lost.

82 (*Colour*) Lévy-Dhurmer: *Marsh Birds in Landscapes*. New York, Metropolitan Museum (Harris Brisbane Dick Fund).

83 (*Colour*) De Feure: *Les Fleurs du Mal*. Paris, Coll. Lesieutre.

84 Filiger: *Notation chromatique*. London, Piccadilly Gallery.

85 John Strudwick: *The Ramparts of God's House*. London, Courtauld Institute.

86 Nicholas Kalmakoff: *Chimera*. London, Lynne Thornton Coll.

87 Carl Strahtmann: *Dante on his Deathbed*. London, Piccadilly Gallery.

88 Delville: *La Fin d'un Règne*. Paris, Coll. Pont.

89 Moreau: *Le Dragon* (drawing). Paris, Musée Gustave Moreau.

90 Khnopff: *A Blue Wing* (print). Paris, Bibliothèque d'Art et d'Archéologie.

91 Luc Olivier Merson: *Pan et la Chimère*. New York, Schweitzer Gallery.

92 Arthur Rackham: *Andromeda* (watercolour). London, Fine Art Society Ltd.

93 Delville: *Orphée*. London, Private Collection (ex Piccadilly Gallery).

94 Arnold Böcklin: *The Sirens*. Berlin, Staatliche Museen.

95 (*Colour*) W. Holman Hunt: *The Lady of Shalott*. Hartford (Conn.), Wadsworth Atheneum (Ella Gallup Sumner and Mary Catlin Sumner Coll.).

96 (*Colour*) Delville: *Portrait of Madame Stuart Merrill*. Paris, Coll. Delville.

97 Böcklin: *Rocky Gorge*. Munich, Schackgalerie.

98 Kubin: *Black Flowers* (ink and wash). London, Piccadilly Gallery.

99 Georges Clairin: *La Grande Vague* (engraving). London, Fine Art Society Ltd.

100 Augusto Giacometti: *Night*. Zurich, Kunsthaus.

101 Paul Gauguin: *Figure de Spectre* (charcoal drawing). Paris, Louvre (Cabinet des Dessins).

102 William Rimmer: *Evening: Fall of Day*. Boston, Museum of Fine Arts.

103 Henry de Groux: *Lohengrin*. Paris, Coll. Pierre Élie Flamand.

104 Alphonse Mucha: *Sarah Bernhardt et son Fils*. Paris, Bibliothèque Nationale (original lost; ex Coll. Robert de Montesquiou).

105 Beardsley: *Siegfried* (drawing). Paris, Bibliothèque Nationale.

106 Maxwell Armfield: *Faustine*. Paris, Musée National d'Art Moderne.

107 Thomas Theodore Heine; *The Caterpillar*. Munich, Neue Pinakothek.

Index

Italic numerals indicate references to plates